# HISTORY OF THE EAST SURREY REGIMENT, VOL. II

# HISTORY
*of the*
# EAST SURREY REGIMENT

BY

COLONEL H. W. PEARSE, D.S.O.

AND

BRIGADIER-GENERAL H. S. SLOMAN, C.M.G., D.S.O.

VOLUME II
(1914-1917)

HISTORY OF THE EAST
SURREY REGIMENT, VOL. II

LONDON
THE MEDICI SOCIETY, LIMITED
MCMXXIII

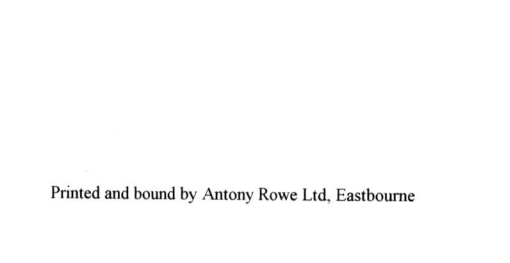

Printed and bound by Antony Rowe Ltd, Eastbourne

# INTRODUCTION

BY

MAJOR-GENERAL SIR JOHN R. LONGLEY, K.C.M.G., C.B.,
Colonel of the East Surrey Regiment

THE late Colonel H. W. Pearse, D.S.O., author of Volume I of the History of the East Surrey Regiment, which was published in 1916, had hoped to bring out Volume II of the work before the end of 1920.

The fulfilment of that hope was unfortunately prevented by his death after an operation in October, 1919. The loss that the Regiment sustained by the death of this able writer, who had ever placed his services freely at its disposal, is felt by all its members.

After the death of Colonel Pearse it was my task to find a member of the Regiment in a position to complete its history down to December, 1919, and in March, 1920, Brigadier-General H. S. Sloman, C.M.G., D.S.O., who had already in September, 1919, been approached on the subject by Colonel Pearse, consented to undertake the work.

The documents connected with the History left by Colonel Pearse included the records, as prepared by him, of the 1st, 2nd, 7th, 8th, 9th, 12th and 13th Battalions from August, 1914, or, in the case of the Service Battalions, from the date on which they were raised. Needless to say, these prepared records terminated abruptly at various dates prior to or near that of the Armistice. They were based mainly on the Battalions' War Diaries, supplemented by information supplied by individual officers, N.C.O.'s and men. Colonel Pearse had come to the conclusion that the records as left by him would require to be considerably abridged.

A perusal of these records made it evident that the first step towards the required compression must be the elimination of the long casualty lists. After consultation with many senior officers of the Regiment the following arrangement was agreed upon, viz. the casualties to be stated by name in the case of officers only, the totals of the casualties in other ranks to be recorded periodically. Lists of the men of other ranks who lost their lives in the Great War will be found in the Appendix at the end of Volume III, and it is a matter of great regret to me that it has not been found possible to give nominal rolls also of those other ranks who were wounded.

## INTRODUCTION

Another question, which arose when the story of the Regiment in the Great War approached completion, and it was realized that it must be published in two volumes, was whether it was advisable to devote Volume II to the records of the permanent battalions of the Regiment, and Volume III to those of the Service battalions, or whether it was preferable to include the records of all the battalions up to a certain date in Volume II, Volume III containing their continuation to December, 1919. Senior officers were again consulted, and it was finally decided, in accordance with the views of the majority, to adopt the latter plan. Volume II accordingly contains the records, up to March, 1917, of all the battalions which served overseas, and in addition, in Chapter I, the services up to December, 1919, of those battalions which had not that good fortune; while Volume III contains the continuation of the records up to December, 1919, of those battalions which were then serving overseas.

Each volume is divided into sections treating of different periods, such periods being so defined as to bring out the successive phases of the war on the Western Front, and the successive chapters in each section deal with each battalion in the order of its seniority.

In the text generally the names of the battles and other engagements are in accordance with the Report of the Battles Nomenclature Committee, as approved by the Army Council and published in 1921.

The contents of each section, which appear in the text in the form of sectional headings, are as follows:—

Volume II.

*Section I.*
August, 1914, to September, 1915.

The component units of the East Surrey Regt. at the commencement of the Great War, and the units added to it during the War; the Retreat from Mons; the Battles of Le Câteau, of the Marne, 1914, of the Aisne, 1914, and of La Bassée; the despatch of Territorial battalions overseas to relieve Regular battalions; the Battles of Ypres, 1914 and 1915.

*Section II.*
September, 1915, to June, 1916.

The Battle of Loos and the subsequent actions of the Hohenzollern Redoubt. Operations in Salonika.

*Section III.*
July, 1916, to March, 1917.

The Battles of the Somme, 1916, and the advance to the Hindenburg Line, 1917. Operations in Salonika.

# INTRODUCTION

VOLUME III.

*Section I.*
April, 1917, to March, 1918.

The Battles of Arras, 1917; the Battle of Messines; the Battles of Ypres, 1917; the Battle of Cambrai, 1917. Operations in Italy, Salonika, Mesopotamia and Aden.

*Section II.*
March, 1918, to July, 1918.

The German Offensives, 1918, including the First Battles of the Somme, 1918, and the Battles of the Lys. Operations in Salonika.

*Section III.*
August, 1918, to November, 1918.

The Advance to Victory, 1918, including the Battle of Amiens; the Second Battles of the Somme, 1918; the Second Battles of Arras, 1918; the Battles of the Hindenburg Line; the Battle of Ypres, 1918; the Battle of Courtrai; the Battle of the Selle; the Battle of Valenciennes; and the Battle of the Sambre. Operations in Salonika and Mesopotamia. The Armistice.

*Section IV.*
November, 1918, to Dec., 1919.

After the Armistice. Disbandment of the Service Battalions. Operations in North Russia and Mesopotamia.

In conclusion, I desire, on behalf of the Regiment, to thank, firstly, Brigadier-General H. S. Sloman, C.M.G., D.S.O., for all his work in the compilation of this History; secondly, those officers and other ranks who have so ably assisted him. Practically all the surviving Commanding Officers have been good enough to supply material for and revise the record of each battalion during the period of their command; and many other officers and other ranks have helped the compiler by the loan of reports, maps, etc.

The names of them all are too numerous to be set down here, but I must thank by name Colonel H. D. Lawrence, C.M.G., who has carefully revised the whole of the text; Major (now the Rev.) W. H. Baddeley, D.S.O., M.C., who completed the record of the 8th Battalion; Captains H. V. Bayliss, D.S.O., M.C., R. E. C. Adams, M.C., and E. R. Gould, who dealt with the records of the 3rd, 1st and 2nd Battalions respectively; also Captain K. Anns, M.C., who has given frequent help in the preparation of the Maps and Plans.

JOHN R. LONGLEY,
*Major-General,*
Colonel, The East Surrey Regiment.

# CONTENTS

INTRODUCTION — PAGE v

By Major-General Sir John R. Longley, K.C.M.G., C.B., Colonel of the East Surrey Regiment

## SECTION I
### August, 1914, to September, 1915

**Chapter I** — 3

The component units of the East Surrey Regiment; the records of those units, other than the regular battalions, up to the year 1914, and the services during the Great War of 1914–1919 of those units which took no part in the fighting overseas.

**Chapter II** — 30

August and September, 1914: The 1st Battalion lands in France with the British Expeditionary Force; in the Battle of Mons and the Retreat from Mons, including the Battle of Le Câteau.

**Chapter III** — 44

September, 1914: The 1st Battalion in the advance to the Aisne, in the Battle of the Marne, 1914, and in the Battle of the Aisne, 1914.

**Chapter IV** — 52

October, 1914, to March, 1915; the 1st Battalion in the Battle of La Bassée, in action at Richebourg L'Avoué and Lorgies; four and a half months of trench duty in Flanders between Armentières and Ypres.

**Chapter V** — 67

April to September, 1915; the 1st Battalion in the defence of Hill 60; two months and a half in the trenches south of Hill 60 during the Battles of Ypres, 1915; on transfer with the 5th Division to the X Corps, the Battalion serves two months in the line between Maricourt and the River Somme.

**Chapter VI** — 87

August, 1914, to September, 1915; the 2nd Battalion brought home from India and allotted to the newly formed 28th Division, with which it proceeds to France. In the Ypres Salient, heavy losses in action near St. Eloi; in the Battles of Ypres, 1915; three months' trench-duty near Wulverghem and St. Eloi.

**Chapter VII** — 108

October, 1914, to December, 1916: the 1/5th and 1/6th Battalions embark for India; garrison duty in India during 1915 and 1916.

# CONTENTS

**CHAPTER VIII** — 111

June, 1915, to September, 1915: the 7th Battalion sees its first active service in the trenches near Armentières.

**CHAPTER IX** — 114

July to September, 1915: the 8th Battalion arrives in France and performs its first tours of trench duty near Albert.

## SECTION II
### SEPTEMBER, 1915, TO JUNE, 1916

**CHAPTER X** — 119

September, 1915, to June, 1916: the 1st Battalion passes four months in the line between the River Somme and Maricourt; and another four months in the line in the Arras area.

**CHAPTER XI** — 129

September, 1915, to June, 1916: the 2nd Battalion in the Battle of Loos; the defence of the Hohenzollern Redoubt. The 28th Division proceeds to Egypt and thence to Salonika. Work on the Salonika Defences. The 28th Division advances to the Struma River. The Battalion in the outpost line near Lake Butkovo. Malaria epidemic.

**CHAPTER XII** — 142

September, 1915, to June, 1916: the 7th Battalion moves to the Loos area and takes part in the later phases of the Battle of Loos and the subsequent actions of the Hohenzollern Redoubt: after three months in the line, north of the La Bassée Canal, the Battalion returns to the Hohenzollern Redoubt area, where it takes part in the defence of the craters: at the end of two months' rest and training behind the line it moves to the Albert area.

**CHAPTER XIII** — 156

September, 1915, to June, 1916: the 8th Battalion passes five months in the front line near Albert; moves to Vaux on the River Somme; after a month's rest near Amiens, returns to the front line near Carnoy, and prepares for the Battles of the Somme, 1916.

**CHAPTER XIV** — 164

September, 1915, to June, 1916: the 9th Battalion arrives in France. In the Battle of Loos suffers heavily in action south-east of Hulluch. Eight and a half months in Flanders, in the trenches near St. Eloi, near Hooge and near Wulverghem.

**CHAPTER XV** — 183

May and June, 1916: the 12th Battalion arrives in France and takes its first tour of trench duty near Ploegsteert Wood.

CONTENTS

## SECTION III

### July, 1916, to March, 1917

**Chapter XVI** — page 187

July, 1916, to March, 1917: the 1st Battalion in the Battles of the Somme, 1916; at Longuéval in the Battle of Delville Wood; in the Battle of Guillemont, in and near Leuze Wood; in the Battle of Morval; six months in the line in the La Bassée Canal area.

**Chapter XVII** — 203

July, 1916, to March, 1917: the 2nd Battalion with the British Salonika Army on the Struma Valley front, between Lake Butkovo and Lake Tahinos.

**Chapter XVIII** — 209

July, 1916, to March, 1917: the 7th Battalion in the Battles of the Somme, 1916; at Ovillers in the Battle of Albert, 1916, and in the Battle of Pozières Ridge; six weeks in the line south of Arras; at Gueudecourt in the Battle of the Transloy Ridges; five months in the line about Arras.

**Chapter XIX** — 222

July, 1916, to March, 1917: the 8th Battalion in the Battles of the Somme, 1916; in the Battle of Albert, 1916, at Montauban; in the Battle of Thiepval Ridge at the Schwaben Redoubt; in the Battle of the Ancre, 1916, captures Desire Trench; in the winter operations on the Ancre, in action near Miraumont; transferred to the Hazebrouck area.

**Chapter XX** — 241

July, 1916, to March, 1917: the 9th Battalion in the Battles of the Somme, 1916; its attack on a strong point near Guillémont, and its heavy losses in the Battle of Delville Wood; in the trenches on the Vimy Ridge and near Hulluch and Liévin.

**Chapter XXI** — 252

July, 1916, to March, 1917: the 12th Battalion in the line near Ploegsteert Wood: in the Battles of the Somme, 1916; the capture of Flers; five months in the line near St. Eloi.

**Chapter XXII** — 259

June, 1916, to March, 1917: the 13th Battalion arrives in France; in the trenches opposite Lens and north of Albert; the Battalion moves to the Somme Valley and is in the front line near Bouchavesnes when the German retreat to the Hindenburg Line commences.

# ILLUSTRATIONS

|  | FACING PAGE |
|---|---|
| PHOTOGRAPH OF HILL 60 | 78 |
| PHOTOGRAPH OF THE STRUMA VALLEY | 140 |
| PHOTOGRAPH OF BOULEAUX WOOD AND MORVAL TAKEN FROM THE AIR | 198 |

# LIST OF MAPS

| | |
|---|---|
| GENERAL MAP OF NORTHERN FRANCE | *Front of volume* |
| GENERAL MAP OF THE YPRES SALIENT | |

| | PAGE |
|---|---|
| THE 1st BATTALION IN THE BATTLE OF MONS, 1914 | 33 |
| THE 1st BATTALION AT THE PASSAGE OF THE MARNE, 9TH SEPTEMBER, 1914 | 47 |
| THE 1st BATTALION IN THE DEFENCE OF HILL 60, 19TH TO 21ST APRIL, 1915 | 69 |
| THE 2ND AND 8TH BATTALIONS IN THE BATTLES OF YPRES, 1915, 1917 | 96 |
| THE DEFENCE OF THE HOHENZOLLERN REDOUBT BY THE 2ND BATTALION, ON SEPTEMBER 27TH TO OCTOBER 1ST, 1915 | 130 |
| THE 7TH BATTALION AT GUN TRENCH | 145 |
| THE 7TH BATTALION AT THE HOHENZOLLERN REDOUBT, MARCH, 1916 | 150 |
| THE 9TH BATTALION IN THE ATTACK BY THE 72ND BRIGADE NEAR HULLUCH, 26TH SEPTEMBER, 1915 | 167 |
| THE 7TH BATTALION IN THE BATTLES OF ALBERT, 1916, AND POZIERES RIDGE | 211 |
| THE 12TH BATTALION IN THE BATTLE OF FLERS-COURCELETTE, SEPTEMBER, 1916, AND THE 7TH AND 12TH BATTALIONS IN THE BATTLE OF THE TRANSLOY RIDGES, OCTOBER, 1916 | 217 |
| THE 8TH BATTALION IN THE BATTLES OF THIEPVAL RIDGE AND THE ACRE, SEPTEMBER TO NOVEMBER, 1916 | 231 |
| THE ATTACK OF THE 9TH BATTALION ON STRONG POINT NEAR GUILLEMONT, AUGUST 16TH, 1916 | 245 |

| | |
|---|---|
| GENERAL MAP OF THE SOMME FRONT | *End of volume* |
| GENERAL MAP OF THE SALONIKA FRONT | |

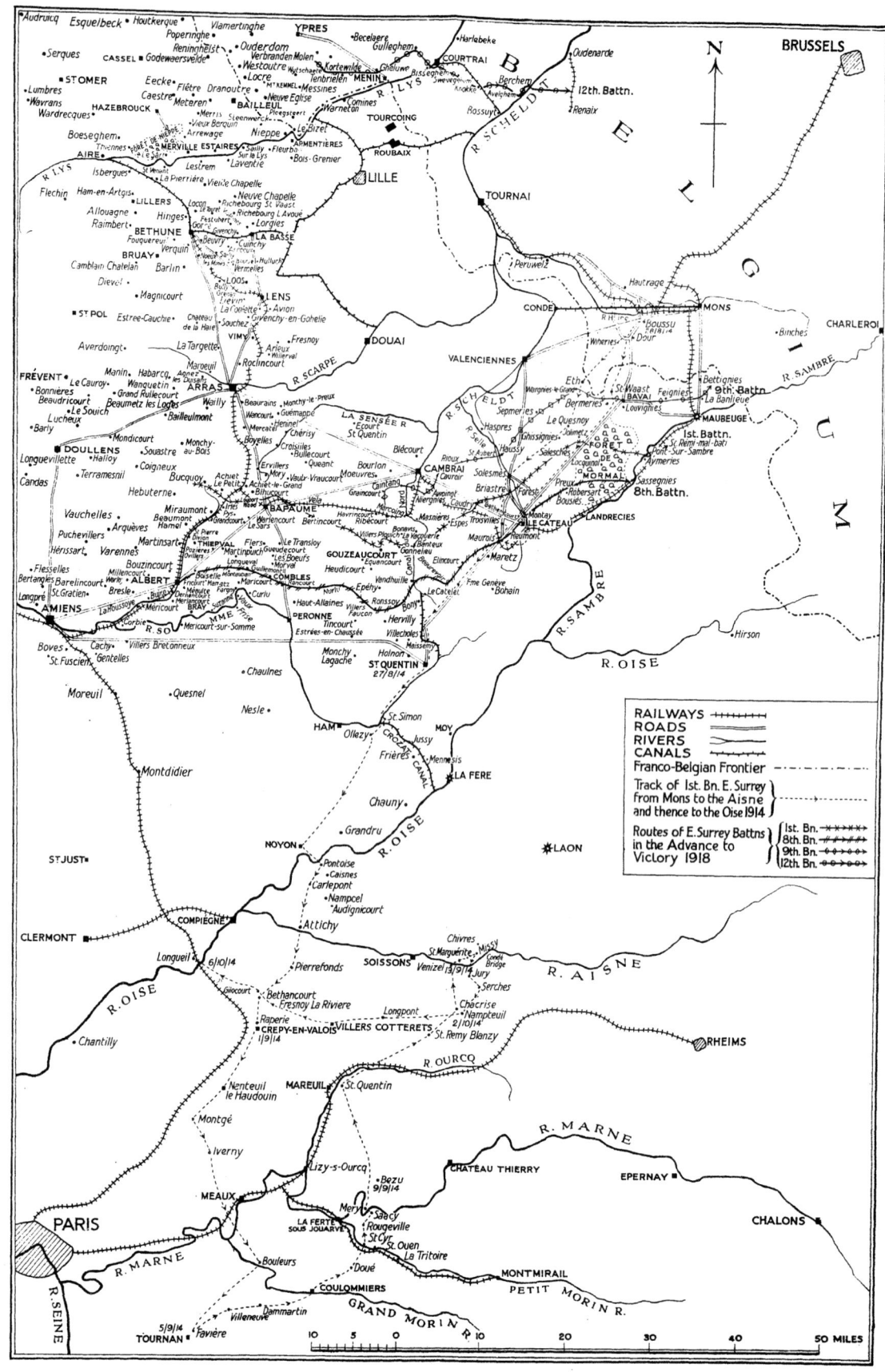

GENERAL MAP OF THE BRITISH POSITION ON THE WESTERN FRONT, SHOWING ROUTES OF 1st BATTALION IN AUGUST AND SEPTEMBER, 1914, AND OF 1st, 8th, 9th, AND 12th BATTALIONS IN THE ADVANCE TO VICTORY, 1918

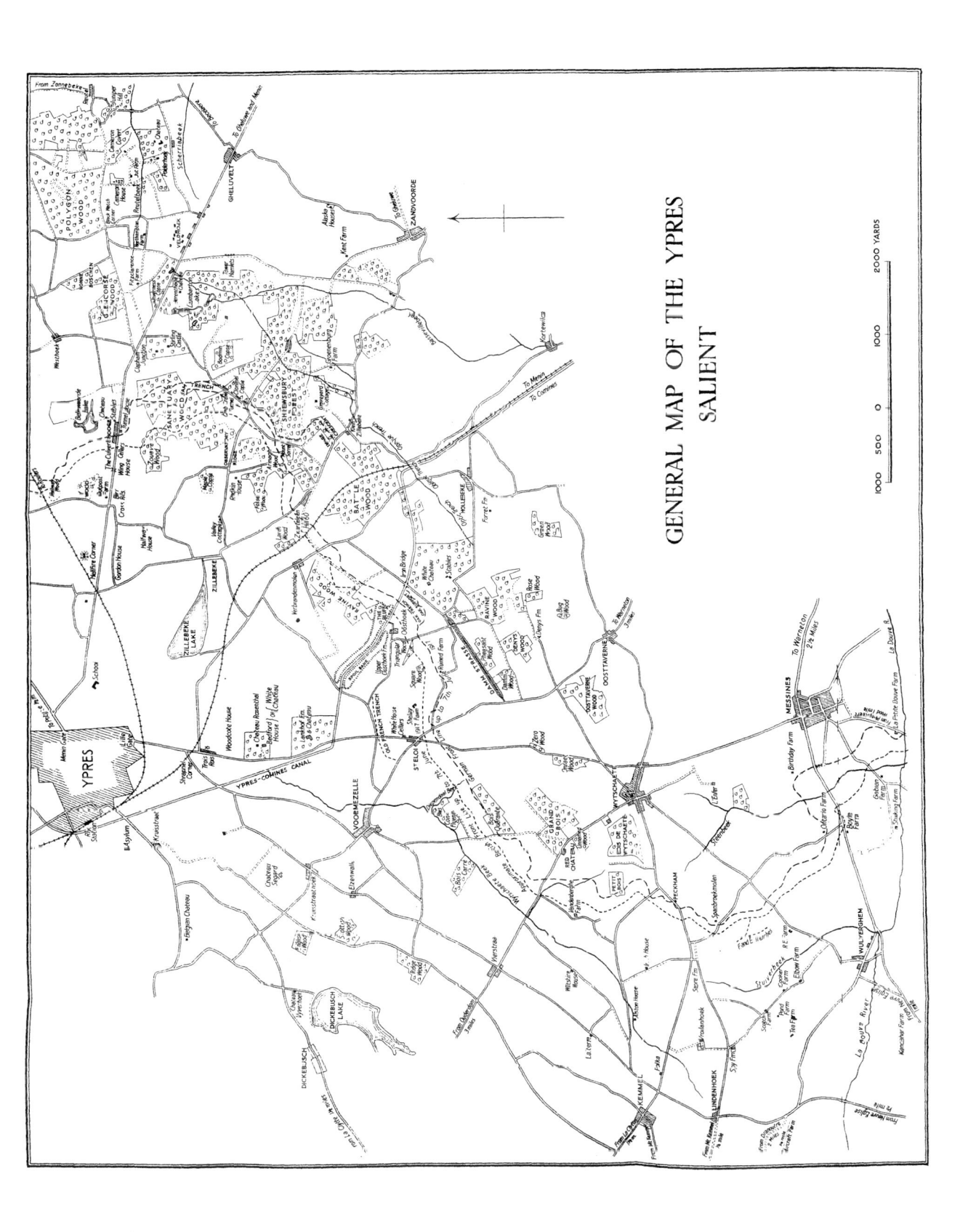

GENERAL MAP OF THE YPRES SALIENT

# SECTION I

### AUGUST, 1914, TO SEPTEMBER, 1915

THE COMPONENT UNITS OF THE EAST SURREY REGIMENT AT THE COMMENCEMENT OF THE GREAT WAR, AND THE UNITS ADDED TO IT DURING THE WAR: THE RETREAT FROM MONS; THE BATTLES OF LE CATEAU, OF THE MARNE, 1914, OF THE AISNE, 1914, AND OF LA BASSEE: THE DESPATCH OF TERRITORIAL BATTALIONS OVERSEAS TO RELIEVE REGULAR BATTALIONS: THE BATTLES OF YPRES, 1914 AND 1915.

# CHAPTER I

THE COMPONENT UNITS OF THE EAST SURREY REGIMENT; THE RECORDS OF THOSE UNITS, OTHER THAN THE REGULAR BATTALIONS, UP TO THE YEAR 1914 AND THE SERVICES DURING THE GREAT WAR OF 1914–1919 OF THOSE UNITS WHICH TOOK NO PART IN THE FIGHTING OVERSEAS.

AT the outbreak of the Great War in August, 1914, the East Surrey Regt. comprised the following units:—

        1st Battalion (Regular).
        2nd Battalion (Regular).
        3rd Battalion (Reserve) (A).
        4th Battalion (Extra Reserve) (B).
        5th Battalion (Territorial Force) (C, D, E).
        6th Battalion (Territorial Force) (F, G, H).
        The Regimental Depôt at Kingston-on-Thames (I).

To the above units were added the following, as the new Armies were gradually formed:—

        7th Battalion (Service) (J).
        8th Battalion (Service) (K).
        9th Battalion (Service) (L).
        10th Battalion (Service, later Reserve) (M).
        11th Battalion (Service, later Reserve) (N).
        12th Battalion (Service) (O).
        13th Battalion (Service) (P).
        14th Battalion (Reserve) (Q).

Also, from the existing Territorial Force battalions, there were formed so-called Second Line and Third Line Battalions, so that at one time there were six Territorial battalions of the East Surrey Regt., designated the 1/5th, 2/5th, 3/5th, 1/6th, 2/6th and 3/6th Battalions.

Of the nineteen units thus comprised in the East Surrey Regt., nine battalions only saw active service in the field overseas, and their war record is given in the succeeding chapters. In this chapter it is proposed to give a brief account of the origin and history down to the year 1914 of all the units except the two Regular battalions, and the record of services during the Great War of those units which did not proceed overseas.

### (A) *The 3rd (Reserve) Battn. East Surrey Regt.*

The 3rd Battn. East Surrey, which for nearly a century prior to the introduction of the Territorial system in 1881 was known as the 1st Royal Surrey Militia, can trace its descent from the "Fyrd" of Saxon times, through the "Posse Comitatus" of the Normans and Plantagenets, the trained bands of the Tudor dynasty and the Militia of the Stuarts. All these forces were county organizations, and, as no standing army existed prior to the Great Civil War of the seventeenth century, they furnished the men who fought under Alfred against the Danes, at Stamford Bridge and Hastings in 1066, at Crécy and Agincourt, in the Wars of the Roses and in the earlier years of the Great Civil War.[1]

The earliest document in the Public Record Office relating to the Surrey County Force is an incomplete Muster Roll dated 1522, when Henry VIII was king. Fuller records exist regarding its services during Elizabeth's war with King Philip of Spain. In 1587 it was present, with a strength of 1900 of all ranks, in the camp at Tilbury formed in anticipation of the coming of the Spanish Armada. At Tilbury it was specially selected to furnish 500 men as bodyguard for the Queen. Disembodied in the year following, the Surrey Force furnished several contingents during the remainder of Elizabeth's reign for service overseas. In 1592 Captain Taxley with 100 Surrey men served in the army which the Earl of Essex led to the assistance of Henry IV, King of France and Navarre, in his struggle against the League and the Duke of Parma's Spanish Army in Northern France. Four years later another strong Surrey contingent served under the Earl of Essex at the relief of Calais and the capture of Cadiz. In 1598 Surrey men served in the Home Counties Force engaged in suppressing a rebellion in Ireland, and also in Flanders against the Duke of Parma.

James I, who came to the throne in 1603, at once commenced to reorganize the trained bands which were known thenceforward as Militia. The control of the force was taken out of the hands of the Lords-Lieutenant of counties, a change which later on was one of the causes of friction between King and Parliament.

For nearly forty years the Surrey Militia from time to time furnished contingents to the various expeditionary forces despatched overseas, till in 1642 the outbreak of civil war between Charles I and his Parliament provided it with employment on active service in this country. The Surrey Militia was almost solid for Parliament and joined the Parliamentary Army which was covering London. Its headquarters were at Tottenham Court, with detachments at Farnham and Kingston; consequently it took no part in the fighting which resulted from Charles' attempt to break through the cordon at Brentford.

---

[1] For the history of the 3rd and 4th Battalions up to 1902, the writer is indebted to Capt. J. Davis's "Historical Records of the Second Royal Surrey Regt. of Militia," and Colonel G. J. Hay's "Epitomised History of the Militia (The Constitutional Force)."

## ITS EARLY HISTORY

In July, 1543, an Association was formed, embracing Kent, Surrey, Sussex and Hampshire, to raise a mobile force for service in the Field Army out of the County Forces which were still tied down to the defence of London. To this mobile force Surrey contributed 850 men. In 1645 Cromwell commenced to form his New Model Army, to which the Surrey Militia sent 350 men in that year and 200 in 1646. The New Model Army did not replace the Militia, which remained embodied.

A year after the execution of Charles I, his son, afterwards Charles II, who had fled to the Continent, reappeared at the head of an army in Scotland. Cromwell, who had moved north with his Ironsides to attack it, called up the Surrey Regiment of Militia to join his army. The regiment, under the command of Sir Richard Onslow, set out accordingly, but before it could reach him Cromwell had defeated Charles at Dunbar, thirty miles east of Edinburgh. The Surrey Regiment then moved to Dunstable, and thence to Oxford to join the major general's force collected to meet another Scottish army which had invaded England and was defeated at Worcester in 1651.

One result of this frequent association of the Militia and the New Model Army was that the red coats of the latter were adopted by the Surrey Militia, which is mentioned in a contemporary record as wearing green coats at Farnham in 1643.

Soon after the Restoration, in 1660, the Militia Acts of Charles II vested the control of the national Militia, which was estimated at 130,000 men, solely in the hands of the Crown and made provision for the better discipline of the force. The men were to be provided, armed, equipped and paid by persons who owned property above a certain value. In those days a musketeer was armed with a musket having a barrel of not less than three feet in length, a collar of bandoliers and a sword; while a pikeman carried an ash pike not under sixteen feet in length and a sword, and was equipped with breastpiece, backpiece and headpiece. The mustering of the regiment, which lasted four days only, and company musters of two days each four times a year, were recognized at the time as quite inadequate for proper training.

During the Great Fire of London, in 1666, Charles II ordered the Lords-Lieutenant of Middlesex, Hertfordshire and Surrey "to draw together the Militia at the most fitting rendezvous," and the Surrey Militia marched accordingly to Lambeth with carts containing implements for coping with the fire.

Though the Militia Army saw most of the fighting in the rebellion of the Duke of Monmouth in 1685, and captured the Duke after the Battle of Sedgemoor, it was then beginning to yield its place as the principal military organization of the kingdom to the new standing army, which absorbed most of the money and attention of both King and Parliament. In consequence, for nearly a century preceding the year 1756 the Militia was practically untrained and unorganized.

A muster roll of the Surrey Militia for 1697 has been preserved. The Duke of Norfolk was then in command, and there 15 companies, each averaging 150 strong and having their headquarters at Croydon, Leatherhead, Reigate, Guildford, Chertsey, Kingston, Putney, Godalming, Farnham and Southwark, the latter place accounting for six of the companies.

The outbreak of the Seven Years' War and the introduction by George II in 1756 of Hessian and Hanoverian troops into the United Kingdom, in consequence of the menace of a French invasion, once more directed public attention to the Militia Army. The English people, humiliated by the presence of the foreign mercenaries, were, on the whole, in favour of the reorganization of the force, and in the year following an Act was passed for that purpose. Active measures were quickly taken by the Lords-Lieutenant, who were responsible for raising the personnel, and, in the case of Surrey, companies were formed at the towns mentioned in the preceding paragraph, their combined strength amounting to 850 men. Their uniform consisted of a cocked hat, a long red coat with the skirts hooked back to show the white facings, a red waistcoat, red breeches and white gaiters. The hair was powdered and tied in a queue. Their arms were musket, bayonet and sword. Colours were presented to the Regiment, one a Union, the other white, bearing the Arms of the Lord-Lieutenant, Lord Onslow, who commanded for a short time until he was succeeded by Sir Nicholas Carew.

Drilling was carried out with enthusiasm by the companies, which were occasionally also assembled as a battalion, with such good results that at the close of 1758 Smollett recorded that the Regiment rivalled the Regulars in the perfection of their exercise and seemed as fit for active service. The nation was proud that the old Constitutional Force was preparing itself with such energy for its defence.

Early in July, 1759, the Regiment was embodied and distributed in quarters in Rochester, Strood, Dartford and Gravesend. Later in the year it was divided into two battalions, each of five companies. The 1st or Eastern Battalion, commanded by Sir N. Carew, was quartered at Kingston; the 2nd or Western was quartered at Fulham, Putney and Wandsworth under Colonel G. Onslow, who had as his Adjutant Francis Grose, the author of the well-known work *Military Antiquities*.

Until the disembodiment of the Regiment in 1762, at the close of the Seven Years' War, these two battalions had frequent change of quarters, and their duty of guarding and escorting French prisoners of war took them to various towns, first in Kent and Surrey, and later on, in 1760, to Salisbury and Northampton, whence they moved again to Dover and Deal, and then to Brighton and Lewes. They returned to Surrey for disembodiment in December, 1762, and were reformed into a single battalion two months later. Sir N. Carew had recently died, and Sir G. Onslow commanded until 1765, when he was succeeded by Major Jeremiah Hodges.

During the ten years following on the conclusion of the Seven Years' War the high standard of training and organization which had been reached by the Militia during that conflict was maintained; so that when, owing to the possible imminence of war, the Militia was embodied in 1773, the force was efficient and up to establishment. Two years later the American colonies revolted, and in

1776 the Surrey Militia earned the approbation of King George III by volunteering for whatever duty His Majesty might think proper.

In 1778 France came to the assistance of the revolted American colonies, and in March of that year the Surrey Militia was embodied and two years later was stationed at Ringwood in the south of Hampshire. Already involved in the war with France and America, the British Government had now to meet a new danger at home. On the 2nd June, 1780, Lord George Gordon marched with a mob of some 60,000 men to the Parliament House to present a petition against the recently passed Act which had repealed the Penal Laws against Roman Catholics in England. Unaccountable delay on the part of the authorities in dealing with the mob led to the Gordon Riots, and for four days London was given over to anarchy. The prisons were broken open, Roman Catholic churches and chapels and the houses of prominent citizens of that Faith were pillaged and burned.

The part taken by the Surrey Militia in quelling the riots is described in the following extract from the "British Army Despatch, Press and West End Courier":—

> "And for their deeds and conduct in modern times, our fathers have told us how during the Gordon Riots, when they, who should have protected the State and Commonwealth, hesitated and looked coolly on, the Surrey Militia cleared with the bayonet the City and bridges, and, rolling back the flood of anarchy and rebellion, saved the metropolis of the Empire from pillage and fire."

At the time when the Regiment rendered this service it consisted of twelve companies, and its establishment was 45 officers and 1040 other ranks.

Soon after the Peace of Versailles in 1783 the Surrey Militia was disembodied, but the system of an annual training for one month of the Militia generally was introduced, and the records of the Surrey Regiment show that it carried out this training every year until 1793, when it was again embodied owing to the French Republic having declared war against Great Britain, Holland and Spain.

At the end of 1799 the Battalion was disembodied, but was re-embodied in 1801, when, according to the regimental records, it was first granted the title of the 1st *Royal* Surrey Militia. The earliest known authority for this honour, however, is a War Office letter dated the 23rd April, 1804, which gives a list of the Militia regiments permitted by His Majesty to bear the appellation of Royal. This list includes the 1st and 2nd Surrey Regiments,[1] and it is believed that the honour was conferred on them for having volunteered in 1798 for service in Ireland. The 1st Royal Surrey Militia served for several years in that country, from which it returned to England in 1811, under the command of Lord Grantley.

During 1813 the headquarters and right wing were stationed at Dorking,

---

[1] The 2nd Royal Surrey Militia is now the 3rd Bn. The Queen's (Royal West Surrey) Regt.

while the left wing was at Reigate. Early in the following year the Battalion supplied a draft of thirty men under Captain Whitby to the First Provisional Battalion of Militia, which left Portsmouth on the 10th March and disembarked at Pauillac, near Bordeaux, only to find that the war was over. Meanwhile the 1st Royal Surrey Regt. was quartered first at Horsham and then at Brighton, whence in June, 1814, it returned to its own county for disembodiment.

During the preceding fifty years considerable changes had been introduced in the uniform of the rank and file, and at the end of the Napoleonic Wars the men wore sugar-loaf hats, red jackets, white breeches and black gaiters.

Following on the escape of the French Emperor from Elba, the 1st Royal Surrey Militia was re-embodied on the 29th June, 1815, after a large number of its recruits had been drafted to the Guards and Line regiments. These recruits were hurried off to the theatre of war before they could be clothed in the uniform of their new corps, and they consequently fought at Waterloo in their Surrey Militia jackets. After re-embodiment, the 1st Royal Surrey Militia, reduced by the loss of its recruits to a strength of 350 men, was stationed first at Portsmouth and then at Fermoy, whence it returned to England and was disembodied on the 30th April, 1816.

During the next five-and-thirty years there is but little to record. Trainings took place at long intervals until 1831, when they were discontinued. The headquarters of the Battalion moved in 1826 to Richmond, where the staff was gradually reduced by discharges and deaths, as no fresh appointments were made. In 1852, however, the re-establishment of the French Empire once more directed attention in England to the almost forgotten Militia, and by an Act passed in that year Queen Victoria was empowered to raise 80,000 Militia men and to cause them to undergo an annual training for a period of fifty-six days. The reorganization of the 1st Royal Surrey Militia was at once commenced by Colonel William Holme-Sumner, and the Battalion was assembled for training in Richmond and its vicinity on the 3rd May, 1853. Owing to the raising of the 3rd Royal Surrey Militia (afterwards the 4th Battn. East Surrey Regt.) at Kingston-on-Thames in 1853, the recruiting area of the 1st Royal Surrey Militia was somewhat curtailed.

In consequence of the war with Russia, the Battalion was embodied at the end of 1854. In April of the year following it was issued with double-breasted tunics in place of the short-tailed coatees. In May the Battalion moved into C and D Lines, South Camp, Aldershot, and was one of the first two corps sent to Aldershot, the other being the 1st Royal Middlesex Militia in the adjoining Lines.

In September the 1st Royal Surrey Militia was quartered in Portsmouth, where it remained embodied until the end of the war. The outbreak of the Indian Mutiny brought about its re-embodiment in 1857, when it proceeded for a few months to Clonmel. Disembodiment followed on the suppression of the Mutiny, and in succeeding years the Battalion reassembled annually for its training. In 1860 Colonel G. Evelyn succeeded to the command on the death of Colonel Holme-Sumner. In 1872 the 1st Royal Surrey Militia was affiliated to the 70th (Surrey) Regiment, now the 2nd Battn. East Surrey, and four years later its headquarters were moved back to Kingston.

With the introduction of the Territorial system, in 1881, the 1st Royal Surrey Militia became the 3rd Battn. East Surrey Regt., and its facings were changed in consequence from Royal blue to white.

It is of interest, however, to note that the present badge of the East Surrey Regiment was designed from those of the 1st and 3rd Royal Surrey Militia, those of the 31st and 70th Regiments forming no part of it. The badges of the 1st and 3rd Royal Surrey Militia were respectively, the Arms of Guildford surmounted by a crown, and the Star of the Order of the Garter. To form the East Surrey badge the former was superimposed on the latter; but in recognition of the association of the Regiment with Kingston-on-Thames, the Arms of that town, three fishes and an R., were substituted for the Royal Arms of England in the small shield on the central tower of the castle in the Guildford Arms.

In the year 1882 the 3rd Battn. East Surrey was armed with the Martini-Henry rifle in place of the Snider, and in 1884 was presented with new colours at Aldershot by the Countess of Lovelace, the Commanding Officer at the time being Colonel Carleton-Smith. His successor in the command was Lieut.-Colonel T. W. Lemmon, who was promoted to that rank in 1887.

In 1890 a change in the training period was introduced, and thenceforth the recruits assembled for musketry training before the trained men.

Soon after the commencement of the South African War the Battalion was embodied for five months in 1900, when it was quartered at Perham Down Camp under the command of Lieut.-Colonel Sir G. D. Clerk, and again in May, 1901, when it volunteered for service at the front. The Battalion embarked in the hired transport *Idaho*, with a strength of 23 officers and 617 other ranks, at Southampton on the 5th June, 1901, and disembarked on the 1st July at Port Elizabeth. It was at first employed on the Lines of Communication, its headquarters being at Colesberg, with a detachment later near Stormberg, where 2nd Lieut. Lyon was killed in action while on reconnaissance duty. At the end of 1901 the Battalion moved to Beaufort West and garrisoned the blockhouse line from that town to Victoria Road. While in charge of a convoy Major Crofton was killed in action at Uitspanfontein on the 5th February, 1902. From Beaufort West the Battalion was transferred in March, 1902, to Simon's Town, where it furnished guards for the prisoners-of-war camp. From Simon's Town Colonel Sir G. D. Clerk proceeded to England, and Major J. C. Worthington assumed command.

The Battalion embarked for England early in July, 1902, arrived at Southampton on the 26th and was disembodied at Kingston the same day.

In July, 1904, the Battalion, which was then commanded by Lieut.-Colonel Worthington, sent 16 officers and 300 other ranks from Cowshot, where it was undergoing its annual training, to attend the ceremony of the unveiling of a tablet placed in St. Saviour's Collegiate Church, Southwark, in memory of the officers and men of the Battalion who had lost their lives in South Africa. In

December of the same year His Majesty the King conferred on the Battalion the distinction " South Africa, 1901–1902."

From 1904 to 1914 training was carried out annually. In 1908 the Militia was replaced by the Special Reserve, and in the 3rd Battn. East Surrey 425 N.C.O.'s and men transferred to the new force, 35 elected to remain Militiamen and 122 exercised their right of taking a free discharge.

When the Great War broke out in August, 1914, the Annual Training had already been completed under Lieut.-Colonel C. O. Shipley, who had assumed command in 1912. The 3rd Battn. East Surrey was then the only Special Reserve battalion with a full complement of officers, of whom all the juniors had been trained by the 1st Battalion.

On the 8th August the 3rd Battn. East Surrey was embodied at Kingston-on-Thames and proceeded the same night to the Grand Shaft Barracks and Land Defences at Dover. At that station, where it remained until the Armistice in 1918, the Battalion, in addition to its garrison duties, was employed as a training and draft-finding unit, its first draft of 93 other ranks, under 2nd Lieut. V. Booth, being sent out to the 1st Battalion on the 26th August.

During September and October, 1914, the Battalion, in spite of the frequent despatch of drafts overseas, rapidly increased in strength, its numbers at the close of the latter month being 46 officers and 1972 other ranks. It had been in the meanwhile reorganized on the four-company basis, and, in order to absorb the new arrivals, additional training companies composed of recruits were formed as necessary whenever the strength exceeded the war establishment of 1019 of all ranks.

On the 1st November three of these companies—G, H and I—were transferred bodily to form the nucleus of the 10th Battn. East Surrey. This loss to the 3rd Battalion was rapidly made good, and the strength increased gradually until the maximum of 113 officers and 2756 other ranks was reached in August, 1915.

During the period of the War 911 officers served with the Battalion and 19,040 men passed through its ranks. Of the latter, 13,029 were despatched overseas, and 6011 were transferred to other units in the United Kingdom.

The distribution of the 13,029 men sent abroad was as follows:—

|  |  |
|---|---|
| To the 1st Battn. East Surrey | 3,695 |
| ,, 2nd ,, ,, ,, | 1,268 |
| ,, 7th ,, ,, ,, | 1,276 |
| ,, 8th ,, ,, ,, | 778 |
| ,, 9th ,, ,, ,, | 158 |
| ,, 12th ,, ,, ,, | 697 |
| ,, 13th ,, ,, ,, | 321 |
| ,, Base (France) for posting as ordered | 4,261 |
| ,, ,, (Mediterranean) ,, ,, | 558 |
| Sent overseas individually | 17 |
|  | ——— |
|  | 13,029 |

The foregoing figures give some idea of the task accomplished during the Great War by the 3rd Battn. East Surrey, which was the training, clothing and equipping for service in the field of over 750 men in every succeeding three months. That this heavy task was accomplished so successfully reflects the greatest credit on all ranks, especially when it is remembered that many of the officers, N.C.O.'s and men were recovering from wounds or illness contracted on service and, when recovered, were replaced by others suffering from similar disabilities. In recognition of his services Colonel Shipley was awarded the C.B. in 1915. He left the Battalion in February, 1918, and was succeeded by Lieut.-Colonel A. J. D. Hay, who did not, however, actually take over the command till May, 1919.

On the 19th November, 1918, the 3rd Battn. East Surrey left Dover, under the command of Colonel E. F. Sulivan, for Bridge of Allan, and in February, 1919, was stationed at Glasgow during the Labour troubles in that city. From Glasgow the Battalion proceeded to Clipstone Camp in Nottinghamshire, where it was disembodied on the 31st July, 1919.

With the limited space at disposal it is not possible to give here a list of all the officers and other ranks of the 3rd Battn. East Surrey who were awarded honours for gallant service in the field or who met their deaths while serving with other corps overseas. Where 3rd Battalion officers are mentioned in the succeeding pages, which give the records of other battalions of the East Surrey Regiment, as having received a decoration or as having been killed in action, a note is added to their names—it is hoped in every case—stating that they belonged to the 3rd Battalion. Other 3rd Battalion officers, however, saw active service with battalions of other regiments or in other corps, such as the Royal Flying Corps, and the lists subjoined show, firstly, those who met their deaths, and, secondly, those who were awarded decorations while so attached:—

(i) OFFICERS OF THE 3RD BATTN. EAST SURREY WHO MET THEIR DEATHS DURING THE GREAT WAR WHILE SERVING WITH OTHER CORPS.

2nd Lieut. T. S. Arnold. Died 11/10/17 of wounds received while serving with the 2/7th Battn. Lancashire Fusiliers.
Captain C. H. Becker. Killed 8/8/18, while serving with the Royal Fusiliers.
Lieut. S. C. H. Begbie. Died 22/4/18, while serving with the Royal Air Force.
Captain E. W. Bowyer-Bower. Killed in action 19/3/17, while serving with the 59th Squadron Royal Flying Corps.
Lieut. J. V. Card, M.C. Killed in action 25/3/19, while serving with the British Mission in the Caucasus.
Captain A. T. Chapman. Killed in action 26/4/15, while serving with the Hampshire Regt.
2nd Lieut. D. H. A. Cheers. Killed 17/4/18, while serving with the Royal Air Force.
2nd Lieut. R. D'Albertanson. Died 8/8/16 of wounds received while serving with the 6th Battn. Dorset Regt.
2nd Lieut. P. J. Gibbons. Killed in action 7/10/16, while serving with the 11th Battn. Royal West Kent Regt.

2nd Lieut. H. L. Gopsill. Killed in action 15/2/18, while serving with the Royal Flying Corps.

2nd Lieut. St. J. L. Hartnell-Sinclair. Killed in action 25/9/15, while serving with the 2nd Battn. Welsh Regt.

2nd Lieut. V. B. Haskins. Killed in action 20/11/15, while serving with the 5th Battn. Shropshire L.I.

2nd Lieut. S. J. Jennings. Killed in action 30/3/18, while serving with the Field Survey R.E.

2nd Lieut. W. S. Mansell. Killed in action 11/9/17, while serving with the Royal Flying Corps.

Captain A. E. Norman. Died 11/5/15 of wounds received while serving with the Army Cyclist Corps.

2nd Lieut. P. G. W. O'Hara. Killed in action 14/8/16, while serving with the 1/4th Battn. Royal Berkshire Regt.

Lieut. R. Q. Scott. Killed in action 16/4/17, while serving with the 20th Battn. Royal Fusiliers.

Captain H. Tripp. Killed in action 16/8/17, while serving with the 1/4th Battn. Royal Berkshire Regt.

2nd Lieut. F. C. D. Williams. Killed in action 19/7/16, while serving with the Royal Berkshire Regt.

Captain W. H. Williams. Killed in action 18/5/15, while serving with the Bedford Regt.

(ii) OFFICERS, W.O.'S AND N.C.O.'S OF THE 3RD BATTN. EAST SURREY WHO WERE AWARDED DECORATIONS NOT RECORDED ELSEWHERE IN THIS VOLUME.

*Distinguished Service Order:*

Captain S. C. W. Smith, while serving with the R.A.F.

*Military Cross:*

Lieut. J. V. Card, December, 1918, and January, 1919, while serving with the British Mission in the Caucasus.

Captain G. C. W. Gregory, 1st November, 1918, while serving with the 4th Battn. Royal Berkshire Regt. in Italy.

Lieut. O. Lloyd, October, 1918, while serving with the 4th Battn. North Stafford Regt. at Kappelhoek, near Courtrai.

2nd Lieut. G. C. Millis, October, 1917.

*Order of the British Empire:*

Major C. E. New, O.B.E.

Major R. H. H. Jackson, O.B.E., attached Machine Gun Corps.

*Meritorious Service Medal:*

Regtl. Sergt.-Major W. Emerson.

Company Qr.-Mr.-Sergt. E. H. Harwood.

Regtl. Sergt.-Major T. R. McCarthy.

Regtl. Sergt.-Major H. J. Parsons.

Company Sergt.-Major T. E. West.

Company Sergt.-Major R. Williams.

(B) *The 4th (Extra Reserve) Battn. East Surrey Regt.*

The unit, which in 1881 received the title of the 4th Battn. East Surrey, was raised in 1852 as the 3rd Royal Surrey Militia. A battalion of the same name had been raised in 1798 and disbanded in the year following.

The Battalion served in 1902, under the command of Lieut.-Colonel E. F. Sulivan, in South Africa, where Battalion Headquarters and four companies formed part of the Namaqualand Field Force in the relief of Ookiep, and took part in the attack on the Boer position at Steinkop on the 28th April. The remaining four companies formed the garrison of a blockhouse line in the Sterkstroom district.

After the proclamation of peace on the 31st May, 1902, the Battalion was employed in guarding prisoners of war at Green Point and Simon's Town until its return to England, when it was granted the distinction " South Africa, 1902."

The Battalion, then under the command of Lieut.-Colonel R. F. Peel, had already assembled at Kingston-on-Thames on the 3rd August, 1914, for its annual training when it received the order to mobilize on the outbreak of the Great War. Within a few days it was made known that extra Reserve battalions would not be sent overseas as complete units, but would be employed on garrison duty in the United Kingdom and to supply drafts to the line battalions in the field.

In accordance with the above decision, the Battalion, after mobilization, moved on the 9th August to Plymouth, and after a week spent in billets relieved a battalion of the Royal Irish Regiment in South Raglan Barracks, and, in addition, furnished garrisons in Tregantle and other forts, besides guards on wireless and cable stations along the South Coast.

During September the Battalion received many strong drafts of recruits, the greatest number in one day being about 1760; and in October the surplus personnel was drafted to the newly formed 10th and 11th Battns. East Surrey, leaving the 4th Battalion with a strength of about 1500 of all ranks.

A large number of young officers joined the Battalion from the Universities and Officers' Training Corps, most of whom, as will be seen in the records of other battalions of the Regiment, gained distinction later on in France and other theatres of the War. Lieut.-Colonel E. F. Sulivan and Captain B. G. F. Garnett, who had both been in command of battalions before the War, joined the 4th Battn. East Surrey as company commanders

Early in 1915 the Battalion commenced to send drafts overseas, one of 250 other ranks being despatched to the 2nd Battn. East Surrey in February, and by the 4th August—that is, twelve months after the outbreak of the War—the total numbers drafted were as follows:—

| | |
|---|---:|
| Other ranks to 1st Battn. East Surrey | 200 |
| ,, ,, 2nd ,, ,, | 931 |
| | 1131 |
| Officers sent overseas, of whom by the 4th August, 1915, 12 had been killed and 3 wounded | 34 |

It should be mentioned that the drafts furnished by the Battalion were invariably reported on as being highly trained and of excellent material.

In April, 1915, the Battalion moved to Saltash in Cornwall, and while at that station furnished a special detachment of 150 men for the parade on the Hoe in connection with the Centenary Celebrations. Among the numerous parties from the sea and land services attending this parade, the East Surrey detachment well upheld the reputation of the Regiment for smartness and steadiness.

The work of training and despatching drafts overseas, in addition to the performance of garrison duty, went on at Saltash, the Battalion being inspected as a unit of the Plymouth garrison by His Majesty the King in July, 1916, and by Field-Marshal Sir John French on the 13th September, 1917.

At the end of September the 4th Battn. East Surrey was transferred to Felixstowe, where it took over a section of the Harwich Defences. At Felixstowe the Battalion occupied billets which were spread over a wide area, no less than five canteens having to be provided for the use of the different detachments.

On the 9th November, 1918, a War Office telegram was received ordering demobilization, which commenced forthwith and proceeded until Battalion Headquarters and the few remaining details moved to the regimental Depôt at Kingston-on-Thames in January, 1919. Before they left Felixstowe, Colonel F. R. Peel received the following letter, which is quoted as a record of the highly creditable reputation of the Battalion at that station:—

HEADQUARTERS,
FELIXSTOWE SECTION,
9.12.18.

Officer Commanding,
    4th Battn. East Surrey Regt.

On the demobilization of the 4th Battn. East Surrey Regt., the G.O.C. desires me to express to you and all under your command his high appreciation of the good work done by all during the whole course of the War.

The Battalion has been a happy one, has worked with a splendid spirit; the discipline has been excellent, the men smart and well turned out, and the good work done at the Front by the thousands who have passed through its ranks reflects the greatest credit on those who trained them and imbued them with a fine regimental spirit. The G.O.C. wishes every success to those who are now leaving his command on demobilization.

(Signed) M. R. WHITAKER,
Capt., Brigade-Major.

As will be seen by the following table of drafts sent overseas during the War, the sentence "the thousands who have passed through its ranks" is no exaggeration, and it was the boast of the 4th Battn. East Surrey that never once did it fail to furnish in any draft the total number of men called for:—

## DRAFTS FURNISHED DURING THE WAR

| | | |
|---|---|---|
| Other ranks sent to 1st Battalion | | 178 |
| ,,    ,,    ,,   2nd    ,, | | 947 |
| ,,    ,,    ,,   7th    ,, | | 396 |
| ,,    ,,    ,,   8th    ,, | | 80 |
| ,,    ,,    ,,   9th    ,, | | 190 |
| ,,    ,,    ,,   12th   ,, | | 86 |
| Other ranks sent to units of the various Expeditionary Forces, inclusive of East Surrey battalions not specified | | 2855 |
| | | 4732 |

To individual soldiers of these drafts a considerable number of Distinguished Conduct Medals and Military Medals were awarded; while one officer, Lieut. H. B. Geary, received the Victoria Cross, and nearly thirty other officers received the Military Cross.

In his successful work of training, Colonel Peel had the assistance of Major M. J. A. Jourdier, Major M. J. Minogue, Lieut. Kennedy and Lieut. G. Milner, who held in succession the appointment of Adjutant of the Battalion; and another tribute is paid to the result of their joint efforts in the subjoined letter from the C.-in-C. the Forces in Great Britain:—

G.H.Q. THE FORCES IN GREAT BRITAIN,
HORSE GUARDS, LONDON, S.W.,
*24th June*, 1919.

DEAR COLONEL PEEL,

I write to you on the occasion of the demobilization of your Battalion, to express my warm appreciation of the work done by the 4th Reserve Battalion East Surrey Regiment since mobilization.

The high standard of the drafts sent overseas by your Battalion, due to the hard work of all concerned, contributed materially to the splendid achievements of the battalions which fought under my command.

Will you please convey to all who have served in your Battalion my high appreciation of their work in the past, and my most hearty thanks for the splendid service which they have rendered during the Great War?

Believe me,
Yours sincerely,
(Signed)   D. HAIG,
Field-Marshal,
Commanding-in-Chief,
The Forces in Great Britain.

Bt.-Colonel R. F. Peel,
4th East Surrey Regt., Harwich.

Following the plan adopted in the record of the 3rd Battn. East Surrey, two lists are subjoined. The first list gives the names of those of officers of the 4th Battn. East Surrey who met their deaths during the Great War while serving with other corps. The second list gives the names of officers and other ranks of the 4th Battalion who were awarded decorations not recorded elsewhere in this History.

In these lists the names of 4th Battalion officers who met their deaths or were awarded decorations while serving with other battalions of the East Surrey Regt. do not appear, as they are mentioned in the records of the battalion with which they were serving at the time, and a note that they belonged to the 4th Battalion is there added to their names.

(i) OFFICERS OF THE 4TH BATTN. EAST SURREY WHO MET THEIR DEATHS DURING THE GREAT WAR, WHILE SERVING WITH OTHER CORPS.

Major C. F. H. Rumbold. Killed in action 22/11/15, while serving with the 2nd Battn. Norfolk Regt.

Lieut. A. N. Joseland. Killed in action 22/9/17, while serving with the Nigeria Regt.

Lieut. W. H. Mitchell. Drowned 15/4/17, in the loss of H.T. *Arcadian*, while *en route* to Egypt to join the Royal Flying Corps.

2nd Lieut. E. T. Covington. Killed in action 9/3/17, while serving with the 6th Battn. Loyal North Lancashire Regt.

2nd Lieut. V. C. Howard. Drowned 15/4/17, in the loss of H.T. *Arcadian*, while *en route* to India to join the Indian Army.

2nd Lieut. A. G. E. Todd. Killed in action 23/4/17, while serving with the 2nd Battn. Hampshire Regt.

(ii) OFFICERS AND OTHER RANKS OF THE 4TH BATTN. EAST SURREY WHO WERE AWARDED DECORATIONS NOT RECORDED ELSEWHERE IN THIS HISTORY.

*C.M.G.:* Lieut.-Colonel R. F. Peel.

*Distinguished Service Order:*

Captain (acting Lieut.-Colonel) A. White, while serving with the 4/5th Battn. South Staffordshire Regt.

*Order of the British Empire:*

Captain A. W. Bowyer (O.B.E.); Captain L. H. Chidson (M.B.E.), while serving in the Machine Gun Corps.

*Military Cross:*

Lieut. E. H. Collinson, while serving in the Machine Gun Corps.

2nd Lieut. L. Roberts, while serving with the 6th Battn. R. West Surrey Regt.

*Distinguished Conduct Medal:*

Pte. T. J. Jack, while serving in the Machine Gun Corps.

### (C) *The 5th Battn. East Surrey Regt. (T.F.).*

The 1st Administrative Battn. Surrey Rifle Volunteers was formed in 1862 from various Rifle Corps then in existence at Wimbledon, Epsom, Streatham and Sutton. In 1880 the title of the Battalion was altered to "3rd Surrey Rifle Volunteers," and again, in 1887, to "2nd Volunteer Battalion, The East Surrey Regt."

During the South African War the Battalion sent a service company to the 2nd Battn. East Surrey and a detachment to the City Imperial Volunteers. In recognition of the services in the field of these detachments, the 2nd Volunteer Battn. East Surrey was granted the distinction "South Africa, 1900–1902."

On the formation of the Territorial Force in 1908 the 2nd Volunteer Battn. East Surrey received its present title "5th Battn. East Surrey Regt. (T.F.)," and was included in the Surrey Brigade of the Home Counties Division, the other battalions of the Brigade being the 4th and 5th Battns. "Queen's" R. West Surrey Regt. and the 6th Battn. East Surrey. On the 19th June, 1909, His Majesty King Edward VII presented the King's and Regimental Colours to a party of officers of the 5th Battn. East Surrey, sent to Windsor to receive them.

At the end of July, 1914, the Battalion assembled at Bordon for training with the Home Counties Division and marched to Salisbury Plain. On arrival there, on the 4th August, it was ordered, owing to the outbreak of the Great War, to return at once by rail to its headquarters at Wimbledon.

On August 5th the Battalion mobilized at Wimbledon and proceeded the same day to its War station at Chatham. Its Depôt was formed at Wimbledon, and recruiting continued there up to the end of August, by which time the Battalion was up to establishment. From Chatham the 5th Battn. East Surrey moved for a short time to Maidstone, and thence to Canterbury, where the Surrey Brigade was concentrating.

At Canterbury all ranks were invited to volunteer for service overseas, and, with the exception of a small number, at once accepted the liability for General Service. Orders were then received for the formation of a "Second Line" Battalion, and those members of the original Battalion—thenceforward to be designated the 1/5th Battn. East Surrey—who had not volunteered for General Service, were transferred as the nucleus of the newly formed 2/5th Battn. East Surrey.

On the 17th October it became known that the "First Line" Home Counties (44th) Division would shortly proceed to India, and soon afterwards the Division was inspected at Canterbury by His Majesty the King. The 5th Battn. East Surrey, with a strength of 28 officers and 800 other ranks, under the command of Lieut.-Colonel R. K. Harvey, T.D., left Canterbury on the 29th October, 1914, for embarkation at Southampton, and its subsequent history is continued in Chapter VII.

### (D) *The 2/5th Battn. East Surrey Regt. (T.F.).*

The 2/5th Battn. East Surrey Regt. was raised at Wimbledon in September, 1914, its original personnel being those members of the 1/5th Battn. East Surrey

Regt. who had not volunteered for General Service. Lieut.-Colonel W. A. Gillett was appointed to command the new battalion.

Recruiting proceeded briskly, and by November the Battalion was some 800 strong and moved to Windsor for training with the Second Line (67th) Home Counties Division. In May, 1915, the Battalion moved to Tunbridge Wells, and in the following month was temporarily at Wrotham for work on the London Defences. About this time those members of the Battalion who had not volunteered for General Service were tranferred to a Provisional Battalion, leaving the 2/5th Battalion composed entirely of General Service men. In August orders were received for the formation of a Third Line Battalion, and the necessary personnel were transferred from the 2/5th Battalion to the new unit, which was designated the 3/5th Battn. East Surrey Regt.

The winter of 1915–1916 was spent by the Battalion in billets at Reigate, whence it moved into camp at Sevenoaks at the end of June. After a fortnight at Sevenoaks the Battalion marched to Gore Street, in the Isle of Thanet, and in August furnished drafts for the Expeditionary Forces. During the winter of 1916–1917 the Battalion was employed on Coast Defence duty in the Isle of Thanet.

In the spring of 1917 the Battalion was raised to war establishment and commenced special training at Gore Street with a view to proceeding to France. This hope, however, was not realized, as the Battalion was disbanded in August, 1917, and the personnel sent overseas as drafts to the Expeditionary Forces.

(E) *The 3/5th Battn. East Surrey Regt. (T.F.).*

The 3/5th Battn. East Surrey Regt. was raised at the Territorial Depôt in Wimbledon by Major R. G. Hué-Williams towards the end of August, 1915, as the Third Line unit of the 5th Battalion. The nucleus of the new battalion consisted of 5 officers and 107 other ranks, including transfers from the 2/5th Battalion.

From the start the Battalion staff was fully occupied with the double duty of training and recruiting. Training presented many difficulties owing to the paucity of experienced instructors; while recruits came in but slowly, mainly owing to the fact that a R.F.A. Brigade was being raised simultaneously in the 5th Battalion's recruiting area. During October, however, nine more officers were posted to the 3/5th Battalion, and in December it was formed into two companies each consisting of about 150 of all ranks.

On the 1st January, 1916, the Battalion moved, with a strength of 22 officers and 396 other ranks, to Cambridge, where it joined the Third Line Group B of the Home Counties Division. On the 22nd March sufficient progress had been made with training to allow of the despatch by the Battalion of a draft of 7 officers and 375 other ranks to join the 1/5th Battn. East Surrey in India.

Early in April the Battalion, with the rest of the Home Counties Division, moved from Cambridge to Crowborough in Sussex. The strength of the Battalion at that time was 17 officers and 115 other ranks only. Shortly afterwards a draft of 105 recruits was received and another draft of 1 officer and 52 men was sent out to the 1/5th Battalion. During June and July some 400 other ranks were drafted into the Battalion, and a third draft 100 strong was sent to the 1/5th Battalion.

On the 22nd August, 1916, orders were received that the 3/5th and 3/6th Battns. East Surrey were to be amalgamated to form a new unit, which was to be designated the 5th Reserve Battn. East Surrey Regt. The latter battalion was formed on the 1st September, with a strength of over 1700 of all ranks, and Lieut.-Colonel Hué-Williams was appointed to the command.

The new battalion formed part of the Home Counties Reserve Brigade and was stationed at Crowborough until the 24th October, 1916, when it marched to Tonbridge. After a year's stay at Tonbridge it returned to Crowborough.

From Crowborough the Battalion moved at the end of September, 1918, to Tunbridge Wells, where its disbandment was ordered on the 13th November, 1918. The order for disbandment was, however, suspended on the 17th December and the Battalion continued in existence till the 18th April, 1919, when it was finally disbanded.

During the two and a half years of its existence the 5th Reserve Battn. East Surrey was a training and draft-finding unit and despatched overseas numerous drafts, some to India to join the 1/5th and 1/6th Battalions, and others to join the Expeditionary Forces in France, Italy and Salonika. The total strength of the drafts so despatched amounted to some 400 officers and 3700 other ranks, and the favourable reports received regarding them prove that the good spirit and efficient training prevailing in its youngest draft-finding unit added much to the credit of the Regiment to which it belonged. Lieut.-Colonel Hué-Williams was awarded the O.B.E. in recognition of his services as Commanding Officer, while Sergt.-Major C. T. Owen received the Meritorious Service Medal.

(F) *The 6th Battn. East Surrey Regt. (T.F.).*

The 6th Surrey Rifle Volunteers were originally formed as a battalion in 1862 from various Volunteer Rifle Corps then existing at Esher and in its vicinity. In 1880 the title of the Battalion was altered to "5th Surrey Rifle Volunteers," and again, in 1887, to "3rd Volunteer Battalion East Surrey Regt." The formation of the Territorial Force in 1908 gave the Battalion its present title, "6th (Territorial) Battn. East Surrey Regt."

The Battalion had been awarded in 1905 the honorary distinction, "South Africa, 1899-1902," in recognition of its services in supplying a large number of officers and men to various units, including a detachment to the City Imperial Volunteers, and a Volunteer company which served for a time with the 2nd Battn. East Surrey Regt. in the South African War. In 1913 the Battalion accepted the liability for foreign service and was granted the distinction "Imperial Service."

The Home Counties Division, to which the Battalion belonged, having been selected in 1914 for training as a Division, the Battalion reached Salisbury Plain on August 3rd. The same day, owing to the imminence of the Great War, it received orders to return immediately to Kingston-on-Thames, and on arrival there by rail on the 4th it was ordered to mobilize.

Mobilization was completed by the afternoon of the 5th August, and the Battalion left Surbiton that evening and after five days' special duty reached Maidstone, where it remained carrying out training till the 22nd August. The Battalion then moved to Canterbury, where the Surrey Brigade was concentrating, and later on orders were received to form a Second Line Battalion. Accordingly a number of officers and N.C.O.'s were detailed as the *cadre* of the new unit, designated the 2/6th Battn. East Surrey Regt.

On the 17th October it became known that the Home Counties Division would shortly proceed to India, and before leaving Canterbury it was inspected by His Majesty the King. The 1/6th Battn. East Surrey Regt., under the command of Lieut.-Colonel A. P. Drayson, embarked at Southampton, with a strength of 30 officers and 805 other ranks, as part of the First Line (44th) Home Counties Division, on the 29th October, 1914, and its record thereafter is continued in Chapter VII.

(G) *The 2/6th Battn. East Surrey Regt. (T.F.).*

The 2/6th Battn. East Surrey Regt. was raised in September, 1914, by Lieut.-Colonel and Hon. Colonel J. Leslie G. Powell, V.D., at Peace Headquarters, Kingston-on-Thames. The nucleus of the new battalion consisted of details taken over from the 1/6th Battalion prior to its embarkation for India in October, 1914.

In November, 1914, the Battalion moved in billets at Windsor for training with the Second Line (67th) Home Counties Division. The command of the Battalion was now taken over by Major W. Merrick, T.D., with Major F. Lester as Second-in-Command, Captain R. J. McNair as Adjutant, and Lieut. F. C. Robinson as Quartermaster.

As the result of recruiting marches of a picked detachment throughout its recruiting area in Surrey the Battalion speedily reached its establishment, and was inspected with the remainder of the 67th Division in Windsor Great Park by His Majesty the King in December, 1914, and by Field-Marshal Lord Kitchener at Runnymede in January, 1915.

In June, 1915, the Battalion moved into billets in Tunbridge Wells, whence in the month following it sent a draft of 5 officers and 57 other ranks to the newly formed 3/6th Battalion at Kingston-on-Thames.

In October, 1915, the Battalion moved to billets in Redhill, and was inspected by Field-Marshal Lord French at Godstone.

In July, 1916, the Battalion moved into camp at Sevenoaks, but was transferred almost immediately to Gore Street, in the Isle of Thanet, where it was selected to give a display of the attack from trenches to representatives of the American Army.

In the autumn of 1916 the Battalion was heavily depleted, two drafts, one of 500 and the other of 400, being sent overseas. On the 27th October, 1916, the

Battalion moved into billets at Margate, and having been brought up to establishment was, in January, 1917, with the rest of the Surrey Brigade placed under orders for service overseas. During its period of Coast Defence duty in Margate the Battalion came under hostile shell fire from the sea, but sustained no casualties.

In April, 1917, the Battalion returned to camp at Gore Street, where it remained until the autumn. Then, in common with other units of the 67th Division, it was disbanded and the personnel was sent overseas in two drafts. The transport and certain specialist officers and other ranks were transferred to a Young Soldiers' Battalion which replaced the 3/6th Battn. East Surrey at Gore Street. Lieut.-Colonel Merrick was attached to the 1st Battn. East Surrey, which was then serving in the Ypres salient, and the remaining officers were transferred to units overseas.

It should be mentioned that for the years 1915-1916 and 1917 the average of the individual scores made by members of the Battalion in the general musketry course exceeded the figure of qualification for First Class Shot.

(H) *The 3/6th Battn. East Surrey Regt. (T.F.).*

The 3/6th Battn. East Surrey was raised as the Third Line unit of the 6th Battalion at the Territorial Depôt, Kingston-on-Thames, on the 21st July, 1915, by Captain J. C. Eales-White, who received a commission in the 6th Battalion in 1910, after twelve years' service in the London Scottish. He had recruited about 20 men when he received from the 2/6th Battalion a draft of 5 officers and 57 other ranks.

As in the case of the 3/5th Battalion, the Battalion staff had the double duty of training and recruiting. In the latter work valuable assistance was given by the County Association, by Mr. T. P. O'Connor, M.P., and by Mr. George Cave, K.C., M.P. (now Lord Cave), with the result that by the middle of November two companies at full establishment had been formed.

Like the 3/5th Battalion, the 3/6th moved on the 1st January, 1916, to Cambridge, where it also joined the Third Line Group B of the Home Counties Division. The strength of the Battalion was now 51 officers and 420 other ranks, and on its way across London the newly formed band played through the City, by special permission of the Lord Mayor.

On the 16th February Major H. C. Watts, who had recently arrived home from the 1/6th Battalion in India, took over command of the 3/6th Battalion from Captain Eales-White, who was appointed Adjutant. Later in the month a draft of 5 officers and 100 other ranks was sent out to the 1/6th Battalion in India.

On the 3rd April the 3/6th Battalion moved with the Home Counties Division to Crowborough in Sussex, and within the next four months sent two more drafts, totalling 150 to the 1/6th Battalion and others totalling 11 officers and 80 other ranks, to France. On the 27th July Lieut.-Colonel Watts was transferred to the T.F. Reserve, and Captain Eales-White was reappointed to the command.

Amalgamation with the 3/5th Battalion to form a new unit was ordered shortly afterwards, and on the 1st September, 1916, the 3/6th Battalion, with a strength of 927 of all ranks, was merged into the 5th Reserve Battn. East Surrey, the history of which has already been recorded.

### (I) *The East Surrey Regimental Depôt.*

The mobilization of the other units of the East Surrey Regt. at the beginning of August, 1914, caused the withdrawal from the Regimental Depôt at Kingston-on-Thames of the whole of the personnel who were serving with it prior to the outbreak of the Great War. Lieut.-Colonel H. P. Treeby, D.S.O., was appointed under mobilization orders to the command of the Depôt and the 31st Regimental District Recruiting Area on the 4th of August, with Major F. White as his Second-in-Command. Both these officers had served in the Regiment and had retired from it after the South African War. Colonel Hyde Edwards, V.D., at the same time took over the duties of Headquarters' Recruiting Officer.

The staff with which these officers had to carry on their work was at first practically non-existent, and in order to complete it the Officer Commanding the Depôt was authorized to select officers and civilians and to re-enlist ex-N.C.O.'s for the vacant appointments.

During the first eighteen months of the War, the period during which the strength of the British armies was maintained by voluntary enlistment, the duties of the personnel of the Depôt were to obtain recruits and to pass them on to other units in the United Kingdom.

Following on Lord Kitchener's appeal for recruits for the New Armies, great recruiting meetings were organized throughout the 31st Regimental District Recruiting Area. At these meetings, two or three of which were held each day, appeals to men to come forward for enlistment were made by influential gentlemen of the county and by officers of the Depôt. Later on recruiting demonstrations were arranged, in which bodies of troops marched through the various towns in the area, and special meetings were held, when addresses were delivered by prominent local men. Many of these meetings were also addressed by Pte. E. Dwyer, V.C., of the 1st Battalion.

By these means recruits were collected at Kingston Depôt at the rate, on the average, of 315 a day. At first the pre-war practice of clothing and equipping recruits at the Depôt was retained, but as their numbers increased and the new Service units were formed, it became necessary to limit the stay at Kingston of the newly joined recruits to twenty-four hours, after which they were passed out to their units without uniform or arms. Attempts to prepare their documents before departure placed a heavy strain on the civilian clerks, who were few in number and new to the work.

In the autumn of 1915 National Registration, under Lord Derby's Scheme, came into force, and the Local Government Board forwarded to the Depôt the "Pink Forms" of 160,000 men of military age in the county area. For each

Pink Form three cards (white, red and blue) had to be completed with full particulars of each man's registration. In this work the Depôt authorities were assisted by a large number of voluntary helpers throughout the area, and by October, 1915, 200,000 Registration Forms, with the necessary cards, were completed and indexed, and "Military Representatives" and "Military Tribunals" were appointed. The first application of the new organization was the Royal Proclamation of the 14th December, 1915, which called up Groups 2, 3, 4 and 5 (single men).

The Derby Recruiting Scheme was in its turn superseded by the Military Service Act, which came into force on the 1st March, 1916, and continued until the cessation of hostilities.

In August, 1917, the Ministry of National Service was formed and took over from the military authorities the work of obtaining recruits. Under the new Ministry the 31st Regimental Recruiting Area ceased to exist as such and was divided between the new London and Guildford areas.

It is estimated that, prior to the formation of the Ministry of National Service, 97,000 recruits joined the Colours from the 31st Regimental District Area. Of this number, 84,000 passed through the Kingston Depôt. The balance of 13,000 is accounted for as the number of men who enlisted outside the area between the dates of registration and of the cessation of voluntary enlistment.

Two new organizations for the benefit of members of the East Surrey Regt. were formed at the Depôt during the War and were maintained until its termination rendered their continuance unnecessary. The first organization was the East Surrey Depôt Comforts Fund, which collected funds by means of subscriptions, concerts and fêtes, and was thus able to furnish a continuous supply of "comforts" of all kinds to the various battalions of the Regiment. The second organization was the East Surrey Prisoners of War Fund, presided over by Lady Longley. Subscriptions and funds were obtained by the same methods as for the Comforts Fund, and the committee, with the kind assistance of the Regimental Agency, packed and despatched to those members of the Regiment who had the ill-fortune to become prisoners of war, supplies of clothing and food which did much to mitigate the hardships of their captivity.

### (J) *The 7th (Service) Battn. East Surrey Regt.*

On the augmentation of the Army by the first 100,000 men demanded by Lord Kitchener, one of the first battalions to be raised was the 7th Battn. East Surrey Regt. Major C. C. G. Ashton, commanding the Depôt of the Regiment at Kingston-on-Thames, was appointed to the command, with Major R. H. Baldwin as Second-in-Command. Captain the Hon. Cuthbert James, formerly of the Regiment, was appointed senior company officer, with the rank of Major, Lieut. E. H. J. Nicholls (2nd Battalion) was promoted Captain and appointed Adjutant, and Sergt.-Major G. W. H. Rowe, from the regimental Depôt, was appointed Lieutenant and Quartermaster.

The Battalion was raised at Colchester, sharing the Goozerat Barracks with the 6th Battn. Royal West Kent Regt., and was rapidly completed with officers and men. On the 29th August the Battalion moved into camp at Purfleet, where musketry instruction was the chief consideration. Here several changes took place in the composition of the Battalion, many of the officers passing to other units or to the staff, while a number of old soldiers were transferred to the 3rd Battalion at Dover, and a considerable number of men were discharged as medically unfit. On the formation of the 37th Infantry Brigade the Battalion was posted to it, together with the 6th Battn. "Queen's," 6th Battn. "The Buffs" and 6th Battn. Royal West Kent Regt. Training proceeded vigorously, early deficiencies in the matter of blankets, clothing, boots and rifles being gradually made good, and in a surprisingly short time the Battalion attained a degree of steadiness and discipline which promised great things for the future.

On the 24th November the 37th Brigade, under Brigadier-General C. A. Fowler, left Purfleet for Sandling, Kent, where it was quartered in huts. Here the Brigade joined the remainder of the 12th Division, commanded by Major-General James Spens. The huts were of very bad construction and had been built in boggy ground, quite unsuitable for a camp, and much unnecessary discomfort was the consequence. Company training was at once begun, but after about three weeks the huts were perforce abandoned and the Battalion moved into billets at Sandgate.

Here training continued through the winter, until on the 22nd February, 1915, the Division marched for Aldershot, where it was quartered in Albuhera Barracks.

At Aldershot more advanced training at once began, the whole of the First New Army, comprising the 9th, 10th, 11th, 12th, 13th and 14th Divisions, being assembled in and around the camp, under General Sir Archibald Hunter. The units of these Divisions were put successively through battalion, brigade and divisional training. In March, Major-General Spens was appointed to a command in Egypt, and Major-General Wing took over the command of the 12th Division.

On the 17th April Lieut.-Colonel C. C. G. Ashton left the Battalion on appointment to command the 2nd Battn. East Surrey in place of Major Le Fleming, who had been severely wounded. Lieut.-Colonel Ashton was succeeded in command of the 7th Battalion by Lieut.-Colonel Baldwin, the original Second-in-Command of the Battalion, who had for several months been in command of the 9th Battalion at Shoreham.

Throughout its period of training all ranks of the Battalion had worked splendidly. Though disappointed at being kept so long at home while the Expeditionary Force was suffering heavily, and was urgently in need of reinforcement, all ranks fully appreciated the benefit that they had received from the very careful training given them. This appreciation they had shown by their excellent behaviour, for serious misconduct had been practically non-existent. At last, on the 28th May, 1915, the orders for embarkation arrived, followed by the transport animals and vehicles on the field service scale. A farewell message from His Majesty the King, wishing success to the 12th Division and expressing a desire to be informed of its achievements, gave great pleasure to all ranks.

On the 31st May the Battalion transport, machine guns, etc., left Aldershot by train under Major C. James and crossed from Southampton to Havre without incident. The Battalion followed on 1st June, 1915, embarking at Folkestone at midnight. The s.s. *Victoria*, in which the Battalion crossed the Channel to Boulogne, was escorted by two destroyers. The further record of the Battalion is continued in Chapter VIII.

### (K) *The 8th (Service) Battn. East Surrey Regt.*

The 8th Battn. East Surrey Regt. was formed as a unit of the Second New Army at Purfleet on the 10th September, 1914. On the 11th September, Lieut.-Colonel H. L. Smith, D.S.O., who had commanded the 1st Battn. East Surrey previous to his retirement in 1911, was appointed to command the 8th Battalion, which was then over 1000 strong, quite a third of the rank and file being Norfolk or Suffolk men. The 7th Battalion, which was at that time also at Purfleet, had lent to the 8th Battalion seven officers, including Major R. H. Baldwin, and also some N.C.O.'s. Lieut. Irwin was acting Adjutant, and Lieut. MacMillan was Quartermaster. Major F. White, also a retired officer of the East Surrey Regt., was shortly afterwards appointed to the Battalion as Second-in-Command.

In the early stages of training the men were without arms or uniforms, but this in no way interfered with their keenness to learn, and selections of the most promising for non-commissioned rank were quickly made. On the 16th October the camp, close to Purfleet Rifle Range, was vacated, owing to its waterlogged state, and the Battalion moved to Belhus Park Camp, near Aveley. The Battalion now formed part of the 55th Brigade of the 18th Division, the other three battalions of the Brigade being the 7th Battn. "Queen's," the 7th Battn. "The Buffs" and the 7th Battn. Royal West Kent Regt. At Aveley some rifles were received and training went on apace. On the 1st December the Battalion moved into huts near Purfleet village. January, 1915, was occupied with range practices and brigade inspections, and shortly afterwards Major H. G. Powell, D.S.O. (Loyal North Lancashire Regt.), took over command from Lieut.-Colonel Smith, who, as also Major White, was found medically unfit for service overseas.

At the end of March the Battalion moved to Colchester for ten days' brigade training. The 18th Division was then concentrated at Codford, where brigade training was continued, followed by divisional training. In the middle of June the Division was inspected by His Majesty the King prior to its departure to France. The 8th Battn. East Surrey embarked for France on the 26th July, 1915, and its further record is continued in Chapter IX.

### (L) *The 9th (Service) Battn. East Surrey Regt.*

The 9th Battn. East Surrey Regt. came into existence at Shoreham (near Brighton) about the middle of September, 1914, Major R. H. Baldwin, who had recently arrived in England on completion of a tour of duty in West Africa, being appointed to the command with the temporary rank of Lieut.-Colonel. Men arrived very rapidly, and on the 19th September the Battalion was over

1000 strong. In the ranks were a large number of old soldiers, but over 300 of these were sent off about three weeks later to complete the 1st Battalion, which had suffered heavy losses at Mons and in the subsequent fighting.

The 9th Battn. East Surrey, with the 8th Battn. "Queen's," 8th Battn. "The Buffs" and 8th Battn. Royal West Kent Regt., formed the 72nd Brigade, under Brigadier-General B. R. Mitford, C.B., D.S.O., an officer on the retired list, who had seen much active service. Brigadier-General Mitford's regimental service had been passed in "The Buffs" and East Surrey Regt. The 72nd Brigade, with the 71st and 73rd, belonged to the 24th Division, under Major-General Sir J. G. Ramsay, K.C.B., an officer on the retired list of the Indian Army.

The divisional and brigade staffs arrived at Shoreham on the 19th September, on which date, as has been mentioned, the 9th Battn. East Surrey was up to establishment; but there were as yet no arms available for the men. Tents and cooking pots had been provided, but no other camp equipment; there was a great shortage of blankets. The camp lay on the southern slopes of the Downs; the nights were frosty and very cold. An appeal to the local population brought in a large number of blankets, but even then there was not more than one per man. Lieut.-Colonel Baldwin organized the Battalion on a sound basis, and the thousand men soon assumed the air of soldiers.

On September the 24th the 72nd Brigade shifted camp to the Oxenfield, just south of Buckingham House. The weather was fine, and the field looked a good camping site. A week later, however, rain came on and the ground became a bog, which all efforts failed to solidify. Consequently, after much discomfort, the 72nd Brigade moved to billets in Worthing, the 9th Battn. East Surrey being quartered in the northern portion of the town. Here the winter was passed in steady training, relations between the rank and file and the civilians being uniformly pleasant throughout this period.

On the 2nd April, 1915, the Brigade moved by rail to Redhill and Reigate, the 9th Battn. East Surrey being quartered about Redhill. Here, until April 18th, the units of the Brigade were employed on trench-work, on a line marked out as part of the London defences. On April 17th Lieut.-Colonel Baldwin was transferred to the 7th Battn. East Surrey Regt., to take the place of Lieut.-Colonel Ashton, who had been sent to Ypres to take over command of the 2nd Battalion, which had lost all its senior officers. Major F. L. Sanders, the senior Major of the 9th Battalion, was promoted to the command, Major H. V. Welch becoming Second-in-Command. On April the 19th the Battalion entrained at Redhill and returned to Shoreham, where the 72nd Brigade was accommodated in newly built and incomplete huts on the site of its former camp. Here the Brigade remained for two months, finally leaving Shoreham by march route on June 21st, halting that night at Horsham, on the 22nd at Guildford, and arriving on the 23rd at Blackdown Camp, near Aldershot.

After completing very full instruction in Battalion, Brigade and Divisional work, the 9th Battn. East Surrey, with the remainder of the 24th Division, embarked at Folkestone on the 31st August, 1915, and arrived at Boulogne at about midnight. The subsequent record of the Battalion commences in Chapter XIV.

### (M) *The 10th (Service) Battn. East Surrey Regt.*

The 10th Battn. East Surrey Regt. was originally formed at Dover on the 26th October, 1914, as a Service Battalion in the 95th Brigade of the Fourth New Army. It was at first composed of about 400 N.C.O.'s and men, the overflow of the 3rd Battalion. Of the new recruits, about 95 per cent came from the London district, principally South London, Croydon and Richmond. Major A. J. Hay (3rd Battalion), with Captain A. E. Couper (late 2nd Battalion) as his Adjutant, was in temporary command until the appointment of Lieut.-Colonel E. Sulivan on the 18th November, 1914.

The Battalion was in camp on the Glacis at Dover until the middle of November, and it moved into the Oil Mills Barracks for the winter. The Battalion continued training for service overseas until April, 1915, when, owing to the impending departure overseas of the Service battalions of the first three New Armies, fresh arrangements had to be made to meet their inevitable war wastage. For this purpose the infantry battalions of the Fourth and Fifth New Armies were converted from "Service" to "Reserve" battalions, their purpose thenceforth being to furnish drafts for the older "Service" battalions.

The 95th Brigade was accordingly converted into a 2nd Reserve Brigade, and from that time the Battalion was designated the 10th (Reserve) Battn. East Surrey Regt. On the 18th May it moved to Purfleet and shortly afterwards sent its first draft overseas. The Battalion moved to Shoreham on the 21st September, 1915, and on the 15th March, 1916, returned to the Oil Mills Barracks at Dover. Later on it moved into Maxton Road Camp at Dover until the 31st August, 1916, when it was converted into the 30th Training Reserve Battalion.

### (N) *The 11th (Service) Battn. East Surrey Regt.*

The record of the 11th Battn. East Surrey Regt. is very similar to that of the 10th Battalion. It was first formed at Devonport on the 1st November, 1914, as a Service Battalion in the 100th Brigade of the Fourth New Army, the original personnel, some 750 other ranks, being drawn from the excess strength of the 4th Battalion.

Colonel E. F. Sulivan, of the 10th Battalion, was temporarily in command of the 11th until the 18th November, when he was appointed to the command of the 10th Battalion, and was succeeded in command of the 11th by Lieut.-Colonel C. G. Carnegy, M.V.O., of the Indian Army.

After some six weeks at Devonport the 11th Battalion moved in the middle of December, 1914, to Dartmouth, where it continued to train as a unit for service overseas. In April, 1915, however, for the reasons stated in the record of the 10th Battalion, the 11th Battalion also ceased to be a Service Battalion and became the 11th (Reserve) Battn. East Surrey Regt. It was shortly afterwards transferred to Colchester, posted to the 93rd Brigade, and commenced its new duties of supplying drafts for the battalions overseas. About the 15th September,

1915, the Battalion moved to Shoreham-by-Sea, where it served as a draft-finding unit for another twelve months.

On the 1st September, 1916, the Battalion ceased to exist as a unit of the East Surrey Regt., as it was amalgamated with the 9th Battn. "Queen's," and the two units were then converted into the 21st Training Reserve Battalion.

### (O) *The 12th (Service) Battn. East Surrey Regt.*

In February, 1915, the mayors of the boroughs of London were approached by the recruiting authorities with a view to obtaining additional units for the New Armies. The Mayor of Bermondsey, Mr. Hart, undertook to raise a battalion of infantry, which for Territorial associations was to receive the title of the 12th Battn. East Surrey.

The new battalion was formed at Rotherhithe on the 24th May, 1915, and Lieut.-Colonel L. F. Beatson, formerly a lieutenant in the Royal Warwick Regt., was appointed on the 31st to command it. Recruiting for the Battalion commenced in Bermondsey without delay, and considerable assistance was rendered by Sir Harry Lauder. The 3rd Battalion supplied a number of Regular N.C.O.'s who had been wounded in France while serving with the 1st or 2nd Battalion, and a certain number of officers joined from the Inns of Court O.T.C.

Training was carried out in Southwark Park until the beginning of September, 1915, when the Battalion moved to Witley Camp and joined the 122nd Brigade of the 41st Division. The Battalion was now augmented by the arrival of drafts from Kingston and of a number of officers from the Inns of Court O.T.C. The General Musketry course was fired at Aldershot under very unfavourable conditions.

During the early months of 1916 a number of lads who were under age were replaced by older men and battalion, brigade and divisional training were proceeded with. Towards the end of March, Major H. H. Lee, D.S.O., of the Cameronians, relieved Lieut.-Colonel Beatson in command of the Battalion. Shortly afterwards "final" leave was opened, and the 41st Division was inspected by His Majesty the King at Aldershot prior to its departure on May 1st, 1916, for active service in France. The record of the Battalion is continued in Chapter XV.

### (P) *The 13th (Service) Battn. East Surrey Regt.*

The 13th (Service) Battn. East Surrey Regt. was raised at Wandsworth, largely through the exertions of the mayor of the borough, Lieut.-Colonel Sir Archibald Dawnay, J.P., and was composed almost entirely of local men. The first recruit was posted on the 3rd June, 1915, and by the end of the second month the Battalion had been completed. Early in September it was sent, under Lieut.-Colonel A. T. W. Burton, who had been appointed to the command on June 15th, to Witley in Surrey, where training began in earnest. The Battalion, on arrival at Witley, was posted to the 41st Division, and while the rank and file was passing through the various stages of recruits' training most of the officers went in turn to classes of instruction. In October the Battalion moved to Barossa Barracks, Aldershot, on transfer to the 39th Division, commanded by Major-General N. W. Barnardiston. While at Aldershot the organization of the Battalion was completed, and section, platoon and company training successively proceeded. Early in November the 39th Division marched to Witley Camp for brigade training, the 13th Battn. East Surrey, together with the 20th and 21st Battns. Middlesex Regt. and the 14th Battn. Argyll and Sutherland Highlanders, forming the 118th Infantry Brigade.

On the 15th December, 1915, Major W. C. Newton, Middlesex Regt., was appointed to the command, with the temporary rank of Lieut.-Colonel, vice Lieut.-Colonel Burton, transferred to the 14th Battn. East Surrey. Musketry training was now in progress, and in January, 1916, the 39th Division fired its course on the Ash rifle ranges. In February the 39th Division proceeded on active service, but certain battalions being found to be insufficiently trained, the 118th Brigade was left behind and, after being transferred to the 40th Division, commanded by Major-General H. G. Ruggles-Brise, was broken up. The 13th Battn. East Surrey and the 14th Battn. Argyll and Sutherland Highlanders were transferred to the 120th Brigade, which was completed by the 11th Battn. King's Own Royal Lancaster Regt., and the 14th Battn. Highland Light Infantry.

The 40th Division remained at Blackdown, near Aldershot, training hard until orders came for it to prepare to proceed overseas. It was inspected soon afterwards by His Majesty the King, who expressed his pleasure at the steadiness of the men on parade and said he was sure that the same discipline would assert itself under more strenuous circumstances in days to come—a prophecy which, as later pages will show, was nobly fulfilled.

On the 3rd June, 1916, the 13th Battn. East Surrey entrained at Frimley for Southampton and embarked for France in the afternoon. The history of the Battalion is continued in Chapter XXII.

### (Q) The 14th (Reserve) Battn. East Surrey Regt.

The story of the 14th Battn. East Surrey is a brief one. It was formed at Wandsworth as the reserve battalion to the 13th Service Battalion from the overflow of the latter unit. Lieut.-Colonel A. T. W. Burton was appointed to the command, and Captain F. Alexander as his adjutant, both officers having been transferred from the 13th Battalion.

On the 1st November, 1915, when the 14th Battn. East Surrey had attained a strength of between 500 and 600 of all ranks, it was moved to Gravesend and remained at that station until it was disbanded at the end of June, 1916. The duty of finding drafts for the 13th Battalion was then taken over by the newly formed 5th Reserve Battn. East Surrey, *vide* sub-section (E) of this chapter.

Lieut. T. G. Poland, who was transferred from the Battalion to the Royal Flying Corps, was subsequently awarded the Distinguished Service Order.

# CHAPTER II

AUGUST AND SEPTEMBER, 1914: THE 1st BATTALION LANDS IN FRANCE WITH THE BRITISH EXPEDITIONARY FORCE; IN THE BATTLE OF MONS AND THE RETREAT FROM MONS, INCLUDING THE BATTLE OF LE CATEAU.

ON the outbreak of war with Germany and Austria the 1st Battalion was stationed at Dublin, under the command of Lieut.-Colonel J. R. Longley, and was in a high state of efficiency, being recognized by the military authorities in Ireland as one of the best disciplined and most efficient battalions then in the country. The Battalion formed part of the 14th Brigade, 5th Division. The Brigade was commanded by Brigadier-General S. P. Rolt, the other battalions in it being the 2nd Battn. Suffolk Regt., the 1st Battn. Duke of Cornwall's Light Infantry and the 2nd Battn. Manchester Regt.

The Battalion, which was in its summer quarters at the Curragh Camp, received orders to proceed to Dublin on the 29th July, 1914, and further orders to mobilize on Tuesday the 4th August. The first draft, of 400 reservists, arrived from Kingston-on-Thames on the 6th, and mobilization was completed on the 8th, with the Battalion at war establishment, in addition to a first reinforcement of 99 men, under Captain J. K. T. Whish.

Embarkation was postponed until the 13th August, and the delay was utilized to the full in musketry practice and march discipline. To the special attention paid to the last-named essential branch of military training, and the good marching of the Battalion, its slight losses in prisoners in the first weeks of the War is largely to be attributed.

On August 13th the Battalion fell in at 9 a.m. and marched from Wellington Barracks through the streets of Dublin to the North Wall. After a long wait on the quay the Battalion embarked on the transport *Botanist* and, sailing at 6 p.m., arrived at Le Havre, after a calm passage, at noon on August 15th. After disembarkation the Battalion had a long march in heavy rain to the rest camp, though the tremendous enthusiasm of the populace largely discounted the inclemency of the weather. The following day, Sunday, was fine and sunny, and the men were able to get the camp in good order and clean their uniform and equipment.

The Battalion paraded at 4 a.m. on Monday the 17th and marched to the railway station, where after some delay it entrained at 11.30 a.m. The first stop was at Rouen, where coffee was provided by the French authorities. Amiens was reached at 9 p.m., and at 4 a.m. on the 18th August the Battalion detrained at Le Câteau. Here preserved rations were served out, and at 7 a.m. the Battalion marched to Landrécies, a distance of 7½ miles. The road ran chiefly through woods, and the day being very hot and still the march was a trying one. The men had had little rest since August 4th, the first day of mobilization, and the reservists had not yet got accustomed to the heavy weight of their equipment, which was new to most of them; while the overwhelming hospitality of the inhabitants, who at every halt had pressed food, wine and cigars on the soldiers, now began to show its effects. At Landrécies the Battalion was accommodated in Biron Barracks, and the officers were billeted on families in the town, who received them with great kindness.

The concentration of the 5th Division in the neighbourhood continued during the next two days, and the Headquarters of the Division and the Brigade arrived at Landrécies.

The Battalion was chiefly occupied in route-marching, though it found time for bathing in the canal, where it sustained its first casualty, Pte. Walters, a reservist, being drowned.

On the 20th August the Battalion was addressed on parade by Major-General Sir Charles Fergusson, commanding the 5th Division, who made a most stirring and excellent speech, in the course of which he warned the men that the coming campaign would be no child's play.

On Friday the 21st the Battalion fell in at 6.25 a.m. and marched as the rear battalion of the 14th Brigade northwards through the Forêt de Mormal to Bermeries, about 13 miles. Bermeries was reached at 2 p.m., and here in the course of the evening all preparations for immediate action were made. It was known that fighting was at hand, and all were most cheerful and confident.

The Battalion was ordered to parade at 4 a.m. on the 22nd August, but this hour was changed to 7.30 a.m., when the 14th Brigade fell in and quickly marched off. At the first halt the officers were called to the front and told to warn their men that they might meet the enemy any time after noon. No fighting, however, took place; the Franco-Belgian frontier was crossed at 9 a.m., and after a hot march of 18 miles the head of the Brigade at 3 p.m. reached the Mons–Condé canal, along which it was ordered to take up an outpost line. The 1st Battn. East Surrey, which had again marched as the rear battalion of the Brigade, passed the other three battalions and, turning to the right, marched along the towing path towards Mons. The Battalion, now on the right of the Brigade, held the line of the canal, with its right resting on and including the bridge by which the Mons–Tournai railway crossed it at Les Herbières. The left of the Battalion included the road bridge over the canal nearly a mile to the west. This front formed the right section of the outpost line of the 14th Brigade, the D.C.L.I. holding the left section. On the right of the East Surrey were the King's Own Scottish Borderers, the left battalion of the 13th Brigade. The 15th Brigade was in reserve.

The dispositions of the 1st Battn. East Surrey were as shown in the sketch map on page 33, and the ground was thus distributed among the companies:—

*Right bridge-head:* C Company, under Captain J. P. Benson, and machine-gun section, under Lieut. T. H. Darwell.

*Left bridge-head:* B Company, under Captain E. M. Woulfe-Flanagan.

*Centre:* D Company, under Captain M. J. Minogue, held the south bank of the canal and connected B and C Companies.

*Reserve:* A Company, under Captain H. P. Torrens, was posted in a small wood about 500 yards in rear of Battalion Headquarters, which were in a cottage on the south bank of the canal between D and B Companies.

Major H. S. Tew, who was in charge of the right bridge-head, established his headquarters at a point covered by the canal and railway embankments, the former of which was about 10 feet high and the latter 25 feet.

It will be seen from the sketch that C Company, on the right, held several small trenches generally parallel to the canal and 150 to 200 yards north of it. This position was weakened by the line of houses which ran down to the road bridge close on its right, held by the K.O.S.B.'s. It was understood that the houses nearest to the canal were to be blown up by the Engineers, but from some unknown cause this was not done.

The three East Surrey companies in the outpost line were all in position by 6 p.m. and soon started work on their positions.

At dawn on the 23rd August a patrol under Captain R. C. Campbell went forward and examined the woods and the railway as far as Hautrage Station. No Germans were seen, and the railwaymen were busily engaged in removing locomotives and railway carriages to the rear of the British line.

The Commanding Officer, finding at his early morning inspection how much foreground there was to be cleared in front of the right bridge-head, ordered the reserve company, A, forward and placed it under Major Tew's orders. The Brigade was also asked to send up two companies of the Suffolks, who were in Brigade Reserve, with the Brigade tools, to assist in the work of clearing. With the help of A Company and one of the Suffolk companies, a clear field of fire varying from 300 to 500 yards was obtained by noon, and the trenches, $4\frac{1}{2}$ fete deep, were well hidden.

The morning had opened misty and wet, but about 10 a.m. the sky cleared. Soon after midday firing began further away to the right of the East Surrey position, and by 1 p.m. fire also was opened against C Company's trenches. Part of the Suffolk company which was clearing the ground in front was consequently drawn into them. It must be mentioned that shortly before the German attack opened Major Tew sent Lieut. Schomberg across to the road bridge on his right, held by the K.O.S.B., and arranged with that battalion that neither it nor the East Surrey would withdraw without first informing the other. Major Tew immediately reported this arrangement to Lieut.-Colonel Longley, who further arranged that each battalion should hold on to its position till after dark, and issued orders to that effect to the Battalion. He then sent to the D.C.L.I. on his left, to propose a similar pact with them, but found that this battalion had already fallen back from the canal, in accordance with orders received, to take up a position south of the Haine, a small river to the south of the canal. He then arranged that Major Tew should blow up the railway bridge, when compelled to retire, without waiting for further orders, and that this should be the signal for the road bridge held by B Company to be blown up also.

As soon as the German attack opened Captain Benson, commanding C Company, who had been in consultation with Major Tew, went forward with the officer commanding the front platoon of A Company, Lieut. D. Wynyard, to decide on the best way of reinforcing the right fire trenches when necessary. The two officers crossed the canal by means of a barge which had been moored

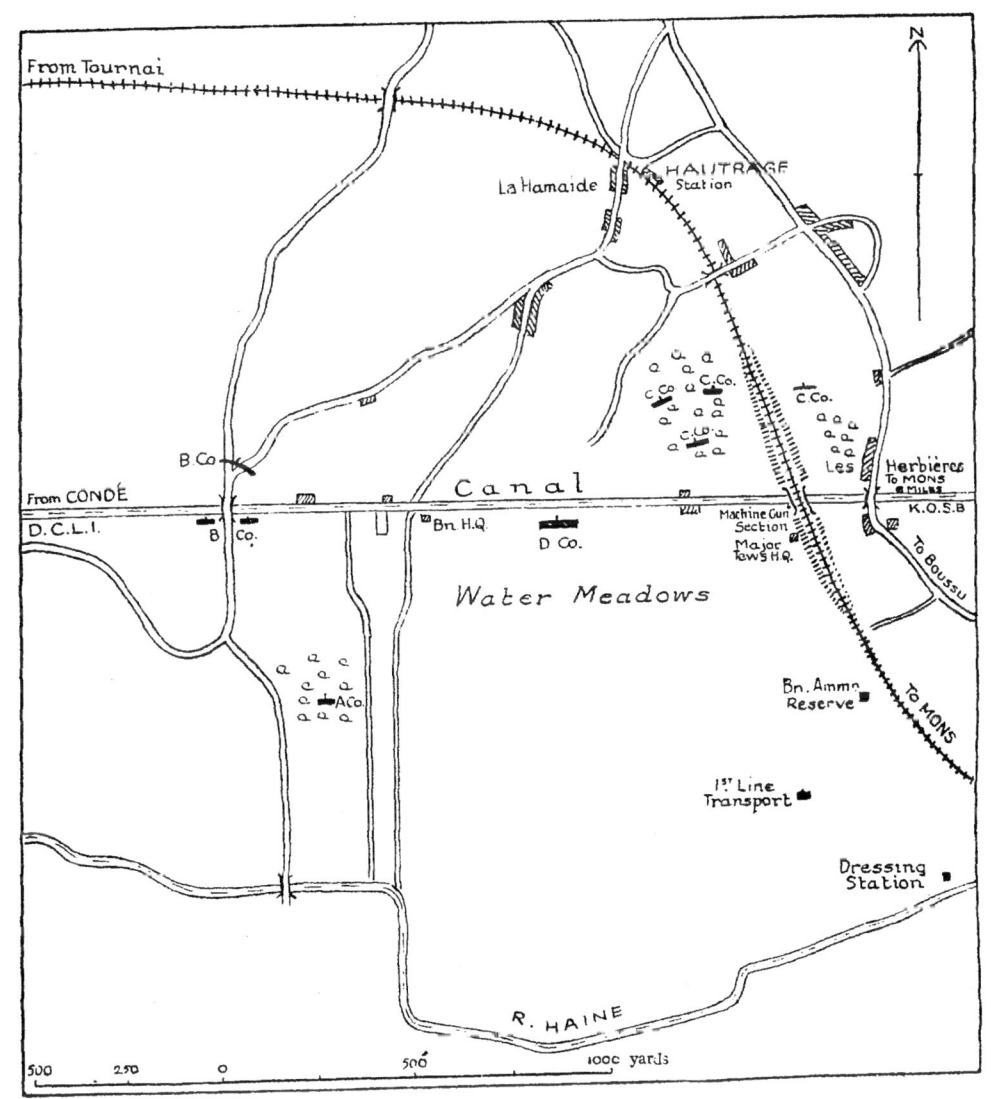

THE 1ST BATTALION IN THE BATTLE OF MONS, 1914

across it under the railway bridge and walked forward towards the nearest fire trench. When they had advanced about fifty yards, machine-gun fire was directed on them and Captain Benson was hit at once and fell to the ground mortally wounded. He was put on a stretcher by Lieut. Wynyard and two men

II.—D

under a heavy fire by which one of the men was presently wounded, a third man taking his place. With great difficulty Captain Benson was carried to the dressing station, whence he was taken later to a Belgian convent at Boussu, where he received every care, but died during the night.

Captain J. P. Benson had retired from the Army shortly before the War with the intention of entering the Church. He rejoined on mobilization and, at his own urgent request, went on active service with the Battalion. He was a first-rate soldier, a worthy member of a military family, and had previously done good service in the 2nd Battalion in the South African War, in which he was wounded. His death was deeply regretted by officers and men.

When Captain Benson became a casualty, the command of C Company devolved on Captain R. C. Campbell, who was at the time in charge of the fire trenches of the company on the west of the railway embankment. In accordance with an order conveyed to him by Company Sergt.-Major Thompson, Captain Campbell proceeded to Major Tew's headquarters close to the railway bridge. On the fire in front becoming much brisker, Captain Campbell asked leave to go up to his fire trenches again, and was permitted to do so. He went first to the left of his line, where he found 2nd Lieut. Ward coolly controlling the fire of his men, who were holding two trenches.

Throughout the morning various contradictory orders were received by the Battalion as to the holding of the canal position and as to when a retirement would take place, and owing to the rapid development of the attack it would seem that the officers and men in the trenches on the west of the railway were not aware that retirement might, under certain circumstances, take place before darkness came on.

On the east of the railway the German attack was heavy, their infantry coming on extended at one pace interval and supported by a large number of machine guns. The 1st Battn. East Surrey, however, held their ground firmly and inflicted heavy losses on the Germans. Attempts by the latter to cross the railway embankment, in order to attack the left trenches of C Company in flank, were also defeated with heavy loss by the machine-gun section excellently handled by Lieut. Darwell.

At about 4 p.m. the attack on the trench east of the railway became serious, and Lieut. Wynyard advanced, as had been arranged by Captain Benson, with about fifty men and reinforced the trench at a critical moment. Fighting at very close quarters took place, and Lieut. Wynyard was severely wounded in the arm, but the position was held.

At about 6 p.m. the battalion on the right of the East Surrey was suddenly compelled to fall back from the road bridge which it was holding, its defences having been destroyed by artillery fire at close quarters. In consequence of this retirement, Major Tew saw that it was necessary to withdraw his troops to the south bank of the canal, and also to retire the machine-gun section from the position which had enabled it hitherto to sweep the railway.

The order to retire was signalled to C Company by Lieut. Darwell. The signal was seen by the troops in the trenches on the east of the railway, and the portions of A and C Companies occupying them were successfully withdrawn, crossing the canal by the barge mentioned above, their retirement being covered by the fire of the remainder of A Company, which had been posted on the south bank of the canal. It would appear, however, that the signal to retire was not observed by 2nd Lieut. Ward's and Lieut. Morritt's platoons, who, on the west of the railway, had successfully held their trenches against heavy attacks throughout the afternoon, and the evacuation of the trenches on the east of the railway enabled the German infantry to swarm over the embankment and advance against their right and rear.

Captain Campbell, whose visit to the left trenches of his company has already been mentioned, was making his way from 2nd Lieut. Ward's trenches towards those held by Lieut. Morritt's platoon at the moment when the Germans opened fire from the railway embankment. Being in the open, he was immediately wounded in the neck. He was thrown to the ground by the shock, but was not stunned and got up again at once. 2nd Lieut. N. L. Ward saw the Germans on the embankment at the same moment, and promptly ordered his men to retire by rushes towards the canal. Captain Campbell was now hit by a second bullet, this time in the face, his tongue also being severely injured by the wound; but he gamely struggled on after Ward's platoon, receiving two more wounds in quick succession, the last one breaking his arm and bringing him again to the ground. In his own words: " I felt about done, and I saw Ward waving his sword and dashing forward with his men. He must have fallen dead almost at that moment. He showed very great coolness and pluck, and died like a hero."

Lieut. Morritt and his men, who occupied three trenches on the right of those held by 2nd Lieut. Ward's platoon, behaved with equal gallantry. Morritt, at the moment when the Germans appeared on the railway embankment, was walking to his centre trench from the right, and so did not at first see the enemy. The men in the right trench saw them, however, and some began to retire. Morritt at once rallied them, and they returned to the trench. Presently Germans in large numbers appeared in the little wood between Morritt's trenches and the canal, so his retreat was cut off. Quite undaunted, he sent a messenger to warn Captain Campbell of what had happened, and then ordered his men to fix bayonets and charge through the Germans to the canal. The order so gallantly given was as gallantly obeyed; but the task was an impossible one, and it is doubtful if a man got through from the fire trenches, though those under Company Sergt.-Major Thompson in the support trench, being nearer the canal, contrived to escape. Lieut. Morritt himself, after leading his men for about twenty yards, was brought down by a bullet wound above the right knee. He had already been seriously wounded in the right wrist, and less gravely in the leg. When on the ground Lieut. Morritt saw a German aiming his rifle carefully at him at a range of about twenty yards, but fortunately the shot hit his sword, breaking it in half.

When all resistance was over the Germans took the unwounded prisoners and made those of the wounded who could walk fall in and march off, leaving the two officers and a number of dead and severely wounded men on the ground. The wounded bandaged one another as best they could, and in the morning Lieut. W. G. Morritt and eight of his men were carried by Belgians to a convent, where they all received the kindest and most skilful attention. Eventually they were removed as prisoners to Germany, where, after several plucky attempts to escape, Lieut. Morritt was killed on his last attempt at Schwarmstadt, in Hanover, on the 27th June, 1917.

Captain Campbell, who did not discover where Lieut. Morritt was, crossed the canal in the morning of the 24th August with two wounded men who could walk, and they found their way to another hospital. This was under German management, but Captain Campbell was removed to a house near at hand, where he was most hospitably treated and nursed by a Belgian and his wife. Later in the day he was visited by two German officers, both wounded, who brought him a bottle of wine as a present and complimented him on the fine shooting of his men. A pleasant and chivalrous episode. A week later he was taken to a hospital at Cologne.

We must now go back to the moment when Major Tew ordered Lieut. Darwell to signal the retirement. Darkness was fast coming on, and Major Tew, after seeing the troops on the east of the railway begin to withdraw, turned his attention to the arrangements for the destruction of the bridge and the organization of a rearguard to cover the further retirement to the River Haine. By the time that these matters had been attended to all British troops had ceased crossing the canal, and A Company, on the south bank of the canal and west of the railway, had opened a heavy fire on the ground in front of them—that is, on the position once occupied by Lieuts. Morritt's and Ward's platoons. Major Tew therefore concluded that all his men had recrossed the canal, and, having withdrawn A Company from the vicinity of the railway bridge, he gave orders for it to be blown up. This was done, and the explosion was followed immediately by another to the west, which announced the destruction of the road bridge held by B Company. After the destruction of the railway bridge Major Tew, hearing that part of A Company was still on the canal bank, went back to within 100 yards of the wrecked bridge, but all that he could hear were orders shouted in German on the north bank of the canal. It was not until next morning that he learnt that the greater part of the troops on the west of the railway had been cut off.

The destruction of B Company's road bridge was effected none too soon, for the last man had only just quitted the house, which had been fortified as a bridge-head, when a German shell completely destroyed it. Then the right and left half-battalions, in accordance with their orders, retired steadily by their respective routes to the south bank of the River Haine. Thence they marched to Boussu, a distance of less than three miles; but the road was so congested with troops and the night so dark, notwithstanding the glare of burning houses, that it was 2 a.m. on August 24th before the weary troops reached their destination and threw themselves down to rest in a factory yard. So ended for them the first day's fighting of the Great War.

The Battalion rested but two hours at Boussu, parading at 4 a.m. on the

## TWO COMPANIES SEPARATED FROM THE BATTALION

24th August and marching to Dour, the streets of which town, a densely populated mining settlement, were crowded with men, women and children flying panic-stricken from the sound of the guns, which were now close at hand. The 1st Battn. East Surrey was posted in reserve, the remainder of the Brigade, which had been only lightly engaged on the previous day, taking up a defensive position outside the town. Lieut.-Colonel Longley and his Adjutant, Captain Bowring, were presently ordered to examine the ground in case the Battalion might be required to reinforce any portion of the Brigade.

While they were so employed the Battalion, under Major Tew, was ordered to Wiheries to act as left flank-guard during the retirement of the 5th Division. This order was eventually modified, B and D Companies, under Lieut.-Colonel Longley, being detailed to act as rearguard, and being ordered later across the frontier to St. Waast, near Bavai, which they reached about 7 p.m. after a very hot and trying day. This was the third place to which they were ordered within an hour, so quickly was the situation changing at that time.

The two other companies, A and C, under Major Tew, were kept out on the flank at Wiheries by direct order of an officer of the divisional staff, who later gave precise instructions as to the route by which they were to proceed to Eth, four miles west of St. Waast. The result of these orders was that Major Tew's two companies were separated from the Battalion for a considerable time. Their experiences will be related presently.

On the 25th August the Battalion Headquarters, with B and D Companies, together with the 2nd Battn. Suffolk Regt. and two companies of the 2nd Battn. Manchester Regt., the whole under Leut.-Colonel Longley, were ordered to form a rearguard to cover the retirement of the Division through Bavai. The Germans advanced rapidly, especially on the right flank. No sooner had shrapnel begun to burst over the rearguard than Uhlans, followed by infantry, pressed on, so that our troops were cut off from the road through Bavai by which the main body had retired. Having reinforced his right, Lieut.-Colonel Longley was able to disengage his rearguard and withdraw across country, striking the line of retreat south of Bavai. The Suffolks and Manchesters then joined the main body, while a battery of R.F.A. and the D.C.L.I. joined the rearguard, which proceeded along the western edge of the Forêt de Mormal, in which bodies of Uhlans were constantly reported. The two East Surrey companies, with the battery, formed the rear party of the rearguard, and a very hot and dusty march it was for the East Surrey, with the guns constantly trotting past them to take up successive positions throughout the retirement.

On arriving near Le Câteau, the Suffolks and Manchesters were found taking up an outpost position north of the town, and the rearguard was ordered to pass through to the east of the town, where it bivouacked at dusk, D Company furnishing the outposts on this flank. The day had been an exhausting one and the Battalion had marched twenty miles since daybreak, but the men had not flagged and were in good heart.

During the night of the 25th/26th August an order was received at the 14th Brigade Headquarters, which were situated close to those of the 1st Battn.

East Surrey, for all troops to take up the defensive positions allotted to them; but these defensive positions were not specified in the order, nor had they been previously communicated. Lieut.-Colonel Longley, on being consulted by the Brigade Staff regarding this order, at once asked where their defensive position was, and, finding that it was not even known whether any such position existed, he declined to rouse his wearied troops to set out on a dark night in search of the unknown. He said, however, that he would rouse his men at 3 a.m. and strengthen the outposts at that hour, and, as no further information was received as to the defensive position, this was the action finally taken. In the early morning of the 26th fresh orders were received to rejoin the main column at a point five miles south-west of Le Câteau by 8.45 a.m., and at dawn the Brigadier started to join the two other battalions of his Brigade, leaving Brigade Headquarters to follow with Lieut.-Colonel Longley's party.

Hearing that the town was very congested with British troops, Lieut.-Colonel Longley decided to allow ample time for the march to the point named, and his column was formed in readiness to move at 6.30 a.m., Brigade Headquarters leading, when suddenly a heavy fire was opened on it from houses in the eastern outskirts of the town. This unexpected attack was made by a body of German troops disguised in khaki, a form of surprise for which our men were at that time not prepared.

Lieut.-Colonel Longley at the moment was at the rear of the column giving orders to the commander of the rear party, to which he had attached all available cyclists of the East Surrey and D.C.L.I. He met the emergency with great coolness and, riding promptly to the head of the column, formed a firing line on the high ground overlooking Le Câteau astride of the road to Catillon. Under cover of its fire he gradually moved his troops across the railway, which ran nearly parallel to and some 300 yards south of the road. The Battalion transport, however, with about 100 men under Lieut. Lawton, did not succeed in crossing the railway until they had retired in an easterly direction for a considerable distance. They eventually joined the 1st Division, with which they had to remain for a fortnight before they were able to rejoin the Battalion during the Battle of the Marne.

Having got his troops south of the railway, Lieut.-Colonel Longley endeavoured to skirt the southern end of the town, but found his way barred by a German force concealed in a wood. This force proved to be too strongly posted to be dislodged, though a spirited counter-attack by B and D Companies East Surrey, supported by one company D.C.L.I., considerably reduced the volume of the enemy's fire and increased its wildness. In this action Lieut. G. E. Swinton and several men were wounded.

Lieut.-Colonel Longley was thus compelled to move in a more southerly direction, but before doing so ordered Captain Stacke, with one platoon of D Company, to take up a position south of the railway, in order to cover the withdrawal of the last D.C.L.I. company across it. This duty was carried out by Captain Stacke in the most able manner, which earned for him the grateful thanks of the officer commanding the D.C.L.I.

After the fight had continued for some hours, each move becoming more and more difficult, since the Germans from their covered positions maintained a heavy rifle fire on our men crossing their front over the open fields, the 3rd Cavalry Brigade at last came in view from the east. Having joined hands with them, the column succeeded in rejoining the Division at Maurois, where it reported at 2.30 p.m. The two East Surrey companies were at once ordered to strengthen the right flank-guard, as the retirement of the II Corps was about to be resumed.

The companies remained out on the flank till after dark, when they joined the troops on the road, which was choked with guns, transport wagons and ambulances. Every vehicle carried its load of wounded men, many with wounds not yet dressed. So dense was the press of retreating troops on the road south of Maurois that all formation was lost and men, horses and vehicles moved in one solid mass with constant halts and checks. The weary march continued in a south-westerly direction till nearly 10 p.m., when, being unable to get into touch with either the 5th Division or 14th Brigade, Lieut.-Colonel Longley turned the companies into a farm by the roadside, "Ferme Genève," east of Beaurevoir. Here the farmer made them welcome, giving them shelter in his commodious stables and outhouses, and as much straw as they wanted. He refused all offers of payment, only asking that in return Captain Bowring would write to him occasionally. The night was wet, and the men were so footsore and dazed from the strain of continuous marching, fighting and lack of sleep, that these few hours' rest were most beneficial.

At 3 a.m. on August 27th Lieut.-Colonel Longley ordered the companies to turn out and take up a position on high ground astride the road while the tired troops, transport and ammunition columns were once more set in motion. The East Surrey companies then fell in and resumed their march also, halting presently to cook and eat some bacon which they found by the roadside. Refreshed by this long-deferred meal, the companies marched cheerily on, singing as they went.

On arrival at St. Quentin at 1.45 p.m., it was found that the 14th Brigade had moved on and that the 15th Brigade was about to start. Lieut.-Colonel Longley's column therefore followed the latter, acting as rearguard as before, south-westwards along the upper reaches of the River Somme. On nearing St. Simon he was directed to take up an outpost position to cover the bivouac of the 15th Brigade, being at the same time assured by the Brigadier that he would be relieved at 7 p.m. Relief, however, never came, so at 4 a.m. on the 28th August Lieut. Darwell was sent to report to Brigadier-General Count Gleichen, who ordered the East Surrey to cross the Crozat canal at 6 a.m. and to instruct the R.E. officer on duty at the bridge to blow it up when all had crossed. This done, the companies marched on a short distance until, by a recently vacated camping ground, a supply of biscuit, bread and meat was found, presumably deposited by the Army Service Corps. Breakfast was then cooked and eaten, and at 9 a.m. the march was resumed with renewed vigour. An hour later the companies arrived at Noyon, where they found the 14th Brigade, and were rejoined by the two companies so long detached under Major Tew. The Battalion then continued its march with the Brigade and, after crossing the River Oise, bivouacked at Pontoise, on the southern bank of that river.

We must now trace the history of Major Tew's companies, whose separation from the Battalion at Wiheries on August 24th will be remembered. In accordance with the orders given him by a staff officer on that occasion Major Tew marched to Eth, a mile on the French side of the frontier, which place was reached after dark, the men much exhausted by the heat and their previous exertions. Here the companies found an entrenched position just south of Eth held by the 4th Hussars and 16th Lancers, whom they relieved, spending the night in the trenches.

Next day, at early dawn, Major Tew was informed by the officer commanding the 4th Hussars that all infantry was to clear out as quickly as possible, as the defensive position was not going to be held; but he could get no information as to route, objective or position of other troops and was compelled to march off without food or water. Soon after starting, however, water was found in a farm, and in a deserted wagon some food was found, and also a bicycle which subsequently proved most useful. The food was distributed, and a little later a quantity of supplies were found " dumped " by the roadside, from which the rations were completed.

Major Tew's companies continued to march throughout the day, arriving much fatigued about 5 p.m. at Briastre, some five miles north-west of Le Câteau. At Briastre they found billets in a farm, but after one hour's halt orders were received from a brigade of the 4th Division, which was also in Briastre, to continue the retirement, no route being given, and late at night the companies arrived at Troisvilles, three miles west of Le Câteau, where the men lay down to sleep in the streets. About midnight Major Tew ascertained that the 14th Brigade was at Le Câteau, but decided to wait till daylight before moving off to join it.

On August 26th the detachment marched at 4 a.m. towards Le Câteau, but soon afterwards, on the Montay–Reumont road, met Brigadier-General Rolt, who ordered it to fall in in rear of the 14th Brigade when it came by. This order was presently changed in consequence of General Sir Horace Smith-Dorrien's famous decision to halt and deliver battle. Of this the troops knew little or nothing, but it was announced that the 5th Division was going to stand and fight, and, after consultation with Lieut.-Colonel Bond, of the King's Own Yorkshire Light Infantry, Major Tew took up a position facing north-east with his two companies in the front line on the east of the Montay–Reumont road, just south of its junction with the Troisvilles–Le Câteau road.

The East Surrey companies, formed in five lines, took up a frontage of about 200 yards and entrenched themselves, A Company in front, with C Company in support. On their left were the 2nd Battn. K.O.Y.L.I., on their right the 2nd Battn. Manchester Regt. and to the right front, on a spur, there was another battalion, the Suffolks. In the intervening valley were several batteries of artillery.

A heavy shrapnel fire was soon opened on the two East Surrey companies, and after about an hour some unsteadiness was shown by a part of the rear company, which had suffered severely and had lost five of its six officers at Mons. These men were immediately rallied by Captain A. R. Hewitt, who for this and other gallant services was afterwards awarded the Distinguished Service Order. The two companies then held firmly to their trenches until, after very severe fighting, all the troops on their right, including the artillery, had been withdrawn from the field. Finally, in accordance with orders, the K.O.Y.L.I. on their left commenced to retire, and Major Tew's companies remained entirely unsupported and without orders. He himself at this time was wounded in the right hand, but took no notice of the injury.

It was now obvious that an immediate retirement was necessary, and as there were no troops to cover the movement, and the shrapnel and machine-gun fire of the enemy was concentrated on the two companies, an orderly withdrawal was out of the question. The companies therefore were directed to rush from cover to cover, making the best of their way south-west towards Maretz. During the early part of the retirement the German artillery continually advanced and pursued the companies with its fire, but eventually the men got clear. Major Tew, with Captain Hewitt and Lieut. Roupell, then gradually collected the companies and the retirement continued all through the night, with the exception of a two hours' halt at Ferme Genève. It will be remembered that the remainder of the Battalion was also at Genève that same night, but in the darkness the two wings failed to meet.

The conduct of Major Tew's companies at Le Câteau was admirable. They were exposed for nearly five hours to an incessant and severe shrapnel fire in shallow trenches hastily constructed with their entrenching implements. The men were exhausted with continuous marching, day and night, since August 23rd, yet they steadily held their trenches until ordered to retire, and remained unshaken at the end of that movement.

St. Quentin was reached in the early morning of the 27th August, where rations were found, and just south of that place an hour's halt was made for breakfast. Orders were received, however, to continue the retirement at once, the enemy being close at hand, and the two companies marched a distance of nine miles via St. Simon to Ollezy on the south bank of the River Somme, where they found the 14th Brigade.

On August 28th the Brigade marched through Noyon and bivouacked near Pontoise, on the south bank of the River Oise. The march was long and hot. During a halt Sir John French came up in his car and got out to tell the men that their efforts had not been in vain, as they had saved the left flank of the French Army which had been in imminent danger. Just before reaching Noyon the Brigade was joined by Lieut.-Colonel Longley's column, and the Battalion was consequently reunited.

The British Expeditionary Force had now succeeded in placing a serious obstacle, the River Oise, between itself and the pursuing enemy, and it was at Pontoise that the Battalion had the first breathing-space since the commencement of the retreat.

The Battalion rested at Pontoise during the night of August 28th and until 7 p.m. on the 29th, when the 14th Brigade was suddenly ordered to march three miles southwards to Carlepont. The column was continually checked for long periods, and after marching about two miles bivouacked at 11.30 p.m. on the roadside. At 3.30 a.m. on August 30th it proceeded via Carlepont towards the River Aisne. The weather was extremely hot, and about midday the Brigade halted for two hours. Tea was made and issued, after which the men marched in good spirits till, at 6 o'clock, they bivouacked near Attichy beside the River Aisne. The 2nd Battn. Suffolk Regt., which had been reduced by casualties to a strength of 280 men, was now attached to the Battalion.

Next morning the Brigade fell in at 10 a.m. and, after crossing the Aisne, marched through Pierrefonds and Béthancourt to Raperie, just north of Crépy-en-Valois. The march was badly managed and extremely hurried owing to false alarms.

As soon as day broke on the 1st September firing was heard on all sides, and the 5th Division commenced to take up a position in expectation of immediate attack. The 13th Brigade was posted just north of Crépy, and the 14th Brigade was ordered to hold a ridge south of that town in order to cover its retirement. The 1st Battn. East Surrey accordingly took up a position east of the railway and the 13th Brigade retired through it, while the 15th Brigade passed by on the left. The Germans, however, did not pursue closely, and after the 14th Brigade had retired to another position it resumed its march, with the North Irish Horse and East Surrey as rearguard. As darkness came on heavy firing was heard away to the east; but Nanteuil-le-Haudouin was reached at 8 p.m., and the 1st Battn. East Surrey passed a peaceful night there in bivouac.

On the 2nd September the 14th Brigade moved off at 3 a.m. and marched via Le Plessis to Montgé, where the 1st Battn. East Surrey, as a change from its usual bivouac in a cornfield, had comfortable billets, Battalion Headquarters being in a château from which the outskirts of Paris could be seen some twelve miles to the south-west. Next day the 14th Brigade, acting as rearguard to the II Corps, was on the move at an early hour. As there was no pursuit by the Germans, column of route was soon formed and the march continued via Iverny to the River Marne, which was crossed near Meaux. On reaching Bouleurs the Battalion bivouacked, the officers' mess being established in the house of the deputy mayor, who with great kindness provided wine and fruit.

The following day, September 4th, was spent in Bouleurs until 11 p.m., when the 14th Brigade moved off towards Tournan, which lies eighteen miles south-east of Paris. The 1st Battn. East Surrey spent the following day and the night of the 5th/6th September on outpost duty near Favières, covering the 5th Division in and about Tournan and in touch with the outposts of the III Corps on the left. With this march to Tournan ended the Retreat from Mons, for on the morning of the 6th September, to the great satisfaction of all ranks, the 5th Division marched in a north-easterly direction towards Villeneuve. The Battalion received its first reinforcing draft of Captain Whish and 98 other ranks prior to marching off, and with the rest of the 14th Brigade it bivouacked

# THE CASUALTIES

for the night at Dammartin. Here Major Tew was admitted to hospital in consequence of the wound which he had received at Le Câteau.

The casualties of the Battalion in the Battles of Mons and Le Câteau and in the Retreat from Mons were as follows:—

*Killed :*    2 officers and 27 other ranks.
*Wounded :* 3    ,,    ,, 82    ,,    ,,
*Missing :*  2    ,,    ,, 117   ,,    ,,

Of the latter, both officers and at least 50 other ranks were wounded.

## CHAPTER III

SEPTEMBER, 1914: THE 1st BATTALION IN THE ADVANCE TO THE AISNE, IN THE BATTLE OF THE MARNE, 1914, AND IN THE BATTLE OF THE AISNE, 1914.

ON September 7th the 14th Brigade continued its eastward march to Coulommiers on the Grand Morin river, the 1st Battn. East Surrey arriving there after dark and bivouacking in mass in a field on the left of the road. The knowledge that the enemy was now retreating raised the enthusiasm of the men to the highest pitch, though it may be remarked that their spirits had never fallen in proportion to the gravity of the situation. Notwithstanding that many men marched bootless and with bleeding feet and with no equipment beyond their arms and ammunition, all were eager for a chance to strike back at the enemy. During the march to Coulommiers, and while passing through that place, it was evident by the many traces which the Germans had left behind them that the British force was rapidly closing on the enemy. Shops had been looted wholesale, and the streets were littered with broken wine bottles.

On September 8th the retreating Germans were holding the line of the Petit Morin river with a strong rearguard, which was attacked by the British I Corps at La Tretoire, and by the II Corps about St. Cyr and St. Ouen.

The 5th Division stood to arms early and then waited for some time while the cavalry, with a good stiffening of artillery, moved forward. Finally, the Division also advanced with the 14th Brigade in the centre. After passing through Doué, the 1st Battn. East Surrey was ordered to push on ahead of the Brigade, moving up on the right of the 13th Brigade, with B and C Companies, under Captain J. K. T. Whish, in first line and A and D Companies in second line. While advancing in this formation orders were received that the 13th Brigade was to attack St. Cyr, and the 14th Brigade St. Ouen, the latter place being then out of sight on the far side (the right bank) of the Petit Morin river. The lower portion of the village of St. Ouen lay right in the valley; the upper portion was quite separate, being near the top of the slope on the far bank.

The D.C.L.I. moved up on the right of the East Surrey, and the advance continued over open ground which rose slightly till within a mile of the river, when it fell sharply down to the flat meadows through which the river flows. The downward slope into the valley was densely wooded, particularly where the 1st Battn. East Surrey advanced, and it was therefore necessary to close and move through the wood in single file. The companies extended again on reaching the foot of the slope, in order to cross the railway and the open fields beyond. The D.C.L.I. found the wood less dense on their line of advance and so arrived first at the river, and had already begun to cross when the East Surrey arrived on the left bank.

The river here flowed in two channels, one only being bridged, and there was but one small and rickety boat, by means of which the two battalions could cross the other channel, which was unfordable with high, steep banks. The crossing of the river was a lengthy process, and it was arranged between the two commanding officers that the whole of the East Surrey should be ferried over after half the D.C.L.I. had crossed.

While waiting on the south side of the river Lieut.-Colonel Longley was informed of the exact position of the German trenches. As they were somewhat to the east of the crossing place, he directed the Battalion after crossing to take ground to the right, in order to come in on the right flank of the enemy's position, promising the men that they should get at the Germans with the bayonet. As soon as B, C and D Companies had crossed he pushed on with them up the slope, leaving A Company to follow on as quickly as possible. The men were greatly cheered at the prospect of closing with the enemy.

The slope leading up from the river valley was covered with orchards and small woods, through which the Battalion rapidly advanced, finally reaching more open ground at the summit. Here it suddenly encountered some German cavalry, who at once turned about and galloped off to a flank behind a wood. A hurried fire was opened on them with little effect; but some of the enemy's retreating infantry were fired on with better result. The advance continued, and the German trenches were soon under oblique and partly reverse fire from the East Surreys, whose firing line was being thickened preparatory to a further outflanking movement. Unluckily, our artillery (both 3rd and 5th Divisions) now opened fire all along the ridge, making any further advance impossible, and thus depriving the Battalion of the full reward of its rapid advance. Though the shelling brought the East Surrey attack to a standstill, it also pinned the enemy to their trenches and prevented their getting away, and by nightfall a considerable number of prisoners had been captured.

The Battalion bivouacked for the night near Rougeville, where it was joined by Lieuts. Lawton, Stoneham and Relton, with Sergt.-Major Hyson and 110 rank and file. Most of this party were men of the First Line Transport who had been separated from the Battalion since the Battle of Le Câteau on August 26th, as already described. The losses of the Battalion on September 8th were Captain J. K. T. Whish and two men killed; Lieut. J. O. G. Becker and six men wounded. Captain Whish's death was generally regretted in the Regiment. He was a zealous and experienced officer who had served with the 2nd Battalion in the South African War and had also seen service in East Africa with the King's African Rifles.

On September 9th the passage of the River Marne was forced by the I and II Corps, the III Corps, which met with strong opposition about La Ferté, also getting across during the night. In the II Corps the 14th Brigade moved off at 5 a.m., forming the advanced guard and taking the road to Saacy on the River Marne, about 10 miles south-west of Château-Thierry.

After a short advance the advanced guard and main body were halted for a considerable time, and during the halt the officers of the East Surrey saw a big column of troops moving along the road which led over the high ground northwards from La Ferté. This column was unfortunately held by the authorities to be part of the III British Corps which was reported to have crossed the river at that place, but it was in fact a large body of German troops in retreat. But for this mistake the Germans would have suffered heavy loss from our artillery.

On reaching Saacy the bridge over the Marne was found intact, and the 14th Brigade crossed it and moved through thickly wooded country towards Méry (see Map opposite). The advance of the Brigade was strongly opposed, and a short halt was made by the infantry until some guns to the northward had been silenced. The 1st Battn. East Surrey then received orders to advance in support of the Manchester Regt. and the D.C.L.I. in a northerly direction along the high ground on the east side of the main valley. The 15th Brigade, which had crossed higher up the Marne, was advancing on the right rear of the 14th, while the 13th Brigade was in support to its left rear.

In accordance with the orders received, Lieut.-Colonel Longley now moved the Battalion along the wooded slope north of Méry towards Bezu, and then, changing direction to the left, crossed the St. Aulde–Bezu road and began to ascend the wooded ridge north of it. Halting the Battalion at A in the sketch before it reached the open ridge, the Commanding Officer gave the two leading company commanders their frontage and direction. No sooner had Captain Stacke extended two platoons of D, the leading company, than a German battery across the valley, at B in the sketch, opened an enfilading fire which it maintained all day. It was not until six in the evening that this battery was located and silenced. Several casualties having occurred in D Company, Lieut.-Colonel Longley ordered it to move to its left, determining to continue the advance along the wooded and more sheltered lower slopes. Captain Stacke was very severely wounded in the thigh while helping wounded men to cover, and Captain Bowring, the adjutant, was also wounded in the head while similarly employed, but remained at duty till ordered to take Captain the Hon. A. R. Hewitt back after the latter had been dangerously wounded when going forward with the Commanding Officer to reconnoitre.

The two battalions in front were no longer making headway: the Manchesters, inclining to the right during their advance, had joined the 15th Brigade; while the D.C.L.I.'s left had been forced back off the ridge on to the Les Maillons road. A few Germans pushed on far enough to discover in a cottage by the roadside the East Surrey medical officer with Captains Hewitt and Bowring; the latter, who was asleep, awoke to find himself surrounded, and he and the medical officer were marched off by the Germans. They left Captain Hewitt, who, in spite of the severity of his wound, feigned delirium and convinced them that he was dying.

The 1st Battn. East Surrey now advanced into the gap on the right of the D.C.L.I., reinforcing the firing line under Captain Woulfe-Flanagan, as the machine-gun and rifle fire from the German trenches south of the Bezu–Montreuil road was taking effect.

The Battalion eventually reached the edge of a narrow clearing close to the enemy's position, where it met with such a heavy fire that the Commanding

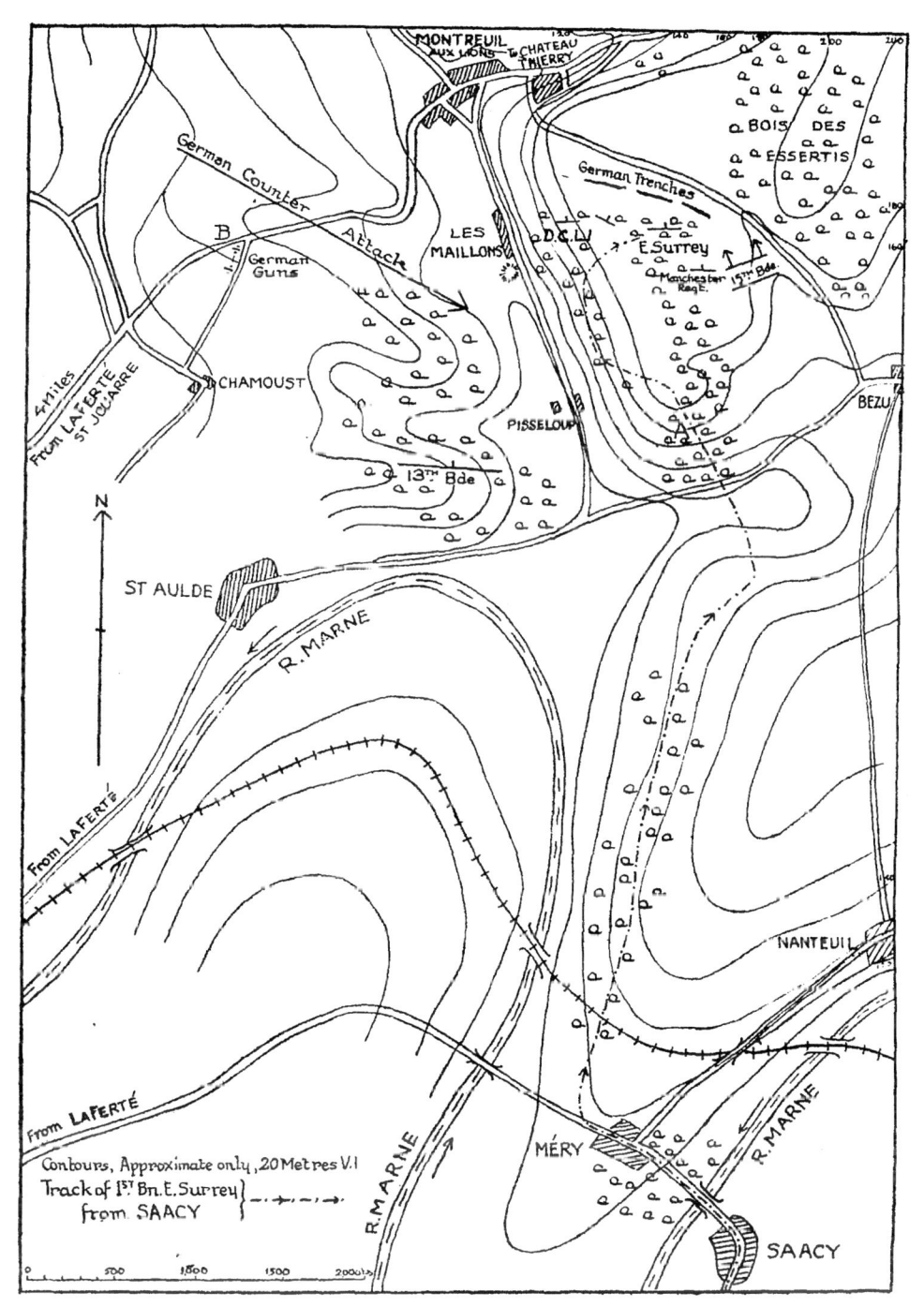

THE 1ST BATTALION AT THE PASSAGE OF THE MARNE, 9TH SEPTEMBER, 1914

Officer, after twice leading forward reinforcements, decided that a further frontal advance was at the time impossible. He then went across to the 15th Brigade to secure their co-operation on the enemy's left flank, but their attempt to turn the enemy's position also met with no success.

Late in the afternoon the enemy launched from the west side of the valley a counter-attack which was stopped by the 13th Brigade, assisted by the East Surrey, who threw back their left flank to support it by their rifle fire; while the machine-gun section under Lieut. Darwell again put in some very useful work against the enemy's guns and infantry, taking heavy toll of the latter as they emerged from a concealed trench in the woods. Nightfall found the enemy still in position, but evidently very much shaken, as he was soon on the run, and after dark the 2nd Battn. Suffolk Regt. moved forward and furnished outposts for the Brigade. The 1st Battn. East Surrey then closed and bivouacked along the Bezu–St. Aulde road.

The casualties during the day had been twenty other ranks killed; Captains the Hon. A. R. Hewitt, F. A. Bowring and H. H. Stacke, and Lieuts. E. G. Lawton and H. F. Stoneham and 95 other ranks wounded.

Among those who distinguished themselves at the passage of the Marne was Sergt.-Major G. E. Hyson, who took forward a horse and cart along the road towards Les Maillons in order to bring in some of the wounded. The sergeant-major was fired at by a party of some twenty Germans under an officer, who killed the horse and wounded its driver, the sergeant-major narrowly escaping. For his gallant services on this occasion Sergt.-Major Hyson was afterwards awarded the Distinguished Conduct Medal.

The 14th Brigade continued its advance northwards on September 10th, forming the reserve of the 5th Division. Parties from each battalion were left behind to bury the dead and collect wounded, many of whom were found awaiting removal along the road, which had formed part of the battlefield on the previous day. The Brigade halted at about 7 p.m. and bivouacked near a small village called St. Quentin, not far from the left bank of the River Ourcq. Many German prisoners were taken during the day.

On September 11th the Ourcq was crossed after slight opposition and the pursuit was continued in cooler weather to St. Rémy-Blanzy, ten miles south of Soissons. Heavy rain fell during the afternoon. The German retreat had become more rapid, and but few prisoners were taken.

On September 12th the weather was very wet and the roads were consequently in a bad state. The recently formed Sixth French Army on the British left was heavily engaged to the west of Soissons, and it was apparent that the Germans were preparing to dispute the passage of the River Aisne to the utmost. The Battalion reached Chacrise, seven miles south-east of Soissons, in the evening, where it went into billets.

After a wet night the early morning of September 13th was fine but very cold. The 14th Brigade moved off at 4.30 a.m., with the 2nd Battn. Manchester Regt. acting as advanced guard. About 10 a.m. the British artillery came into action for about two hours, during which time the Royal Engineers made a small raft by which the Manchester Regt., followed by the 1st Battn. East Surrey, crossed the River Aisne at Venizel, three miles east of Soissons. The two battalions were across by 3 p.m. and at once advanced north-eastwards in very widely extended lines under shrapnel fire across the absolutely open meadows to St. Marguérite. This was the first occasion on which widely extended lines were used in France by the Battalion, as the ground had never before been so entirely devoid of cover. At St. Marguérite a brigade of the 4th Division was met, advancing eastward, and this necessitated a change of direction. Brigadier-General Rolt consequently ordered the East Surrey to advance up a wooded spur north of St. Marguérite, and by 9 p.m. the Battalion had moved through the wood and bivouacked on its northern border close behind the outposts of the 4th Division. The casualties this day were only eight men wounded.

On September 14th the Battalion moved down from the ridge in the early morning and advanced eastwards with the D.C.L.I. on Missy over open country and rather across the German front. Casualties therefore soon began. By noon B, C and D Companies of the East Surrey were in occupation of the north end of the village, and A Company was closely engaged with the enemy at the eastern end while keeping touch with the 13th Brigade. A patrol sent forward from D Company by Captain Minogue discovered a portion of the main German position north of the Aisne on the wooded spur above the village of Chivres. It was naturally very strong and greatly strengthened by a high wire fence and wire entanglements. A search was made through the village for wire-cutting instruments, and with them openings were made through the wire fence and entanglements by men from the front companies. The 15th Brigade had been ordered to attack the German position from the east, and a frontal attack from the northern end of Missy was directed against it by a needlessly mixed force of three companies of the Norfolk Regt., three of the Bedford Regt., one of the D.C.L.I. and three of the 1st Battn. East Surrey, with two companies of the Cheshire Regt. in support in the village. These troops were not in position till after 4.30 p.m. The East Surrey companies then advanced, with the Norfolks on their right and the Bedfords on their left. The wire was crossed without loss, and a short, steep slope was ascended. On reaching a clearing in the wood some way up this slope the East Surrey and Norfolk companies came under a heavy fire at close range from the Germans entrenched just above them on their right front. It was almost dark at the time, and immediately afterwards the companies belonging to the 15th Brigade were withdrawn by order of their Brigadier. The three East Surrey companies and the leading company of the Bedford Regt. were therefore left in a dangerously isolated position. Support was offered by the officer commanding the two Cheshire companies, and at Lieut.-Colonel Longley's request two platoons of that regiment advanced in close support. The company of the Bedford Regt. just referred to was commanded by Major Allason, who elected to remain where he was, on the left flank of the East Surrey. Here he was found by Lieut.-Colonel Longley when going along the firing line and collecting some East Surrey men who had got mixed up with the Bedfords. When nearing the right flank Lieut.-Colonel Longley received a message from

Lieut. Montanaro, who was in command of B Company, since Captain Woulfe-Flanagan had been wounded during the morning, to the effect that he had advanced on the right and required reinforcement. The Commanding Officer then went forward with some men, but finding that the Germans above Lieut. Montanaro were increasing in strength and threatening to turn his right, he threw back his line on that flank and made good his position on the edge of the clearing. He then reported the situation to the Brigade and asked that rations and water might be sent up to the Battalion. After a time, however, orders were received for the East Surrey to withdraw to St. Marguérite, where the Battalion bivouacked about 10 p.m.

The casualties this day were as follows:—

*Killed*: Lieut. G. L. Relton and 15 other ranks.

*Wounded*: Captain E. M. Woulfe-Flanagan, Lieut. H. St. G. Schomberg and 81 other ranks.

During the morning of September 15th the Battalion moved into a line of dugouts on the rising ground west of the Chivres spur and north of Missy. The day was spent in improving and extending these shelters, and about eight o'clock in the evening the East Surrey was ordered to take over the outposts covering Missy then being found by the 15th Brigade. On arrival at Missy the main street was found to be blocked with ambulances and troops; it was pitch dark and heavy rain was falling. The Battalion therefore experienced great difficulty in taking up its new position. Heavy fire broke out on the right about midnight while the troops which had been relieved were still in the village, where for a time there was much congestion and some confusion, so it was not until near dawn that the Battalion was finally settled in the outpost position, with two companies holding the eastern outskirts of the village and two the western. Two men were wounded during the relief.

The position held by the Battalion was much cleared and strengthened during September 16th; part of the ground on the right was taken over by the West Riding Regt. lent by the 13th Brigade. A welcome reinforcement of seven officers made good some of the recent casualties. On this day one man was killed and two wounded.

On September 17th the Battalion remained in the same position. There was a good deal of sniping, and five men were wounded. Wet weather continued on the 18th, on which day one man only was wounded and Major H. S. Tew rejoined from hospital. On the 19th the defences, which had been much strengthened, were heavily shelled, as was the village of Missy. The German fire failed, however, to find the East Surrey trenches. The day's casualties included Captain A. de V. Maclean killed, and twelve rank and file wounded. Captain Maclean, who had joined the Battalion only three days previously, had served with the 2nd Battalion in the latter part of the South African War and was a fine officer.

On September 20th the enemy's artillery did not open fire till the afternoon, when one man was killed and five wounded; but on the 21st Missy was heavily shelled and Battalion Headquarters were wrecked. One man was killed and twelve wounded by this fire. On the 22nd the defences were again under heavy fire, but there were no casualties, and next day the Battalion was relieved by the Dorset Regt. and moved into bivouac outside St. Marguérite. Six men were wounded during the relief.

On September 24th the Battalion received a draft of two officers and 201 men; and on the 25th recrossed the Aisne to Jury and joined the 14th Brigade in billets in that village. Major-General Sir Charles Fergusson, commanding the 5th Division, visited Battalion Headquarters and expressed his very high opinion of the services of the Battalion. On September 26th General Sir Horace Smith-Dorrien, Commanding II Corps, also visited the Battalion informally and talked to the men of B Company about the good work of the East Surrey.

On September 27th, at 3 a.m., the Battalion was ordered to fall in at once, a report having been received that the enemy was crossing the River Aisne in force at Condé Bridge. The 1st Battn. East Surrey then marched with the 14th Brigade to Serches, whence, on receipt of further information to the effect that the first report was a false one, it returned at once to its billets in Jury.

On the march to Serches, Lieut.-Colonel Longley had been obliged, owing to high fever, to fall out and go to the Field Ambulance in Serches, so Major Tew took over command of the Battalion, which remained in Jury till the end of the month. Opportunity was taken during these few days of comparative quiet to remedy defects and deficiencies in clothing and equipment, which naturally had suffered in the continuous marching and fighting since the 21st August.

## CHAPTER IV

OCTOBER, 1914, TO MARCH, 1915; THE 1st BATTALION IN THE BATTLE OF LA BASSEE, IN ACTION AT RICHEBOURG L'AVOUE AND LORGIES; FOUR AND A HALF MONTHS OF TRENCH DUTY IN FLANDERS BETWEEN ARMENTIERES AND YPRES.

VERY early in October the British Army on the suggestion of Field-Marshal Sir John French, was secretly withdrawn from its position on the Aisne and transferred to the left flank of the Allied front, where it was to be joined later by the 7th Division and the 3rd Cavalry Division, which were operating between Ypres and Bruges with the object of assisting the Belgian Army in its withdrawal from Antwerp. The new arrangement had the advantages of improving the British line of supply and of restoring the British Army to its normal position on the French left. Sir John French also desired to make an effort to turn the German right, then about Lille, and thus aid the French frontal attack on the Aisne position. It may also be assumed that he desired to anticipate the attempt to reach the shores of the British Channel which was known to form part of the German plan of campaign.

The move from the Aisne to the line of the River Lys was carried out with great secrecy, the troops marching by night and hiding from aeroplane observation in villages and woods by day. The 1st Battn. East Surrey received no hint of their destination when at 6.30 p.m. on October 1st they were ordered to march out of Jury one hour later. After a march of about six miles in the dark the Battalion arrived at Nampteuil at 11 p.m. and went into billets. Night marches followed—on October 2nd to Longpont, about fifteen miles, and on the 3rd via Villers-Cotterets to Fresnoy, a long and trying march of eighteen miles.

On the 4th the Battalion rested in billets till 3 p.m., when it made a short march to Gilocourt and again went into billets, remaining there on the 5th. On October 6th the Battalion was directed to entrain at Longueil station for Crécy. The train left at 1.30 a.m. on the 7th and arrived at Crécy an hour later, whence it proceeded to Noyelles-sur-Mer, near the mouth of the River Somme. At Noyelles the Battalion detrained at 11.30 a.m. and marched to its billets at Château Bois De L'Abbaye, two miles east of Abbeville.

At 6.30 p.m. on the 8th October the 14th Brigade marched seventeen miles north-eastward to Vaulx, arrived there early next morning and remained in billets during the day. At 6 p.m. the 1st Battn. East Surrey was ready at the appointed place for the motor-buses which had been ordered to meet it. The buses, however, went astray, and a start was not made until 3 a.m. on the 10th. That evening the Battalion was assembled, ten miles south-west of Béthune, at Diéval, where Lieut.-Colonel Longley and Lieut. Schomberg rejoined from the Base hospital.

# THE BATTLE OF LA BASSEE

On the 10th October the 2nd British Cavalry Division came into contact with the German cavalry north of the Aire–Béthune canal and thus commenced the Battle of La Bassée. On the following day the 14th Brigade reached the Aire canal at Hinges, three miles north of Béthune, having met on their way a large number of refugees from Belgium and Northern France. At 4 p.m. the 1st Battn. East Surrey entrenched itself on the west bank of the canal, with two companies holding the bridge Pont Lévis. In front of them, and forming an outpost line in Locon on the far side of the canal, was the 1st Battn. Devon Regt., which had replaced the 2nd Battn. Suffolk Regt. in the 14th Brigade, the last-named battalion having been withdrawn to reorganize after its heavy losses in the Retreat from Mons.

On the left or northern flank of the East Surrey was the 3rd Division. South of the East Surrey was the Manchester Regt., and beyond them the 15th Brigade in touch with the French left a few miles east of Béthune.

On the 12th October the 14th Brigade crossed the Aire canal by the Avelette bridge and marched eastward via Locon by a very winding road through a flat and densely populated country. On their way they met numerous French mounted troops, including several regiments of Cuirassiers with bright steel breastplates and red breeches. These regiments had just been relieved by British cavalry. In rear of the French mounted troops came some Chasseurs Alpins, wearing tam-o'-shanters, knickerbockers and stockings and taking their wounded along in wheelbarrows. One of their officers informed Lieut.-Colonel Longley that the Germans were close at hand.

On arrival at the forked road about two miles west of Richebourg L'Avoué the 14th Brigade deployed in order to continue its advance on a wider front, owing to the reports of the proximity of the enemy. The 1st Battn. East Surrey now found itself on the left of the Brigade, and moved forward by the left-hand road leading towards Richebourg St. Vaast.

As soon as the last of the Chasseurs Alpins had passed, two of the East Surrey companies were extended on the left of the road, and shortly afterwards Major Tew was sent forward to take command of them. They soon met a German skirmishing line, which was at once engaged. Major Tew was then ordered to attack, keeping touch with the Worcester Regt. on his left. As soon as the attack started it was met by a hot shell fire, while the Worcester Regt. was checked by enfilade machine-gun fire.

The country in which the 14th Brigade was now operating was perfectly flat and intersected by numerous ditches, some of which were serious obstacles, only to be negotiated by ladder bridges. The trees lining the ditches limited observation in any direction to a few hundred yards. Thus Major Tew's party, when advancing on the left of the road, were unable to see the remainder of the Battalion, which at a bend in the road sighted the Germans marching confidently towards them in pursuit of the Frenchmen. The opportunity was one not to be missed. Captain Minogue, commanding D, the leading company, lost no time in occupying a farm and orchard on either side of the road, from which position the rifles of the company and the machine guns of the Battalion wrought havoc in the enemy's ranks and scattered them in search of cover. The machine-gun section put three German machine guns out of action and by its accurate fire prevented their removal, though they were too far away to be captured.

The advance was then resumed just as the light began to fail, but was very soon countermanded, owing to the Brigade on the left being held up by enfilade fire as already mentioned, and as soon as it was dark the 1st Battn. East Surrey commenced to entrench itself in its position about a mile due west of Richebourg L'Avoué. Except for an abortive dash made by a party of Germans on D Company before it was quite dark, possibly to cover the withdrawal of their machine guns, the night passed quietly.

The total casualties this day were 2nd Lieut. W. Thompson wounded and 21 other ranks killed or wounded, a very small loss compared with the casualties inflicted on the enemy.

The advance of the 5th Division was resumed on the 13th October, the 1st Battn. East Surrey moving forward at 5.30 a.m. followed by a section of 18-pounders under 2nd Lieut. Davidson, R.F.A., whose close co-operation was of the greatest assistance to the East Surrey during the whole period that it was attached to the Battalion. Three companies under Major Tew were in front, followed by A Company held in reserve by the Commanding Officer. The direction taken was north-eastward towards Richebourg St. Vaast, and at first in the darkness there was no sign of the enemy. After a time, however, fire was opened on the companies from their right front, and D Company pushed forward eastward to an enclosed farm half a mile south of Richebourg St. Vaast. From that position the enemy was located in some buildings, 500 yards to the east, which formed a strong position, the capture of which by direct assault would have entailed considerable losses. It was therefore decided to await a turning movement by the 3rd Division on the left. At this juncture, however, 2nd Lieut. Davidson brought his guns into action and with almost the first round hit one of the houses, bolting about fifty Germans. C and D companies then advanced from the farm in widely extended lines and started to dig themselves in about 100 yards beyond houses which had been held by the Germans and just east of the road running south-east from Richebourg St. Vaast. In this position, facing east and astride of the Rue des Berceaux at a point midway between Richebourg St. Vaast and Richebourg L'Avoué, the Battalion remained, with two companies in the trenches and two in billets in rear, until the 16th October, as the 14th Brigade stood fast during that period while the 3rd Division moved forward in conformity with the half-right wheel which the II Corps was making with its right pivoted on Givenchy.

The casualties on the 13th October had been 42 other ranks killed or wounded, while 4 officers had been wounded, viz. Lieuts. H. Baddinsell (3rd Battn. attd.) and W. S. Ford, and 2nd Lieuts. O. M. James and A. H. King (4th Battn. attd.). Lieut. Ford and 2nd Lieut. King had joined the Battalion only three days previously.

On the 14th October, after a very wet day, the relief of the front companies was being carried out at seven o'clock in the evening, when the Germans opened a terrific musketry and machine-gun fire all along the Brigade front. This fire, the noise of which resembled a *feu-de-joie*, continued until 10.30 p.m., when it slackened somewhat and towards morning died down completely. It was afterwards ascertained from an intercepted message that the Germans had opened this fire in order to cover their intended retirement, but so vigorous was the British reply that they were forced to cancel their plan. The Battalion sustained a number of casualties, Captain M. J. Minogue, the last remaining captain, being wounded and 32 other ranks killed or wounded.

The 15th October was a quiet day, and the rest which it afforded was thoroughly appreciated. At 5.30 a.m. on the 16th the advance was resumed by the 14th Brigade, and, after a series of complicated movements across country in a fog, the 1st Battn. East Surrey reached at 9 p.m. the Ferme du Biez, near the southern corner of the Bois du Biez and about a mile and a half due east of Richebourg L'Avoué. Two companies were billeted in the farm, while A and D Companies formed the outpost line in touch with the outposts of the Brigade on the left. Major F. G. Jackson with 2 other officers and 65 other ranks joined during the day.

The advance was continued at 6 a.m. on the 17th October in a south-easterly direction, the 1st Battn. East Surrey being still on the left of the 14th Brigade and in touch with the 3rd Division. The German rearguard was soon encountered, but in no great strength, and Lorgies, a village two miles north of La Bassée, was made good by ten o'clock with but few casualties. Orders were then received to attack La Bassée, and the 1st Battn. East Surrey and the D.C.L.I. on its right were formed up in extended lines in the open near the southern outskirts of Lorgies preparatory to a further advance, which, however, was held up owing to the troops on both flanks of the East Surrey being checked by enfilade machine-gun fire. When darkness came on, A and D Companies, under Major Jackson, entrenched and held a position just south of Lorgies, the other two companies being billeted in the village. Next day the 1st Battn. East Surrey went back into Brigade Reserve at La Tourelle, near the Ferme du Biez, leaving behind, in support of the Manchester Regt., two companies, which rejoined the Battalion on the 19th October.

Meanwhile on the 18th, the enemy, strongly reinforced, in turn assumed the offensive and from that date till the 31st October the II Corps carried on a most gallant fight in defence of its position against very superior numbers.

While the 1st Battn. East Surrey was in reserve at La Tourelle and the adjacent distillery, Lieut.-Colonel Longley took over temporary command of the 14th Brigade, and Major Tew that of the Battalion. Next day, the 21st, Major W. H. Paterson joined from the 2nd Battalion in England and took over command of D Company.

Meanwhile, on the 20th October, heavy fighting had been in progress just south of Lorgies, and the Manchester Regt. had suffered considerable losses. At eleven o'clock that night Major Tew received orders to relieve the Manchester Regt. in the Lorgies defences and to continue supporting the K.O.S.B.'s with one company. For the latter duty D Company, under Major Paterson, was detailed, while Battalion Headquarters and the remaining companies proceeded to Lorgies. The relief was completed by 4 a.m. on the 21st October, and the Manchester Regt. passed back through the village.

The trenches now held by A and B, the two front East Surrey companies, ran roughly in a south-westerly direction from a point on the Lorgies–La Bassée road about 500 yards south of Lorgies; while C Company was in support in a trench, also on the west side of the road, on the southern outskirts of the village. To the east of the road were the D.C.L.I., and on their left again was a battalion of another brigade. Against these two battalions the Germans about 7 a.m. on the 21st October launched an attack, which overwhelmed the battalion furthest from the East Surrey on the left of the D.C.L.I., and the left of the D.C.L.I. became involved in its retirement.

At the first indication of the German attack Major Tew had sent off an urgent message to Major Paterson to bring D Company to Lorgies, a request that was promptly complied with. The first platoon, under Lieut. Schomberg, reported to Major Tew just when the situation on the exposed left of the East Surrey was becoming more and more critical, and the platoon was despatched round the eastern outskirts of Lorgies to a position whence it was able to enfilade the Germans who had reached that side of the village. This relieved the situation for the moment until Major Paterson, arriving with his second platoon, reinforced Lieut. Schomberg and, with the assistance of some of the D.C.L.I. and of the East Surrey machine guns firing from a house in the village, finally expelled the Germans and completely restored the situation.

Major Paterson, with his two platoons of D Company, then occupied a trench to the east of the Lorgies–La Bassée road, some 200 yards in rear of B Company's left, which, as we have seen, rested on the other side of that road. A Company of the West Kent Regt. arrived later and extended on Major Paterson's left. The remaining platoons of D Company were retained as Battalion Reserve in the southern end of Lorgies.

Though the village was now secure, the left of the line held by B and C, the two front companies, was completely in the air, and, as it was impossible to communicate with them by daylight, their situation was a cause of grave anxiety at Battalion Headquarters throughout the afternoon, which wore on with heavy shell fire and incessant sniping. Eventually, however, a report came through after dark that all was well with the three front companies.

In view of the situation that had developed during the day on the left of the 1st Battn. East Surrey, that unit about midnight received orders to make a short retirement and occupy a new line on a level with the position which C Company had held during the day near the southern edge of the village. This change of position was effected by 4 a.m. on the 21st October. The casualties on the 20th had been 5 other ranks killed and 2nd Lieut. J. O. Carpenter and 15 other ranks wounded.

At daybreak on the 22nd the Germans captured Violainés, a small village about a mile and a half south-west of Lorgies, and, in order to assist a counter-attack for its recapture, the 1st Battn. East Surrey maintained throughout the day a heavy rifle and machine-gun fire on the Germans to its right front. The casualties during the day were Lieut. N. L. Bridgland, an excellent young officer, and 4 other ranks killed and 7 wounded.

As the II Corps had now received orders to take up a line which was shorter and less exposed, the 14th Brigade was withdrawn from Lorgies at midnight, 22nd/23rd October. In this retirement the 1st Battn. East Surrey was not molested by the enemy, and by 3.30 a.m. it had taken up a position facing southeast some 500 yards south of Richebourg L'Avoué, where the work of digging new trenches began at once. Soon after daybreak on the 23rd advancing German infantry was sighted, and sniping immediately commenced.

On the 24th October, Brigadier-General F. S. Maude took over command of the 14th Brigade and Lieut.-Colonel Longley resumed command of the Battalion. Heavy shell fire continued throughout the day and another attack was made at 4 p.m., but again was not pressed. One man was killed and 4 wounded.

October 25th, a fine bright day, was utilized to the full by the German heavy guns, which shelled the trenches and village of Richebourg incessantly, killing 3 men and wounding 10. The Battalion was reinforced by the arrival of Captain L. J. Le Fleming with 3 officers and 80 other ranks. Next day the reserve trenches and village were again heavily shelled all the afternoon, but only two men were wounded. October 27th was a less fortunate day, for, although the enemy chiefly directed his efforts against the 3rd Division on the left and captured Neuve Chapelle, the 1st Battn. East Surrey had 1 man killed and 11 of all ranks wounded, including Lieut. M. S. Benning, who died of his wounds on the 1st November. He had been with the Battalion only two days when he was mortally wounded. On the 28th heavy shelling again continued from 7.30 a.m. till 5 p.m., but the Battalion remained unshaken, and an attempted assault at 5.30 p.m. was easily repulsed at the cost of 4 killed and 17 wounded. The next day much resembled previous ones. There was again very heavy shell fire which caused some casualties, viz. Captain L. J. Le Fleming and 4 other ranks wounded.

The following " Special Order " was published on the 29th October: " On October 22nd, 1914, Lieut.-General Sir Charles Ferguson, on relinquishing command of the 5th Division, wrote to Lieut.-Colonel Longley as follows:—

" I only write to say how grateful I shall always be to you and your Battalion for the splendid example and unfailing good work which has always characterized you all, and of which you may well be proud. No regiment has done better, and in none have I ever had more confidence. Please say good-bye to all for me, and you know I shall always remember them with pride and affection."

Battalion Orders of October 29th also published the following list of decorations awarded to the 1st Battn. East Surrey Regt.: Captain the Hon. A. R. Hewitt, Distinguished Service Order; Captain E. M. Woulfe-Flanagan, Legion of Honour (Croix de Chevalier); Sergt. H. W. Hunt, Médaille Militaire.

The following were mentioned in despatches, dated 18th October, 1914:

Lieut.-Colonel J. R. Longley; Major H. S. Tew; Captains E. M. Woulfe-Flanagan, Hon. A. R. Hewitt, M. J. Minogue and F. A. Bowring (Adjutant); Sergt.-Major G. E. Hyson; C.Q.M.S. J. V. Woolgar; Sergts. H. W. Hunt, R. H. Hunt and M. L. Hill; Pte. J. Wilkins.

The two Sergts. Hunt were brothers, most gallant soldiers, natives of Chertsey in Surrey. They were both killed in action at the Battle of the Marne on the 9th September, 1914.

For conspicuous services in the fighting round Richebourg L'Avoué and Lorgies, the Distinguished Conduct Medal was afterwards awarded to the following: Q.M.S. W. Fisher; Sergts. W. C. Edwards and M. L. Hill; Ptes. J. E. Healey and J. Wilkins.

On the 29th October news was received that the Indian Corps was about to relieve the II Corps, some units of which were to be withdrawn into reserve, while the others were to remain in support of the Indian Corps. In accordance with this arrangement, Lieut.-Colonel Swiney, formerly an East Surrey officer and now commanding the 2nd Battn. 39th Garhwalis, arrived at 9 p.m. with his company commanders to inspect the position held by the East Surrey. At 2 a.m. on the following day the 2nd Battn. 39th Garhwalis arrived and had just begun to take over the trenches when a heavy fire was opened, which lasted about forty minutes, and a second outburst about 4 a.m. again delayed the relief.

The 1st Battn. East Surrey at last moved off about 5.30 a.m. and marched to billets at Les Glatignies, near Locon. The first day's rest was broken by an order to move about two miles to fresh billets at La Couture. The Battalion arrived there about 6 p.m., and just as the leading company was moving into its billets a howitzer shell fell at the head of the Battalion, killing 2 men and wounding Lieut. H. St. G. Schomberg and 7 rank and file.

On the 31st October Battalion Headquarters, though changed on the previous night, were shelled. The billets of the Battalion were then transferred to the further end of the village, but were again shelled during the night. These incidents illustrate the efficiency of the enemy's spy system at this period of the war. Major Paterson took over the duties of Second-in-Command from Major Tew, who went to hospital suffering from an injury to his knee.

On November 1st the 14th Brigade moved a short distance to new billets at Le Touret, and in the afternoon marched to Lestrem, seven miles north of Béthune, arriving at 6 p.m. While on the march several N.C.O.'s and men of the 2nd Battn. East Surrey, who had arrived from India with the Meerut Division, greeted the Battalion. On November 2nd the Battalion, with the D.C.L.I., marched northwards *en route* to Ypres, but immediately on arrival at Bailleul were sent back to Lestrem in thirty-three motor-buses to support the Indian Corps.

On November 3rd the Battalion marched at 7 a.m. towards Vieille Chapelle and billeted in farms about two miles west of it, where it received a draft of 3 officers and 35 other ranks. The morning of November 4th was spent in refitting, and at 3.45 p.m. the Battalion moved to billets at Laventie in close support of the Lahore Division. Here Captain P. C. Wynter with 2 subaltern officers and 54 other ranks joined the Battalion. On November 5th the Battalion marched back to its billets near Vieille Chapelle and completed refitting.

The 14th Brigade again took over a sector of the front line on November 6th, relieving the 8th Brigade near Vieille Chapelle, and the 1st Battn. East Surrey marched at 5.45 p.m. to take over the trenches occupied by the Royal Scots. The relief was effected by midnight without loss, and the Battalion remained in the trenches on this occasion for eight days, being relieved at a late hour in the night of November 14th. While in the front line there was an incessant rifle fire from the Germans and a considerable amount of badly aimed shell fire. A few casualties occurred daily, the total losses during the eight days being 2 killed and 23 wounded.

The 14th Brigade now recommenced its move northwards, and the 1st Battn. East Surrey marched in wet and very cold weather to Meteren a mile west of Bailleul. After only one night's rest the Battalion crossed the frontier into Belgium and took over on November 16th the trenches east of Lindenhoek, near Mt. Kemmel, held by the 153rd Regiment of the 39th French Division. The relief was a difficult one, as the German trenches were from 50 to 100 yards from the French ones, and on slightly higher ground. On November 17th the support trenches of the Battalion were persistently shelled. During the night and early morning of the 18th there was a sharp frost and some snow, after which the weather improved. Shelling continued, causing several casualties, and Major Paterson had a narrow escape, a shell striking one end of his dugout as he left by the other. The 19th and 20th were bitterly cold, with heavy snow on the former date, and the trenches were shelled each day. On the 21st the frost was very hard. The machine-gun section put out of action a German machine gun, this being the sixth time that they had performed the feat.

On November 22nd the support trenches were subjected for three or four hours to a heavy and accurate shell fire which covered the ground around with craters and destroyed the communication trenches. For conspicuous gallantry on this day Cpl. F. Camis was awarded the Distinguished Conduct Medal. When his section had been shelled out of a trench he remained behind under heavy howitzer fire to bandage the wounded. The history of the 23rd was similar, all the Battalion trenches being heavily shelled and several men killed. On this day, however, it is recorded that the British field-guns and howitzers fired vigorously and made excellent practice, which greatly cheered the troops.

November 24th ended the tour of trench duty, the Battalion being relieved at midnight by the Dorset Regt., when the companies marched to billets at Dranoutre. The total casualties during the eight-day tour in the trenches were 2nd Lieut. H. Housecroft and 17 other ranks killed and 40 other ranks wounded. 2nd Lieut. Housecroft had been less than a month with the Battalion.

The men were given a late morning on November 25th, and the rest of the day was spent in refitting. Fur jackets were served out and found most comfortable in the severe cold. Several men had suffered from frostbite during the last tour in the trenches. The men were also much pleased by the distribution of a large number of presents sent out by friends of the Battalion in England, and at their request a grateful acknowledgment of the gifts was published in *The Times* and other newspapers. On November 26th the Battalion rested, and arrangements were made for 200 men at a time to bathe at the lunatic asylum at Bailleul. Next day experiments were made by the staff to ascertain the best method of carrying the considerable amount of warm clothing now in possession of the men, and at dusk on the 28th the Battalion again marched up to the trenches, its position on this occasion being near Wulverghem.

November 29th to December 1st were quiet days, the casualties being 3 men killed and 3 wounded. The Royal Engineers provided some iron loopholes during this period and began much-needed draining operations. At 6 p.m. on December 1st the Battalion was relieved by the Dorset Regt. The night was wet and, the relief being completed about 8 p.m., the companies assembled at Neuve Eglise and thence marched about seven miles west into billets at St. Jans Cappel. As a result of trench duty the men could not now do more than $2\frac{1}{2}$ miles in the hour, and did not reach billets until 1.30 a.m. on December 2nd. On this date Lieut.-Colonel Longley, Lieuts. Darwell, Clarke and Roupell, Sergt.-Major Hyson and Q.M.S. Rodgers left for England on seven days' leave, Major Paterson assuming command of the Battalion.

In the afternoon of the 2nd December the Battalion (14 officers and 633 other ranks) paraded for inspection by the Commander-in-Chief, Field-Marshal Sir John French, who addressed them as follows:—

" 1st Battn. East Surrey Regt., I am very glad to have the opportunity of addressing you to-day and of thanking you for the work you have done. On the way here I asked your Corps Commander, Sir Horace, what special occasion I could mention in which you have distinguished yourselves. ' Whatever you mention, and whatever you say,' he said, ' it will not be too much. They have been splendid throughout.' No regiment could wish for higher praise than this, and I thank you personally for what you have done and the way you have helped me. The 5th Division have had more than their share of the fighting in this campaign. On the terrible retirement after Mons and Le Câteau you had the brunt of the fighting, and immediately after, at the Battle of the Marne, you had to attack the most difficult section of the line, and the attack was brilliantly carried out. Not a week later you were engaged on the Aisne and held the extremely difficult position of Missy, into which an incessant rifle and shell fire was poured from the commanding German position above. Less than a month after this the Regiment was in the thick of the terribly severe fighting round La Bassée, where you were faced by three if not four times your numbers and experienced some of the fiercest fighting of the War. Lately in the trench fighting you have gallantly defended your lines against the most determined attacks and the most vigorous shelling. In fact, you have crowded into the four months of this campaign enough fighting to fill the battle honours of an Army Corps, and by your conduct throughout you have not only upheld, but greatly added to the fame of a grand old Regiment. In conclusion, as Commander-in-Chief, I wish once more to thank you for your endurance and for the splendid work you have performed and to tell you how glad I am to have this opportunity of being able to tell you so."

On December 3rd the visit of His Majesty the King to the Army in the field took place, and the 1st Battn. East Surrey was represented by one company, which paraded at Brigade Headquarters. His Majesty presented Distinguished Conduct Medals to a number of N.C.O.'s and men whose names have already been recorded, and on the conclusion of the inspection three hearty cheers were given by the troops on parade.

The Battalion marched to Neuve Eglise on December 5th and remained there in Brigade Reserve until the 10th, when, under Lieut.-Colonel Longley, who had rejoined from England, it relieved the Devon Regt. in the trenches at Wulverghem. The period of rest, longer than usual, had considerably improved the health of all ranks.

The first three days in the line were quiet and the casualties were few. 2nd Lieut. R. J. Hillier and 160 N.C.O.'s and men joined the Battalion on the 11th. On the 14th an attack was made on Wytschaete by the 3rd Division and a French Corps on the left of the 5th Division, which supported the attack by its fire. The operations continued on the 15th and 16th and had little success, the attacking troops being unable to move in the deep mud. The enemy's artillery fire became very heavy, and the Battalion lost 11 men killed, Lieut. W. H. M. Simpson mortally wounded and 27 other ranks wounded. For gallantry in repairing the telephone wires under heavy fire on the 16th, Pte. E. W. Peacock was afterwards awarded the D.C.M.

On December 17th the 1st Battn. East Surrey was held in readiness for another demonstration, but its services were not required, and at 9 p.m. it was relieved in the trenches by the Dorset Regt. and marched back to billets at St. Jans-Cappel. During this week of trench duty, in addition to the loss of 13 killed and 35 wounded, the number of sick increased considerably owing to very wet and cold weather. The trenches were waterlogged, and enteric fever made its first appearance.

The Battalion remained at St. Jans-Cappel in cold and unpleasant weather until the 23rd December. During this period of rest Captain and Quartermaster W. Ford left the Battalion after thirty-one years of valuable service, his place being filled by the promotion of Sergt.-Major G. E. Hyson. A draft of 40 rank and file joined on December 21st, and on the 23rd the Battalion marched to Dranoutre, where it was billeted with the D.C.L.I., while the Devon and Manchester Regts. took over trenches from the 13th Brigade.

On Christmas Eve a draft of 108 men joined, and a dry day was employed in cleaning and drying the uncomfortable billets. Christmas Day was very cold and foggy, but the distribution of the cards and gifts sent by their Majesties the King and Queen and by Princess Mary gave great pleasure.

For the next three days companies were employed separately in trench digging, and in the afternoon of the 29th the Battalion marched up to the trenches and relieved the Devons, who reported that the Germans had made frequent attempts to leave their trenches and fraternize on Christmas Day and were not finally discouraged until one or two had been shot. On December 30th much work was done in draining the trenches, which were deep in water. There was no heavy fire, yet 3 men were killed and 7 wounded. On the last day of the year there was little fire and no casualties occurred.

The New Year began with a heavy bombardment of the German trenches, to which the enemy's guns presently replied. A large shell fell in a support trench occupied by part of A Company, burying 5 men. Pte. C. Owen and another man proceeded at once to dig these men out, when, a second shell falling near, the second man desisted. Pte. Owen continued digging, and was in the act of dragging out one of the buried men when a third shell killed him. For this act of devoted gallantry Pte. Owen was recommended for reward. Captain D. Wynyard, who had recovered from his wound received at Mons, rejoined and took over the duties of Adjutant.

The Battalion remained in the trenches till the night of January 4th, losing altogether during the tour 11 men killed and 2nd Lieut. C. G. Watson (Royal Berkshire Regt. attd.) and 21 men wounded. The relief was effected without loss, though the Germans opened machine-gun fire on the trenches while it was in progress. The Battalion then marched to billets at Bailleul, arriving there about 1 a.m. on January 5th and remaining until the 9th. Major Paterson went to England on short leave on the 5th, and on the 9th Colonel Longley, who, except for three short periods of extra-regimental duty, had been in the Battalion throughout his service, and had commanded it with high distinction from the beginning of the campaign, left on appointment as Brigadier-General of the 82nd Brigade. He had no time to take farewell of his old regiment before leaving, but sent them the following message at the first opportunity with a request that it might be read out to them on parade and afterwards published in orders:—

"3.2.15.

"Officers, Non-commissioned Officers and Men,

"My orders on the 9th January to join and take command of the 82nd Brigade gave me no time for any leave-taking. I had quite intended coming over to see you while my brigade was in reserve, but that unfortunately has not been possible, so I am writing this message instead.

"You have a record second to none, and I have every confidence in your fully upholding that glorious record and adding to it as the years go by. To do that, however, you must continue the same whole-hearted devotion to duty, setting yourselves the same high standard as in the past; and fostering a right spirit of self-sacrifice without which no soldier is worth his salt. Bear these things in mind, and God speed you in your work.

"I wish to express my very sincere thanks to the Battalion staff and to all company officers for the great assistance they have unfailingly given me at all times, likewise to the N.C.O.'s for their co-operation on all occasions. As for the men, I have nothing but admiration for the thoroughness they put into all their work, and for their cheeriness however trying that work may be. The sympathy and good feeling that exists between all ranks has been a marked feature in the Battalion for many years, and long may it continue so.

> "My task is taught,
> Your swords are wrought,
> So forward, though not
> Farewell, but 'au revoir.'"

"J. R. LONGLEY,
"Brigadier-General,
"Commanding 82nd Infantry Brigade."

On January 10th the Battalion marched to new billets at Neuve Eglise, and on the following day Major Paterson returned from England and assumed command. On the 13th a draft of 91 men joined, and on the 16th the Battalion relieved the Devon Regt. in the trenches at Wulverghem. The relief began at 6 p.m. in heavy rain and pitch darkness, and was not completed before half-past ten.

The 17th January was a quiet day in the line, only one man being wounded; but on the following day the trenches occupied by A Company were shelled and two men were buried by the explosion of two shells which fell close together. Cpl. R. Williams and two other men went to the assistance of the buried men, and while the two men worked in the trench Cpl. Williams jumped up on the parapet to remove the head cover. This he did knowing that earlier in the day a man had been killed on the same spot by a German sniper. He was almost immediately shot through the leg and at the same moment struck by fragments of a shell. For this gallant conduct Cpl. Williams afterwards received the Distinguished Conduct Medal.

On January 19th, in consequence of a readjustment of the sector, part of the Battalion was relieved by the West Riding Regt. and the Queen Victoria's Rifles, and Headquarters and two companies marched into billets at Neuve Eglise. On the 20th D Company, which had remained in the trenches, was shelled and had 1 man killed and 6 wounded.

The periods of rest between the tours of duty in the trenches in these early days of the War were of short duration, and on the 21st January the Battalion again moved up to the line and relieved the D.C.L.I. in the trenches just north of the River Douve. The weather was terrible, and, owing to the river having overflowed its banks, men walking to and from the firing line were up to the waist in water. The Commanding Officer was ordered to report if the Battalion could hold the trenches for two complete days. On the 22nd the weather was clear and bright, and the whole flooded country was frozen hard. Company commanders reported that their men, though wet and very cold, wished to "stick out" the two days. The trenches were shelled without effect, but 1 man was killed and 2 wounded by German snipers. On the 23rd several men were found to be suffering from frostbite, and that evening the Battalion was relieved by the Devons and marched into Neuve Eglise. Next day it was complimented in Brigade Orders on its excellent work in the trenches.

On January 25th news was received that the 2nd Battn. East Surrey, which had recently arrived in France, was billeted at Flêtre, eight miles west of Neuve Eglise. Greetings were interchanged by message, and on the 26th the Commanding Officer and two other officers rode over to visit the 2nd Battalion.

On January 28th Captain A. Huth (4th Battalion) and a draft of 90 men joined. On the 29th German aeroplanes came over the billets, and in the afternoon two shells fell in them, killing 1 man and wounding 9. In the evening two companies went into the reserve trenches, while the remainder of the Battalion finished the month in billets.

On February 1st the Battalion relieved the D.C.L.I. in A sector opposite Messines. The weather was favourable, the night being fine and dry with slight frost. About daybreak on the 3rd a fire broke out in a farm occupied as Battalion Headquarters. The building was in full view of the Messines Ridge, but by great exertions the fire was extinguished before the German artillery could locate it.

The trenches were shelled on the 4th and German snipers were active, 2 men being killed and 2 wounded. The Battalion was relieved by the Devon Regt. in the evening and marched to billets at Neuve Eglise, where it remained till February 11th, one man being wounded by shell fire, in the village. On the 8th the Battalion was joined by Captain J. C. May, 2nd Lieut. Dymott (Indian Army attd.) and 80 men. February 10th being Sobraon Day, was celebrated by special meals, a football match with the Devons in the afternoon and a concert in the evening.

On February 11th the Battalion relieved the Manchester Regt. in the B sector trenches in front of Messines, and was relieved by the D.C.L.I. on the night of the 15th. During this tour of duty the weather was stormy and wet, and the casualties were 2 killed and 8 wounded. On being relieved the Battalion returned to billets at Neuve Eglise, where it spent the next four days. This village, being close to the line, was subjected to periodical shelling by the enemy, and on this account was not much safer than the trenches. Fortunately for the Battalion, no shelling took place until the last day of its stay, and on the evening of the 19th the Battalion again took over A sector opposite Messines. This tour of trench duty was quiet and only six men were wounded. On the 23rd the Battalion was relieved by the Devons and went back at night into billets at Neuve Eglise.

On February 24th a draft of 50 men joined. On the 26th the following awards to officers and men of the Battalion for conspicuous service up to and including the actions of the River Aisne appeared in Orders:—

Lieut.-Colonel Longley was promoted Brevet Colonel, and Major Tew Brevet Lieut.-Colonel. Captain M. J. Minogue, Lieut. R. A. F. Montanaro and Lieut. and Quartermaster G. E. Hyson received the Military Cross.

# PATROL WORK

The following were mentioned in despatches:—

Lieut.-Colonel J. R. Longley; Majors H. S. Tew and W. H. Paterson; Captain M. J. Minogue; Lieuts. T. H. Darwell, R. A. F. Montanaro and G. R. P. Roupell; Sergt. W. Parkes; Lce.-Sergt. H. Bousfield;[1] Lce.-Cpl. G. Bosten; Ptes. A. Quesnel, J. Hudson, J. Burton, Gutsall, H. Ward, W. Glock.

Shortly after noon on February 27th the Germans began shelling the north end of the village, and the Battalion was ordered to evacuate all its billets immediately and clear the village. Before this could be carried out a shell wrecked a house occupied by part of C Company, burying a number of men, of whom 7 were killed and 5 more or less severely wounded. Pte. Gould, who had joined with the last draft, was partially buried, and on being released at once assisted in digging out eight of the buried men. At 4 p.m. the shelling, having apparently ceased, the Battalion was ordered to remove kits from the billets, platoon by platoon. Shelling began again at once, and the men were again ordered to leave the village. At night the Battalion marched to the trenches in sector B and relieved the Manchester Regt. The month ended with snow and a violent storm of wind.

March 1st was a quiet day with no casualties, but on the 2nd the farm occupied by Battalion Headquarters was heavily shelled. Fifty-three shells, of which thirty-six were howitzer shells, fell on or round it, but without causing any casualties. One man was killed in the trenches. March 3rd was again quiet, and the Battalion was relieved at night by the D.C.L.I., A Company moving into billets in Neuve Eglise, and the remaining companies into newly constructed huts about a mile south of that village.

On March 4th the Battalion was busily engaged in making roads and drains. Neuve Eglise was shelled and A Company was moved out of it into huts, having one man wounded. On the 5th Neuve Eglise was again heavily shelled about midday: two shells fell into the Field Ambulance, killing Major Richards, R.A.M.C., and four men, two of whom belonged to the Battalion, while two East Surrey men were wounded. On March 6th Neuve Eglise was heavily shelled all day, and Battalion Headquarters moved into the huts. The 7th was a day of rain with more shelling; at night the Battalion relieved the Manchester Regt. in sector A opposite Messines.

On March 8th there was little sun and a very cold wind, with a hard frost at night. Several officers' patrols went out close to the German lines and threw grenades into their trenches. One man was wounded. March 9th opened fine and was a quiet day, with a fall of snow in the afternoon. At night a smart exploit was performed by a patrol of four men under Lieut. G. R. P. Roupell, accompanied by Lieut. R. A. Abercrombie. The patrol went to a farm about 300 yards from our trenches and occupied by Germans as part of their line. To reach the farm the patrol had to crawl for a considerable distance owing to the clearness of the night. On arriving close to the farm they remained for some time lying flat and listening to the Germans talking in, and in rear of, the farm.

---

[1] Lance-Sergeant Bousfield was appointed 2nd lieutenant in the Regiment on March 14th, 1915.

II.—F

Eventually they saw five men leave the farm, and very soon after five men came back. Lieut. Roupell decided that they had seen the relief of a listening post. Presently a flare showed that they were close up against a thick wire entanglement running down to a hedge from the direction of which the relief had come. They crawled down the side of the entanglement to the hedge, and had got to within ten yards of it when they were twice challenged by a German whose head and shoulders could be seen against the sky. As they were prevented by the wire from rushing the post, they opened rapid fire on it with rifles and revolvers. The Germans replied; one of them shrieked out, and two were seen running away towards the farm. As there was no further sign or movement from the post it was presumed that the three other Germans had been killed. The patrol then opened out and retired quickly to their trench under heavy fire from the German position. Lieut. Roupell was slightly wounded in the arm, but the remainder of the patrol were untouched.

On March 10th a trench mortar burst in the trench occupied by C Company, wounding one man. The next night the Battalion was relieved by the D.C.L.I. and went into billets at Neuve Église, where it remained till the 15th; but in consequence of the exposure of the village to shell fire, the days were passed in fields on the Bailleul road, the companies returning to their billets after dark. In consequence of this sensible though somewhat uncomfortable arrangement no casualties occurred. On March 15th the Battalion marched after dark straight from the fields on the Bailleul road to relieve the Manchester Regt. in sector B trenches before Messines. During this tour of trench duty the weather was mostly fine but dull, the casualties being one man killed and one wounded. Snow fell on the 19th, on which day the Battalion was relieved after dark by the D.C.L.I. and marched to Neuve Eglise. Next day was very fine, and the companies moved into huts west of the Bailleul road.

March 21st was a bright, warm day and Church service was held in the camp. In the afternoon the Commanding Officer, acting adjutant and company commanders went to Kemmel to inspect new trenches to be taken over by the Battalion. On the 23rd Neuve Eglise was shelled and six men employed there were wounded. The Battalion paraded at 5.50 p.m., marched northward to Kemmel and relieved the Wiltshire Regt. and parts of the 4th Battn. Gordon Highlanders and the Suffolk Regt.

On the first day in the new position the trench occupied by A Company was heavily bombarded, 11 men being wounded, and the total casualties during the day were 3 killed and 12 wounded. On the 25th there was little shelling, but a considerable amount of sniping, and at night an organized rifle and machine-gun fire was carried out which silenced the German musketry fire.

On March 27th the Battalion was relieved by the Manchester Regt. and marched to Locre, where it remained for four days in bright and sunny but very cold weather. During the night of the 31st the Battalion relieved the Manchester Regt. in the trenches north-east of Mt. Kemmel. The total casualties during March were 11 men killed and 1 officer and 30 other ranks wounded.

## CHAPTER V

APRIL TO SEPTEMBER, 1915: THE 1st BATTALION IN THE DEFENCE OF HILL 60; TWO MONTHS AND A HALF IN THE TRENCHES SOUTH OF HILL 60 DURING THE BATTLES OF YPRES, 1915; ON TRANSFER WITH THE 5TH DIVISION TO THE X CORPS, THE BATTALION SERVES TWO MONTHS IN THE LINE BETWEEN MARICOURT AND THE RIVER SOMME.

THE first four days of April were passed in the trenches north-east of Mount Kemmel and a good deal of shell and rifle fire was directed on the trenches each day, the casualties being 2nd Lieut. J. Nash (4th Battn. attd.) and 4 men killed and 17 men wounded.

As the 5th Division was now being transferred to another part of the line, the 1st Battn. East Surrey was relieved during the night of the 4th April by the Gordon Highlanders and Royal Scots, and went back to billets at Locre. It marched next morning to hutments east of Zevecoten, remaining there until the 7th, when it continued its march northward to Ypres, where it remained in Brigade Reserve, being quartered in the cavalry barracks. The town had been heavily shelled during the day, and about 100 casualties had occurred in various regiments. There was more shelling on the 9th April, and the 1st Battn. East Surrey had three men wounded in the streets.

On the 10th April the 2nd Battn. East Surrey marched through Ypres and was heartily cheered by the men of the 1st Battalion, who were lined up in the square near the Cloth Hall. This meeting of the two battalions aroused the greatest interest throughout the East Surrey Regt.

On the following day the 1st Battn. East Surrey took over from the Manchester Regt. the trenches a quarter of a mile south-east of Verbranden Molen and on the opposite side of the Ypres–Comines railway to Hill 60, which was soon to become the scene of one of the hardest fights that the Battalion has experienced. While inspecting these trenches during the night of the 13th Brigadier-General F. S. Maude was severely wounded, the casualty being recorded in the Battalion Diary as "a grievous loss to the Brigade." During this tour of trench duty 6 men of the Battalion were killed and 19 wounded; while Captain J. C. May received severe injuries from a fall, which resulted in his being invalided to England. On the 15th the Battalion was relieved by the Manchester Regt. and returned as Brigade Reserve to the cavalry barracks, where it was joined by a draft of 18 men.

On the 18th April, Colonel G. H. Thesiger, who had assumed temporary command of the 14th Brigade, was ordered to send a battalion to reinforce the 13th Brigade at Hill 60. The 1st Battn. East Surrey was selected for this duty, and Battalion Headquarters and A and B Companies moved off at 4 p.m. to a position one mile short of Hill 60, followed two hours later by the remainder of the Battalion. While waiting for orders in this position the Battalion had its first experience of gas and its unpleasant effect on the throat and eyes.

Before proceeding with the narrative it is advisable to give a short description of Hill 60 and the circumstances of its capture by the British. East of Verbranden Molen the ridge which runs south-west from Mount Sorrel to the Bluff is crossed by a deep cutting, in which runs the railway from Ypres to Comines. On the northern edge of the cutting stands Hill 60, which has been described aptly as a pimple near the western crest of the ridge. As will be seen by reference to the sketch map opposite, the 60-metre contour indicates approximately the base of this pimple. To its position, therefore, rather than to its elevation, is due the value which Hill 60 had for the Germans as an artillery observation post overlooking the lower ground to the west and north-west towards Ypres, which lies some two miles distant and 120 feet below it.

On the 17th April the British front line ran along the road which leads from the hamlet of Zwarteleen round the northern base of the pimple and crosses the railway by the bridge. About 6 p.m. on that date the Royal Engineers exploded the mines which they had driven under the German fire-trenches on the hill, with the result that five craters were formed, occupying practically the whole area, which had once been the summit of the hill. Following on the explosion of the mines, the 1st Battn. Royal West Kent Regt. and 2nd Battn. K.O.S.B., of the 13th Brigade, captured and occupied the German support trenches, which ran round the southern slope of the pimple, a short distance below the crest-line. During the night of the 18th/19th April the 15th Brigade relieved the 13th on both sides of the railway cutting, and the 1st Battn. East Surrey, now attached to the 15th Brigade, took over a portion of the Brigade front, viz. the Hill 60 position, at 5 a.m. on the 19th April.

Before proceeding with the description of the Hill 60 defences it is necessary to indicate the situation and dimensions of the mine-craters referred to in the preceding paragraph, as some of these craters played an important part in the subsequent defence. Three of the craters lay, approximately in a straight line, close to the southern crest-line of the hill and, having regard to the position of an observer on the hill looking southwards towards the new German front line, are referred to hereafter as the left, middle and right craters respectively. The left, or easternmost, crater formed with the middle crater a figure of eight, as their lips intersected at one point where their junction was below ground level. The left crater was about 30 yards in diameter and had a depth of some 20 feet; while the middle crater was of slightly greater dimensions. The right crater, a smaller one, was separated by a few yards from the middle one. Two other smaller craters lay in rear—that is, near the northern crest-line of the hill.

The defences of Hill 60 consisted, roughly speaking, of two lines of trenches both of which started from a point near the railway bridge. The advanced line of trenches ran from the bridge up the slope of the pimple towards the right crater, where a gap existed, beyond which the old German support trenches were held as the British front line and extended as far as the front of the left crater.

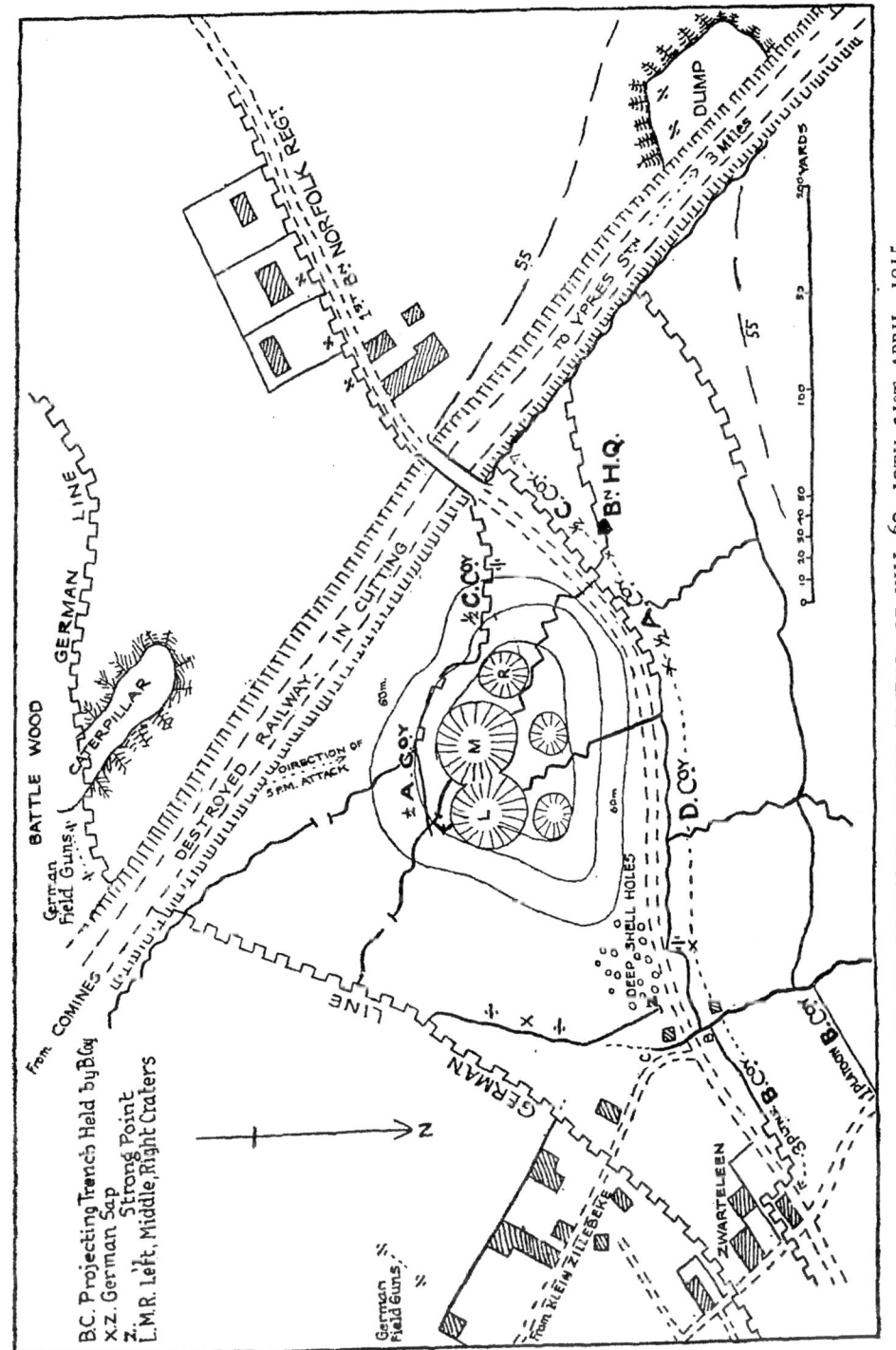

THE 1ST BATTALION IN THE DEFENCE OF HILL 60, 19TH–21ST APRIL, 1915.

Into these trenches opened two old German communication trenches which crossed No Man's Land from the German front line, one of which continued through the left extremity of the British front line past the left crater into the middle one, while a branch from it ran direct to the left crater. Both the old German communication trenches were "blocked" in No Man's Land at some distance from the British front line, and both branches of the continuation of the left-hand trench were blocked again between the advanced line and the craters.

The left of the British advanced line was thus completely in the air, and the danger to this flank was increased by the existence of the German sap XZ. When the Battalion took over the position, C Company, under Captain A. H. Huth, occupied the whole of the advanced line from the bridge to the left crater.

The other line of trenches followed roughly the road which ran from the bridge round the northern base of the pimple to Zwarteleen. At first A Company, commanded by Lieut. G. R. P. Roupell, occupied the right trenches as far as the communication trench running up to the left crater. D Company, under Lieut. E. G. H. Clarke, was on A's left, and B, under Captain P. C. Wynter, held the left of the Battalion's front as far as the point of junction with the 1st Battn. Cheshire Regt. near Zwarteleen. B Company had three platoons in the front line and one, under 2nd Lieut. O. I. Nares, in the support trench about 50 yards in rear of its left. At the base of the pimple, opposite the junction of D and B Companies, the ground was pitted with large shell holes; and a little further to the left was the German strong point Z, distant only 20 yards from B Company's right. Further again to the left and at right angles to the general front was the short trench B.C., also held by B Company, with two ruined houses alongside it, which obscured the view into the shell-hole area.

The machine-gun section under Lieut. Darwell had five machine guns, four of which were with B and D Companies sweeping the eastern slopes of the hill, and one with C Company near the bridge. The Bedfords were in support in a line of trenches with dugouts about Larch Wood, which was on the railway some 500 yards in rear of the hill.

Throughout the 19th April, which was spent in clearing the trenches of dead and wounded and in improving the defences, the position was shelled continuously by the Germans, their fire being directed chiefly on the support and communication trenches in rear of the hill. About 5 p.m. the shelling increased to a heavy bombardment of all the trenches by trench mortars and heavy howitzers. It was answered by the British guns and ceased after half an hour, but during that period it had wrought great destruction. No infantry attack followed, and the Battalion commenced at once the task of repairing the damaged defences.

About 10 p.m. an important change took place in the distribution of the two companies on the right, when half of A Company, under Lieut. Roupell, relieved the two platoons of C Company which had originally occupied the old German support trenches on the forward slope of the pimple. Thereafter C Company on the extreme right and A Company on its left had each two platoons in the advanced line and two in support in the trenches along the road.

The work of repairing the defences continued throughout the night, and, in spite of the enemy's continuous shelling and bombing, the men worked magnificently, and all damage was made good by dawn of the 20th. Captain Huth, an excellent officer whose death was regretted by the whole Battalion, was killed while superintending the extension of C Company's trench in the advanced line up the slope to the right crater.

The early morning of the 20th, which like the previous day was fine and hot, passed fairly quietly as far as the advanced line was concerned; but in rear of the hill the fire of the enemy's heavy howitzers was very accurate and caused much damage to the parapets. On the left, No. 5 platoon of B Company, under Lieut. A. C. T. Evanson, observed a party of the enemy working on their sap at X and tried to bomb them from C, the end of the trench BC, but without success. The end C was then broken down by German field-guns in action just beyond Zwarteleen. It was eventually blocked again by some very brave men of No. 6 platoon, under the direction of Sergt. P. Griggs, who subsequently received the D.C.M. and later on was killed in one of the battles of the Somme, 1916. These men saved the trench BC, which otherwise would have remained completely exposed.

The worst thorn in the side of B Company, however, was the strong point at Z, which had been completed by the Germans during the night and was now provided with steel loopholes. Situated as it was only 20 yards from the British trench, B Company suffered severely from its bombers and snipers. Every time one of the East Surrey men looked over the parapets near the strong point a German bullet went into or near his head, and in one place five men in succession were killed in this way while an attempt was being made to bring rifle fire to bear on the above-mentioned German working party at X.

About 11 a.m. a heavy bombardment started on the position generally and again caused great destruction. In places the trenches were obliterated and many men were killed or buried by the explosions. During this bombardment the Commanding Officer, Major W. H. Paterson, with the Adjutant, Captain D. Wynyard, visited D Company's trenches. Captain Wynyard, noticing that some men were helping the wounded in a specially exposed portion of a trench, ran to the spot and moved the men along the trench away from the danger zone. He then returned to the wounded men and attended to them until he was himself killed by a shell. His body and those of the men who were killed with him were at once buried by a party under Lieut. Norton. Major Paterson then returned to the headquarters dugout, which was situated in a communication trench a short distance in rear of C Company, and directed 2nd Lieut. B. K. Dymott, the second machine-gun officer, to take over the duties of adjutant.

About this time the right of B Company and the left of D were being badly raked by shrapnel from the German field-guns in action just beyond Zwarteleen. As the few bridge traverses in these trenches had been knocked down, many men were wounded. They were carried into a dugout, which unluckily was destroyed shortly afterwards by a shell.

Soon after midday the bombardment died down and the weary work of repairing the damaged trenches under sporadic shell fire was resumed. Indeed, the bombardments seem to have been regarded by some of the men in the less exposed defences as affording an opportunity for relaxation in the form of card games. About 2.30 p.m. Captain P. C. Wynter, who had received orders to move B Company forward at dusk and relieve A Company in the advanced line beyond the hill, went up to reconnoitre his new position. While so engaged he was wounded in the head and was removed unconscious into a dugout for shelter. This dugout also was destroyed afterwards by a shell, and Captain Wynter was killed.

About 3 p.m. the Germans attempted to advance from their sap near the strong point Z to the shell-hole area in front of B Company's right. Protected as they were by their snipers in the strong point the situation was for a moment full of danger. It was saved, however, by Pte. E. Dwyer, who, instead of putting his head over the parapet, jumped boldly on to it and flung bombs into the strong point. His brave action enabled his comrades to man their parapet and deal with the enemy moving into the shell holes, while D Company also brought a cross-fire to bear on them from the right.

About this time No. 8 platoon was brought up from the support trench as a reinforcement and took up its position in the front line as the left platoon of B Company. Here its commander, 2nd Lieut. O. I. Nares, found himself, by a curious coincidence, next in the line to his brother, Captain E. P. Nares, who commanded the right company of the Cheshire Regt. of the 15th Brigade.

So far the German activities against the defenders of Hill 60 had been of a preliminary nature, but soon after 4 p.m. their real concerted attempt to recapture the lost position began to develop. The first phase of this attack was an intense concentrated bombardment of the whole position by guns of all calibres, including those of field batteries near Zwarteleen and the Caterpillar, those in the latter position firing direct into A Company's trenches in the advanced line.

The bursting of shells was incessant and the noise was deafening. The little hill was covered with flame, smoke and dust, and it was impossible to see more than ten yards in any direction. Many casualties resulted, and the battered trenches became so choked with dead, wounded, debris and mud as to be wellnigh impassable. Every telephone line was cut and all communications ceased, internal as well as with sector headquarters and the artillery, so that the support afforded by the British guns was necessarily less effective.

One of the first victims of the bombardment, it would seem, was Major Paterson. A quarter of an hour before it commenced he had sent 2nd Lieut. Dymott to Lieut. Darwell, who was with the machine guns near the junction of B and D Companies, with a message that the last-named officer was to come and take over adjutant's duties. After delivering the message 2nd Lieut. Dymott returned to Battalion Headquarters, and Lieut. Darwell followed a few minutes later. On arrival at the headquarters dugout, he found that it had been destroyed by a shell. Major Paterson, the Commanding Officer, was lying near it dead, and 2nd Lieut. Dymott was severely wounded. Of the rest of the Headquarters personnel only the corporal and one man of the signallers were fit for duty. With these two soldiers Lieut. Darwell, seeing the necessity for reinforcements and failing to obtain news of Captain Wynter, the next senior officer, tried to tap the wires in the communication trench alongside the railway in order to get in touch with sector headquarters, but without success. After this failure, Cpl. Harding, of the signallers, made his way there with a message notifying the death of Major Paterson and asking for reinforcements. Another messenger got through to the artillery observation post at the Dump.

Meanwhile in the advanced line the two platoons of A Company, under Lieut. Roupell, had suffered heavy losses and their trenches were much battered. 2nd Lieut. Davis was in command of the platoon on the left in front of the left crater, while Lieut. Watson's platoon held the right trench which bent back to join C Company's trench. This bend was badly raked by the German field guns, and when Lieut. G. L. Watson and some twenty men had been killed, Lieut. Roupell sent back orders to Lieut. Abercrombie to bring up his platoon as a reinforcement. Lieut. Abercrombie had literally to cut his way through the remains of Lieut. Watson's platoon, who had all been buried by the explosions which had wrecked their trench. Under the continued fire of the German field guns he lost many men while doing so, but he and the survivors of his platoon behaved most gallantly and kept their trench open, thus providing the only means of communication to Lieut. Davis's platoon on the left, who had no other exit from their trench.

So far the German infantry had not shown any activity since the commencement of the intense bombardment, and from the statements of German prisoners it would appear that they were withdrawn, during its first phase, from the trenches adjacent to the hill. Soon after 5 p.m., however, the bombardment lifted off the southern and eastern slopes of the hill, and the fire of the German artillery was thereafter directed on to the communication and support trenches as well as on to the remainder of the hill.

Shortly after this lift a strong party of German infantry deployed from the railway cutting near the Caterpillar and advanced across the open in the direction of the right crater. It was quickly stopped and driven back by the concentrated fire of the British artillery, the machine guns of the 1st Battn. Norfolk Regt. on the far side of the cutting and the machine gun in C Company's trench. Cpl. F. W. Adams, who was in charge of the latter machine gun, was at the time single-handed, as during the bombardment both his gunners had been killed, while he himself was severely wounded. He continued nevertheless to fight his gun, though a portion of his jaw had been shot away, for more than half an hour, until, soon after the German infantry attack was dispersed, he was killed by a bullet through the head. For his heroism his name was subsequently submitted by the Battalion for the award of the Victoria Cross.

Simultaneously with this attack two others developed, one against A Company in the advanced line, and the other opposite B and D Companies on the left of the hill. In the attack on A Company parties of bombers crawled up the old German communication trenches, supported by parties of infantry who from time to time attempted to advance by short rushes across the open ground. The men of A Company, though suffering heavy losses from bombs and rifle fire, put up a very brave defence. Unable to use their long-handled bombs, owing to the narrowness of their trenches, they gallantly picked up the German bombs and hurled them back before they exploded, and each rush of the enemy's infantry was stopped by rifle fire.

The other attack opposite B and D Companies was evidently an attempt to isolate A Company's left in the advanced line by obtaining possession of the left crater and the communication trench leading up to it from D Company's right. Fortunately, a platoon of the latter company, under 2nd Lieut. Norton, had already occupied this communication trench, and the cross-fire of the two companies once more defeated the German attempts to advance through the shell-hole area. These attempts were made from the sap XZ after the British trenches opposite Z had been subjected to a heavy enfilade fire from the field batteries beyond Zwarteleen. In the sap itself two machine guns had been installed which commanded the approach to the left crater and A Company's left. It will be seen shortly how, in spite of the new menace, the occupation of the left crater by British reinforcements enabled A Company to continue its marvellous defence of the advanced line.

Meanwhile, in response probably to Lieut. Darwell's appeal for reinforcements, which had been carried to sector headquarters by Cpl. Harding, Major W. Allason, with reinforcements from his battalion, the 1st Bedfords, had arrived at the foot of the hill about 5.45 p.m. and at once assumed local command.

At this moment, under stress of heavy casualties, Lieut. Roupell called for reinforcements for A Company in the advanced line, and Major Allason sent forward a party of his men, who somehow found their way to and occupied the left crater. The call for help also reached 2nd Lieut. Geary, of C Company, who forthwith collected his platoon and led them forward. Unable, owing to the battered condition of the right communication trench to reach the advanced line by that route, he looked through a gap in the debris, saw the Bedford men in the left crater and, followed by his platoon, rushed across the open to join them. The arrival of this much-needed reinforcement was greeted by the Bedford men with loud cheers.

That the left crater was now one of the enemy's objectives on this flank was evident from the fact that it was not under hostile artillery fire, although shells were pouring into the middle crater. Also the machine guns in the sap took a heavy toll of the reinforcements that came up from time to time. These reinforcements included further parties of the Bedford Regt., 2nd Lieut. Norton with his platoon of D Company, which had previously manned the communication trench, and Lieut. G. W. Kennedy with the last platoon of A Company. As had been the case with 2nd Lieut. Geary, Lieut. Kennedy had been unable to join A Company in the advanced line. The latter officer was shortly afterwards severely wounded in the head, but with great fortitude he stayed on with his men until 2nd Lieut. Geary persuaded him to allow himself to be taken back. 2nd Lieut. T. A. Norton fought gallantly for another half-hour until he was killed by a shot through the head while firing over the lip of the crater. The

German rifle fire and grenades had caused many casualties in other ranks also, and the crater was fast filling up with dead and wounded. The latter were being attended to by Capt. G. D. Eccles, R.A.M.C., and his orderly Lce.-Cpl. Fitzgibbons, who subsequently received the Military Medal.

Meanwhile A Company in the advanced line, in spite of very heavy losses, was still holding on most gallantly to its trenches. The enemy's attacks were frequent and never varied in form. On each occasion, after a hail of grenades from the two old communication trenches, the supporting infantry charged across the open, hoping, no doubt, to find the trench deserted or full of dead, but they were always met and stopped by the rapid fire of the few survivors. But A Company was sadly in need of reinforcements. The intense bombardment and the resulting destruction of all telephone wires had rendered communication between the various groups of the defence a matter of the greatest difficulty, and we have seen how the reinforcements intended for A Company had been diverted to the left crater owing to the battered state of the hill.

Fortunately, when darkness came on, soon after seven o'clock, the intensity of the bombardment diminished somewhat and Lieut. Roupell, realizing that without reinforcements he could not continue to hold the position himself, came back from the advanced line to explain the situation. Though wounded in eight places, he made his way to sector headquarters, and there, at 7.30 p.m., he gave a full report to Lieut.-Colonel Griffiths of the Bedford Regt., the sector commander, who promised further reinforcements. After having his wounds dressed, Lieut. Roupell gallantly went forward again to resume command of his company in the advanced line.

Meanwhile a dangerous situation had arisen in A Company's portion of the advanced line, when, soon after eight o'clock, the German bombers, crawling forward along the left communication trench, had penetrated into the extreme left of A Company's trench. The fire of 2nd Lieut. Davis's platoon along this trench, which was practically straight with no traverses, prevented the Germans from establishing themselves in it; but they in their turn kept A Company's men back by constant bombing, and the extremity of the trench remained untenable for both sides.

A certain number of Germans managed, however, to slip across into the prolongations of their communication trench which led into the middle and left craters respectively. From the communication trench leading to the middle crater some commenced firing into the backs of the defenders of the left crater, while others advanced in single file along the branch trench leading into it. The latter were shot down at close range as fast as they came on, and finally they abandoned their attempts to capture the crater from this direction and fell back to the junction of the communication trench with the advanced line.

After repelling this attack 2nd Lieut. Geary, who was anxious regarding the situation on his flanks, sent three messengers to Lieut. Clarke to ascertain how D Company was getting on, while he personally made his way across the summit to the advanced line. To anticipate as regards the messengers, no answer came from Lieut. Clarke as no one of them reached him.

On reaching A Company's trench, Lieut. Geary was relieved to find there 2nd Lieut. Davis and an officer of the Bedford Regt. with men of both regiments still full of fight and in possession of the greater portion of their trench. A conference of the three officers led to the decision that they must not think of sacrificing the hill until they had made sure that there was no one behind to support them, and 2nd Lieut. Geary left to make further investigation of the situation.

On his way he met Major P. T. Lees, who was bringing forward his battalion, Queen Victoria's Rifles, with orders to recapture the portion of the advanced line reported to be occupied by the Germans. Major Lees, who had not seen the position by daylight, after hearing 2nd Lieut. Geary's account of the situation, arranged for a joint attack by 2nd Lieut. Geary's men and the Q.V.R., on a signal to be given later, with the object of driving the Germans from the left of the advanced line. As events turned out, however, this attack was not needed.

Meanwhile the defenders of the left crater were still holding their own against constant attacks and bombing, and further to the left B and D Companies opened fire whenever the enemy was seen moving in the shell-hole area in front of them, where he made at least three unsuccessful attempts to advance between dark and dawn.

On the hill itself measures were now being taken to repair the damage caused by the bombardment and to strengthen the position. Telephone wires between companies were repaired, and under the direction of 2nd Lieut. Geary a trench was commenced on the summit of the hill, near the lip of the middle crater and commanding it, by men hastily collected who worked under a pitiless fire. While this work was in progress a German flare light went up and revealed the fact that from a point close to the new trench the Germans at the left extremity of the advanced line were visible. Fire was promptly opened on them, and another position was prepared from which fire was brought to bear along the old communication trench down which they must retire. As the Germans were crowded together with but little cover, they presented a target which it was hard to miss, and they were forced well back into the old communication trench, from which, however, they continued to hurl bombs into the left of the British advanced line. Having completed these arrangements, 2nd Lieut. Geary returned to the left crater, picking up on his way a party of Q.V.R. with ammunition, of which he found the men in the left crater to be in urgent need.

While these events had been taking place on the summit and left of the hill there had been no cessation of the attacks on A Company in the advanced line. That these attacks were still unsuccessful was due to the stubborn pluck of all ranks of the company. C.S.M. Reid rendered valuable service by going back several times after dark to bring up ammunition, and Lieut. Roupell again went back soon after 11 p.m. and brought up a party of the Bedford Regt., a much-needed reinforcement.

After the retirement of the Germans from the left of the advanced line, which took place not long before midnight, the situation became easier and only four fresh attacks were delivered against A Company in the next three or four hours. In the left crater, however, the casualties continued to be heavy, and shortly before dawn 2nd Lieut. Geary went back for reinforcements. On his way down the hill he received a severe wound which eventually caused the loss of his left eye.

At dawn on the 21st the worn-out men in the trenches were roused with difficulty in expectation of a renewed attack, which mercifully never came, and at 6 a.m. the Hill 60 position, intact as it had been taken over by the 1st Battn. East Surrey on the 19th, was handed on to the 1st Battn. Devon Regt. The relief was not effected without further casualties, and 2nd Lieut. W. A. Davis, who had been with A Company throughout the defence of the advanced line, was amongst the killed.

After relief, the 1st Battn. East Surrey, sadly reduced in numbers and with six officers left out of the twenty-one who had gone into action on the 19th, marched back, under the command of Lieut. Darwell, to billets at Kruisstraat, carrying with them the body of their lamented commander, Major Paterson, which was buried later in the day in the Convent grounds at Ypres. It may be noted here that Major Paterson was promoted to the rank of temporary Lieut. Colonel after his death. He was a soldier of rare merit. Highly courageous, prompt and determined, he was trusted implicitly by his battalion, which would have followed him anywhere, and his unfailing cheerfulness had the happiest influence on those around him.

The casualties in the defence of Hill 60 were as follows :—

*Killed:* 7 officers and 106 other ranks.

*Wounded:* 8 officers and 158 other ranks.

The officers killed were Major W. H. Paterson, Captains P. C. Wynter, A. H. Huth (4th Battn. attd.) and D. Wynyard, Lieut. G. L. Watson (3rd Battn. attd.), and 2nd Lieuts. W. A. Davis and T. A. Norton (both 4th Battn. attd.). Those wounded were Lieuts. G. R. P. Roupell and G. H. Wigston, 2nd Lieuts. B. H. Geary (4th Battn. attd.), G. W. Kennedy, C. P. Emmett, C. E. Lugard, A. R. Abercrombie (The Queen's attd.) and B. K. Dymott (Indian Army attd.).

On arrival at Ypres, the following telegram was received from Colonel Thesiger, commanding the 14th Brigade, which the Battalion had now rejoined: " Deeply deplore loss of your C.O., so many officers and men, but congratulate the Battalion on the gallant example they have set to all." This struck the right note. The defence of Hill 60 had indeed cost the East Surrey Regt. dearly, and the strain on every man had been great but nobly met. In the words of Brigadier-General Northey, who then commanded the 15th Brigade, " the Bedfords and East Surrey, suffering enormous losses, never budged nor even complained." In a war abounding with glorious deeds the defence of Hill 60 has been regarded as among the finest, and the memory of the 19th to 21st April, 1915, and of those who fell during those grim days and nights will ever be cherished by the Regiment.

On April 22nd the 1st Battn. East Surrey was ordered to Ouderdom to attend a parade for the Commander-in-Chief. Before the Battalion started, Sir

Charles Fergusson, the Corps Commander, addressed it, congratulating it on its fine performance, and adding: " It was the most magnificent thing yet in the whole war." In the afternoon at Ouderdom Field-Marshal Sir John French spoke to the Battalion and the other units which had taken part in the fight at Hill 60 on their glorious achievement.

Though the gallant deeds performed by individual officers, N.C.O.'s and men at Hill 60 were many, most of the officers who might have brought them to notice were either dead or in hospital. In course of time, however, those cases that could be verified were reported to the proper authorities and were then recognized by the award of decorations.

Lieut. G. R. P. Roupell, 2nd Lieut. B. H. Geary and Pte. E. Dwyer received the Victoria Cross, and the notification of the awards in the *London Gazette* recorded their services as already described in these pages. The Military Cross was awarded to Lieuts. T. H. Darwell and E. G. H. Clarke, and the Distinguished Conduct Medal to Company Sergt.-Major A. J. Reid, Sergts. P. Griggs and W. E. Packhard, Cpl. W. H. Harding, Lce.-Cpl. F. S. Martin and Ptes. A. Hotz and F. Grimwood. The following were mentioned in despatches: Major W. H. Paterson, Captain D. Wynyard, Lieuts. Darwell and Clarke, Sergt. Griggs, Cpl. F. W. Adams, Ptes. J. Brown, S. Elliott and Owers. Lieut. Roupell and Ptes. E. Dwyer and G. M. May also received the Russian Cross of St. George.

The capture and defence of Hill 60 are not now officially included in the battles of Ypres, 1915. The first of this series of battles, viz. the Battle of Gravenstafel, was fought on the 22nd and 23rd April, and in commencing it the Germans adopted the hitherto unknown gas attack, which overwhelmed the right division of the French troops holding the line north of Ypres. The whole of the Ypres salient was thus threatened, and on the 23rd April the 1st Battn. East Surrey, amongst other units, was ordered to be ready to move at a moment's notice. On this date Captain R. D. F. Oldman, of the Norfolk Regt., took over temporary command of the Battalion.

On the 24th April the Germans opened the Battle of St. Julien and in the afternoon succeeded in capturing the village of that name, which lies about three miles north-east of Ypres. At 5.30 p.m. on that day the 1st Battn. East Surrey moved forward into the second line and worked till midnight on a new inner defence line which was being hastily constructed in rear of Ypres.

At two o'clock in the morning of the 25th the Battalion went into billets at Kruisstraathoek, and soon afterwards B Company's billets were shelled and 1 man was killed and 4 wounded. The remainder of the day was spent in bivouac in the fields outside the village; but the shelling all round Ypres was incessant and nine more men were wounded. The Battalion relieved the Manchester Regt. at night in the trenches which it had already occupied earlier in the month on the far side of the railway opposite Hill 60. Here it remained until the night of April 30th, the weather being fine and sunny: it sustained a loss of 7 men killed and 25 wounded, mainly from shell fire, which was continuous and heavy.

During the last two days of the month the Battalion received strong reinforcements by the arrival of Captain E. M. Woulfe-Flanagan with a draft of

HILL 60

FROM A PHOTOGRAPH TAKEN FROM THE DUMP NEAR THE RAILWAY LOOKING SOUTH-EAST

# IN THE LINE SOUTH OF THE RAILWAY NEAR HILL 60

300 men and of 6 subaltern officers. On relief by the Manchesters on April 30th the Battalion marched back to billets in Kruisstraathoek.

May 1st and 2nd were spent in bivouac in a field south-west of Ypres. Drill and training of sappers, bombers and machine gunners was carried out in spite of frequent shelling, which caused a casualty list of fourteen men wounded. On the 4th May half the Battalion, under Captain Woulfe-Flanagan, went up to the trenches south of the railway near Hill 60 and relieved the Norfolk Regt. and 6th Battn. Liverpool Regt.; the remainder of the Battalion, under Captain Oldman, remained in bivouac. On May 5th the two companies in the trenches had gas pumped against them on three occasions, the Germans at the same time opening heavy rifle fire. Respirators were promptly put on and the fire returned. There was further fighting on Hill 60 during the day and much artillery fire on both sides, the casualties numbering 2 killed and 7 wounded, and the half-battalion under Captain Oldman was brought up into reserve to Brigade Head-quarters. Lieuts. T. H. S. Swanton and R. Streatfeild-James joined from England. These officers had previously served in Flanders with the 2nd Battalion.

May 6th was a fine day and the wind blew towards the enemy. New respirator pads were issued to the half-battalion in the trenches. The half-battalion under Captain Oldman returned to its bivouac during the morning, and two officers and sixty-four bombers were formed into a separate tactical unit. Various appliances for combating gas were issued and instructions given for action during gas attacks.

Meanwhile an Order of the Day had been published by G.O.C. II Corps, Lieut.-General Sir Charles Fergusson, confidently calling on the Corps to resist all the efforts of the German Army to break through the British line. This confidence was echoed by Major-General Morland, commanding the 5th Division, and in communicating the call to his brigade General F. S. Maude, who had rejoined from England with his wound still unhealed, wrote the following memorandum, which gave deep satisfaction to every man in the Battalion:—

> "In circulating the above for communication to all concerned, the Brigadier-General Commanding expresses his conviction that the Brigade will continue to emulate the proud record which it has already created for itself, a record which has during the past few weeks been enhanced on Hill 60 by the resourcefulness, devotion to duty, cool temerity and endurance of the Devons, and by the magnificent and glorious heroism of the East Surreys.
>
> "(Signed) F. S. Maude,
> "Brigadier-General Commanding 14th Infantry Brigade.
>
> "*May 7th*, 1915."

On May 7th the Headquarters and remainder of the Battalion joined the two companies already in the trenches, and for two and a half months from that date the 1st Battn. East Surrey remained in the line unrelieved, so few were the troops available for the defence of the Ypres salient. During May the battles of Frezenberg Ridge and Bellewaarde Ridge were fought further to the north, and the German artillery shelled continuously the portion of the line held by the Battalion, its fire being chiefly directed on the battery position and roads in rear, while Ravine Wood close behind the Battalion came in for its full share. Consequently the supply of food and ammunition, though carried out at night, was extremely hazardous, but no serious attacks were made on this portion of the line. The casualties during the period May 10th to 22nd amounted to 3 men killed and 28 wounded, and on the latter date Lieut. J. Newington (3rd Battn. attd.) was also killed. He was the son of Captain Newington, formerly of the 1st Battalion. His death, which was instantaneous, was caused by a stray rifle bullet in the wood.

On the 23rd, a fine and warm day, several changes occurred. The Battalion was ordered to hand over its trenches to the Norfolk Regt. and to take over trenches on its right from the D.C.L.I. The move was effected with some difficulty owing to the reduced accommodation now allotted to the Battalion. On this day Lieut. Darwell was ordered to attend a machine-gun course at St. Omer, and handed over the acting-adjutancy to Lieut. Streatfeild-James.

Between the 23rd and 31st May 7 men were killed and 38 wounded. These constant casualties are thus explained in the Battalion War Diary: "The usual sniping going on. We hope shortly, when loopholes are completed, to cope with this more effectively. At present by day enemy snipers have things a good deal their own way as they are well provided with loopholes." On the 29th, Brevet Lieut.-Colonel H. S. Tew rejoined from England and took over command from Captain Woulfe-Flanagan, who had commanded since Captain Oldman rejoined his own regiment on May 16th. Officers continued to join from England throughout the month, and gradually the gaps caused on Hill 60 were filled.

Although the conclusion of the Battle of Bellewaarde Ridge on the 25th May marked the end of the battles of Ypres, 1915, the Battalion Diary for June tells a similar story to that of May, of unresting vigilance and steady endurance, and also records the daily improvement of the trenches under the experienced eye of Lieut.-Colonel Tew. One day of this month was so like another that to record its events in detail would be monotonous. It seems preferable to mention events of special interest and to conclude with a statement of casualties.

On the 10th June short leave to England was opened to N.C.O.'s and men, but on a very small scale, parties of four being allowed to go home for five days, which included the journeys. On the 11th a small draft of twenty-five men joined the Battalion. On the 22nd three Vickers' guns were issued in place of Maxims. On the 24th General Maude addressed a representative party of the Battalion on the occasion of his vacating command of the 14th Brigade on appointment to the command of a division. Three sides of a small square were formed in the fir wood. General Maude thanked the Battalion for the splendid work it had done. He remarked on the good commanding officers that it had had throughout the campaign, and said that he considered the late Major Paterson the ideal commanding officer that a battalion could wish for.

On June 27th Brigadier-General Compton (from Lieut.-Colonel, Somerset

Light Infantry) assumed command of the 14th Brigade, and leave was sanctioned for eight instead of four N.C.O.'s and men. There were then about 100 of all ranks who had been with the Battalion from the first day of the War. On the same day the Battalion was completed with one "smoke-helmet" per man, and the issue of a second helmet was begun.

The weather throughout the month was generally fine and suited to trench work, dry but not too hot. A great deal of work was carried out in strengthening and draining the trenches and in improving the mile and a half of communication trenches in charge of the Battalion. All were inspected by the new Brigadier on the last day of the month.

The casualties during June were: 8 other ranks killed and 2nd Lieut. H. H. E. Massey and 54 other ranks wounded.

The 1st Battn. East Surrey had still more than three weeks of trench duty before it, for it was not until the night of the 24th July that its share in the defence of the Ypres salient came to an end. The record of the first three weeks of the month is somewhat monotonous, as was that of June, but it sets forth a tale of steady and progressive work, of a regular development of war organization, and of an approach to perfection in the construction of the section of field defences held by the Battalion. In this last respect perfection would have been reached much sooner but for the difficulty of obtaining material in adequate quantities. Thus on July 6th the Battalion Diary records that the supply of sandbags was limited to 1000 per battalion per night, work being consequently limited; and on July 12th, when the whole Brigade was engaged in improving its barbed-wire defences, the Battalion required and could have used twenty rolls of wire daily, but could only obtain ten. Time and industry, however, worked wonders, and before the Battalion finally left its section of the defences its trenches had reached a very high standard as regards security from fire, strength in defence, convenience of access and sanitation. The support trenches had been reconstructed much closer to the fire trenches, so that rapid reinforcement was always practicable; loopholes had been provided in abundance; and by the construction of a double line of communication trenches the work of relieving the front companies was greatly facilitated. On July 19th the Diary records: "The Battalion snipers" (most ably trained by 2nd Lieut. R. Hillier, himself a first-rate shot) "are thirty-two in number, and by dint of constant practice are becoming more and more efficient. By firing at the enemy's loopholes they have rendered several useless, and have taught the German snipers behind the loopholes to be very careful. Consequently we are in a fair way to gaining a superiority of fire over the enemy." On the same day the admirable work done by Sergt. Cooper and his Pioneers is recorded. They had produced notice-boards, loopholes, benches, tables, "knife rests," trip wires, periscopes and many other useful articles, of good workmanship and at wonderful speed. The "knife-rests" were portable barbed-wire obstructions, the framework of which resembled the domestic article so named.

There was, throughout the month, a considerable amount of artillery and rifle fire in the sector, but, owing to the greatly increased security of the trenches and the superiority of our fire already mentioned, the total casualties were only as follows: Killed or mortally wounded, 7 other ranks; wounded, Brevet Lieut.-Colonel H. S. Tew and 38 other ranks.

On July 23rd a notification was received that Brevet Lieut.-Colonel Tew had been selected for promotion to Lieut.-Colonel and to command the Battalion in succession to Brigadier-General J. R. Longley, whose period of command expired on June 20th. The promotion consequently bore date June 21st, 1915. General Longley's connection with the East Surrey Regt. was thus officially closed, but his memory long dwelt and will dwell with those who served in it with him and under his command. Throughout his regimental career General Longley had shown himself a soldier of the best stamp. Strict and conscientious in the performance of his duties, cool and highly courageous and enterprising in the field, he had earned the entire confidence of his battalion and a reputation second to none among the commanding officers of the original Expeditionary Force of August, 1914.

The relief of the Battalion, owing to the transfer of the 5th Division to the X Corps, after its long tour of duty in the line took place on the night of July 24th, when the 2nd Battn. Royal Scots took over the trenches. The headquarters of the Battalion left the trenches at 12.30 a.m. on the 25th and followed the companies to Reninghelst, distant ten miles.

On arrival at Reninghelst the companies were accommodated in huts for the remainder of the day. The Battalion transport moved on at 4 p.m., and at 7.50 p.m. the Battalion marched via Godewaersvelde to Eecke, distant about 10½ miles. Eecke was reached about midnight, and the men were soon settled in billets.

The next day was devoted to rest and cleaning up, and at 10 a.m. on the 27th the 14th Brigade was formed up in three sides of a square for inspection by General Sir Herbert Plumer, Commanding the Second Army, whose address is thus recorded in the War Diary of the 1st Battn. East Surrey:—

"The Army Commander said that he had not come there to hold an inspection parade, but rather to say a few words to the Brigade before it left to join the New Army, to which it was being transferred. He was glad to see that the long period during which the men had been engaged in trench warfare had not caused them to forget how to stand still and to handle their arms. Their clothing was against them, and would not have pleased those who were used to Aldershot parades, but those who *really knew soldiers* were able to judge in spite of clothing, and the Brigade had turned out as it ought to have done.

"The General went on to say that he need not remind his hearers of what they had done in the past, for that would be written in the records which would form the history of the War. Those, however, who were acquainted with the facts knew the part which the 5th Division and the 14th Infantry Brigade had taken in the early part of the War, and they knew that that part had been at least an arduous one. During the period that the Brigade had been in the sector which it was then leaving it had been occupied with trench warfare rather than with active operations against the enemy, with one or two exceptions, as when (although not actually employed as a brigade) two of its battalions—the East Surreys and Devons—had been very hotly engaged at Hill 60, and by their efforts had contributed very greatly to the retention of that hill. Since that time the Brigade had continued to be engaged in trench warfare; but trench warfare was not to be rated that dull sort of fighting that some were prone to think it. Comparisons, the General remarked, were odious, but he had no hesitation in saying that as far as the Second Army was concerned, and for that matter as far as the Expeditionary Force was concerned, no brigade had won so high a reputation for trench warfare as had the 14th Brigade under General Maude. . . . While commanding the V Corps he (General Plumer) knew that the line occupied by the Brigade was absolutely safe.

"The Army Commander concluded by saying that the Brigade was going to a new Army (the Third), under General Monro, and to a new Corps (the X), under General Morland, both of whom knew full well the reputation of the Brigade. On those whom he was addressing would fall the responsibility of living up to the reputation which they had made, and of forming the nucleus of the new Army; for they would be the veterans, and the 14th Brigade standard would be the standard which other brigades would emulate. It must and it would be a high one, and if all the other brigades reached it, both the Corps and Army Commanders would have confidence. The General then expressed his sorrow that the Brigade was leaving the Second Army and wished them the best of luck."

The weather continued fine and sunny. Company parades were ordered for instruction in close order drill. The Battalion Diary records that from two and a half months of trench duty the drill of the men had become rusty, and that recent drafts, though of excellent quality, had not received training up to the peace standard. This was unavoidable, owing to the very short time the men had served at home before being sent out.

The total casualties incurred during the two and a half months' trench duty were 28 killed and 177 wounded. Of these, 8 per cent were wounded by shell fire in the wood, the remaining casualties occurring in the trenches or during reliefs. Most of the men killed were shot in the head by German snipers whilst looking over the parapet.

The Battalion remained at Eecke until July 31st, on the afternoon of which day it marched to Godewaersvelde and entrained for Corbie, near Amiens. The troop train reached Corbie at 7.30 a.m. on the 1st August, and two hours later the Battalion marched through the town to Daours, distant about four miles. Here it remained in comfortable billets during the 2nd and 3rd, completing clothing arrangements and carrying out various drills. Full advantage was taken of excellent bathing in the River Somme. The climate was found to be considerably warmer than that of Flanders, and shades were provided to give protection from the sun to the back of the head and neck.

During the afternoon of August 4th General Monro, commanding the new Third Army, inspected the 14th Brigade, which at 8 p.m. marched out of Daours eastward, the Devons leading and the 1st Battn. East Surrey marching next. The destination of the Battalion was Ville-sur-Ancre, distant twelve miles, where good billets were found. No British troops had as yet been operating in the Somme area, and the inhabitants welcomed the Brigade with every form of hospitality. On the 6th to the 8th August the Battalion ammunition was tested, an opportunity not wasted by the snipers, now well provided with telescopic and orthoptic sights.

On the morning of the 8th the Commanding Officer and the company commanders went forward to inspect the trenches which were to be taken over, and at 10.20 p.m. the Battalion marched 5½ miles to Bray, on the Somme, arriving there about midnight. The road was much choked by troops and transport moving in the opposite direction. The billets at Bray were found to be very dirty, nevertheless the troops were confined to them till 4 p.m. on the 9th, in order to rest the men thoroughly before going into the trenches.

At midnight the Battalion left Bray on its way eastward to the line. Unfortunately, heavy rain fell before the start, and consequently that part of the road between Suzanne and the trenches, being only a country track, was very heavy going. The distance marched was about five miles, and the Battalion was quickly settled in its new trenches, thanks to the excellent arrangements made by the outgoing French troops, the 1st Battalion of the 99th Regiment. Maps and orders, translated into English, were ready, and guides led each company to its trenches. By 5.30 a.m. on August 10th the whole relief had been completed.

The neighbouring country proved to be undulating, with steep slopes falling abruptly to the marshes of the Somme. The portion of line taken over by the Battalion (known as Sector A.2) had a frontage of nearly 2000 yards. The right of the sector lay in low ground about the Moulin de Fargny on the Somme and ran thence north-west up a steep slope to the Bois de Fargny. From this wood it ran north, along the eastern side of the crest of a long spur running north and south, cutting the Maricourt–Peronne road about 500 yards east of Maricourt, and ending on the Maricourt–Hardecourt road north of this. Except on the right the advantage of the ground was with our trenches; but the Moulin de Fargny lay right under the enemy's position, and was much exposed to bombs, trench mortars and light guns. The sector was covered by two batteries and was well provided with defensive mines. The communication trenches were very deep and the bomb-proof shelters were excellent, strongly constructed and worthy of their name. The parapet of the fire trenches was, however, weak, and those trenches appeared to have been little used.

The Battalion remained in the Maricourt trenches during the rest of August working hard at the defences, the first thing taken in hand being the strengthening of the parapets and the provision of fire platforms. On August 15th two companies of the 6th Battn. Northampton Regt. were attached to the Battalion for instruction.

On the 16th the Battalion Diary mentions the rations issued that day, viz. honey, cheese, tea, sugar, bacon, five sacks of onions, 850 lbs. of fresh meat, bread, biscuits, milk, salt, coal and candles. "Rations," the Diary adds, " have been continuously good, and there has never been any lack. Clothing has always been available, as well as facilities for washing clothing. The tailors' and shoemakers' shops have worked well, and the Battalion during the last nine months has been kept well-booted and cleanly turned out."

On August 17th one man of a German patrol was wounded and taken prisoner. He was questioned by Lieut.-Colonel Tew, but gave no information of value. He had on him no documents of any kind, no identity disc, and the numeral 16 on his shoulder-strap might or might not have indicated the number of his regiment. On the 22nd the 6th Battn. Northampton Regt. completed their period of instruction and returned to Suzanne. They had had only three men wounded by grenades while in the trenches.

On August 26th Lieut.-Colonel Tew went to England on short leave, and Major Woulfe-Flanagan assumed command of the Battalion. The remainder of the month passed without special event, there being a gradual increase of artillery fire on both sides, but no resulting increase of casualties on our side.

The following casualties occurred during the period of trench duty near Maricourt: an average of one a day:—

*Killed:* 3 other ranks.

*Wounded:* 2nd Lieut. A. W. Goolden and 17 other ranks.

On the 1st September the Battalion was relieved in the trenches by the 1st Battn. Norfolk Regt. and marched to billets at Morlancourt, a distance of ten miles. No casualty occurred during the relief. On September 2nd and following days 6 officers and 300 men were detailed for work on a second line of defence. On the 4th Lieut.-Colonel Tew returned from leave and resumed command, and in the afternoon the divisional band played for the first time to the troops, and was a great success. The Battalion had been presented with five baths and a boiler by the Red Cross Society, a valuable addition to comfort in view of the approach of colder weather. Another article of equipment received at this period was a catapult which threw a 2-lb. bomb 180 yards, and a 1-lb. bomb 260 yards.

The corn being now cut, there was ample ground available for open-order movements, and the opportunity was not lost. With drills and fatigue duties and football matches in spare time, the period of rest quickly passed, and in the evening of September 10th the Battalion marched back to the same sector of the Maricourt trenches in relief of the 1st Battn. Norfolk Regt. The machine-gun section went on in advance and took over its positions in daylight. The machine-gun section now consisted of four guns belonging to the Battalion, with three guns of the 5th Battn. Cheshire Regt. attached. The disposition of companies was three in the firing line and one in reserve.

On September 11th, Lieut. Roupell, V.C., arrived from England and took over the adjutancy. The usual routine of trench life followed, no casualties occurring till the 16th, when two men were wounded by shell fire and one, accidentally, by a bomb. On the four days following there was an increase of artillery and rifle fire on both sides; and on September 20th Captain Streatfeild-James and Lieut. Wigston were wounded by the same bullet. It came through a loophole and wounded Captain Streatfeild-James in the left arm, in which he had previously been wounded while serving with the 2nd Battalion, and Lieut. Wigston through both thighs. This was also Lieut. Wigston's second wound.

The Battalion was relieved without casualties by the 2nd Battn. Manchester Regt. in the afternoon of September 22nd, two companies and Battalion Headquarters going into billets at Maricourt, and the other two companies, under Major Woulfe-Flanagan, into billets at Suzanne. Maricourt, though much damaged by shell fire, accommodated the D.C.L.I. as well as the East Surrey wing. The village was shelled on the 23rd September, and the Battalion lost 4 men killed and 9 wounded, mostly belonging to A Company.

## CHAPTER VI

AUGUST, 1914, TO SEPTEMBER, 1915: THE 2ND BATTALION BROUGHT HOME FROM INDIA AND ALLOTTED TO THE NEWLY FORMED 28TH DIVISION, WITH WHICH IT PROCEEDS TO FRANCE. IN THE YPRES SALIENT, HEAVY LOSSES IN ACTION NEAR ST. ELOI; IN THE BATTLES OF YPRES, 1915; THREE MONTHS' TRENCH-DUTY NEAR WULVERGHEM AND ST. ELOI.

THE outbreak of the War with Germany found the 2nd Battn. East Surrey stationed at Chaubattia, in Northern India, and the first mobilization of British Infantry Divisions for active service in Europe did not include it. The Battalion was at first detailed for defensive duties in the Meerut area, but as the crucial nature of the struggle in Europe soon became evident, and the vast majority of the people of India emphatically declared their loyalty to the Empire, the white garrison of India was reduced to a very small force left to guard the north-western frontier. The 2nd Battn. East Surrey consequently was soon moved to Jhansi and Nowgong, and two months later embarked on the transport *Malda* for England, there to mobilize. The voyage home, with a great fleet of transports and its escort, took thirty-seven days, which seemed interminable to the impatient soldiers. Disembarking at Devonport on December 23rd, the Battalion entrained for Winchester the same evening, arriving there early on Christmas Eve, 1914, and going under canvas on Magdalen Hill in very cold weather. The Battalion, with a strength of 21 officers and 908 other ranks, now formed part of the 85th Brigade of the 28th Division, and on being medically inspected were all found fit for active service with the unfortunate exception of the Commanding Officer, Lieut.-Colonel H. D. Lawrence, who was found to be incapacitated by an internal injury. On December 26th a draft of thirty men joined the Battalion from the 3rd Battalion at Dover. On the 30th the colours were sent, under escort, to the Depôt at Kingston-on-Thames, and on the last day of the year Lieut.-Colonel Lawrence handed over the command to Major W. N. R. Gilbert-Cooper. Lieut.-Colonel Lawrence, a very keen soldier and devoted to the Regiment, had served in it for 32½ years and had commanded the 2nd Battalion with marked success. The deep regret with which he parted with the Battalion was shared by all ranks, who felt that in him they had lost a firm friend and a trusted Commanding Officer.

Mobilization continued somewhat slowly and was not completed until the last day in England, January 17th, 1915; but on the 12th the 28th Division was inspected by His Majesty the King, and presented a very fine appearance. On the 18th January the Battalion, with a strength of 27 officers and 966 other ranks, left Winchester by march route for Southampton, arrived there at noon and, embarking immediately on the s.s. *Maidan*, sailed at 6.30 p.m. for France.

The Battalion arrived at Havre at noon on January 19th, disembarked and marched to No. 1 Rest Camp. On the following morning an advanced party entrained for Hazebrouck, followed at 9.30 p.m. by the remainder of the Battalion. The route ran via Rouen, Abbeville, Boulogne and Calais. Hazebrouck was reached at 1 a.m. on the 22nd, and the remainder of the night and day were passed in billets there. At 9.30 a.m. on the 23rd January the Battalion marched for Caestre and Flétre, and was billeted in the two villages. Here the remainder of the month was spent in assiduous preparation for active service. Several of the officers were detached for a spell of duty in the trenches; the machine-gun section received the latest form of instruction and the latest developments of trench digging were assimilated. On January the 28th the Brigade and Battalion were visited by the Commander-in-Chief, Field-Marshal Sir John French.

The first day of February ended the brief preparation of the Battalion for active service, and on February 2nd the 85th Brigade, headed by the 2nd Battn. East Surrey, marched from Flétre at 8.30 a.m., the destination being Ouderdom, distant thirteen miles. Here the Brigade went into billets as Reserve Brigade to the 28th Division, which now formed part of the V Corps. On February 3rd a German aeroplane flew over Ouderdom and was greeted with rifle fire. This was the first view of the enemy. The boots that had been issued at Winchester were by now found to be of very bad quality and gave much trouble. These, it is fair to add, had been bought under great difficulties, owing to the immense quantity of boots that had been supplied to our Allies at the beginning of the War. This assistance was necessary, but our soldiers suffered for it.

On February 4th, after a day spent as usual in various forms of training, the Battalion marched at 6.30 p.m. from Ouderdom for Ypres (eight miles), and was posted at the headquarters of the 83rd Brigade, as reserve to it. C and D Companies were detailed to carry food and water to the front-line trenches during the night, and had one man wounded while performing this duty. This was the first casualty of the Battalion during the War.

During the night of February 4th the Battalion was ordered to march back to Ouderdom, and reached its billets at 7.45 a.m. On February 5th orders were received that the men were to rest during the day, and in the evening orders of immediate readiness to move were issued. The order to march came at 1.30 p.m. on February 6th, and the Battalion arrived at Ypres at 4.15. Two hours later B and C Companies, under Captain Anson and Lieut. Heales, marched to take over a portion of the front-line trenches between St. Eloi and the Ypres-Comines canal, near Oost Hoek. These trenches were lettered " M " to " T," from St. Eloi eastward. The parapets of some of them were only two feet high, and in consequence the men had to lie flat, with the result that their rifles were constantly clogged with mud. It was found that C Company and one platoon of B and half the machine-gun section, under Lieut. J. Gurdon, was all that was required to relieve two companies of the 3rd Battn. Middlesex Regt., which was holding the sector at the time, and the remaining platoons of B Company marched back at 4 a.m. on February 7th to billets at Kruisstraat (about two miles south-west of Ypres), to which village the remainder of the Battalion had been sent in reserve.

The 7th February passed quietly at Kruisstraat until 5 p.m., when an intermittent shelling opened. Four privates were killed and two wounded by this fire. At 5.10 p.m. the remainder of B Company and two platoons of D marched, under Captain C. S. Reeve, to relieve C Company and the platoon of B Company in the trenches. A Company also marched under orders to dig second-line trenches. Nothing special occurred on February 8th, the portions of the Battalion not in the trenches being mainly employed in carrying supplies to the platoons in the trenches and to the 3rd Battn. Middlesex Regt. Four other ranks were wounded during the performance of this duty. The billets at Kruisstraat were intermittently shelled during the day, but no casualties occurred there. On February 9th the Battalion was ordered to relieve the 3rd Battn. Middlesex Regt. in the trenches, but the order was subsequently cancelled, and supplies were carried to the trenches as on February 8th. While employed on this duty 2nd Lieut. R. G. Milburn (4th Battn. attd.) was mortally wounded, dying on February 10th. Four privates were also wounded.

On February 10th, at 6 p.m., the Battalion marched to relieve the 3rd Battn. Middlesex Regt. in the front-line trenches between St. Eloi and the canal. Two men were wounded during the relief. B Company (less one platoon), two platoons D Company and half machine-gun section, which had been in the trenches since February 7th, were now relieved and returned to billets, where they were attached to the 3rd Battn. Middlesex Regt.

On February 11th 6 men were killed and 17 wounded in the trenches. German saps were observed and reported, and on February 12th these were seen to have extended during the previous night. On this day 4 other ranks were killed and 2 wounded. On the night of the 12th the Battalion was relieved in the trenches by the Middlesex Regt. and the detachment as above of B and D Companies. After relief the Battalion was detained in support of the 3rd Battn. Middlesex Regt. and was employed in the special trench digging which was being carried out as a counter-measure to the German sapping. At 4.30 a.m. on February 13th the Battalion left for its billets at Kruisstraat, arriving at 6 a.m., after ninety-six hours in the front line under very trying weather conditions. B Company, less one platoon and two platoons of D Company, however, remained in the trenches, attached to the Middlesex Regt. Two men were wounded this day.

About 7.30 a.m. on the 14th February a telephone message directed the Battalion to march as soon as possible to Brigade Headquarters at Trois Rois. The men were quickly assembled from their billets and marched to Ypres, where extra bandoliers were served out. The ammunition cobs, which were stabled at Ypres, were ordered to follow the Battalion as soon as possible. On arrival at Brigade Headquarters a halt was called, which enabled the cobs to join the Battalion. The halt was also much needed by the men, many of whom had been out all night digging support trenches, while others had their feet so swollen by trench duty that they had been marching in their socks. These good fellows had been told they might fall out, but had replied that they would get along somehow.

Information was presently received that the Brigadier and his staff had gone forward, and the march was therefore continued. On approaching Lankhof, it was seen that the road was being heavily shelled. Major Gilbert-Cooper therefore continued the advance by platoons in single file, with fifty yards' interval between platoons, the files marching along the very wet and slimy ditch at the foot of the road embankment. On reaching the Ypres–Comines canal the Battalion moved in similar formation close under its north bank and in complete cover. Many shells passed overhead, but no loss was incurred. Under this cover a halt of an hour was made, during which time it was raining hard and there was a bitter wind blowing. This told on the men, who had become very hot while ploughing their way through the heavy mud.

At about 1 p.m. the Battalion, apparently unseen by the enemy, crossed the canal by a temporary bridge near the western end of the Spoil Bank (*vide* Ypres map) and formed up in close column under protection of the Spoil Bank. Here were assembled the 2nd Battn. "The Buffs" and a half-battalion of the Royal Fusiliers.

Half an hour later Major Gilbert-Cooper received orders that two front-line trenches situated near the western angle of Triangular Wood and known as "O" and "P.1," which previously had been held by the Battalion, but had been lost on the 13th by the battalion which relieved it, were to be retaken, and that the 2nd Battn. East Surrey would form the firing line and supports, the remaining troops above mentioned forming the reserve. As the Battalion, when previously holding the trenches to be attacked, had moved into and out of them by night, it was a difficult matter to determine by daylight their exact position with regard to the place of assembly. An officer of the battalion which had lost the trenches accompanied the firing line as a guide, but was unfortunately killed early in the advance. Owing to the absence of the five platoons already in the adjacent trenches, to previous casualties and to frostbitten men and those sick from other causes, the Battalion went into action with no more than half its normal strength.

Major Gilbert-Cooper called his officers together and, using a small cowshed as a post of observation, explained to them the plan of attack and decided on the line of advance, which was to be southwards to some old trenches across the road about 200 yards south-east of Upper Oosthoek Farm, which was the headquarters of the battalion holding the sector. On reaching these trenches each platoon of the leading company was to extend and advance rapidly across the 300 yards of open ground which separated them from "O" and "P.1" trenches.

A Company, under Lieut. Swinton, formed owing to its weakness in two lines only, led the advance, supported by C Company similarly disposed, under Captain Anson. Two platoons of D Company and one of B formed the Battalion Reserve. Captain A. T. Robinson, acting senior major, was in charge of the advance, which commenced at 2 p.m. The early part of the advance was successfully carried out without loss, the configuration of the ground affording complete cover for about half the distance from the place of assembly to Upper Oosthoek Farm. At this point, however, when the leading company was passing through the ruins of the farm buildings, a heavy rifle and machine-gun fire was directed on them, and several men were hit. The advance, however, continued without any hesitation, though officers and men fell rapidly. The distance from the farm buildings to the lost trenches was about 500 yards. A hedgerow running north and south afforded some light cover for the first 200 yards of this distance, but the last 300 yards lay over an open turnip field with deep clay soil. While struggling knee deep in the mud across this field A Company was practically wiped out, and C Company, following in close support, fared little better. A handful of brave men of A Company, most gallantly led by 2nd Lieut. Coker, got to a point about eighty yards distant from the German position, but all were either killed or disabled, 2nd Lieut. Coker himself receiving five severe wounds. The leading half of C Company, under Captain Anson, coming immediately under the fire described, advanced by short rushes for about 100 yards to a point where there was an old German trench. It lost heavily in crossing this belt of fire, and the second half, under Lieut. Heales, suffered similarly. Here the survivors of the company were brought to a standstill, all the officers and the company sergeant-major being killed or wounded, while it was evident that A Company in their front had been annihilated. The Battalion Reserve of about sixty men was not brought forward from the farm, as it was evident that so small a number could not carry the position.

The facts as described sufficiently explain the failure of the attack and the decision to bring forward no more troops to attempt at the time to carry the position. It may, however, be added that it had been necessary to order the Battalion to advance without firing, as the trenches on both flanks of those attacked were still held by British troops. The attacking companies were therefore exposed to a destructive fire to which they could make no reply, and moreover they received but little artillery support owing to the shortage of ammunition. Whoever may have been to blame for the failure of the attack, it certainly was not the brave men who attempted to carry it out. As soon as dusk enabled the Battalion stretcher-bearers to get to the front they moved up and collected those of the wounded who were unable to crawl in unaided. Of the whole attacking party only 2 officers and about 25 men remained unwounded and able that night to stand to their arms.

Meanwhile the three platoons of B Company and two of D Company which were with the 3rd Battn. Middlesex Regt. had also been in action at " M " trench close to St. Eloi, and among other casualties had lost three officers killed, viz. Captain Reeve and 2nd Lieuts. Tagg[1] and Shone.

The total casualties therefore on this unfortunate day were as follows:—
*Officers killed or died of wounds*: Captain C. S. Reeve, 2nd Lieuts. C. H. Tagg, D. H. Beatty (4th Battn.), E. J. W. Birnie and R. F. Shone.

---

[1] 2nd Lieut. C. H. Tagg had recently been promoted from sergeant in the Battalion, and is reported to have behaved splendidly in the action in which he fell.

*Officers wounded:* Captains A. T. Robinson and E. St. G. Anson; Lieuts. G. E. Swinton, A. G. Heales and K. Bell-Irving; 2nd Lieut. W. Coker.

*Other ranks:* Killed, 35; wounded, 81.

A total of 40 killed and 87 wounded.

The Battalion held its ground until 3.30 a.m. on the 15th February, when it received orders to march back to Kruisstraat. On reaching its billets in that village at about 6 a.m., the Battalion, which now numbered barely 200 of all ranks, was in sore need of rest and reorganization. It must not be forgotten that the men, who had left India a little more than two months previously, suffered especially from the trying weather conditions in the trenches, and the vacancies in the officers' and N.C.O.'s ranks caused by the recent heavy casualties needed to be filled.

Unfortunately, however, the general situation on the Ypres front at this period afforded few opportunities for resting the troops, and at 5.15 p.m. the Battalion was called upon to take part in a night attack for the recapture of the lost " O " trench. The rendezvous of the three battalions taking part in the attack was at the cross-roads 500 yards north of St. Eloi, and Colonel Geddes, of " The Buffs," who was in command of the operation, detailed his own battalion for the attack with the 2nd Battn. East Surrey (strength about 130 of all ranks) in support and the Northumberland Fusiliers in reserve. The position of deployment, Upper Oosthoek Farm, was reached in good time and the two leading battalions deployed for the attack. At 9 p.m. " The Buffs " advanced, followed by the 2nd Battn. East Surrey at a distance of forty yards. The enemy at once sent up flares and opened a heavy fire with rifles, machine guns and artillery, the last of which caused the greater part of the casualties in the East Surrey and Northumberland Fusiliers.

" The Buffs," who had got clear of the zone beaten by the enemy's artillery just before it opened, succeeded in capturing one-third of " O " trench from the Germans, who, however, managed to retain the far end of the trench with an unoccupied gap between the opposing forces.

The casualties sustained by the 2nd Battn. East Surrey in this night attack were as follows:—

*Officers:* Killed, 1 (2nd Lieut. F. P. Greener).

*N.C.O.'s and men:* Killed, 11; wounded, 38.

A total of 12 killed and 44 wounded out of 130 of all ranks engaged. In addition to these heavy losses in action, one officer and a considerable number of men had been placed on the sick list between the 7th and 15th February through frostbite, contracted in the waterlogged trenches.

The Battalion returned to billets after the night attack on the lost trench at 5.30 a.m. on the 16th February, and marched at 3 p.m. to billets at Vlamertinghe. A draft of 1 officer and 55 other ranks joined on this date.

On the 17th, Major Gilbert-Cooper was admitted to hospital, suffering from frozen feet, and the command devolved on Captain Fuller, who (but for the Adjutant, Captain Bayliss) was the only remaining officer of that rank. At 1.45 the Battalion paraded and marched into Ypres, where it was ordered to

# THE 85TH BRIGADE TRANSFERRED TO THE 3RD DIVISION

hold the canal during the night while fresh trenches were dug for the defence of the city. The Battalion was relieved by the 4th Battn. Royal Fusiliers at 5 a.m. on the 18th February and marched back to billets at Vlamertinghe.

On the 19th February the 85th Brigade was temporarily transferred to the 3rd Division, and on relief in the 28th Division by the 13th Brigade marched to Locre, three miles north-east of Bailleul. The Battalion remained at Locre, resting and refitting, until the evening of the 2nd February, when it marched to take over trenches east of Kemmel. The Battalion found two companies for the trenches, with two in reserve at Laiterie on the Neuve Eglise road, and during the three following days lost 1 man killed and 2 other ranks wounded, while 5 subaltern officers joined for duty. The 26th February was also a quiet day. There were no casualties, and the Battalion was relieved at night by the Wiltshire Regt. and returned to billets at Locre by midnight. On February 27th the Battalion was resting and refitting. On the 28th it was on duty. Church parade was at noon, and at 4 p.m. the Battalion was inspected by the Brigadier.

On March 1st the Battalion received a welcome reinforcement of 330 men with 3 officers; all of the 3rd Battalion. On March 2nd the Battalion was inspected by Major-General Haldane, Commanding 3rd Division, and on the 3rd Captain L. J. Le Fleming (who had served with the Battalion in the South African War and had been wounded while with the 1st Battalion in 1914) arrived from England and took over the command. Captain the Hon. A. R. Hewitt, who had distinguished himself in the early portion of the War with the 1st Battalion and had been severely wounded, also joined for duty. In consequence of the dearth of experienced officers, Captain Hewitt took over command of C Company in addition to acting as Second-in-Command. A draft of 46 men arrived on March 4th from the base, mostly sick and wounded men returning to duty. In the evening the Battalion proceeded to the trenches, three-quarters of a mile north of Wulverghem, with headquarters at Scotch Farm. Two companies were in the trenches, one at headquarters, and the fourth in reserve at Lindenhoek.

On March 5th the two reserve companies relieved the companies in the trenches. So far the only casualties had been 2 men killed and 1 wounded; but on the morning of the 6th Scotch Farm was shelled, and Headquarters and A Company were compelled to vacate the buildings and take cover in a ditch alongside the side road 200 yards north of the farm. The wounded were at first left in the cellars of the farm-house, but the shell fire eventually set fire to the buildings. Captain Le Fleming, with other officers and some men, then went back and removed the wounded, who were all safely conveyed to Lindenhoek. The farm was only 1200 yards from the German trenches and in full view of them. Rain set in in the afternoon, and Battalion Headquarters were moved back to Lindenhoek and A Company to another farm. Casualties this day were 1 killed and 9 wounded, all by shell fire.

From the 7th to 11th March the companies in the trenches were relieved daily by those in reserve, and during this period the Battalion sustained the following casualties:—

*Killed:* Lieut. C. E. E. Wells and 7 other ranks.

*Wounded:* Lieut. R. Streatfeild-James and 18 other ranks.

On the 9th, Battalion Headquarters moved after dark into Pond Farm, about 200 yards south-west of Scotch Farm. On the 10th a draft of 125 men arrived.

On March 11th three trenches held by the Battalion were evacuated by order, to facilitate shelling the German trenches close in their front. These trenches were reoccupied after dark without mishap. In the evening orders were received by the Commanding Officer concerning an attack on Spanbroek Molen to be made on the following day by the 7th Infantry Brigade, through the line held by the Battalion. For the purpose of this attack all barbed wire was to be removed in front of certain portions of the line, and flying bridges were to be made where required. All these preparations were completed before dawn on the 12th.

March 12th was an unfortunate day for the Battalion, which suffered heavy losses through the course of events in an attack in which it was not intended to take an active part. The early morning was very misty, and for that reason the preliminary bombardment of the German trenches, timed for 7 a.m., did not commence till 2.30 p.m. The attack was consequently postponed from 8.40 a.m. to 4.10 p.m. Units were duly informed of the postponement. Trench E.1 left was evacuated at dawn, as ordered, and E.1 right (the southernmost of the trenches held by the Battalion) became very crowded owing to some of the assaulting brigade having worked up into it. This trench was heavily shelled by the enemy and was also swept by the fire of two machine guns on its right front, so that the trench became choked with dead and wounded, 2nd Lieuts. J. O. G. Becker and J. P. de Buriatte being among those killed. Our own guns unfortunately also shelled the trench, and 2nd Lieut. J. Kirtland then gave the order for unwounded men to retire. The order was obeyed, but 2nd Lieut. Kirtland was killed by a rifle bullet, and the men lost heavily. Sergt. Bull and four men at the extreme right of the trench, who were engaged with the two German machine guns, did not retire and succeeded in holding their ground. Captain Le Fleming reported to Brigade Headquarters that the Battalion was being heavily shelled by our own guns, but the telephone line was just then cut by a shell. Captain Hewitt, who was in command of the Battalion supports, fearing that Trench E.1 right might be rushed by the enemy, ordered 2nd Lieut. L. G. B. Crabb with twenty-five men to reoccupy it. The order was gallantly obeyed, and the party had nearly reached the trench when a machine gun opened on them, killing or wounding all but three. 2nd Lieut. Crabb was killed by a shot through the head. Reoccupation of the trench by daylight being obviously impossible, Captain Hewitt waited till dark, and then sent 2nd Lieut. Walliker with twenty-five men to the trench. This party arrived without loss.

When the attack of the 7th Brigade developed the 2nd Battn. East Surrey covered the advance by rapid fire and rifle grenades. While firing over the parapet in the performance of this duty, Captain J. H. L. Haller (3rd Battn. attd.) was shot through the head and killed. Captain Haller was a very good officer and a man of talent. He had served with the 1st Battalion in the early part of the War. Three other casualties to officers occurred this day: 2nd Lieut. H. Strong, who had been recently promoted from Band Sergeant in the Battalion and was temporarily attached to the 3rd Battn. Middlesex Regt., was killed by a shell; 2nd Lieut. R. H. H. Jackson was wounded; and 2nd Lieut. J. A. H. Wood was slightly wounded and returned to his trench after having had his wound dressed. The behaviour of all the officers on this trying day was beyond praise.

The total casualties of the Battalion were as follows:—

*Officers:* Killed, 5; wounded, 2.

*N.C.O.'s and Men:* Killed, 36; wounded, 39.

On March 13th our artillery was again active. The Battalion was informed that it would be relieved on the following day, but this order was presently cancelled. After dark it was found that the Germans had brought up a searchlight which swept the ground in rear of our fire-trenches and made relief very difficult. This was at once reported and the position of the searchlight indicated. A Company relieved C in the trenches, 1 man being killed and 3 wounded. On March 14th Trench F.2 was partially vacated to enable our guns to bombard the German trenches. This was effectually done, and the German searchlight was destroyed. Casualties, 1 killed and 4 wounded. On March 16th the Battalion was relieved by the 3rd Battn. Worcester Regt. and marched back to Locre, arriving at 11.30 p.m. Casualties, 2 killed and 3 wounded. A draft of 117 men arrived.

In spite of the heavy losses sustained, it will be seen that the numbers in the ranks were well maintained; but there was a want of experienced officers and of time for training the newly arrived drafts in trench duty. The situation was too strained for any long period to be granted for training, but the Battalion was left entirely to the Commanding Officer until the 24th March, and he made excellent use of the time. The men were fitted out with fresh clothing and, after hot baths all round, were given (in Major Le Fleming's words) " a good deal of stiff drill as a battalion, in addition to practising the attack, physical training, bayonet work, etc." Selected men also, one section per company, were instructed in the use of hand grenades under battalion arrangements after receiving only one hour's instruction from the Royal Engineers. Major Le Fleming pointed out that this amount of preliminary instruction was inadequate, but more could not be given, so the Battalion had to make the best of it. One accident unfortunately occurred, by which 2 sergeants and one man were killed and 11 were wounded. On the evening of March 24th the Battalion marched to billets at Dickebusch, where training, combined with trench digging and other fatigue duty, continued till the 28th. On the 25th March the Divisional Commander presented the Military Cross to Lieut. J. A. H. Wood, who was thus the recipient of the first honour awarded to the Battalion, for his excellent work in guiding the Battalion in the night attack of the 15th/16th February

On the 27th March the Battalion furnished carrying parties to the trenches, and 2nd Lieut. E. W. Sheppard (Royal West Kent Regt. attd.) and four men were wounded. On the day following a draft of 90 men arrived.

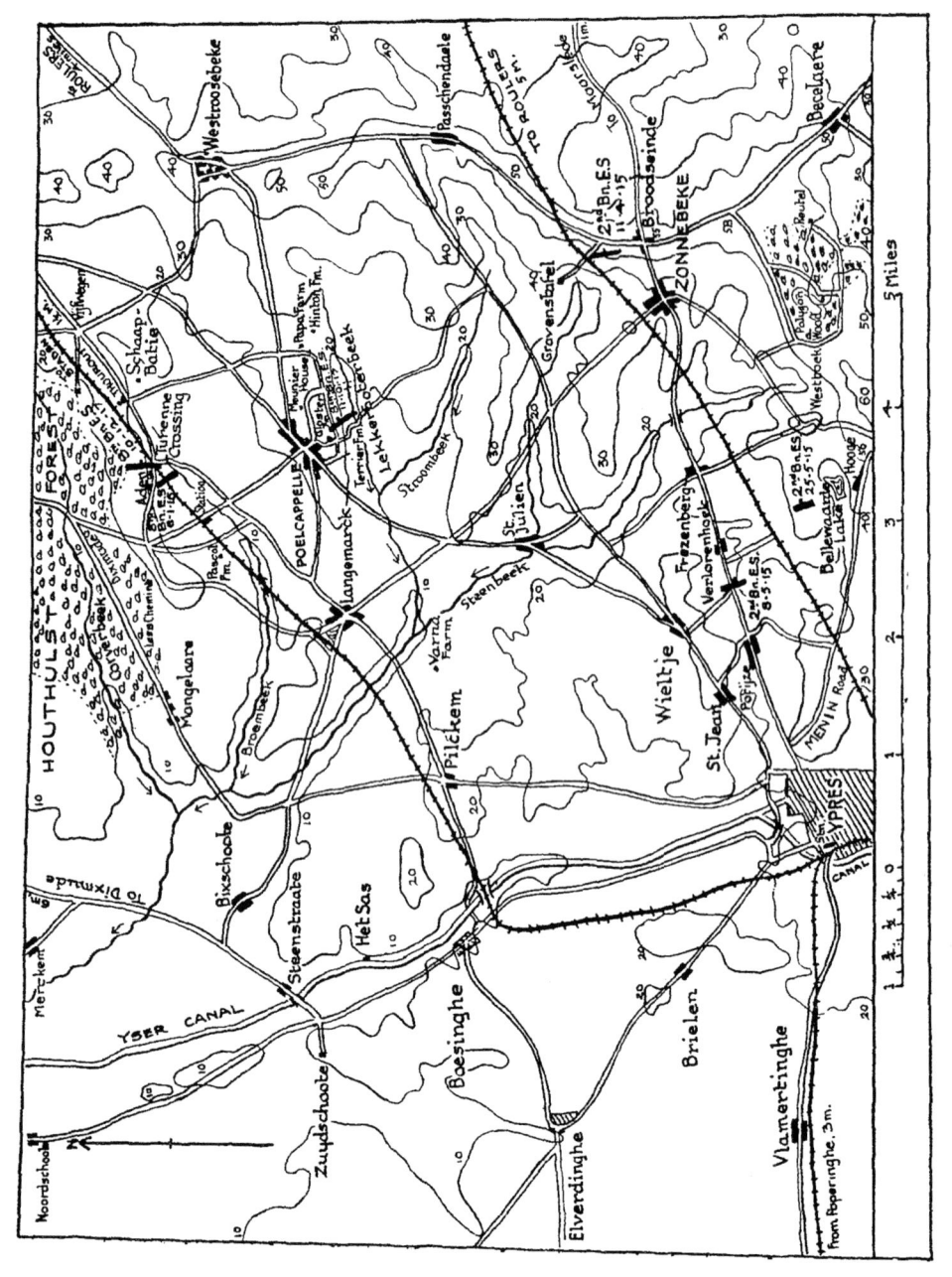

THE 2ND AND 8TH BATTALIONS IN THE BATTLES OF YPRES, 1915, 1917.

## THE 85TH BRIGADE REJOINS THE 28TH DIVISION

The 85th Brigade was now under orders to move to the St. Eloi sector. On the 14th March the trenches about that village, then held by the 27th Division, had been the scene of a great German attack, during which the enemy obtained a footing on the mound lying south-east of the village. Another German attack at the same point had been repulsed with heavy loss on the 17th March, and the 85th Brigade was sent to St. Eloi with orders to make the position impregnable. This meant work day and night for all ranks.

During the evening of the 28th March the 2nd Battn. East Surrey took over the St. Eloi trenches from the 3rd Battn. Middlesex Regt. One N.C.O. was killed on the 28th, and on the following day 2nd Lieut. R. Wilson-Rae (3rd Battn. attd.) and 4 men were killed and 2nd Lieut. C. G. Bayne and 11 men were wounded.

On March 30th the Battalion was relieved in the trenches by the 3rd Battn. Middlesex Regt. and returned to Dickebusch, having lost this day 7 men killed and 5 wounded.

On March 31st Major-General Haldane, Commanding 3rd Division, presented medals for distinguished conduct in the field to Sergt. A. Bull and Ptes. A. J. Doyle and F. Ruffell for their gallant behaviour on March 12th. Two months later this decoration was also awarded to C.S.M. W. Blackman for his services in the same action.

On April 1st the Battalion returned to the St. Eloi trenches, relieving the 3rd Battn. Middlesex Regt. It remained in these trenches till the night of the 3rd April, when it was relieved by the 1st Battn. Lincoln Regt. and returned to Dickebusch. In these three days it lost 7 killed and 15 wounded.

On the following evening (April 4th) the Battalion marched through Ypres and took up its position as battalion in support about Château Rosenthal, about two miles south of Ypres. The 85th Brigade had now been retransferred to the 28th Division, and on the evening of April 5th the Battalion was relieved by the Liverpool Scottish and marched back through Ypres to Vlamertinghe, arriving at the huts about 4 a.m. on the 6th. Here the Battalion remained, training hard, till April 10th. On the 8th the Battalion was inspected in its lines by General Sir Horace Smith-Dorrien, Commanding the Second Army. The General expressed high approval of the soldierly bearing and scrupulous cleanness and neatness of the Battalion after two and a half months of incessant hardships and fighting and very heavy casualties. Major-General Haldane also expressed his approval of the conduct of the 85th Brigade while under his command in the 3rd Division.

On April 10th the Battalion marched from Vlamertinghe through Ypres to relieve the French 153rd Infantry Regt. in trenches about three-quarters of a mile north-east of Zonnebeke (see Map opposite). As the 2nd Battalion passed the famous Cloth Hall of Ypres the 1st Battalion turned out in the square and the men of each battalion cheered the other—a moving incident.

The French battalion from which trenches were taken over stood on the left of its division. North of this French division was another French division which was about to hand over its trenches to the Canadian Division. The French Commanding Officer told Major Le Fleming that the Germans had been very quiet since they had been there, but were continually enquiring when the British were coming to take over.

The trenches taken over by the 2nd Battn. East Surrey extended southwards from the point where the Gravenstafel road crosses the railway to within a quarter-mile of Broodseinde. The relief was completed by 2 a.m. on the 11th, and very soon afterwards the German fire sensibly increased, two or three men being killed by snipers quite early in the morning. The men were in excellent spirits and returned the fire vigorously. In the afternoon it was reported that the Germans were mining towards our trenches in two places and were getting unpleasantly close. Major Le Fleming started round the trenches about 6 p.m. to give instructions about dealing with these mines, and while passing from one company to another he was hit by a German sniper and severely wounded. He handed over command of the Battalion to Captain Hewitt and was taken back after dark to the regimental aid-post at Zonnebeke. Major Le Fleming's services to the Battalion from the 3rd March to the 11th April, 1915, were invaluable. Very quiet and collected in manner, he possessed much decision of character and proved himself in time of great stress an ideal commanding officer. In a short narrative of the events of his period of command Major Le Fleming spoke most highly of Captain Bayliss; Lieutenant and Quartermaster Percy; Lieut. Gurdon, the machine-gun officer; Lieut. Land, the medical officer, " who showed great devotion to duty, especially during the shelling of Scotch Farm"; and, finally, of his Second-in-Command, Captain Hewitt, " who was a magnificent example of devotion to duty."

On the 13th April the trenches held by the Battalion were heavily shelled, and on the 14th the Battalion was relieved and went back into billets at St. Jean. The casualties from the 11th to 14th April included 2nd Lieut. H. M. Whitehead (4th Battn. attd.) and sixteen other ranks killed. On the 15th April, in consequence of an expected German attack, the Battalion was sent forward into dugouts west of Zonnebeke. As no attack took place, the Battalion returned to St. Jean. On the 18th April the 2nd Battn. East Surrey again took over the Zonnebeke trenches from the 3rd Battn. Middlesex Regt. Nothing special occurred on the three following days, during which 4 men were killed and 15 wounded.

On the 22nd April, the date of the commencement of the battles of Ypres, 1915, Major (temporary Lieut.-Colonel) C. C. G. Ashton, who had raised and commanded the 7th Battalion, arrived and took over command from Captain Hewitt, who resumed the duty of Second-in-Command. The Battalion was to have left the trenches this day, but the relief was cancelled. About 6.30 p.m. the fire and support trenches were heavily shelled, two men being killed. On this occasion poisonous fumes from the enemy's shells were noticed for the first time.

At midnight of the 23rd/24th April the Germans climbed over their parapets to attack Trenches 23 and 24 in the centre of the line held by the

Battalion. Being, however, caught at once by machine-gun and rifle fire, and also by grenades, their advance was stopped immediately. This German attack was in continuation of their successful gas attack in the Battle of Gravenstafel Ridge on the 22nd April on a French division further north, and its prompt repulse made it possible for the 85th Brigade to detach its two reserve battalions to reinforce the Canadian Division, which was holding the line south of the French Division already mentioned. The losses of the Battalion in this action were 2nd Lieut. H. G. H. Fardell (3rd Battn. attd., and son of Captain Fardell, who served for many years in the 4th Battalion) and 6 men killed and 31 men wounded.

On the 24th April the Battle of St. Julien commenced and continued until the 4th May. Several trench mortars opened on the trenches of the Battalion on the 24th April and kept up a destructive fire all day, inflicting great damage on the trenches. Later in the day the enemy was reported to be preparing an assault, and the trenches were again heavily shelled. A Company of the Middlesex Regt. from Zonnebeke reinforced and was placed in the support trench. No assault was delivered. The day's casualties included 2nd Lieut. R. C. Rottman (3rd Battn. attd.) and 10 N.C.O.'s and men killed and 39 wounded. The night was very quiet, but on the 25th April at 5 a.m. the enemy opened shrapnel fire which continued till 9 a.m., when the trenches were heavily bombarded. The fumes from the shells, against which no protection had as yet been devised, again affected the men and in some cases rendered them unconscious. The casualties to noon had been 4 killed and 18 wounded.

At about 1 p.m. the enemy attacked the whole line held by the Battalion, breaking through Trench 23, the garrison of which had been rendered helpless by the fumes. About fifty Germans occupied a small trench in rear of this, but were dislodged, and eight were captured. The remainder of these men made for the railway, but A Company, which was in the dugouts there, attacked them and captured one officer and twenty-eight men, disposing of the remainder. A Company then advanced to Trench 23 and left an officer and twenty men as reinforcements there. The enemy had also succeeded in occupying the central portion of Trench 24, but were speedily driven out by the Middlesex company at the point of the bayonet. Trench 25, on the left, was also pierced by a strong force of the enemy, who gained possession of the centre of the trench and defeated all attempts to dislodge them. The enemy in attacking were careful not to mask the loopholes of their own trenches, and the fire from these loopholes caused heavy casualties among our men, who, having no loopholes, were obliged to fire over the parapet. Two companies of the Shropshire Light Infantry arrived at 9.15 to endeavour to drive the enemy out of Trench 25, but two attacks made at 12.30 a.m. and 3.30 a.m. on the 26th April were unsuccessful. The general result of the day's fighting in this locality was that the line held by the 85th Brigade remained practically intact, in spite of the formidable nature of the attack and the absence of any available support for the two battalions in the trenches. The Brigade Commander reported: "The 2nd East Surrey have fought with great gallantry all day—much heavy fighting—parapets blown to bits—and men partially asphyxiated. Our losses are heavy, but the enemy's greater."

The casualties on April 25th were very heavy. The officers killed were Captains the Hon. A. R. Hewitt, D.S.O., and F. O. H. Jollie and 2nd Lieut. C. F. Featherstone (3rd Battn. attd.). Those wounded were Lieut.-Colonel C. C. G. Ashton, Lieut. W. H. S. Dunlop, 2nd Lieuts. S. S. Horsley, J. W. L. Ellis and V. Booth; 84 men were reported killed, 119 wounded and 43 missing, the greater part of the latter being ascertained subsequently to have been killed.

The death of all these brave soldiers while making a desperate defence against overwhelming odds makes the 25th April, 1915, a memorable day for the 2nd Battn. East Surrey, and, while all are to be regretted, special reference must be made to the death of Captain Hewitt, D.S.O., while leading one of the counter-attacks. Captain Hewitt was a man of proved gallantry and efficiency, and in him the regiment lost one who was universally liked and respected, and who would assuredly have risen high in his profession. Lieut.-Colonel Ashton was wounded in the head, but in view of the serious situation gallantly remained at his post.

The following message was received by Lieut.-Colonel Ashton from Brigadier-General Chapman, commanding 85th Brigade, at 2 a.m. on the 26th April: " G.O.C. 28th Division wires: 'Your Brigade has done splendidly. I hope that you will clear the remainder out of your trenches to-night. Please congratulate East Surrey from me.' " On the 27th April, Lieut.-Colonel Ashton received the following additional message from the Brigadier:—

*Addressed*: East Surrey—R. Fusiliers.
*From*: 85th Inf. Bde.

" General Bulfin wishes you to know that the conduct of the Royal Fusiliers and East Surrey Regt. has gained the greatest praise of the Commander-in-Chief in the field. He looks to them with confidence to hang on to their position with determination until the present phase of operations admits of their relief. All look to your battalions[1] to save the situation for the British in Belgium and to enable a victory to be won."

After the second attack on the trench held by the enemy in the early morning of the 26th April the remainder of the day was quiet. The enemy was reported to be extending his ground by sapping between the Battalion and the Royal Fusiliers, who were holding trenches on the left of the 2nd Battn. East Surrey.

On the 27th the Brigade was asked to send up some force to drive the enemy from the captured position. The casualties of the Battalion by noon were 14 killed and 19 wounded. At night two companies of the 2nd Battn. Shropshire Light Infantry and 125 men of the 8th Battn. Middlesex Regt. arrived and delivered an unsuccessful attack at 2.40 a.m. on April 28th. The attacking party then returned to their billets. Casualties in the Battalion this day were 12 killed and 18 wounded. In the evening the 3rd Battn. Middlesex Regt. arrived to

---

[1] The two other battalions of the Brigade were still operating near St. Julien.

## THE BATTLE OF FREZENBERG RIDGE

relieve the Battalion, but owing to important digging work the relief was postponed.

April 29th was a quiet day, though an attack was expected in the afternoon. Casualties, 8 killed and 7 wounded. On the 30th April, Headquarters and three companies were relieved and returned to Verlorenhoek, but A Company remained in the left trench. At night B Company relieved A in the left trench. Casualties, 2 killed and 1 wounded. So ended an arduous month.

The 85th Brigade front was heavily shelled during the 1st May, but no casualties occurred in the Battalion from shell fire. D Company relieved B in the trenches at night, 2nd Lieut. W. Thompson, who had only joined the Battalion on the previous day, being wounded during the relief. On May 2nd at 5 p.m. the enemy attacked our line near St. Julien, a veil of greenish yellow gas over the trenches attacked being plainly visible from the position of the Battalion. B and C Companies proceeded to Zonnebeke to support the 3rd Battn. Middlesex Regt. A Company carried supplies to the Royal Fusiliers and Buffs. Four men were wounded.

On May 3rd the 85th Brigade was withdrawn from its trenches to a new line through Frezenberg, about two miles nearer to Ypres, and thence into reserve at Poperinghe. The 2nd Battn. East Surrey consequently left Verlorenhoek at 8 p.m. and reached their bivouac south-east of Brielen that night, the last company not arriving till 4 a.m. on May 4th. The casualties during the move were eight men wounded, while the total casualties during the period 18th April to 3rd May had been as follows: Killed or died of wounds, 141; wounded, 256; missing, 44; a total of 441. Five officers and a draft of 77 men joined on the 3rd and 4th. At 10 a.m. on the latter date the Battalion marched to billets near Poperinghe, where it was inspected on parade on May 5th by Major-General Bulfin, commanding the 28th Division. Major-General Bulfin addressed the Battalion in terms of high praise of its recent gallant conduct.

On May 6th the Battalion was visited by General Sir Herbert Plumer on his relinquishing command of the V Corps on appointment to succeed Sir Horace Smith-Dorrien in command of the Second Army. General Plumer addressed the officers, expressing his satisfaction and pride in the conduct of the corps. The Battalion remained in billets on May 7th, but was held in readiness to move in consequence of German activity against the front held by the 28th Division about Frezenberg since the evacuation of Zonnebeke.

Early on the morning of May 8th a German attack drove back the centre brigade of the 28th Division, and the 2nd Battn. East Surrey and Middlesex were ordered up to the point of danger. The Battalion marched at 11 a.m. and proceeded to the headquarters of the 83rd Brigade, where orders were received to move astride the Ypres-Zonnebeke road and retake the lost front line at Frezenberg. The Battalion was directed to move on the left of the York and Lancaster Regt., with one company south and three companies north of the road. The Battalion moved forward through a reserve line of trenches called the G.H.Q. lines, east of Potijze, and deployed after passing through a gap in the wire entanglement. At 4 p.m. the deployment was completed and the

Battalion advanced. On reaching the road running south-east from Wieltje, machine-gun fire from the left caused many casualties, including Major North, severely wounded in the chest. The enemy's shell fire was also very heavy. A Company, on the south of the road, advanced and reinforced the East Yorkshire in a trench west of Verlorenhoek, but could advance no further. The companies north of the road also advanced, but were held up by the enemy entrenched on a line running north and south through Verlorenhoek.

At 7.15 p.m. information was received that two battalions were deploying for attack and would advance presently on the left of the Battalion. The advance took place, but was not carried beyond the line held by the East Surrey. An advance by the whole line was then ordered for 12.45 a.m. on May 9th, but a reinforcing battalion being driven back by heavy rifle and machine-gun fire, this advance was cancelled, and all battalions were ordered to make good the line that they were then holding. The Battalion consequently remained in its position throughout May 9th, being heavily shelled during the afternoon. In the night A Company was moved to the north of the road, in order to facilitate control. May 10th was a comparatively quiet day, but casualties continued from shell fire.

On the 8th, 9th and 10th May the losses of the Battalion were as follows:—

*Officers killed or mortally wounded*: Captain H. de B. Riordan; 2nd Lieuts. the Hon. R. H. P. Howard (4th Battn. attd.),[1] F. Watson (3rd Battn. attd.) and F. C. Walliker.

*Officers wounded*: Major R. E. N. North; Captain M. J. A. Jourdier; Lieut. C. J. Lonergan and 2nd Lieut. H. Lonergan. Captain Jourdier remained at duty.

*Other ranks killed or mortally wounded*: 96.
*Other ranks wounded*: 129.
*Other ranks missing*: 48.

During the night of the 10th May the Battalion moved to the south of the Ypres-Zonnebeke road and held the northern portion of the 85th Brigade's front, which extended south to the Ypres-Roulers railway. The 11th was a quiet day in the trenches, but 4 N.C.O.'s and men were killed and 4 wounded. A draft of 65 men with 2 officers joined the Battalion. May 12th was also a quiet day, 1 man being killed and 1 wounded, and in the evening the Battalion was relieved by the 1st Life Guards and marched to a field east of Poperinghe.

As the 28th Division was now being taken out of the line for a period of rest, the move was to have been further to the rear, but owing to the activity of the enemy it was necessary to keep the Division in readiness to move up to the Potijze area at short notice. The Battalion consequently remained near Poperinghe until 8.30 a.m. on the 14th May, when it marched across the French border into billets at Houtkerque. On the 15th May a draft of 7 officers and 154 men arrived. On the following day Major-General Bulfin, Commanding the

---

[1] 2nd Lieut. Howard was a grandson of Lord Strathcona, the "grand old man" of Canada.

28th Division, paid an official visit to the Battalion in order to express to it his own appreciation and that of the higher authorities of the good work it had done.

On the 17th May the 85th Brigade was ordered to proceed to Vlamertinghe, but the move did not take place till two days later. On the 18th, Brigadier-General A. J. Chapman gave up the command of the Brigade and issued the following farewell order to the troops which he had commanded in the desperate fighting for the defence of Ypres:—

"In giving up the command and severing my connection with the 85th Infantry Brigade, I take this opportunity of placing on record my high appreciation of its devotion to duty and self-sacrifice. No infantry brigade in the Expeditionary Force has been through a harder or more trying time. Its casualties have been very heavy. The battalions composing it, viz. the 2nd Battn. 'The Buffs,' the 3rd Battn. Royal Fusiliers, the 2nd Battn. East Surrey, the 3rd and 8th Battns. Middlesex Regt., may always look back with pride to this period and know that their sacrifice was not in vain and that they have added fresh glory to the Colours of their regiments.

"My thanks are due to all ranks for their whole-hearted support, which has made my command a very pleasant one.

"I wish you all every good fortune in the future, and shall always remember with pride that I have had the honour to command the 85th Infantry Brigade."

On the morning of the 20th May the Brigade was inspected by Field-Marshal Sir John French, a précis of whose remarks to the brigades of the 27th and 28th Divisions was issued with Army Orders of the 22nd May.

The Field-Marshal spoke as follows:—

"I came over to say a few words to you and to tell you how much I, as Commander-in-Chief of this Army, appreciate the splendid work that you have all done during the recent fighting. You have fought the second Battle of Ypres, which will rank among the most desperate and hardest fights of the war. You may have thought because you were not attacking the enemy that you were not helping to shorten the war. On the contrary, by your splendid endurance and bravery, you have done a great deal to shorten it. In this, the second Battle of Ypres, the Germans tried by every means in their power to get possession of that unfortunate town. They concentrated large forces of troops and artillery, and further than that they had recourse to that mean and dastardly practice hitherto unheard of in civilized warfare—namely, the use of asphyxiating gases. You have performed the most difficult, arduous and terrific task of withstanding a stupendous bombardment by heavy artillery, probably the fiercest artillery fire ever directed against troops, and warded off the enemy's attacks with magnificent bravery. By your steadiness and devotion, both the German plans were frustrated. He was unable to get possession of Ypres—if he had done this he would probably have succeeded in preventing neutral powers from intervening—and he was also unable to distract us from delivering our attack in conjunction with the French in the Arras-Armentières district. Had you failed to repulse his attacks, and made it necessary for more troops to be sent to your assistance, our operations in the south might not have been able to take place and would certainly not have been as successful as they have been. Your colours have many famous names emblazoned on them, but none will be more famous or more well-deserved than that of the Second Battle of Ypres. I want you one and all to understand how thoroughly I realize and appreciate what you have done. I wish to thank you, each officer, non-commissioned officer and man for the services you have rendered by doing your duty so magnificently, and I am sure that your country will thank you too."

The words of Sir John French should be treasured by the 2nd Battn. East Surrey, for they convey the considered opinion of one of the most determined fighters produced by the British Army. The country during the desperate defence of Ypres was necessarily kept in ignorance of the imminent danger of destruction to which the troops holding the salient were exposed owing to their weakness in artillery and in men, and consequently the splendour of the defence has not perhaps received the recognition that was its due.

After Sir John French's visit on May 20th the Battalion was warned that the 85th Brigade would move into the trenches on the following night, taking up a line from the point where the Verlorenhoek road joins the Ypres–Zonnebeke road to Bellewaerde Lake. On the 21st May a draft of 134 men arrived. The Battalion paraded at 7.45 p.m. and marched to Potijze, where it went into support in the G.H.Q. line.

The 22nd passed without incident, but on May 23rd the support trenches were shelled in the morning, 1 man being killed and 7 wounded. In the evening the Battalion relieved the 3rd Battn. Middlesex Regt. in the front-line trenches.

At about 3 a.m. on May 24th, after a heavy bombardment, the whole line of trenches held by the Battalion and by the battalion on its right were attacked by means of asphyxiating gases. All the officers and a large number of men of the right company of the Battalion were overwhelmed by the gas, and this company, together with two companies of the battalion on its right, were driven from their trenches. The remainder of the Battalion held its ground, and by their resolute defence diverted the German infantry attack southwards. The trench vacated was therefore not seized by the enemy, and later in the day was reoccupied by our troops. The following passage describing this attack is extracted from a letter, dated 28th May, 1915, written by an East Surrey officer who was present with the Battalion:—

"In the attack last Monday the Germans attacked on a front of several miles and must have been there in thousands, as there seemed to be no end to them. After a furious bombardment lasting several hours, and after gassing us, the infantry advanced; in front of us they massed in some woods, and then they emerged—it was a wonderful sight; they walked across the fields in our direction without any order, sometimes two or three men together, sometimes five or six or more; there was no attack as we understand it; they simply looked like a crowd coming away from a race meeting, just a mob. They did not double;

they never stopped to fire; they simply moved stolidly forward regardless of losses: they were twice held up and retired, but receiving a fresh impetus from the rear, they came on again; they got to about 200 yards from us and, unable to advance any further, dug themselves in; they are extraordinarily good at this as they disappear into the earth in a very short time. Of course, the infantry advance is covered by an overwhelming fire from their artillery and machine guns, so that our infantry do not have altogether a pleasant time, and it is rather wonderful they inflict the losses they do."

The casualties sustained by the Battalion in this battle, which was the last of the Battles of Ypres, 1915, were as follows:—

Killed or died of wounds, 11 other ranks; wounded, 34; missing, 75; gassed, Lieut. R. Streatfeild-James and 2nd Lieut. L. Jones and 24 other ranks, of whom two died.

The Battalion remained in the trenches until May 28th, losing 4 men killed and 8 wounded. On the 26th, the Medical Officer, Lieut. J. M. Land, R.A.M.C., who had accompanied the Battalion to France and performed excellent work while serving with it, left on relief by Lieut. Macphail.

As the 85th Brigade was now being withdrawn from the front line to refit, the 2nd Battn. East Surrey, when it was relieved by the 4th Battn. Royal Fusiliers on the 28th May, marched back to billets near Vlamertinghe, where it remained until the 3rd June. Drafts totalling 7 officers and 144 other ranks joined it between the 27th and 31st May.

The 2nd Battn. East Surrey Regt., after its hardships and heavy losses in the Battles of Ypres, 1915, was now to experience three months of comparative quiet, during which short tours of duty in the front line alternated with periods well away from the line. These periods were devoted to training and to making good the deficiency in specialists and the non-commissioned ranks.

In the evening of the 3rd June the Battalion marched through Dickebusch to the trenches east of Vierstraat, about four miles south of Ypres. Two men were killed and two wounded on the 4th, after which things were exceptionally quiet until the night of June 7th, when the Battalion was relieved by the 8th Battn. King's Royal Rifles, a battalion of the New Army, and marched to a bivouac at Busseboom, remaining there till the evening of June 8th, when it marched to billets at Houtkerque. Between the 5th and 11th June drafts amounting to 370 men arrived, of whom 20 were trained machine gunners. From the latter date until the 17th June the Battalion had daily route marches and close-order drills.

On the 20th June the Battalion, with a strength of 27 officers and 961 other ranks, marched at 8.30 p.m. from Houtkerque, via Watou and Westoutre, to La Clytte, near Mt. Kemmel, arriving at 9.30 p.m. Headquarters and two companies were accommodated in huts near La Clytte, and the remainder in huts at Rosenhillbeek. Here training continued, and on June 23rd the whole Battalion was placed in huts at Rosenhillbeek and remained there until the 5th July.

On the 5th July the Battalion marched to a bivouac west of Dickebusch. where it remained until the 11th, employed in field training and working parties.

On July 11th the Battalion took over trenches from the 2nd Battn. "The Buffs" between St. Eloi and Vierstraat. On the 14th the Battalion was relieved in the trenches by the 1st Battn. Northumberland Fusiliers and the Liverpool Scottish. The relief was completed by 2.30 a.m. on July 15th, and the Battalion moved back into bivouac near Rosenhillbeek.

At 7.15 p.m. on July 16th the Battalion, with a strength of 27 officers and 1010 men, marched to fresh trenches near Wulverghem in relief of the 4th Battn. Yorkshire Regt. On the 20th the Battalion was relieved by the 2nd Battn. "The Buffs," and proceeded to billets at Dranoutre, where Lieut.-Colonel C. G. Ashton was admitted to hospital, a very arduous period of command having severely tried his health. He was discharged from hospital and resumed command on the 31st July. The Battalion remained at Dranoutre from July 21st to 28th, returning in the evening of the latter day to the trenches at Wulverghem. The casualties during July were 5 other ranks killed and 59 of all ranks wounded, the latter including Captain M. J. A. Jourdier, Lieuts. A. V. Whitehead and G. G. N. Lodge, 2nd Lieuts. F. L. Carter, J. A. Hart and C. Mead, and Regt. Sergt.-Major R. Hussey.

During the month of August and the first three weeks of September the Battalion alternated between the Wulverghem trenches and the billets in Dranoutre. The periods of trench duty averaged six days, and the intervals in Dranoutre were of about the same duration.

In the middle of August the 9th Battn. Leicestershire Regt. was attached to the 2nd Battn. East Surrey for a week's instruction in trench duties, and at the end of that period relieved it in the trenches. On the 22nd August, Lieut.-Colonel C. G. Ashton was invalided to England by a Medical Board, Captain Montague-Bates taking over command of the Battalion with the temporary rank of Major. On August 30th, Lieut.-General Sir H. Plumer, Commanding the Second Army, inspected the Battalion. During August drafts amounting to 2 officers and 78 other ranks joined the Battalion, and its casualties were 3 men killed and 17 wounded.

On September 1st, temporary Major Montague-Bates was promoted Major in the East Surrey Regt. and was granted the temporary rank of Lieut.-Colonel. On the 14th the Battalion paraded near its billets at Dranoutre, when Brigadier-General C. E. Pereira presented to Pte. H. Brown the Russian Cross of St. George (4th Class) for gallantry, a decoration which had also been awarded to Lce.-Cpl. E. Myall.

On the 16th the Battalion entered upon its final tour of duty in the Wulverghem trenches. Excellent use had been made of the long period of comparative rest, and by a well-arranged system of training, exercise and recreation the Battalion had once more been brought into first-rate condition. Its establishment was complete in all ranks, and it was very soon to be given the chance of showing its fighting value.

On the 17th September information arrived that the Battalion would shortly be relieved in the trenches by a Canadian battalion. On the 19th, accordingly, two companies of the 21st Canadians took over half the trenches, and the relief was completed on the night of the 21st September.

The Battalion then returned to Dranoutre, whence it marched on the 22nd September to Strazeele, near Bailleul, round which town the 28th Division was concentrating. This was in preparation for the coming great offensive now known as the Battle of Loos, the 28th Division having been detailed as a reinforcement for Sir Douglas Haig's First Army, which was to open the attack.

# CHAPTER VII

OCTOBER, 1914, TO DECEMBER, 1916: THE 1/5TH AND 1/6TH BATTALIONS EMBARK FOR INDIA; GARRISON DUTY IN INDIA DURING 1915 AND 1916.

THE embarkation for India of the battalions of the Surrey Brigade took place at Southampton on the 29th October, 1914. The 1/5th Battn. East Surrey, the 1/5th Battn. "Queen's" and half the 1/6th Battn. East Surrey were accommodated in the H.T. *Alaunia*, a Cunard liner, while the other wing of the 1/6th Battn. East Surrey was on board the H.T. *Grantully Castle*. These two vessels left Southampton independently the same night, and about noon next day they reached the rendezvous, near the Eddystone Lighthouse, of their convoy, which consisted altogether of nine transports with an escort of two British cruisers. On the 31st October, while in the Bay of Biscay, one of the British cruisers was relieved by a French cruiser and left the convoy, which experienced some rough weather before it passed Gibraltar.

Port Said was reached on the 9th, and, after passing through the Canal, the convoy spent a week off Suez awaiting the arrival of a convoy which was bringing Indian troops from Bombay. This convoy, comprising some sixty transports, reached Suez on the 16th November, and the convoy conveying the Home Counties Division sailed on the day following and arrived at Aden on the 23rd. Two days later another convoy of nearly thirty transports conveying Australian and New Zealand troops and escorted by a Japanese cruiser came into Aden. On the 26th November the Home Counties Division left Aden and that afternoon passed another convoy of transports, in one of which the 2nd Battn. East Surrey was proceeding to England. Bombay was reached on the 1st December.

Both East Surrey battalions disembarked on the 2nd and entrained for their destinations, which were, Cawnpore for the 1/5th Battalion, and Fyzabad for the 1/6th Battalion. The 44th Home Counties Division now ceased for a time to exist under that designation, and the battalions of the Surrey Brigade, together with the 5th Battn. Hampshire Regt., were incorporated into the Allahabad Brigade, commanded by Brigadier-General M. Cowper.

Early in 1915 the East Surrey battalions carried out the "Kitchener Test," the 1/5th Battalion at Barkacha Camp, near Mirzapur, and the 1/6th Battalion near Fyzabad. Both battalions earned most satisfactory reports, and were soon afterwards reorganized on the four-company system, receiving also the new short rifle.

The 1/5th Battn. East Surrey now settled down to garrison duty at Cawnpore, but the 1/6th Battalion moved on the 14th March to Rawal Pindi, near the border of the North-West Frontier province.

During May both battalions despatched drafts of 1 officer and 29 other ranks to the 2nd Battn. Norfolk Regt. in Mesopotamia, followed in August by second drafts each of 20 other ranks, while at various times details were furnished to other corps, such as the Signal Service and Royal Flying Corps. In the case of the 1/5th Battalion, the first draft was commanded by Lieut. H. P. Chadwyck-Healey; while Lieut. G. F. Elmslie was in charge of the corresponding draft from the 1/6th Battalion.

These drafts saw active service in Mesopotamia and sustained heavy casualties as follows:—

|  | 1/5th Battn. | 1/6th Battn. |
|---|---|---|
| Killed in action or died of wounds | 1 | 9 |
| Died of disease in British hospitals | 3 | 9 |
| Wounded | 16 | 5 |
| Captured (many at Kut-el-Amara, 29/4/16) | 12 | 15 |
| Died in captivity, in Turkish hands | 10 | 11 |

The 1/5th Battalion remained at Cawnpore until August, 1915, when it moved, with a strength of 29 officers and about 700 other ranks, to Nowshera in the North-West Frontier province, sending two companies, a short time after its arrival, on to Peshawar. The 1/6th Battalion was more fortunate as regards climate, for it marched at the commencement of the hot weather from Rawal Pindi to a camp in the hills near Murree, returning thence to Rawal Pindi in October.

During this period the 1/5th Battalion was included in the 2nd Infantry Brigade, commanded by Brigadier-General W. Beynon; while the 1/6th Battalion at Pindi was in the 5th Infantry Brigade, commanded by Brigadier-General F. H. Peterson.

It was not until 1917 that the two East Surrey first-line Territorial battalions got their first chance of seeing active service as battalions in the field. There is therefore but little to record regarding them while employed on garrison duty during 1916. For this reason a brief outline of their doings during that period will be given here instead of in the next two sections of this volume.

After training in camp near Cherat in March, 1916, the 1/5th Battn. East Surrey returned to its quarters in Nowshera. In May the Battalion moved by rail to Rawal Pindi and marched thence to a camp at Gharial Spur in the Murree Hills, where it remained during the hot season. In October it returned to Nowshera, strength 559 other ranks, and during the cold weather carried out company and battalion training at Munki Camp.

In November, 1916, the Battalion despatched a draft of 100 other ranks, under the command of Lieut. N. H. Statham, to join the 2nd Battn. Norfolk Regt. in Mesopotamia. This loss was made good in the following month by the arrival of a draft of 99 other ranks, commanded by Lieut. W. R. Taylor, from England.

In April, 1917, the 1/5th Battn. East Surrey moved from Nowshera to Muttra, where it passed the hot weather. In November, Lieut.-Colonel R. K. Harvey handed over the command of the Battalion, which he had held for more than eight years, to Lieut.-Colonel G. A. M. Roe. The record of the Battalion is continued in Chapter III of Vol. III.

Meanwhile the 1/6th Battn. East Surrey, which we left at Rawal Pindi in October, 1915, had undergone training during the cold weather at a camp near Nowshera and had from time to time furnished a company as guard over the railway bridge near Attock. The hot weather of 1916 was spent in the Victoria Barracks at Rawal Pindi. In May there was an outbreak of para-typhoid in the Battalion which, however, caused but one death. Malaria was prevalent at the same time, 50 per cent of the Battalion being infected. The strength of the Battalion had fallen to 650 of all ranks, when it was reinforced by a draft of 5 officers and 244 other ranks on the 2nd May. Two more drafts, totalling 2 officers and 150 other ranks, arrived on the 4th June and 22nd August, while 5 more officers joined in November. These reinforcements, however, barely sufficed to meet the heavy calls made on the Battalion for officers for staff employ and for details furnished for duty with other units, and a draft of 100 other ranks sent to the 1/5th Battn. "Queen's."

In November and December, 1916, the 5th Brigade took part in Divisional Manœuvres near Serai Kala and Hassan Abdul, after which the 1/6th Battn. East Surrey was reported as fit in all respects for active service. Early in January, 1917, it was ordered to join the Aden Field Force, and its services in that theatre of operations will be found recorded in Chapter IV of Vol. III.

## CHAPTER VIII

JUNE, 1915, TO SEPTEMBER, 1915: THE 7TH BATTALION SEES ITS FIRST ACTIVE SERVICE IN THE TRENCHES NEAR ARMENTIERES.

THE 7th Battn. East Surrey Regt. disembarked at Boulogne at 2 a.m. on the 2nd June, with a strength of 30 officers and 837 other ranks, and marched to Ostrohove Rest Camp. Next day it proceeded by train to Lumbres, near St. Omer, whence it marched to Wavrans and went into billets.

Early on June 5th the Battalion marched to St. Leger in great heat. The distance was twenty-one miles and the march tried the men greatly. On the 6th the march was continued through Hazebrouck to Meteren, distance thirteen miles. The day was again very hot and there was no wind, but the marching improved. The 7th was a welcome day of rest. Heavy firing was heard all round. From the 8th to the 20th June the history of the Battalion was uneventful. It remained quietly in billets at Meteren carrying out brisk training to keep all ranks as fit as possible for the coming strain. On the 18th June a draft of fifty-two men arrived from the 3rd Battalion at Dover, and on the 19th a billeting party left for Armentières, where the Battalion was about to be attached to the 82nd Brigade for instruction in trench duties. This brigade was commanded by Brigadier-General Longley, who had commanded the 1st Battn. East Surrey in the early stages of the War.

Marching at 4 a.m. on June 20th the Battalion reached Armentières at 8 a.m. At 2.30 p.m. two companies went into the trenches held by the Royal Irish and Leinster Regts.; while the other two were attached to the battalions in reserve, for instruction in bomb throwing, etc. The companies changed round every twenty-four hours. The sector was a very quiet one, and only one casualty occurred. On the 25th a draft of 60 men arrived from the 3rd Battalion, the strength of the Battalion being raised to 988, with 29 officers. At 8 p.m. this day the Battalion moved to Ploegsteert by companies, arriving at 11 p.m. and going with the 6th Battn. West Kent Regt. into Brigade Reserve. The companies were accommodated in four farms. Battalion Headquarters were shelled without effect on June 26th, and on the 27th A and B Companies at Grand Rabeque Farm were shelled, two men being wounded. The 28th and 29th June were quiet days, and during the afternoon of the 30th the Battalion relieved the 6th Battn. "Queen's" in the trenches, which required much repair. The sandbags were mostly very old and were not bullet proof.

The Battalion remained in the trenches until July 4th, sustaining no casualties and having a very quiet time. Good work was done in improving the parapets, constructing bomb-proof shelters behind the line, etc. On the 4th the Battalion was relieved by the 7th Battn. Suffolk Regt. and marched to billets at Pont de Nieppe, near Armentières. During the night of July 9th the Battalion relieved the 8th Battn. Royal Fusiliers in billets at Le Bizet, where work was at once begun by working parties in the afternoons and nights on a support line of trenches, intended to hold a proportion of the men in the event of a bombardment of the front line. This work was in progress all along the 12th Division front. On July 12th the Battalion sustained its first serious casualties, eighteen men of C and D Companies being wounded by shells while returning from digging, and on the 13th, 2nd Lieut. W. H. T. Armstrong and one man were mortally wounded while on a working party near Carter's Farm. This day D Company's billets were bombarded and razed to the ground, a great quantity of the men's kits being destroyed. Luckily, most of the men were away, and only four were slightly wounded.

On the night of the 16th the Battalion relieved the "Queen's" in the trenches. The tour of trench duty lasted until the night of the 22nd July and was not very eventful. The Battalion was relieved on July 22nd, having lost 1 man killed and 11 wounded, and returned to its old billets at Le Bizet. Here six days were spent in reserve almost without incident. The whole Battalion was required every night for digging, and about one casualty occurred each night. On July 28th the Battalion took over the trenches, as usual, from the 6th Battn. "Queen's." The tour of duty was a very quiet one with only one casualty, the troops opposite being Saxons.

During the month an immense amount of work was done by the Battalion, as by the rest of the Division. The men showed great keenness, were in excellent spirits, and ready for harder trials. The casualties during the month had been limited to 1 officer and 8 men killed and 43 wounded.

The 1st and 2nd August were quiet days, and during the night of the 3rd, which was very wet, the Battalion was relieved by the 6th Battn. "Queen's" and returned to billets at Le Bizet. The 2nd Battalion was only four miles away, and on August 8th, Lieut.-Colonel Ashton, who was in command of it, came over to see the 7th Battalion, which he had previously commanded. On August 9th the 7th Battn. East Surrey returned to the trenches, relieving the 6th Battn. "Queen's." In the early morning following, the trenches held by the Battalion were heavily bombarded and fifteen casualties were sustained. No attack followed. The Diary records that on the 11th the snipers reported that they had killed a German general. On the 13th, Captain J. L. Jones was wounded. The Bishop of Birmingham visited the trenches.

The Battalion was relieved on August 15th and remained quietly in reserve until the night of the 21st, when it returned to the trenches. On the 23rd and 24th the Germans opposite made repeated efforts to communicate with the Battalion, trying the effect of compliments on the shooting of the snipers. These had been carefully trained by Major Wilson, the Second-in-Command and a well-known big game shot, and were very efficient.

The Battalion was again relieved during the night of the 27th by the 6th Battn. "Queen's" after a very quiet tour of duty, and returned to Le Bizet, where the month ended without incident. Casualties to date were: *killed*, 1 officer and 12 other ranks; *wounded*, 2 officers and 60 other ranks. Invalided through sickness, 1 officer and 42 other ranks. The strength on the 31st August was 25 officers and 999 other ranks.

At 2.30 p.m. on the 2nd September the Battalion was formed up in line on the road outside the billets at Le Bizet for inspection by General Sir Herbert Plumer, Commanding the Second Army. In the evening the Battalion relieved the 6th Battn. "Queen's" in the trenches. The 3rd and 4th were very wet, and the men were a good deal tried by having to remain in the waterlogged trenches. The weather improved somewhat on the 5th and 6th, and was fine on the 7th and 8th. In the evening of the latter day the Battalion was relieved by the "Queen's" and returned to billets at Le Bizet, where it remained employed as usual until the evening of September 14th, when it again relieved the "Queen's" in the trenches. The front was exceedingly quiet, neither side showing themselves and hardly a shot being fired by the Germans. A draft of thirty men joined on the 17th. They were men of very good quality, ten being old soldiers of the 1st and 2nd Battalions who had already served in France, and the remainder being New Army cavalry. On the night of the 19th, Captain W. H. Martin was wounded by a rifle grenade. The Battalion was relieved on the 20th by the "Queen's" and returned to its billets at Le Bizet. It had then completed four months on active service without much fighting or heavy loss. For gallantry in patrol work and sniping during this period, Lieuts. R. B. Marshall and J. L. Findlay, Cpl. F. G. Evans and Lce.-Cpl. W. J. Rule were mentioned in despatches. The casualties during the month were 1 man killed and an officer and 4 other ranks wounded.

## CHAPTER IX

JULY TO SEPTEMBER, 1915: THE 8TH BATTALION ARRIVES IN FRANCE AND PERFORMS ITS FIRST TOURS OF TRENCH DUTY NEAR ALBERT.

THE Battalion, under command of Lieut.-Colonel H. G. Powell, D.S.O., left England as follows: The transport and machine-gun section, under Captain A. P. B. Irwin, on the 26th July, 1915, travelling via Southampton and Havre. The remainder of the Battalion crossed the Channel a day later, leaving Folkestone on the evening of the 27th and arrived at Boulogne at 2 a.m. on the 28th July, marching thence to Osterhove Rest Camp, where the arrangements for the comfort of all ranks were excellent. At 2 a.m. on the 29th the Battalion marched to the railway station, entraining at 3.15, and arriving at Bertangles, five miles north of Amiens, at 10.30 a.m. The transport and machine guns had reached that place on the 28th.

The Battalion remained at Bertangles till August 5th, during which time training was pressed on. On August 4th the Battalion, together with the remainder of the 55th Brigade of the 18th Division, was inspected by General Sir Charles Monro, and on the following day marched to La Houssoye. On August 8th the Battalion marched, in company with the 7th Battn. "Queen's," about seven miles to Dernancourt (two miles south of Albert). Here the Battalion remained till the 22nd August. From August 9th to 13th, A and B Companies were attached to the 1st Battn. Bedford Regt. (5th Division) for instruction in trench duty. These were quiet days, and the companies sustained no casualties. From the 13th to the 17th, C and D Companies were similarly attached and had 1 man killed and Lieut. C. R. Cadge and 2 men wounded. On August 21st a draft of 100 N.C.O.'s and men arrived from the 10th (Reserve) Battalion.

On the evening of August 22nd the Battalion relieved the 1st Battn. Bedford Regt. in Trenches 84–94 inclusive, the relief being carried out quickly in fine weather. These trenches formed part of the line east of Albert, and faced the German trenches due west of Fricourt. The tour of trench duty lasted from the 22nd August to the 3rd September, between which dates no operations of importance took place and no casualties occurred until the 28th August, when 3 men were wounded. On the following days 2 men were killed and 10 wounded.

On September 3rd the Battalion was relieved in the trenches by the 7th Battn. Bedford Regt. The night was wet and dark, and the relief consequently took longer than had been anticipated. It was not till 2.30 on the morning of the 4th September that the last company arrived at Méaulte. While the Battalion was in the trenches a draft of forty N.C.O.'s and men had arrived from the 11th Battalion.

The Battalion's billets were at Ribemont (six miles south-west of Albert), and here the Battalion remained until the 18th September. Moves were frequently expected and then cancelled, but good use was made of the period of rest for company training, etc. On September 18th the Battalion moved from Ribemont into billets at Ville-sur-Ancre, on the south bank of that river.

The Battalion was ordered to the trenches on September 21st, but this arrangement was cancelled in consequence of the visit of Field-Marshal Lord Kitchener. The Battalion, together with the 10th Battn. Essex Regt., was inspected by the Field-Marshal outside Bresle. Lord Kitchener expressed himself as being much pleased by the appearance and steadiness of the two battalions. Training continued from the 22nd to the 25th September, on which date the Battle of Loos commenced, some thirty-five miles to the north of Albert. On September 26th the Battalion relieved the 7th Battn. "Queen's" in the trenches. The night passed quietly with only one casualty.

On the evening of September 27th, 2nd Lieut. M. Thorne went out on patrol with Pte. Warby with the intention of bombing a German sniper, and also of ascertaining if certain craters were held. Soon afterwards Pte. Warby returned and reported that 2nd Lieut. Thorne had been shot. Lce.-Sergt. Conquest led three patrols to bring him in, the third of which got well out, in spite of heavy machine-gun and rifle fire, but failed to find the missing officer. Lieut. C. Thorne then went out with Pte. G. E. Hine, found his brother and carried him in on his back. 2nd Lieut. M. Thorne was found to be dead. For this gallant action Lieut. C. Thorne was awarded the Military Cross, and Pte. G. E. Hine the medal for distinguished conduct in the field.

# SECTION II

SEPTEMBER, 1915, TO JUNE, 1916

## THE BATTLE OF LOOS AND THE SUBSEQUENT ACTIONS OF THE HOHENZOLLERN REDOUBT. OPERATIONS IN SALONIKA.

# CHAPTER X

SEPTEMBER, 1915, TO JUNE, 1916: THE 1st BATTALION PASSES FOUR MONTHS IN THE LINE BETWEEN THE RIVER SOMME AND MARICOURT; AND ANOTHER FOUR MONTHS IN THE LINE IN THE ARRAS AREA.

AS already recorded, the 1st Battn. East Surrey arrived in the Somme Valley in August, 1915, and on the 23rd September was in billets at Maricourt, some seven miles south-east of Albert. In the Battalion's War Diary from the 25th to 28th there are many allusions to the Battle of Loos, which commenced on the earlier date, and to the French attack at Vimy. The 14th Brigade fully expected to be called upon to make an advance, but the course of events in the above-mentioned operations decided the matter otherwise. On the 29th September, Maricourt was inspected by Major-General Kavanagh, and on the day following by Major-General Morland, Commanding X Corps.

The first week of October was uneventful. On the 8th of the month the two companies at Maricourt were relieved by the D.C.L.I. and moved back to Suzanne, where the billets were commodious and good, all being situated in one street. The Headquarters offices and those of three companies were in the "Petit Château." Three training grounds were available, and, as the weather was fine, full use was made of them. Three "Barnet-lens" sights, the gift of Colonel Leathem, an old Commanding Officer, proved a most useful addition to the snipers' equipment. The Diary of the 13th contains an account of the system of training in the Battalion in grenade throwing, to which Lieut.-Colonel Tew rightly attached great importance, having foreseen the coming development of the use of this weapon. On October 14th the rifle range was completed, this being the fifth that the Battalion had made in France. On the 15th the Battalion passed from company to battalion training, and the Commanding Officer recorded in the Diary his opinion that it was now in excellent health and highly efficient, having recovered from its exertions and losses in the Ypres salient. On the 16th October, Brigadier-General Compton, commanding the 14th Brigade, inspected the Battalion; 23 officers and 762 N.C.O.'s and men were on parade. The Brigadier expressed himself as well pleased. The eight days just completed were really the first opportunity of steady training that the Battalion had had since it went to France.

On Sunday, October 17th, after Church Parade, Lieut.-Colonel Tew made a short address to the Battalion, telling them of the award of the Victoria Cross to Lieut. B. H. Geary and expressing the hope that his example would inspire them to similar deeds. In the evening the Battalion relieved the 2nd Battn. Manchester Regt. in the same sub-sector as before, viz. A.2, the right of which lay in the Moulin de Fargny, on the right bank of the River Somme. The remainder of the month passed very uneventfully; several warnings were received of German mining close up to the trenches, and precautions were accordingly taken, but no explosion took place. Three companies held the trenches and changed round in succession with the fourth company, which was in reserve. The reserve company was fully employed in various duties, and particularly in assisting the R.E. to prepare shelter for the coming winter in the trenches. There was little firing, and casualties were very light. On the 22nd, Pte. Munro, one of the Battalion snipers, was wounded by a German sniper; he had, according to his own computation, accounted for thirty-three Germans since the beginning of the War. In the evening of the same day one man was killed by a shell, which also wounded 2nd Lieut. Burton and one man. Two men, wounded by shell fire on the 23rd, were the only other casualties during the month.

Various inventions for throwing bombs were under trial at this period, and the Battalion was in possession, on the 25th October, of two "West" bomb throwers, two "catapults" and one "trench mortar." Eight days' leave to the United Kingdom was granted to a number of officers and men during the month.

On the 1st November there was some artillery activity. A patrol went out under 2nd Lieut. Matthews and brought back a specimen of German barbed wire which had been called for by the Division. In the early hours of the next morning three Germans approached one of the Battalion listening posts and one of them was killed by the sentry. He was a fine-looking young soldier, and on his body was found a letter that he had written to his sister, stating that he had examined the position held by the Battalion on the previous night. On the 3rd a German trench-mortar bomb fell in a fire trench near the Moulin de Fargny, killing three men and severely wounding two. The Battalion Diary for the early part of November tells daily of much work on the trenches, which had been taken over in a very bad state, caused by rain and defective construction. This work was much hampered by artillery fire, and eventually it became necessary to carry it on only at night. Three men were wounded in the trenches on November 8th, and that night a patrol under Lieut. Matthews was fired on by a German listening post. Two nights later Lieuts. Topley and Matthews, with Sergt. Whelan and Pte. Herbert, succeeded in getting to within ten yards of the post, into which they threw eight hand grenades. They had heard the Germans talking immediately before they threw the grenades, but not a shot was fired in reply. The raid was well planned and well carried out. No other incident of importance occurred until the Battalion was relieved by the 1st Battn. Devon Regt. in the evening of November 13th. Headquarters and three companies went into garrison at Maricourt, one company, with the snipers and bombers, going into billets at Suzanne. During the twenty-seven days' tour of trench duty the Battalion lost 7 men killed, 2nd Lieut. Burton and 15 men wounded.

The Battalion remained in garrison at Maricourt until the 20th November, when, on relief by the D.C.L.I., it went into billets at Suzanne. While at Maricourt much useful work was done in improving the trenches, and working parties were also supplied daily to assist the Royal Engineers in mining operations.

The 1st Battn. East Surrey remained at Suzanne for a week, devoting as

## DECEMBER, 1915

much time as possible to grenade training, during which Lieut. Topley and two men were wounded by splinters. Special attention also was given to clothing and boots, in view of the approach of winter. On the 26th November the Battalion returned to the trenches, taking over Sub-sector A.3 from the 2nd Battn. Manchester Regt. Three companies were in the trenches, one in reserve in Maricourt Wood, with Battalion Headquarters in Maricourt village. The trenches were found to be better constructed than those in Sub-sector A.2. Their length was 1460 yards and they were held by 500 men, or roughly by one man to three yards. The Diary notes that all men in the trenches were provided with goatskin coats, and fifty steel helmets had been issued, which were worn by the sentries. The Battalion also had about 200 pairs of gum boots.

On the 1st December 2nd Lieut. Lazenby was severely wounded in the forehead by one of our own shells which burst short. A comprehensive system of reconstruction of the trenches was undertaken, as they were in danger of falling in whenever rain came, and as all the work had to be done at night, it entailed great labour. On December 2nd, 2nd Lieut. Wentzel (3rd Battalion) joined with a draft of twenty-six men who had been in hospital in France sick or slightly wounded. On the 3rd, eleven cases of frostbite are recorded in the Diary, some being so severe that the men had to be carried down on stretchers from the trenches. On December 4th, Lieut. Adams left the Battalion for service in the Mediterranean. He was the last of the officers who had landed in France with the Battalion at the commencement of the War, and had been continuously with it since then. He had been Transport Officer since the Battle of the Marne.

A good idea of the state of the trenches is given by the following extract from the Battalion Diary for December 5th: " In one trench on the left of our line the water is practically up to one's thighs, but there is no mud there. In the streets leading to 25 and 26 fire trenches the mud comes up to one's thighs and makes communication with these front trenches almost impossible. Men in these trenches had great difficulty in obtaining their rations." As a result of these conditions thirty-nine men were admitted to hospital with frostbite and " trench feet " between December 3rd and 6th. The German trenches were also in a bad state, and little firing took place at this time. In consequence of the increase of sickness the Battalion was relieved from the trenches on the evening of the 7th December and went into billets at Suzanne. Casualties during the tour of trench duty November 26th to December 7th had been: 1 man killed, 2 officers and 2 men wounded, 77 men admitted to hospital, the majority with " trench feet."

The Battalion remained at Suzanne until the evening of the 12th December, the weather being fairly kind. Every care was taken to restore the men to their usual healthy condition, and stringent orders regarding the drying of socks while in the trenches were issued. At 4.20 p.m. on the 12th the Battalion marched by companies to Maricourt and took over Sub-sector A.4 from the Devons, the relief being completed by 9.30. The trenches in this sub-sector, which included the salient where the British front line bent back westward towards Albert, were found to be flooded and in very bad condition. One man was killed on the 13th December by a German sniper, who fired a single shot at 600 yards. Next evening the Battalion was relieved by the 1st Battn. Devon Regt. and took over the Maricourt defences. Short as had been the tour of duty, ten cases of " trench feet " occurred. " The wet trenches," the Diary states, " are beginning to tell severely on the men, who are, however, sticking to it pluckily." The ensuing week was one of hard weather, and the Devons and East Surrey relieved each other after dusk every third day, the men of either battalion thus spending two nights in the trenches and then returning to Suzanne to dry their clothes.

On the 21st December, Brigadier-General Compton took leave of the 14th Brigade, taking with him the Manchester Regt. and Inniskilling Fusiliers, the latter battalion having been in the Brigade only a few weeks. Brigadier-General Ballard took over command. One man was killed in the trenches by a rifle shot during the night, and on the night of the 22nd a man in a listening post was killed by a German sniper. In the evening the Battalion was relieved by the 15th Battn. Royal Warwick Regt. and went into camp at Suzanne. This camp had its drawbacks, though tents were appreciated, as it stood in a swamp by the River Somme. The Diary adds a pathetic touch: " The officers are in billets of sorts, one being a hen-house the fowls of which are absent, but the smell remains." The Diary proceeds to mention the receipt of a present of 1000 plum puddings from the readers of *The Surrey Comet*. " The men," adds the Diary, " remain wonderfully cheerful, in spite of the mud and discomforts of trench life. There are few sick, and the men won't go sick unless absolutely compelled to." On the evening of the 24th December the Battalion again took over the trenches in Sub-sector A.4. The relief took longer than usual owing to the state of the communication trenches. Some men going to the centre group of trenches got stuck in that avenue and had to be dug out.

At 4 a.m. on Christmas Day a patrol consisting of 2nd Lieuts. E. V. Birch-Reynardson and A. Darrell, Cpl. Clarke and Pte. J. King, went out to examine the enemy's trenches with a view to a future bombing expedition. When close to the enemy's wire the patrol was fired at, and 2nd Lieut. Darrell, Cpl. Clarke and Pte. King were wounded. 2nd Lieut. Birch-Reynardson sent the two latter back, but himself stayed with 2nd Lieut. Darrell. Pte. King could not get in, and Cpl. Clarke went back alone for assistance. A patrol was at once sent out, but daylight came on, and it was obliged to return without finding the missing officers and man. At dusk Lieut. Wight and six men went out for another search, but although Lieut. Wight went on until fired at from the enemy's trenches, he had no better success. There seemed to be no doubt, as afterwards proved to be the case, that all had been killed, and that 2nd Lieut. Birch-Reynardson had sacrificed his life by staying with his wounded brother-officer.

Late in the evening of December 26th the Battalion was relieved by the D.C.L.I. and returned to billets at Suzanne. The Diary of December 27th records the excellent discipline and conduct of the Battalion, and again refers to the admirable good spirits of the men. " There are always any number of volunteers for going on patrol duty at night." On December 28th the Battalion snipers received four rifles fitted with telescopic sights from the Ordnance, and in the evening the Battalion returned to the trenches in the same sub-sector. The Diary records that the Battalion now possessed 490 pairs of gum boots and carried them about with it. Previously these boots had been trench stores, handed over from battalion to battalion. On December 30th the Battalion was relieved from the trenches and went into the Maricourt defences. Here three shifts of 107 N.C.O.'s and men were found for mining operations. On the last day of the year the Germans shelled Maricourt, killing one man and severely wounding C.Q.M.S. Rowe.

The 1st Battn. East Surrey and 1st Battn. D.C.L.I. were now the only battalions remaining of the original 14th Brigade, which was completed by the 1st Battn. Devon Regt., 12th (Service) Battn. Gloucester Regt. and 9th Battn. Royal Scots (T.F.). Another change which took place about this time was the withdrawal from battalions of their machine gunners, who were formed into a Brigade Machine-gun Company.

In the evening of January 1st the Battalion relieved the D.C.L.I. in Sub-sector A.4 and returned to billets at Suzanne on the night of the 3rd, on relief by the same battalion. Thus ended the tour of the Battalion in Sector A., which had been held by the 5th Division since August 10th, 1915. Twenty N.C.O.'s and men killed in action during that period were buried in Maricourt or Suzanne cemeteries.

In the London *Gazette* of the 1st January, Lieut.-Colonel H. S. Tew and Sergt. J. Brown were mentioned in despatches, and (to anticipate slightly) on January 14th, Lieut.-Colonel Tew was awarded the C.M.G., and Company Sergt.-Major J. H. May the Distinguished Conduct Medal.

The 5th Division was now about to enjoy a complete change of scene and occupation for two months, and in the afternoon of January 5th the Battalion marched from Suzanne via Bray to Sailly Laurette, about eleven miles, arriving in the evening with no stragglers. Next day the march was continued to Beaucourt-sur-L'Hallue, about ten miles north-east of Amiens. The men marched well and again no one fell out, which was quite remarkable for a second day's march after so long a spell in the trenches. The Battalion remained at Beaucourt-sur-L'Hallue for five weeks, during which substantial period Lieut. Colonel Tew, an admirable instructor, had a full opportunity of giving the Battalion progressive training. This he did with excellent results, devoting special attention to grenade throwing and field movements. Instruction in these movements was highly necessary, the experience of a large proportion of the officers and men being entirely confined to defensive trench warfare.

A few changes during the month of January have to be recorded, and happily no casualties. On the 10th the 14th Brigade was renumbered the 95th, a change by no means to the taste of its units, but it still remained part of the 5th Division; unfortunately, it lost its Brigade machine-gun company, which was transferred to one of the New Army divisions, and was replaced two months later by the 95th Machine-gun Company from Grantham. On the 21st, Captain

Roupell, V.C., relinquished the adjutancy on appointment as an instructor at the Divisional School. He was succeeded as Adjutant by Captain Montanaro.

On February 13th the Battalion left Beaucourt for a new training area and marched eight and a half miles to Poulainville, where it went into billets. The 1st Devons were also billeted in the village. Here the Battalion remained for two days, but the weather was wet and the ground unfavourable for training, with the result that on the 16th the Battalion marched to Le Mesge, thirteen and a half miles. Here the billets were good, and large tracts of uncultivated ground suitable for training lay close at hand. The 95th Brigade remained in the Le Mesge area until the 24th February, when the 1st Battn. East Surrey marched at a few hours' notice to Berteaucourt, distant nine miles, the Battle of Verdun having commenced on the previous day.

On February 25th the Battalion marched, in the teeth of a north-east blizzard, eleven and a half miles to Gezaincourt. A severe frost during the previous night, followed by the snowstorm during the march, made the road very bad going for the transport. The Battalion remained at Gezaincourt on the 26th, 27th and 28th February, one company working each day on the road to be used in the next march, and a party of officers proceeding on the 27th in motor-buses to Arras, to see the trenches which they were to take over from the French. On February 29th the 95th Brigade marched eleven and a half miles to Grand Rullecourt, considerable delay being caused by one long and steep hill, the frozen surface of which placed a great strain on the horses.

The Battalion rested on March 1st, and in the afternoon received orders to move into the Arras area. Captain A White (4th Battn. attd.) left on appointment to act as senior Major of the 10th Battn. Manchester Regt., which he subsequently commanded with distinction. Captain White, a good and keen soldier, was the " oldest inhabitant " of the officers, having been with the 1st Battalion, except for a short interval caused by illness, since October, 1914. He survived the War, only to be killed by Irish rebels while on special duty in Dublin in 1920.

On March 2nd the Battalion marched to Arras. The last part of the march proved trying, as the men were carrying fur coats and the road was much blocked by transport. The billets in the Rue St. Vaast were very comfortable.

In the morning of March 3rd a party of officers and men visited the trenches in Sub-sector M.2, about two miles north of Arras, to be taken over from the 1st Battn. 88th Regt., French Army. The relief took place at night and was completed at 11 p.m. The Battalion found French troops on its left, the D.C.L.I. on its right and the Devons in support at Roclincourt, where Battalion Headquarters were established. The troops opposite were Bavarians. The Battalion remained in the trenches in Sub-sector M.2 until relieved in the evening of March 6th. These trenches were found generally in good condition, but the disposition of the troops was faulty, as the whole battalion was in the first line, supported only by its snipers, sappers and bombers, and these, owing to the great distance that the rations had to be carried to the front line, were employed almost entirely as carriers. It may be mentioned that the French battalions when holding the sub-sector had always had a company of another battalion in support. On relief, three companies and Battalion Headquarters went into cellars and dugouts in Roclincourt. The remaining company was billeted in Arras. Two men were wounded by a rifle grenade during the relief.

The Battalion remained at Roclincourt, working on the defences, until the evening of the 12th March, when it relieved the Devons in Sub-sector M.2. It now found the 51st (Highland) Division on its left and the 12th Battn. Gloucester Regt. on its right. On March 13th a N.C.O. was wounded by a rifle grenade, and early on the following morning a sentry in one of the listening posts was shot through the head and killed. Later in the day a rifle grenade exploded on leaving the muzzle and unfortunately killed 2nd Lieut. C. C. Pocock and wounded Captain Birch and one man.

The Battalion was relieved by the 1st Battn. Royal West Kent Regt. during the night of March 15th and marched westward to billets at Agnez-lez-Duisans. The Battalion was now "resting" and formed part of the VI Corps Reserve, with orders to move two miles south to Warlus in case of alarm. It remained at Agnez-lez-Duisans until the afternoon of the 21st March, when it returned to the Arras defences, two companies going into the redoubt line in support of the 1st Battn. Devon Regt. in Sub-sector J.1, which was just north of the River Scarpe. Headquarters and the other two companies formed part of the Brigade Reserve in Arras, and were quartered in the cellars of some outbuildings of the destroyed cathedral. Another change in the Brigade had taken place on the 17th March, when the 95th Machine-gun Company arrived from Grantham, where it had been formed and trained.

During the evening of the 25th March the Battalion relieved the 1st Battn. Devon Regt. in the trenches in Sub-sector J.1, the relief being complete by 8.30 p.m. On the 28th two companies returned to billets in Arras and two took up duty in the redoubt line. On the night of the 29th one man was severely wounded when placing wire in front of the trenches. On March 30th, Major Woulfe-Flanagan returned from short leave and resumed duty as senior Major. On the evening of the 31st the Battalion relieved the 1st Battn. Devon Regt. in Sub-sector J.1, three companies being in the fire trenches, and Headquarters and the reserve company in the Oil Works.

On the 1st April, Lieut.-Colonel Tew took over temporary command of the 95th Brigade, vice Brigadier-General Ballard, on short leave. Wiring operations in front of the trenches were steadily proceeding, though at very close quarters with the enemy. On the 2nd a draft of sixty-six men joined the Battalion. During the evening of the 4th April the Battalion was relieved in the Sub-sector J.1 by the 2nd Battn. K.O.S.B., and companies marched independently to their former billets at Agnez-lez-Duisans. On the 5th, Major Woulfe-Flanagan inspected the recently arrived draft and found that it was mainly composed of wounded men of the 1st and 2nd Battalions, returned from duty "down the line." Major Woulfe-Flanagan addressed the draft, expressing his pleasure at seeing them, and his conviction that they would continue to uphold the good name that both battalions had earned in the field to the present time.

On April 7th the Battalion was given a demonstration of the "Flammenwerfer" by the Third Army chemical expert. The instrument, which had been captured from the Germans at Loos, was proved to be harmless enough, provided those against whom it was used kept low. It was, however, necessary that they should be quick to man the fire-step directly the spraying ceased, in order to repel the subsequent attack.

On April 10th, Lieut.-General Sir J. L. Keir, Commanding the VI Corps, inspected the companies on parade. The Battalion remained at Agnez-lez-Duisans, in wet weather, until the evening of the 12th April, when it moved up into support at Roclincourt and Arras. Headquarters and two companies were posted in cellars at Roclincourt, and two companies in good billets in Arras. On the following day Lieut.-Colonel Tew resumed command of the Battalion, and on the 14th Headquarters moved from Roclincourt into Arras. In the evening of April 16th the Battalion relieved the 1st Battn. Devon Regt. in Sub-sector K.2 (previously M.2) and remained there until the evening of the 20th, when the two battalions again exchanged places. The weather during the four days in the trenches was wet and the enemy's trench mortars very active, though only two men were wounded. A draft of thirty-five men from the 4th Battn. joined on the 22nd, and on the 24th the Battalion returned to the K.2 trenches. "At about 2 a.m. on April 26th," the Battalion Diary records, "2nd Lieut. A. J. Reid, of No. 4 Company, was shot through the neck and killed while examining the wire in front of a listening post. He came out with the Battalion as a sergeant, was promoted company sergeant-major on the 28th January, 1915, won the D.C.M. at Hill 60 in April, 1915, and was given his commission in the Battalion on 27th November, 1915. He was buried in the cemetery of the Faubourg d'Amiens. The loss of this keen and cheerful personality is most sincerely regretted by the whole Battalion." The writer feels that it would be a mistake to curtail this charming sketch of the career of a good soldier.

The 1st Battn. East Surrey was relieved by the 1st Battn. Royal West Kent Regt. late in the night of the 28th April, the companies then marching back independently to billets at Agnez-lez-Duisans, where the Battalion finished the month. During April the Battalion system of having an understudy for every officer and non-commissioned officer was completely carried out.

The Battalion remained at Agnez-lez-Duisans until the evening of the 4th May, when it relieved the 7th Battn. King's Royal Rifles in the left sub-sector (I.2) of I Sector, which was just south of the River Scarpe and had recently been taken over from the French. Three companies were in the trenches, and the fourth in reserve near Arras railway station. On the 8th May the Battalion was relieved by the Devons and returned to billets at Agnez. The tour of duty had been quiet and no casualties had been sustained. The Battalion remained at Agnez until May 14th, occupied, as usual, in various forms of instruction and training. On that day Lieut.-Colonel Tew went to the United Kingdom on ten days' leave, and Major Woulfe-Flanagan assumed command. In the evening the Battalion marched off by companies at ten minutes' interval and relieved the Devons in Sub-sector I.2, which they continued to occupy alternately with the

## MAY, 1916

Devons until the 20th June. The periods spent in the trenches lasted six or seven days, and the intervals were passed either in support in Arras or in reserve at Agnez-lez-Duisans. The first day in Agnez was spent in clearing up, the next five at company training. On the last day the men rested, marching up to the trenches in the evening. On working days training began at 7 a.m. and finished at 3 p.m. Great care was taken in training the men in the "assault," especially in the preliminary details of forming up in and climbing out of narrow trenches without confusion, moving through the gaps in the wire and going straight forward to the assault, line after line, with the least possible delay.

The company commanders at this time were Captains Swanton, King and Robinson and 2nd Lieut. Wight. Each of the three companies in the trenches had two platoons in the first line and two in the support line, ready to reinforce at a moment's notice. The Diary notes on the 17th May that 2nd Lieut. S. F. Irwin, the Intelligence Officer of the Battalion, was complimented by the General Officer Commanding 5th Division on the excellence of a report rendered by him on the 16th.

On the 27th May a draft of ninety-two men, which included Lce.-Cpl. Dwyer, V.C., joined the Battalion in Arras, and amongst several officers who also joined during the last three days of the month were Captain R. Streatfeild-James, who had recovered from his second wound, and 2nd Lieut. G. H. W. Clay. The last named was a son of Captain and Quartermaster H. Clay, and, like his father, had been promoted for good service in the field.

While in reserve at Agnez-lez-Duisans during the first week of June the Battalion had a good opportunity for training, and the recently joined officers and men were instructed in anti-gas precautions, being put through the gas chamber. On the 5th June the award of the Military Cross to Regt. Sergt.-Major T. Murden, for his long-sustained devotion to duty and many acts of gallantry, was notified in orders, and about the same date Company Sergt.-Major T. C. Jackson was awarded the Distinguished Conduct Medal. Lieut.-Colonel H. S. Tew, whose services throughout the War had been conspicuous, left the Battalion on the same date, on appointment to the command of the 18th Infantry Brigade. Major Woulfe-Flanagan being on leave, the command of the Battalion devolved on Captain T. S. Swanton.

After the next tour of duty in the trenches the Battalion was in support in Arras, where one company was posted in the cemetery defences. The remaining three found life dull, as the men were confined to their billets except for one hour, 9.30 to 10.30 p.m., when they were allowed in the streets. This confinement was rendered necessary by the German artillery, which shelled the town frequently at varying intervals. Battalion Orders of the 17th June mention that Lieut.-Colonel H. S. Tew, Major E. M. Woulfe-Flanagan and Sergt. J. W. Stacey were mentioned in despatches dated the 30th April, 1916.

On June 20th the infantry of the 5th Division was relieved from the trenches. The three companies of the 1st Battn. East Surrey in Arras were relieved during the night by the 10th Battn. Durham Light Infantry, of the 14th Division, and marched to huts in Wanquetin. C Company (Captain

Robinson), from the cemetery defences, joined the Battalion on the 21st. On the following day Captain Swanton attended a conference of commanding officers at which the general idea of the coming offensive of the Somme was explained, and also the part assigned to the 5th Division. On the 24th there was a second conference, in which the task allotted to the Division was more clearly defined, though its actual performance was to depend on the course of events in another section of the attack.

Major E. M. Woulfe-Flanagan returned from sick leave and took over command of the Battalion on the 26th, while 2nd Lieut. Irwin was appointed Intelligence Officer to the 95th Brigade. The weather was unsettled and interfered with work, especially on the 28th June. During that night the Battalion relieved the 1st Battn. D.C.L.I. in trenches before Wailly, three miles south of Arras. The relief was completed at 2.30 a.m. on the 29th, when the Battalion found on its right the 5th Battn. Liverpool Regt., of the 165th Brigade, and on its left the 1st Battn. K.O.S.B. On the night of the 30th June, after three quiet days in the trenches, the Battalion was relieved by the 1st Battn. Devon Regt. and marched back to billets at Wanquetin.

## CHAPTER XI

SEPTEMBER, 1915, TO JUNE, 1916: THE 2ND BATTALION IN THE BATTLE OF LOOS; THE DEFENCE OF THE HOHENZOLLERN REDOUBT. THE 28TH DIVISION PROCEEDS TO EGYPT AND THENCE TO SALONIKA. WORK ON THE SALONIKA DEFENCES. THE 28TH DIVISION ADVANCES TO THE STRUMA RIVER. THE BATTALION IN THE OUTPOST LINE NEAR LAKE BUTKOVO. MALARIA EPIDEMIC.

THE close of Chapter VI left the 28th Division concentrating about Bailleul and the 2nd Battn. East Surrey at Strazeele, which it had reached on the 22nd September, 1915. At Strazeele the Battalion rested for three days, being warned on September 25th to hold itself in readiness to march at short notice. No order to move came that day; but early on September 26th the Battalion, with a strength of 27 officers and 964 of other ranks, marched via Strazeele station towards Merville. While on the road orders were received to march direct to Bethune, which was reached at 7.30 p.m. The distance covered was seventeen miles, but much delay had been caused through the roads being blocked by the movement of other troops. The Battalion billeted at Bethune for the night, and, although violent fighting was in progress only six miles away, the town, it was noticed, was brilliantly lighted up, the shops were all open and the streets full of people.

It is necessary at this point to describe very briefly the great operation in which the Battalion was now about to take its share. The main attack of this operation, which has become known as the Battle of Loos, was made by the I and IV Corps of the First British Army against the immensely strong German positions running south from the canal at La Bassée to the suburbs of the town of Lens, in co-operation with an attack by the Tenth French Army further south. The whole operation was timed so as to aid the great attack by the French Army in Champagne, by diverting as many as possible of the German reserves from the southern theatre of action. This skeleton outline of the September offensive must be completed by a bald statement that northward of Sir Douglas Haig's attack, and roughly between Ypres and Givenchy, the Second Army, under General Sir Herbert Plumer, made three vigorous attacks on a large scale, with the intention of holding off German reinforcements from the troops opposing General Haig, even as the latter was thus assisting the main French attack in Champagne.

Concentrating our attention north of the Vermelles–Hulluch road on the movements of the I Corps, with which alone we are concerned for the elucidation of our narrative, it may suffice to say that the attack of the I Corps, which commenced at 6.30 a.m. on the 25th September, 1915, met at first with a considerable measure of success. The Hohenzollern Redoubt—a powerful work standing on commanding ground one and a half miles north-east of Vermelles

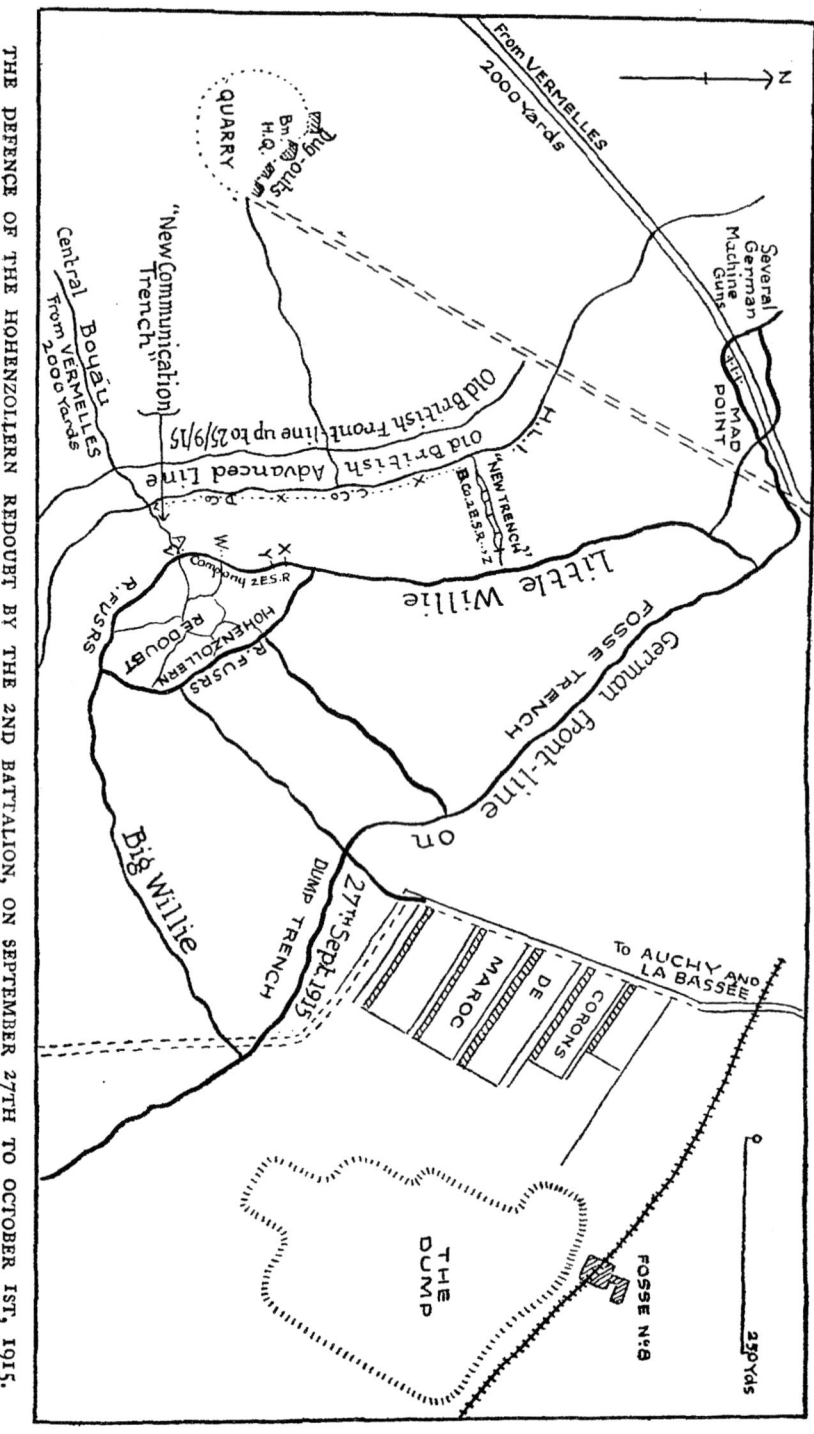

THE DEFENCE OF THE HOHENZOLLERN REDOUBT BY THE 2ND BATTALION, ON SEPTEMBER 27TH TO OCTOBER 1ST, 1915.

and nearly 500 yards in advance of the German front line—as well as Fosse 8, a coal mine with a strongly fortified slap heap 1000 yards north-east of the Redoubt, were captured early in the day by the 26th Brigade of the 9th Division. North of the Redoubt the 28th Brigade of the same division captured the German front line, but was soon afterwards forced back to its own trenches. The British hold on the captured positions was therefore by no means secure, and soon after dawn on the 27th September the garrison of Fosse 8 were driven slowly back in a south-westerly direction until their front was level with the eastern face of the Hohenzollern Redoubt. This development increased considerably the difficulties of the defenders of the Redoubt.

We left the 2nd Battalion at Bethune on the night of the 26th September, on which date the 28th Division was placed at the disposal of the First Army Commander. At 9 a.m. on the 27th the 85th Brigade moved off with orders to take over trenches "east of Vermelles." The western end of this little town, distant seven miles, was reached at 12.30 p.m., and after a halt of two hours, during which hot dinners were eaten, the Brigade left for the trenches. During the halt Lieut.-Colonel Montague-Bates called together the officers of the 2nd Battn. East Surrey for the purpose of explaining the situation and of issuing orders. According to the latest information, parts of the Hohenzollern Redoubt were in the hands of the enemy, who also held a trench called "Little Willie," which connected the northern angle of the Redoubt with the German front line (see Map opposite). The northern portion of the Redoubt and "Little Willie" were in the first instance allotted to the 2nd Battn. East Surrey, and the southern portion to the 2nd Battn. "The Buffs." The 3rd Battn. Royal Fusiliers were to advance through the Redoubt and take Fosse Trench. Before the Battalion marched at 2.30 p.m., however, it became known that the situation had altered, and these orders were accordingly cancelled. To the 2nd Battn. East Surrey was now allotted the task of clearing up the situation as regards the Redoubt and of attacking "Little Willie."

A supply of bombs was drawn from the Brigade Reserve and the advance began, to be interrupted almost immediately by a long halt at the cross-roads in Vermelles. Eventually the Battalion passed through the barricade on the road running eastward from the village, and presently entered the communication trench "Central Boyau" leading to the old British lines opposite the Hohenzollern Redoubt. On the way up heavy hostile shell fire was encountered and Regt. Sergt.-Major E. North was wounded in the head, dying shortly afterwards. Before the Battalion reached its destination 5 other men had been killed and 26 wounded. No guides had been provided, and so great was the uncertainty as to the situation, that Brigadier-General Pereira and his Brigade Major went forward to reconnoitre and were both wounded, probably before they could issue revised orders for the attack.

Eventually Lieut.-Colonel Montague-Bates, after reconnoitring with his adjutant, Captain Bayliss, the ground which separated the old British line from the Hohenzollern Redoubt and "Little Willie," got the Battalion into position at about 1.30 a.m. on the 28th September, the disposition being as follows: On the right A Company (Lieut. Lewis) was in the north-western portion of the Hohenzollern Redoubt, part of the company being held back in support in the "New Communication trench," which was the prolongation of the "Central Boyau" to the Redoubt. B Company (Captain Whitehead) on the left held "New Trench," connecting the old British line with "Little Willie." This trench had been provided on the north side with a fire trench, but both fire and communication trenches were seriously enfiladed from " Little Willie." C Company (Captain Müller) and D Company (Lieut. Voisin) were in reserve in the old British advanced trenches which had been dug for the attack of the 25th September. These advanced trenches were about fifty yards in front of the old British front-line trenches. Battalion Headquarters and the dressing-station were in the quarry a short distance in rear of C Company. The H.L.I. were on the left, and the Royal Fusiliers on the right of the 2nd Battn. East Surrey.

The advance along "Central Boyau" had been led by A Company, then about 200 strong, whose experiences are thus described by one of its officers. "At about midnight (27th/28th September), having moved some distance up 'Central Boyau' and then over-ground, as there was little firing at the time, we came to a trench which was about the place shown on our map as the Hohenzollern Redoubt (V in map). The part of this trench which lay on our right was occupied by some Scottish soldiers who were in a very exhausted condition. They could give us no information as to where they were, nor as to the position of the enemy. We dumped our packs at this point, and waited whilst 2nd Lieut. Woodyear reconnoitred the ground and trench on our left, as our orders were to clear 'Little Willie' trench of the enemy, who was supposed to be cut off at each end of the trench. This, however, proved not to be the case. 2nd Lieut. Woodyear found there was a good length of trench unoccupied, so the company advanced in single file along the right side of the trench (i.e. the north-western face of the Redoubt). Presently we came under fire and a few men were hit, so we got down into the trench. We then moved farther along the trench until we came to a barrier (X in map) about 100 yards from the point where we had left our packs. After placing sentries along the trench and at the barrier, we took a sneak party beyond the barrier and crept round the traverses to see if the further part of the trench was occupied. We could tell that we were now at close quarters from the rifle fire, the flashes appearing to be about thirty yards away. We had now found out that the Germans held 'Little Willie' right up to the Redoubt. They evidently had discovered us, and threw bombs at our part of the trench. We replied by bombing the end of 'Little Willie.' Later we made a short advance, led by Lieut. Lewis, who, having passed several traverses beyond the barrier, had both his legs broken by a bomb which fell at his feet. Several other casualties occurred, and, after removing our wounded with some difficulty behind the barrier (X), we gave up the attempt to advance for the night and decided to wait till daylight. We had thirty casualties that night. Two doctors who were searching out in the open for wounded came to our assistance."

The strength of A Company, only part of which was engaged in this gallant attack, was nearly 200, but it only had three officers present. Lieut. G. H. Lewis, a very brave and valuable officer, belonging to the 4th Battn. East Surrey, was carried back to hospital, but died in a few hours. His place at the head of A Company was taken by Lieut. C. Mead (also 4th Battalion) from D Company.

While A Company was thus maintaining and endeavouring to improve its position in the northern portion of the Redoubt, B Company was similarly employed in " New Trench." Captain Whitehead, who commanded the company, was wounded early in the morning of the 28th, and later Lieut. S. Smith (3rd Battn. attd.), who succeeded Captain Whitehead in the command, was also wounded. The intention was that this company should force its way along " New Trench " to a point whence it could attack the Germans in " Little Willie," but the way was barred by a barricade (Z in map) which could not be passed.

On the whole, the forenoon of the 28th September was fairly quiet. The shelling was not heavy and the bombing attacks were intermittent; but during one of them Lieut. C. Mead, with A Company, was killed. In him the Battalion lost one of its best officers. His place was taken by Captain A. A. B. Dowler, who joined the company at 1 p.m. The whole Battalion was badly in want of sleep, but about noon rations came up, which improved matters considerably.

About 12.30 p.m. the Middlesex Regt. advanced through D Company, moving half-right across the new communication trench to reinforce the "Buffs," who had lost nearly all their officers in their attack on " the Dump." While making this advance the Middlesex were caught by enfilade machine-gun fire from " Little Willie," and soon the " New Communication Trench " was choked with their dead and wounded, greatly hampering the movements of the East Surrey. Captain Dowler consequently moved that part of A Company which had been in this trench into the Hohenzollern Redoubt, and, aided by 2nd Lieuts. Woodyear and Jannson, set his men to work at digging recesses and a firing step in the parados. The attack could not be continued at this time, as the supply of bombs had been exhausted since about 9 a.m., and no more were procurable. The only thing to be done, therefore, was to strengthen the position and hold on till bombs were brought up. This unavoidable lull in the attack enabled the Germans to bring up large quantities of bombs; but Captain Dowler was able to telephone through D Company for artillery support, and " Little Willie " was then shelled very successfully. The German guns directed their fire chiefly on the support trenches, and so A Company was able to hold its ground in the Redoubt. The night of the 28th/29th was comparatively quiet ; some wire was put up by the Engineers, and our position was consolidated generally. The British and German dead, moreover, were buried in the centre of the Redoubt.

Towards dawn on the 29th it began to rain hard, and about 7 a.m. a few boxes of bombs arrived with the rations. The supply of bombs was quite inadequate to meet a heavy bombing attack opened by the Germans at about 8.30 a.m., and as at the same time the German artillery fire became much heavier, it was evident that an attack in force was developing. In spite of heavy casualties, A Company held its ground firmly, headed most gallantly by Captain Dowler, whose personal exertions were conspicuous. Bombing at close quarters continued till about 11 a.m., without advantage to either side, but the Germans then brought up a machine gun which held down part of the East Surrey bombers. This gun was soon afterwards put out of action by a machine gun lent for the purpose by the Royal Fusiliers, and about the same time Captain Dowler shot at close quarters the young German officer who was leading the enemy's bombers.

Fighting continued vigorously in this manner until about 1 p.m., when Captain Dowler was very severely wounded by a bomb. His men, too, suffered heavy losses, and once more the supply of bombs ran short. Rain increased the difficulties of the situation, as many of the bombs had wet fuses and were therefore useless. The Germans naturally realized their advantage and advanced down the trench, throwing bombs in front of them. The East Surrey bombers, being powerless, were compelled to retire before them to the rear of a new barrier (Y in map) which they had built in rear of the original barrier at X. 2nd Lieut. Jannson led some men forward quickly to endeavour to hold this barrier, but found the Germans there before him. He and his men therefore fell back a short distance, out of range of the German bombs, and, getting out of the trench, took up a line at right angles to it (W in map), making use of the shelter of the remains of a disused German communication trench. From this position they opened a hot rifle fire and, being able to enfilade the trench, were enabled to check the German advance. They held their ground, but, being somewhat exposed, sustained many casualties, 2nd Lieut. Jannson, who behaved extremely well, being himself wounded. At this critical period some troops on the right of the Redoubt began to fall back, a movement which exposed the right flank. Some unsteadiness was consequently shown by some of the sorely tried men in the Redoubt, when 2nd Lieut. A. J. T. Fleming-Sandes, who had been sent up with a supply of bombs, rallied them and, jumping up on the parapet, drove back the enemy and saved the situation. 2nd Lieut. Fleming-Sandes, after having his right arm broken by a rifle shot, threw bombs with his left until he was again shot in the face. He well earned the Victoria Cross, which he subsequently received, for this gallant conduct. The danger on the right flank was presently removed by a counter-attack made by the York and Lancaster Regt., and the Redoubt and neighbouring trenches were successfully held. A Company, reduced to 1 officer (2nd Lieut. Woodyear) and about 75 men, was relieved by D Company during the night of the 29th/30th September.

During the 30th September furious bombing continued all day in the Hohenzollern Redoubt, but the 2nd Battn. East Surrey held on to its position without any loss of ground until relieved at 7 a.m. on the 1st October. The relief was completed by 9.30 a.m., when, much fatigued but in high spirits, the sorely tried Battalion proceeded to reserve trenches east of Vermelles. At 4.45 p.m. orders were received that the Battalion was to march four miles westward to Beuvry, but, owing to the blocked state of the road, did not reach its billets until 8 p.m.

## THE 28TH DIVISION IN RESERVE

The losses sustained in the defence of the Hohenzollern Redoubt were as follows:—

| | | |
|---|---|---:|
| Officers: | *Killed and mortally wounded* | 3 |
| „ | *Wounded* | 6 |
| Other ranks: | *Killed and mortally wounded* | 40 |
| „ | *Wounded* | 120 |

The officers killed or mortally wounded were Lieuts. G. H. Lewis and C. Mead and 2nd Lieut. C. R. Chandler. Those wounded were Captains A. V. Whitehead and A. A. B. Dowler, Lieut. S. Smith, and 2nd Lieuts. A. J. T. Fleming-Sandes, J. Jannson and R. A. Kendall.

The Battalion remained in billets at Beuvry on the 2nd October, finding a working party of 500 men, of whom 5 were killed and 10 wounded. At noon on the 3rd October the Battalion marched two miles east from Beuvry to Annequin, arriving there at 1.15. Captain Jourdier joined the Battalion this day and assumed the duties of Second-in-Command. During the night orders were received to move up at once to support the 83rd Brigade in an attack on the Hohenzollern Redoubt, which had been recaptured by the Germans four hours after the 2nd Battn. East Surrey had quitted it. The Battalion accordingly again moved up to the reserve trenches, but returned at 2.50 p.m. to Annequin, where a draft of sixty-nine men joined it.

On October 5th the Battalion went at 8 a.m. into reserve trenches east of Vermelles and remained there until the morning of the 6th. Four men were wounded while in the trenches.

The Battalion returned to its billets at Annequin early on the 6th October, and, as the 28th Division was now being withdrawn from the line to rest, marched at 10 a.m. for L'Eclème, distant about eleven miles. A halt for dinner was made at Bethune, and L'Eclème was reached at 5 p.m. Here the Battalion remained for ten days, resting and refitting on October 7th and training during the remainder of the time. Four officers joined the Battalion to replace casualties, and on the 14th October, Major-General C. J. Briggs, commanding the 28th Division, inspected the Battalion.

On October 17th the Battalion left L'Eclème and marched to new billets at Hingette and Avelette, arriving at noon; and on the 18th moved to Bethune, where it was billeted in the Tobacco Factory. On the 19th the Battalion moved to Givenchy and remained in billets there as reserve to the 85th Brigade; but in the afternoon orders were received that the Brigade was to be relieved from the trenches. The 2nd Battn. East Surrey was accordingly moved to billets at Mont Bernenchon, five miles north-west of Bethune. Officers and men on leave were recalled on account of the impending departure of the 28th Division from France. A draft of 10 men arrived on October 20th, and one of 72 men on the 21st.

The award of the Distinguished Conduct Medal to Sergt. C. Spencer, Lce.-Cpls. D. Donovan and G. Puttock, and Pte. W. Theobald, for gallantry at the Hohenzollern Redoubt, was notified in orders.

On the 22nd October the Battalion marched at 9.30 a.m. from its billets at Mont Bernenchon to Fouquereuil, about five miles distant, and entrained for Marseilles, where it arrived at 6 p.m. on the 24th. The Battalion detrained close to the quay, and A, B and D Companies embarked immediately on the s.s. *Transylvania*, and C Company on the s.s. *Royal George*. The Battalion transport, under Lieut. Voisin, remained temporarily at Marseilles.

Both transports sailed before noon on the 25th October, and dropped anchor in Alexandria Harbour at 11.30 a.m. on the 30th. The Battalion disembarked on the 31st, and moved by train and march to Sidi Bishr Camp, about seven miles east of Alexandria and on the seashore. The camp was practically in the desert, but, on the other hand, the bathing was excellent.

The Battalion reached Egypt at its full establishment in officers and men and in a very fine state of discipline and efficiency. The spirit of all ranks was admirable and quite undimmed by the terrible losses sustained by the Battalion during little more than nine months' service in France. Captain and Adjutant Bayliss, and Lieut. and Quartermaster Percy, both of whom had done admirable work, were the only officers remaining with the Battalion when it reached Alexandria of those who had proceeded with it to France; and of the original non-commissioned officers and men but very few were still serving in it.

The 1st November was occupied in bathing and cleaning up after the voyage. On the 2nd, Lieut. Voisin and the Battalion transport arrived from Marseilles, and a draft of 72 men joined the Battalion.

The Battalion remained in camp at Sidi Bishr until the 25th November, a period entirely without incident. On the 23rd November news arrived that 2nd Lieut. Fleming-Sandes had been awarded the Victoria Cross for his gallant conduct in the defence of the Hohenzollern Redoubt. This was the first occasion on which an officer of the Battalion had won the Cross.

On November 24th the 28th Division received orders to embark at Alexandria, and on the following day the 2nd Battn. East Surrey left camp accordingly at 7.30 a.m. The Battalion, with a strength of 14 officers and 801 other ranks, embarked on the s.s. *Hororata* shortly before noon, the remaining officers and men being left behind to follow on with the regimental transport. The 3rd Battn. Middlesex Regt. and part of "The Buffs" were also conveyed in the *Hororata*.

Early in the morning of the 26th November the *Hororata* left the quay and anchored in the harbour, finally moving out at 4.30 p.m. Orders were issued that troops were to "stand to" daily at dawn, and that lifebelts were always to be worn. The *Hororata* arrived safely at Mudros at 7 a.m. on November 30th and anchored there till 4 p.m., when she sailed for Salonika under cover of night. At 9 a.m. on the 1st December she dropped anchor in Salonika Harbour.

At this point it may be useful to review briefly the course of events on the Salonika front previous to the arrival of the 28th Division. In accordance with an agreement between the Allied Governments, the 10th British Division, commanded by Lieut.-General Sir B. Mahon, which had been preceded by two French divisions, landed at Salonika early in October, 1915. Two more French

## AND JOINS THE SALONIKA EXPEDITIONARY FORCE

divisions arrived before the end of that month. The main object of this Expeditionary Force was to keep open communications with the Serbian Army, and a line was therefore taken up for the protection of the railways leading from Salonika into Serbia. The right of this line, in the neighbourhood of Lake Doiran, which is some five miles south of the point where the Serbian, Greek and Bulgarian frontiers meet, was held by units of the 10th Division.

It soon became apparent, however, that the Salonika Expeditionary Force could not afford any real assistance to the Serbian Army, and, further, that a large concentration of German and Bulgarian troops was taking place in the Strumitza Valley, some twenty miles north of Lake Doiran and near the Greco-Bulgarian frontier. Under these circumstances the advanced troops of the Salonika Force commenced to withdraw, and during the withdrawal the 10th Division was heavily attacked on the 6th to 8th December by superior Bulgarian forces, but succeeded in extricating itself without heavy loss and retired into Greek territory. The advanced troops now covered the disembarkation of the reinforcing divisions, which were at once set to work on the construction of the Fortified Lines of Salonika. These lines extended from the Galiko river, north of Salonika, to Stavros on the sea coast, forty miles east of Salonika.

The record for December, so far as the 2nd Battn. East Surrey was concerned, is one of hard work carried out in a cheerful spirit. On the 2nd December the Battalion disembarked in lighters in the afternoon and marched to a camping ground at Lembet, where they bivouacked for the night. Camp was pitched on the 3rd, and the week following was occupied in camp training, improvement of ground, etc. The Battalion transport and the officers who had been left at Alexandria arrived on the 10th. On the 13th and 14th two companies were employed in digging trenches on the forward slope of the hills overlooking Baldza, about ten miles north of Salonika. On December 16th two companies continued work on the trenches south of Baldza, while the remainder shifted the Battalion camp to "Red House," on the track leading from Lembet to Baldza. The day was very wet. Digging continued on the 17th, and on the 18th camp was again ordered to shift to high ground company by company, so that the working parties should be nearer their work. This was convenient; but the road up the hill was a mere track which quickly became almost impassable. On December 19th, B Company continued work on the Baldza trenches, while A and D Companies began to construct a redoubt at the foot of the hills and just south-east of Baldza. These two companies moved up to the new camp on the 20th, and the work continued on the trenches, the redoubt and the mule track to the camp until the 23rd, which was given as a day of rest. This was spent in cleaning up in the morning, and close order drill in the afternoon. The 24th and the morning of Christmas Day were devoted to digging, and the men had Christmas dinners at 2 p.m. Greetings were received from the Divisional Commander and from Major-General Longley, now commanding the 10th Division. The Brigadier also sent a special message congratulating the Battalion on its hard work on "Bates Redoubt" and the mule track, now styled "Surrey Lane."

From the 26th to the 30th December the Battalion dug support trenches.

At 10 a.m. on the latter day an enemy air raid took place. Bombs fell within 250 yards of the camp of the Battalion. On the last day of the year a small redoubt was begun behind the support trenches. The Battalion line was visited by Lieut.-General Wilson, commanding the XII Corps, to which the 28th Division now belonged.

The Battalion passed the whole of January in its camp near Baldza Pass, and the work of one day so much resembled that of the others that a detailed diary would be wearisome. Changes in the weather alone affected the amount of work done. The normal arrangements were for every available man to walk six miles a day and to dig from 9.30 a.m. to 4 p.m., with an interval of forty-five minutes for dinner. This was a fairly hard and somewhat monotonous life; but the men were in fine health, and as time went on and communications were improved, their small comforts increased. They were either under canvas or accommodated in dugouts, and the nights, therefore, in spite of great cold, were bearable. The enemy made an air raid on the 7th January and dropped bombs near the camp, but did no harm. On the 11th, Captain H. V. Bayliss left the Battalion on appointment as G.S.O. 3 on the staff of the XVI Corps. He had been Adjutant during the whole active service of the Battalion and had worked with the utmost devotion and assiduity.

On the 14th January a draft of 100 men joined Headquarters. On the 18th and 19th the afternoons were devoted to tactical exercises, counter-attacks to recapture lost trenches being practised.

On the last day of the month the Battalion Orders contained a list of decorations announced in the *London Gazette* of the 1st January, 1916, and of those mentioned in despatches on the same date, mainly for services at the Hohenzollern Redoubt. Captain and Adjutant H. V. Bayliss received the Military Cross, and the Distinguished Conduct Medal was conferred on Company Sergt. Major G. H. Coomber and Sergt. R. Forbes. Those mentioned in despatches were Lieut.-Colonel F. E. Montague-Bates, Captain J. Gurdon, 2nd Lieut. (temporary Captain) H. F. B. Garrett, Lieut. C. Mead (killed), Lieut. and Quartermaster H. J. Percy, Company Sergt.-Major G. H. Coomber, Sergt. S. Wootton, Lce.-Cpl. G. Lyons, Ptes. W. Barker and H. Milan.

During February the Battalion remained at Baldza Pass Camp, employed much as it had been during January; but, owing to the progress made on the defences, one company daily was placed at the disposal of its commander for training purposes. The heavy snow of January yielded to frequent rain, varied by snowstorms. Lieut. (temporary Captain) J. O. Carpenter took over the duties of Acting Adjutant on the 10th, and on the 17th Lieut.-Colonel W. N. R. Gilbert-Cooper returned from sick leave in England, Major A. T. Robinson taking over the duties of Senior Major. Lieut.-Colonel Montague-Bates was at the same time appointed to the command of the 12th Battn. Cheshire Regt. in the 22nd Division. On the 24th, Lieut. and Quartermaster Percy went to hospital in consequence of an injury caused by a fall. But for a Brigade field day on the 26th, the rest of the month was devoid of incident.

The first ten days of March had a history much like that of February. Three companies worked daily at the trenches, a good deal hampered by heavy rain, while the fourth company was at training. On the 6th March the Battalion started work on a new second-line trench which it had been detailed to dig, but owing to bad weather not very much had been done when, on the 11th March, the 85th Brigade was relieved by the 83rd, and became Corps Reserve, the 2nd Battn. East Surrey remaining at Baldza Camp. Brigade field days took place on the 15th, 18th and 25th, and a Battalion field day on the 28th, but otherwise steady work continued all the month.

Captain M. J. A. Jourdier, who had held the temporary rank of Major while acting Senior Major of the Battalion, resigned his temporary rank on the 23rd, on appointment as G.S.O. 3 on the staff of the 27th Division. The Battalion Diary records that on the last day of the month a recreation tent was opened in the camp.

Starting from Baldza Pass Camp on the 4th April, the Battalion took part in five days' manœuvres with the remainder of the 85th Brigade. The operations were of a practical nature, an irregular enemy being represented by the Surrey Yeomanry. The weather was warm and fine, and the Battalion returned to Baldza Pass Camp independently on April 8th, arriving at 12.30 p.m.

On the 10th and 11th there were rehearsal parades for the ceremonial parade on April 12th, when General Sarrail, commanding the Allied armies in Macedonia, was invested with the Grand Cross of the Order of St. Michael and St. George. The 2nd Battn. East Surrey was selected to furnish the guard of honour on the occasion, and was complimented on its smartness on parade. The remainder of the month was uneventful, work being continued daily on the second-line trenches.

The month opened with heavy rain, in consequence of which divisional manœuvres were postponed from the 2nd to the 3rd May. On the latter day the 28th Division moved off for a week's manœuvres in the neighbourhood of Langaza. On the 10th May the divisional manœuvres terminated, and the 2nd Battn. East Surrey returned to the Baldza Pass Camp. Rain fell on one evening only during the whole manœuvre period.

After two days' rest, work was resumed on the second-line trenches on May 13th, and continued steadily until the 25th May, when two companies moved to the Besch Chinar Gardens in Salonika, the two remaining companies following on the 25th. The Battalion furnished the Garrison duties in Salonika during the remainder of the month. The populace was much excited on the 28th May in consequence of the Greek Government having allowed Bulgarian troops to take possession of the frontier fortresses. French troops were in readiness to keep order, and the Battalion was held ready to support them at a moment's notice, if necessary. No action, however, was required.

The Battalion was relieved of duty at Salonika on the 2nd June, and marched on the 3rd to its old camp at the Baldza Pass, the weather being very hot. The Battalion was inoculated against cholera on June 4th, and remained on that day and the 5th ready to return, if necessary, to Salonika, which was in a very disturbed state.

Early in June the British Salonika Army was made responsible for that part of the Allied front which covered Salonika from the east and north-east, and advanced, therefore, to occupy positions along the River Struma and its tributary the Butkovo. The 28th Division started accordingly on the 6th June, the day's march being to Ambarkoi, ten miles north of the Baldza Pass. On the 7th the march was continued northwards to Sarigol, in great heat. The 8th was a halt day; but on the 9th the 85th Brigade was ordered to return to Ambarkoi, where it arrived at 12.30 p.m. in excellent condition, in spite of the heat. On the 10th a long and tiring march was made eastwards to Guvesne, on the Salonika–Seres road.

On June 11th the Brigade started at 5.50 a.m. along the Seres road, and arrived at a pleasant bivouac at Likovan. On the march the Army Commander, Lieut.-General G. F. Milne, passed the Battalion and paid Lieut.-Colonel Gilbert-Cooper a very high compliment on its march discipline, adding: " If it were a cold day, I should say the marching was excellent, but in this heat I call it magnificent." On the 12th the Battalion remained in its bivouac till 6 p.m., when it made an easy march to Lahana, arriving at 9.45 p.m. On the 13th June the Battalion reached the right bank of the River Struma at Orljak, and on the following day marched up the right bank of the river to Kopriva, where it bivouacked. The heat was intense, but the men were given the opportunity to bathe in the Struma. On June 15th the Battalion remained in the vicinity of Kopriva.

On the 16th June the Battalion, less C Company, which remained in the bivouac, marched at 5 a.m., and two hours later reached Lozista, a village near the south-western shore of Lake Butkovo. Here French troops were holding an outpost line facing that of the Bulgarian troops, who at the end of May had moved southwards to Demirhissar, about fifteen miles to the east on the far side of the Struma Valley. The outpost line to be taken over by the Battalion was mainly in the low marshy ground by the lake side, which had the reputation of being the most unhealthy part of the Struma front. As the summer was exceptionally hot even for Macedonia, and the only protection against mosquitoes was one square yard of netting per man, the whole Battalion was speedily to become infected with malaria. At 9 a.m. the East Surrey officers reconnoitred the outpost position, which was taken over at 4 p.m. Two companies went into the outpost line, with one in support. One section of the Brigade machine-gun company and one Lewis-gun section were posted in permanent emplacements commanding all approaches from the north and affording an excellent cross-fire. This position was held nightly by the Battalion until June 23rd inclusive, day outposts being taken during that period by the South Nottinghamshire Hussars. On June 18th, Major A. T. Robinson left the Battalion, on appointment to command the 7th Battn. Oxford and Bucks Light Infantry. There was occasional sniping at the cavalry patrols this day.

On the 23rd June the Battalion was relieved in the outpost line by the 2nd Battn. Cheshire Regt. (84th Brigade), and at 4 a.m. on the 24th marched eastward to Big-tree-well, where it bivouacked for the night. At the same hour

THE STRUMA VALLEY, FROM A PHOTOGRAPH

on the 25th June the march was continued to Kurfali, an extremely hot spot in the narrow valley of the Gumus Dere.[1] Here the Battalion, with the 3rd Battn. Royal Fusiliers, formed the Mobile Reserve of the 85th Brigade. The Battalion passed the remainder of June at Kurfali, two companies being employed daily at road-making. Several fresh cases of malarial fever occurred each day, the disease assuming epidemic form by the 29th June, in spite of wholesale quinine treatment which had been started on the 26th.

[1] Dere=valley with stream.

# CHAPTER XII

SEPTEMBER, 1915, TO JUNE, 1916: THE 7TH BATTALION MOVES TO THE LOOS AREA AND TAKES PART IN THE LATER PHASES OF THE BATTLE OF LOOS AND THE SUBSEQUENT ACTIONS OF THE HOHENZOLLERN REDOUBT: AFTER THREE MONTHS IN THE LINE, NORTH OF THE LA BASSEE CANAL, THE BATTALION RETURNS TO THE HOHENZOLLERN REDOUBT AREA, WHERE IT TAKES PART IN THE DEFENCE OF THE CRATERS: AT THE END OF TWO MONTHS' REST AND TRAINING BEHIND THE LINE IT MOVES TO THE ALBERT AREA.

THE 7th Battn. East Surrey had been three days in reserve in its billets at Le Bizet, near Armentières, when on the 24th September it was announced to the Battalion that the British First Army was assuming, in conjunction with certain French armies, the general offensive, which subsequently developed into the Battle of Loos. The task of the British Second Army was to hold the enemy all along its front, and by showing local activity at certain points to puzzle the enemy as to the real point of the main British attack. In accordance with these instructions an attack was planned on the Le Touquet salient, and at 2.30 a.m. on the 25th September the Battalion moved to its allotted position. From 5 to 6.30 the British artillery bombarded the enemy's trenches, and at 5.56 a smoke screen was sent up. Much to the disappointment of the men, however, no attack was made, and at 1 p.m. the Battalion as ordered to return to Le Bizet. Very little news came through on the 26th, except that in the evening the French were reported to have taken Souchez.

The Battalion was to have relieved the "Queen's" in the trenches on the 27th, but instead moved into billets near the railway station at Armentières, remaining there until early on the 29th September and storing all surplus kit. On the 29th the Battalion marched to Steenwerck Station, and entraining there in open trucks, started southwards at 7 a.m. The transport had gone on by road two hours earlier. The destination proved to be Fouquereuil, near Béthune, where the "Queen's" and "Buffs" had already arrived. After awaiting orders from 11.30 to 3 p.m., the Battalion marched to its billets at Verquin. The distance was only 3¼ miles, but the roads were so blocked with troops that the march took two hours. The 12th Division had now joined the British force engaged in the Battle of Loos, which lasted from the 25th September to the 8th October.

At 12.30 p.m. on September 30th the 37th Brigade left for Vermelles, which it was ordered to take over from the 3rd Guards Brigade. This was done at about 4.30 p.m., and the 12th Division had now relieved the Guards Division in the front line from Loos to the Hohenzollern Redoubt. The 37th Brigade was in Divisional Reserve at Vermelles, while the 35th and 36th Brigades held the front line. Shelling was going on night and day, a new experience to the Battalion, the men being greatly impressed by the number of the British guns, which seemed to be almost wheel to wheel and to be numbered by thousands.

Most of the officers of the Battalion paid visits during the 1st October to the battlefields of the 25th and 26th September, and gained valuable information and a fair idea of what the fighting had been like. A good deal of shelling was still going on, but chiefly from the British guns. Bomb practice, under Lieut. Marshall, went on all day, the extreme importance of real efficiency in bomb throwing having been brought home to everyone by the recent fighting. The Diary states: "The 2nd Battalion are on our left and the French on our right, with the Guards Division in support, so being in very good company and the right of the British line our men have every incentive to do well." The 2nd Battn. East Surrey, it may be mentioned, had highly distinguished themselves at the Hohenzollern Redoubt from September 27th to the date on which this entry was made.

On October 3rd the Battalion and the 6th Battn. "Queen's" moved up to the old British trenches three-quarters of a mile north-west of Loos, with the "Queen's" right on the Béthune–Lens road, and the left of the 7th Battn. East Surrey on the Vermelles–Loos road. The trenches were much overcrowded, as the two battalions had only 1000 yards of front, and there were, in addition in the trenches about 1000 dismounted cavalry who were finding burying parties, etc. It was difficult to get water and food to the trenches as the ground between them and Vermelles was heavily shelled all day. The Battalion, however, came off very lightly in casualties, 1 man being killed and 3 wounded; but the 12th Division sustained a heavy loss in the death of its commander, Major-General Wing, C.B., a fine soldier, much liked by all ranks. Major-General A. B. Scott also an artillery officer, succeeded Major-General Wing in command of the Division.

On October 4th the Battalion was subjected to a good deal of shelling, 2 men being killed and 6 wounded. Water, as has been said, could only come up at night, and as most of the men were then out on working parties it was difficult to supply them. On the 5th a battery in D Company's trench was heavily shelled, with the result that 2nd Lieut. A. J. Hastings and 2 men were killed and 9 wounded. At about 6 p.m. the 37th Brigade moved northwards, taking the place of the 3rd Guards Brigade, east of Vermelles. "The Buffs" and Royal West Kent Regt. went into the front line south of the Hohenzollern Redoubt, and the 7th Battn. East Surrey into support, in the old German fire trench, with its right resting on the Hulluch–Vermelles road. The interest aroused by occupying a German trench was discounted by the inconvenience of being so closely packed. The dugouts were found to be very deep and apparently perfectly safe, but there were very few of them.

The difficulty of the position now held by the Guards and 12th Divisions was that the Hohenzollern Redoubt which had been recaptured by the Germans after the 2nd Battn. East Surrey and Royal Fusiliers had ceased to garrison it, not only enfiladed the trenches, but could also take them in reverse. Hard work continued throughout the night of the 6th, communication trenches facing north being converted into fire trenches to meet attacks from that direction. Wiring with German material was also carried out: it was found to be of excellent quality and could be set up without any noise. The 7th October was a quiet day, but Lieut. A. R. B. Owen, the Battalion Transport Officer, was wounded close to the trenches.

At about 1 p.m. on the 8th October the Germans opened a heavy bombardment on all the trenches held by the Brigade, causing a good many casualties in the rearmost trench. These fell mostly on the 6th Battn. "Queen's," the loss of the 7th Battn. East Surrey being 1 killed and 12 wounded. At 6.15 p.m. an attack on a German trench known as Gun Trench (see sketch-map opposite), facing the centre of the Brigade line, was made by the Royal West Kent Regt., supported by two machine-gun teams of the 7th Battn. East Surrey, under Lieut. M. R. Gibson. The trench had been heavily shelled, but was not sufficiently damaged. The attacking party, mostly bombers, got a footing in the trench and bombed their way about half-way along it; but their supply of bombs running out, while the German supply was ample, they were driven out. Lieut. Gibson went forward with one machine gun to the trench and fired at the Germans from their own parapet, doing considerable execution. Lieut. Gibson and Cpl. Wellings were killed, and three of the crew were seriously wounded in performing this gallant action. The attack had to be abandoned, the Royal West Kent Regt. having lost over 100 men. The casualties in the 7th Battn. East Surrey were Lieut. M. R. Gibson and 2 men killed, Captain J. Wyatt and 20 men wounded. Lieut. Gibson was a most gallant officer and a great loss to the Regiment.

On October 9th the Battalion relieved the Royal West Kent Regt. in the front line, having Captain H. J. Dresser and Lieut. H. P. Devenish wounded during the relief. Captain Mackenzie-Penderel was admitted to hospital, and did not rejoin the Battalion. On the 10th and 11th there was a pretty constant bombardment of the trenches, 4 men being killed and 6 wounded.

The 12th was an unusually quiet day, the calm before the storm of October 13th, when the IV and XI Corps delivered an attack. In his despatch to the Secretary of State for War, dated 31st July, 1916, Lord French gives a very brief description of these operations, which consisted of an attack by the XI and IV Corps against Fosse 8, the "Quarries" and the German trenches on the Lens–La Bassée road. He states that the objective of the 12th Division (XI Corps) was the "Quarries," and that at nightfall of the 13th October (the day of the attack) one battalion of this Division had gained the south-westerly edge of the "Quarries." This battalion was the 7th Battn. East Surrey. It should be added that the 12th and 46th Divisions formed the XI Corps, while the 1st Division belonged to the IV Corps.

The preliminary bombardment opened at 12 noon on 13th October, and at 2 p.m. the 1st, 12th and 46th Divisions advanced to attack their several

# THE CAPTURE OF GUN TRENCH

objectives, the capture of which would straighten the line and diminish enfilade fire. The result of the attack may be indicated very briefly, as our interest is concentrated on one battalion. The 46th Division took part of the Hohenzollern Redoubt, but could not complete its task. The 1st Division took their objective, the line of the Lens–La Bassée road, but subsequently lost the northern portion of it, opposite Hulluch. The 12th Division took the north-west corner of the "Quarries," but failed to take the line from the "Quarries" to Gun Trench.

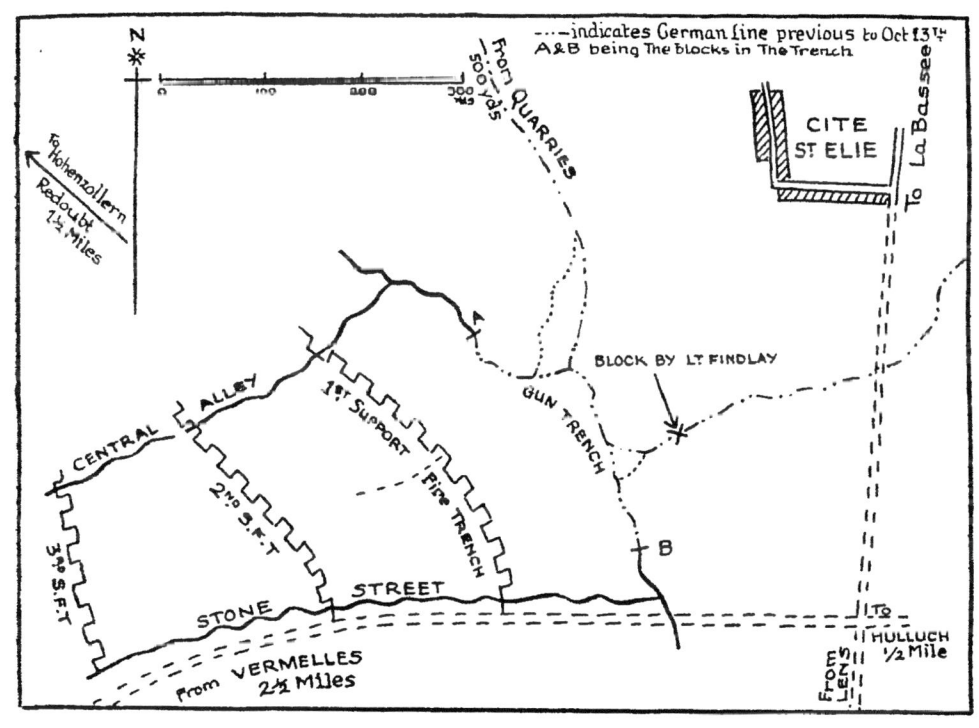

THE 7TH BATTALION AT GUN TRENCH.

The 7th Battn. East Surrey took and held Gun Trench, working out their task as follows:—

At 2 p.m. two platoons of B Company, led by Lieut. J. S. Hewat, made a frontal assault on Gun Trench while bombing parties attacked it from both flanks. The frontal attack got in at once, the Germans running as soon as B Company approached the parapet. A Company, under Captain V. Tomkins, in two lines at fifty yards' interval, followed up, but came under heavy machine-gun fire in the open and suffered severely. The survivors of the company, led most gallantly by Sergt. F. H. Martin, followed up the northern bombing party. Behind A Company came bombers of C Company, under Lieut. J. L. Findlay, their duty being to clear and block for 100 yards the German communication trench to Cité St. Elie. This having been accomplished C Company advanced from its position in second support to the captured trench, and reinforced the garrison, principally on the right. Reinforcements being again quickly necessary D Company went up from the third support trench, followed by Captain Dawson's company of the Royal West Kent Regt. There was much bombing on both sides, and our men suffered a good deal from enfilade fire from the trenches, leading to the "Quarries"; but they stoutly held on to their capture, and did not require further reinforcements though these were brought up in readiness. The night passed fairly quietly, and at 4.30 a.m. on October 14th the companies in the captured trench were reorganized. This was completed by 6 a.m., a German counter-attack on the left being repulsed during the process. The conduct of the men of the 7th Battn. East Surrey in this, their first fight, was very fine; although for five days prior to the enterprise they had been subjected to a heavy bombardment, they attacked with the greatest dash a position which had already successfully resisted the assaults of four other battalions. As a result of their attack the East Surrey men practically annihilated the defenders of Gun Trench, capturing sixteen prisoners, a machine gun and three trench mortars.

The casualties in the capture of Gun Trench were heavy. Captain V. Tomkins, Lieut. T. S. G. Brasnett and 56 N.C.O.'s and men were killed, Lieuts. G. N. Knight and R. B. Marshall and 156 other ranks were wounded, and 33 were reported missing, all no doubt killed or wounded. Captain Tomkins was a fine soldier, and his loss was much regretted in the Battalion.

In the evening of the 14th October the Battalion was relieved by the 11th Battn. Middlesex Regt. and went into billets at Noyelles les Vermelles. The 15th was a day of very welcome rest. Major-General Scott visited the Battalion and told Lieut.-Colonel Baldwin that it had done magnificently. He also conveyed the congratulations of the Corps Commander. In recognition of their services at Gun Trench, Major A. H. Wilson was awarded the Distinguished Service Order; Lieuts. J. L. Findlay and J. S. Hewat the Military Cross; Sergts. F. H. Martin and T. S. Miles, Cpl. F. G. Evans, Lce.-Cpls. F. V. Ritchie and S. Wallis, and Pte. G. Nunn the Distinguished Conduct Medal; Sergt. R. Berry, Lance-Sergt. B. Hanscombe, Lce.-Cpl. A. Saunders, and Pte. A. Woods the Military Medal. The Commanding Officer, the Adjutant (Captain E. H. J. Nicholls) and the Quartermaster (Lieut. G. Rowe) were mentioned in despatches.

A draft of 105 men joined on the 17th October, but the Battalion was still 200 under establishment. There was also a deficiency of 13 officers; and among the wounded were the Regimental Quartermaster-Sergeant, all four Company Sergeant-Majors and 16 other sergeants. On October 19th the Battalion moved into billets at Vaudricourt, where it remained for a week doing steady training. On the 24th a draft of 70 men arrived under Captain L. D. Scott, with 4 2nd Lieutenants who had been left in England as supernumerary officers when the Battalion went abroad.

On October 26th the Battalion marched to Vermelles and took over the trenches at the Hohenzollern Redoubt from the 4th Battn. Grenadier Guards, the 12th Division having taken over the Corps front. The Battalion finished the month in the trenches, sustaining a good deal of shelling by day and working hard at night. Casualties were fortunately light, only 3 men being killed and 2 wounded.

So ended a very strenuous month, which left the Battalion full of confidence as regards meeting future calls on its courage and discipline. The casualties during the month had been:—*Killed*: 4 officers and 102 other ranks. *Wounded*: 6 officers and 251 other ranks. The strength on the 31st October was 23 officers and 891 other ranks.

The Battalion was relieved in the trenches by the 8th Battn. Royal Fusiliers on the 1st November in pouring rain, and went into Divisional Reserve at Sailly-Labourse, about three miles behind the line. The 12th Division had been transferred to the I Corps, commanded by Lieut.-General Hubert Gough. In one respect this was an unfortunate change, as the Division was about to be given a rest of twenty-four days by the XI Corps, whereas the I Corps had all its three divisions in the front line, so a prolonged rest was out of the question. The Battalion rested on the 2nd November, and on the 3rd practised the assault on trenches dug to resemble those near the Hohenzollern Redoubt. This valuable practice was repeated on the 6th, on which day General Sir Douglas Haig conferred its first decoration on the Battalion. This was a Croix-de-Guerre granted to Cpl. F. G. Evans for conspicuous gallantry and good service on October 13th.

On November 7th the Battalion relieved the 7th Battn. Norfolk Regt. in the front line. The trenches were heavily shelled on the 8th and 9th and were a good deal damaged by recent rain, but casualties were almost nil. In the morning of the 10th the Battalion was relieved by the 6th Battn. "Queen's," and was quartered in cellars in Vermelles, remaining there until the 13th November, but getting little rest, as incessant fatigue parties were required to work on the neighbouring trenches owing to the wet weather. On the 13th the Battalion returned to the trenches taking over a sub-sector further south than the Kaiserin Trench, its last charge. After two quiet days the Battalion was relieved here by the 6th Battn. "Queen's" and went into Brigade support, two companies being in the second and third support lines, and Headquarters and the other two companies in Lancashire reserve trenches.

On the 17th November the Battalion was relieved by the 9th Battn. Essex Regt. and went back to its old billets at Sailly-Labourse, where it remained quietly till the 22nd, on which day the 37th Brigade marched to rest billets about Lillers. The weather was very fine, frosty with a bright sun. The distance was eighteen miles, but not a man fell out, which was very creditable after nearly six months in the trenches. The pretty little village of Ames, lying in a valley, was allotted to the Battalion, who found themselves comfortably billeted and welcomed by the inhabitants. Here the remainder of the month was passed pleasantly, and by the 29th November a rifle range had been constructed and musketry training had begun. The casualties during the month were 2 men killed and 10 wounded.

The first week of December passed comfortably at Ames. On the 8th the Battalion marched to Busnettes, distant about six miles; and on the 9th to Béthune. On the 10th trenches near Givenchy-lez-la-Bassée were taken over at night, the relief being a difficult one to carry out. The 37th Brigade put two battalions in the front line ("Buffs" and 7th Battn. East Surrey), with the "Queen's" in support and the Royal West Kent Regt. in reserve. The front held by the Battalion was known as "The Warren" and "The Marches," with Headquarters at "Windy Corner," in a house which was shared with the "Queen's." The enemy was fairly active with machine-gun fire, but otherwise the sector was a quiet one. On December 13th the Battalion was relieved by the Royal West Kent Regt. and went into Brigade reserve at Le Quesnoy. After a day of rest on the 14th the Battalion was replaced here by the 6th Battn. Royal Berkshire Regt., and went into Divisional reserve at Essars, nearer Béthune.

On the 19th the Battalion relieved the 8th Battn. Royal Fusiliers in the trenches near Festubert. Here the front line consisted of islands which were the dry spots in what had once been a trench. There was no communication with the rear except over the open, and of course no lateral movements were possible. The two half-companies in front were therefore relieved every twenty-four hours from Rue de l'Epinette, in the "Village Line." On the 21st the enemy's guns were successfully drawn by a line of fires into shelling an abandoned trench; and on the 22nd a gas attack in front of Givenchy was carried out by our troops, but apparently the Germans knew what was coming. On the 23rd December the Battalion was relieved by the Royal West Kent Regt., and went into Brigade support at Rue de l'Epinette. The men were quartered in ruined houses and were fairly comfortable. On the 24th the British guns kept up an incessant fire, perhaps as a hint that Christmas was not to be used for attempted fraternization; and to avoid any mistake on the subject this was continued on the 25th.

The 26th was uneventful, and on the 27th the Battalion was relieved by the 6th Battn. Royal Berkshire Regt. and went back into Divisional Reserve at Essars, remaining there quietly until the last day of the year, when it took over the Givenchy trenches from the 9th Battn. Royal Fusiliers. At midnight all our field batteries fired salvos to announce the New Year to the Huns, after which all was quiet.

The month had been a very quiet one and casualties slight: 4 other ranks killed and 6 wounded. The health of the Battalion had remained surprisingly good, when it is remembered that the men in the front line had frequently to stand up to their waists in water. The strength on December 31st was: officers, 30; other ranks, 1048.

The Diary for the New Year begins with the following item: "A quiet day. Last night we shot 6 German revellers. They were quite drunk and wandering about on the top of a crater." Lieut.-Colonel Baldwin went home on ten days' leave, and Major Wilson assumed command of the Battalion. On the 2nd January there was a heavy bombardment on both sides, the German fire doing little damage. In the evening the Battalion was relieved by the Royal West Kent Regt. and went into Brigade Reserve at Le Quesnoy.

After a day of rest the Battalion relieved the West Kent Regt. at Windy Corner on the 4th, and had 9 casualties from rifle grenades. On the 5th

# RETURN TO THE HOHENZOLLERN REDOUBT FRONT

the enemy shelled Le Plantin all day. The Battalion had 1 man killed and 4 wounded by shells, and also 4 more casualties from rifle grenades. On January 6th the Battalion was relieved in the trenches by the West Kent Regt. and went into the village line. After three days in the village line, during which it was heavily shelled, the Battalion was relieved by the Berkshire Regt. and moved into Brigade Reserve at Essars on January 10th, remaining there until the 13th, on which day it relieved the 8th Battn. Royal Fusiliers in the trenches in front of Rue de l'Épinette.

After three fairly quiet days here the Battalion was relieved by the 22nd Battn. Royal Fusiliers on the 17th and, as the 12th Division was now being withdrawn from the line to rest, marched to Bellerive, near Gonnehem, for the night. On the 18th a further move was made to billets near Lillers, at La Pierrière, which proved to be mostly under water. The billets, too, were very crowded, and were the worst yet allotted to the Battalion in France.

The Battalion remained training at La Pierrière until January 30th, but from the 26th to 29th inclusive could do little useful work, as it was held in readiness to march at two hours' notice in case of a German attack in force, which was threatened along the front of the I and IV Corps.

On January 30th Divisional manœuvres, which had been postponed in consequence of the situation mentioned, began and the 37th Brigade marched nineteen miles to St. Hilaire. On the 31st the Division returned to La Pierrière, the 37th Brigade forming the advance guard. The casualties in January had been 1 man killed and 30 wounded. The strength on January 31st was 33 officers, 1030 other ranks.

The 1st February was a quiet day, devoted to cleaning up and resting, and the next three days were devoted to training. On February 5th the Battalion marched to Ham-en-Artois and went into billets. Brigadier-General Fowler gave up the command of the Brigade and went to England. The Battalion remained at Ham until the 15th February, finding itself in much better circumstances than at La Pierrière. On February 4th, Major C. James was invalided to England and was unable to rejoin. On the 10th, Major-General Scott, commanding 12th Division, presented medal ribbons to the officers and men already mentioned who had been awarded decorations for conspicuous gallantry at the capture of Gun Trench, and cards to men who had been mentioned in despatches.

On February 15th the Battalion marched to Béthune and went into billets in the Tobacco Factory, where it was inspected on the 17th by Brigadier-General A. B. E. Cator, who had been appointed to command the 37th Brigade. On the 20th the Battalion went to Sailly-Labourse, and on the 21st returned to the Hohenzollern Redoubt front, taking over the following trenches: "Mud Trench," "Sticky Trench," "Hog's Back," "West Face" and "Kaiserin"; also Northampton Trench, the first support line (see sketch-map on page 150). The night was quiet.

On the 22nd the enemy's snipers were very active, but one posted on the "Hog's Back" crater, who had previously been very troublesome, was shot by Cpl. Rule, and his small "fort" was destroyed by our trench mortars. The

## 150 IN THE TRENCHES FACING HOHENZOLLERN REDOUBT

Battalion was in the front line until relieved by the 6th Battn. Royal West Kent Regt. on the 24th February, when it went to the reserve line. There had been no great artillery activity, and casualties had been very light. The Battalion remained in the reserve trenches until the 29th February, when it was relieved by the 8th Battn. Royal Fusiliers and marched back to Béthune. The casualties during the month were 4 other ranks killed or died of wounds and 8 wounded.

The strength on the 29th February was 33 officers, 1003 other ranks.

The Battalion remained quietly in its billets in the Tobacco Factory until the morning of March 4th, when it was moved hurriedly up to Sailly-Labourse preparatory to relieving the 6th Battn. Royal Sussex Regt. on the Hohenzollern

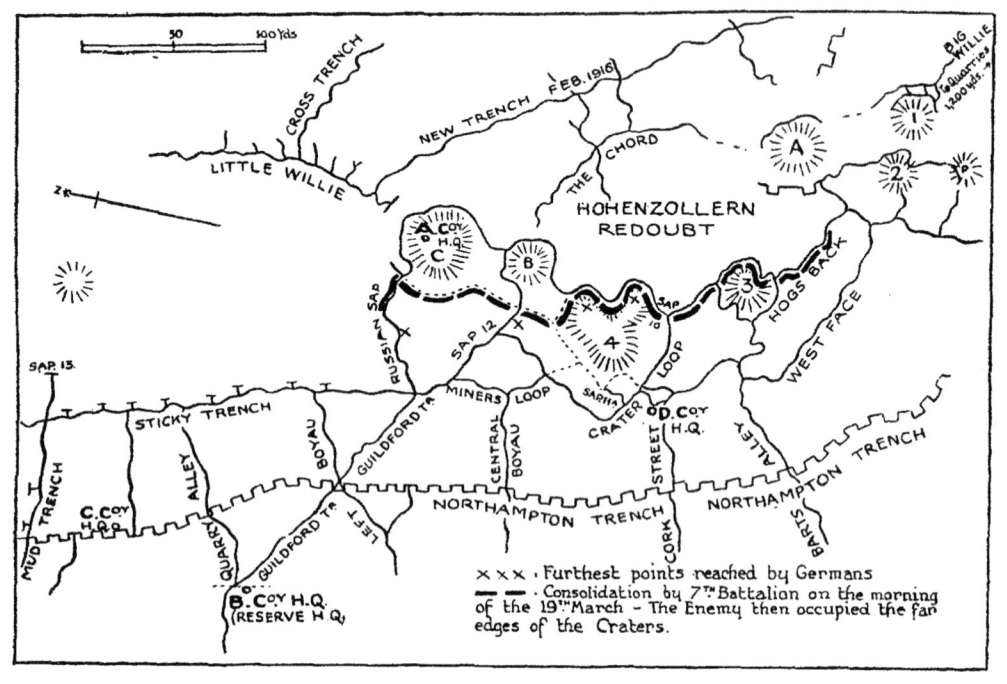

THE 7TH BATTALION AT THE HOHENZOLLERN REDOUBT, MARCH, 1916.

Redoubt front, where a German attack had caused heavy casualties. The relief was carried out on the 5th, and the front line was found to be considerably altered owing to a large number of mine craters in front of and in the enemy line. On the 6th the craters and trenches were all heavily bombarded by the enemy, and at midnight he exploded a mine to the right of the Battalion's position.

On the 7th the 6th Battn. "The Buffs," next on the right to the Battalion, made an attack with the object of taking the line of craters styled the "Chord," but the Germans attacked at the same moment and a deadlock ensued. In connection with this fight the following anecdote is of some interest: During the day Pte. J. Casey, who had joined the 7th Battn. East Surrey after previously serving with the 1st Battalion, was reported "missing, believed killed." He

## THE DEFENCE OF THE CRATERS

rejoined, however, two days later with a note from the Adjutant of "The Buffs" saying that he had rendered them gallant assistance in their bombing attacks. It appears that Pte. Casey had gone off on the 7th to join "The Buffs" in their fight, and at the end of one of the bombing attacks he and a Bavarian were seen standing on their respective parapets throwing stones at one another after having exhausted their supply of bombs.

Between 8 p.m. and 10.30 p.m. on the 7th the enemy made three successive attacks on Crater C, held by A Company 7th Battn. East Surrey, under Captain Richards. All the attacks were repulsed by the garrison of the crater. Communications were good and our guns gave effective assistance. All the lines held by the Battalion were heavily bombarded. Russian Sap, leading to Crater C, was nearly filled in; and Northampton Trench was made almost impassable.

On March 8th the Battalion turned on every available man to repair the trenches, but the work was much interfered with by the German guns. In the afternoon the Battalion was relieved by the 6th Battn. "Queen's" and moved into the reserve trenches. The 9th was a quiet day, carrying parties being found for bombs and rations to the front line; and on the 10th the Battalion relieved the 6th Battn. "Queen's" there in the afternoon. During the night the enemy tried to bomb a post in C Crater, but was easily driven off. The Battalion remained in the front line until the 13th March, the enemy showing great activity all the time, constantly sending over trench-mortar bombs, aerial torpedoes, etc. He was also very active in mining and trenching, and apparently formed a new front line facing the "Chord." In the afternoon of the 13th the Battalion moved to the reserve line, leaving one company in Alexandra Trench in the front line.

On the 15th the reserve trenches were shelled for a short time, and on the 16th the Battalion returned to the front line, taking over the craters, "West Face," etc., from the 6th Battn. "Queen's." On March 17th the Battalion's snipers effectively stopped a German trench gun and also claimed four direct hits on German snipers. On the 18th March the enemy shelled the trenches continuously with 4.2 howitzers and field guns, and at 5.30 p.m. opened a heavy bombardment on the craters, front line and support line. This was the prelude to a heavy attack on all the craters held by the 7th Battn. East Surrey and by the 6th Battn. "The Buffs" on its right. The disposition of the Battalion at the time was as follows: A Company, under 2nd Lieut. L. T. E. Case, held Craters 4, B and C. On the left of A was B Company, under Lieut. H. H. E. Henson, extending as far as the junction of Quarry Alley with Sticky Trench. C Company, under Captain J. L. Findlay, held the remainder of Sticky Trench and Mud Trench. D Company, under Captain L. D. Scott, was on the right of A as far as Bart's Alley. Each company had two platoons in Northampton Trench, and all communication trenches were picketed with bombing posts.

Ten minutes after the bombardment opened all wires had been cut with the exception of those in front of B Company and "the Quarry." At 5.50 Cpl. F. Cushion (A Company) brought a message to Battalion Headquarters saying that C and B Craters were being "badly smashed," and Lieut.-Colonel

Baldwin at once ordered B Company to send a platoon to reinforce C and B Craters, and D Company to send a platoon to 3 and 4 Craters. Cpl. Cushion had volunteered to face what seemed certain death in order to carry his message, and after delivering it he started to return to duty in the front line, but was severely wounded on the way.

At 6.20 p.m. the enemy exploded two mines in the crater line, and shortly afterwards was using "tear" shells freely in and behind our line. At about 7 p.m. Captain Scott, who rendered distinguished service during these operations, reported that the enemy had occupied No. 4 Crater; but at 7.50 he informed Battalion Headquarters that his company (D) had bombed them out of it. A little earlier two platoons of the "Queen's" had been sent up to reinforce West Face, and by half-past eight there was a lull in the attack. The enemy appeared to be consolidating the ground he had gained, and the front line, under Captain Scott, was also consolidating round No. 4 Crater and up to B Crater.

Shortly after midnight orders were issued to Captain Cannon, 6th Battn. "Queen's," to make a counter-attack with the two platoons of the "Queen's" and half B Company 7th Battn. East Surrey, with the East Surrey bombers under Lieut. V. P. Knapp, and to consolidate on the near lip of all the craters. The attack was carried out in due course and was successful; by 3.45 a.m. on March 19th all available men were busy consolidating the position. Pioneers arrived an hour later, but not in time to complete the task.

On March 19th the 37th Brigade was relieved in the line by the 35th Brigade, and the Battalion moved to Sailly-Labourse. Its losses during the very severe fighting between the 7th and 18th March were: *Killed or mortally wounded:* Captain L. J. Jones and Lieut. L. H. F. Robinson (attd. B37 Trench Mortar Battery) and 59 other ranks. *Wounded:* Lieut. H. Gadsby, 2nd Lieuts. Wallis, C. W. Beadle, D. J. Deslandes, J. M. Leahy, G. T. Wilkes and 216 other ranks. *Missing:* 22. Captain L. J. Jones, a very gallant and popular officer, had but recently joined for duty on recovery from a severe wound received in August, 1915.

On March 20th and 21st the Battalion was engaged in reorganizing after its severe strain and losses, and on the following day it moved to billets in Béthune, where the next four days were spent in quiet. On the 27th the 37th Brigade relieved the 36th Brigade in the line, taking up the sector to the south of its last position. The Battalion was posted at Vermelles as Brigade Reserve. On the 29th a welcome draft of 101 men, under Lieut. R. B. Marshall, who had been wounded on the 13th October, 1915, joined the Battalion. Most of the men had already served in France or Flanders with the 1st or 2nd Battalion.

On March 30th the Battalion relieved the 6th Battn. Royal West Kent Regt. in the front line. This day and the 31st were quiet days, but at 7.15 on the evening of the 31st the enemy exploded three mines which shattered the neighbouring trenches, and simultaneously attempted to bomb from two existing craters on the right front. He was, however, bombed back, and before morning all the damaged trenches had been consolidated. About thirty casualties were caused in the Battalion by the explosions and subsequent fighting.

Except for continuous work all day in clearing out the saps and repairing damage done to the defences the 1st April was uneventful. Sapping out to the new crater was continued during the night, and good progress was made. The 2nd was on the whole a quiet day, and on the 3rd the Battalion was relieved by the West Kent Regt. and moved to the support line. Lieut.-Colonel Baldwin went on short leave on April 4th, and Major Wilson assumed temporary command.

On April 6th the Battalion relieved the West Kent Regt. in the front line, and remained on duty there till the 10th. This period of duty was not eventful, but there was considerable artillery activity on the 8th, 9th and 10th. On the latter date the Battalion moved into Brigade Reserve at Annequin, whence on the 11th Major Wilson went home for an Investiture at Buckingham Palace, Captain B. G. F. Garnett taking over temporary command. The last-named officer, it may be mentioned, had formerly commanded the 4th Battalion for four years, but voluntarily rejoined as a captain.

On the 14th the Battalion moved to its old billets in the Tobacco Factory at Béthune, and after two quiet days there relieved the 8th Battn. Royal Fusiliers as left reserve at the Hohenzollern Redoubt, with the Royal West Kent Regt. in front. The next three days are described in the Diary as "quiet and wet," and on April 21st the Battalion relieved the West Kent Regt. in the front line. On April 22nd a successful mine was exploded near C Crater. It rained hard all day and the trenches were getting into a very bad state, which caused heavy work for the men.

The 23rd and 24th April were fairly quiet days during which much progress was made in the strengthening of the position. Next day the 12th Division's tour of duty in the line opposite the craters of the Hohenzollern Redoubt came to an end. The two months during which the tour had lasted had been a period of hard fighting of a nature that tried the strongest nerves. When the Division took over that part of the line there were about five mine craters, and when it handed over there were at least thirty. The men occupying the trenches knew that at any moment a new mine might send their trench and them up in the air, and in the defence of the mine craters they were harassed by the continuous fire of the heaviest trench mortars. Small wonder, then, that an eye-witness has described one of these crater fights as a veritable inferno. How the gallant conduct of the 7th Battn. East Surrey in the defence of the craters was recognized is shown by the following list of decorations awarded:—

*Military Cross:* Captain L. D. Scott and 2nd Lieut. C. W. Cook.

*Distinguished Conduct Medal:* Company Sergt.-Major W. T. Palmer; Sergt. R. W. Burgess; Cpl. F. Cushion, Ptes. W. J. Giles, W. Hewitt and C. Venables.

*Military Medal:* Company Sergt.-Major C. Curtis; Cpls. W. Rule and J. G. Williams; Lce.-Cpls. W. Plant, A. Saunders and G. Searle; Ptes. E. H. Edwards, F. C. Fox, E. F. Lunn, A. E. Turner and A. Woods.

*Mentioned in Despatches:* Lieut. and Quartermaster G. Rowe and Pte. W. Lobar.

In consequence of the withdrawal of the 12th Division from the line, the 7th Battn. East Surrey was relieved on the morning of the 25th by the 12th Battn. Highland Light Infantry and marched six miles in great heat to Noeux-les-Mines, a trial after four sleepless nights and the heavy rain. At 2.5 p.m. the Battalion entrained for Lillers, whence it marched to Allouagne. The billets were only moderately good, but worse had been encountered. The remainder of the month passed quietly, though, owing to repeated attacks by the enemy about Loos, the Battalion was several times under orders to move at short notice. Owing to the heavy work that the Brigade had had during the last two months rest was allowed in the afternoons. A draft of 34 men arrived on the 29th April, half of whom were wounded men returned to duty.

The casualties during the month were 9 killed, 26 wounded and 1 missing. No officer casualty. The strength on 30th April was 37 officers and 998 other ranks.

May, 1916, which completed the Battalion's first year on active service, was entirely devoted to training in peaceful surroundings. The Battalion remained at Allouagne during the first week, carrying out training all the mornings and being left free in the afternoons, with the exception of instructional classes for N.C.O.'s and drills for marked men.

On May 8th the Battalion marched to Flechin, starting at 5 a.m. and arriving at 11 a.m., distance about fourteen miles. Flechin was in the First Army training area, and the ground was very good for the purpose, being hilly and containing a fair-sized wood. All the ground could be used, crops or no crops, an unusual advantage. Company, Brigade and Divisional training went on till the 20th, and from the 21st to the 27th most of the time was devoted to digging instructional trenches, an exact model of the existing British and German trenches near Festubert being constructed on a front of two miles. Having done its usual hard day's work on May 7th, the Battalion was unexpectedly ordered back to Allouagne, and, starting at once, arrived at its billets at 4.30 a.m. on May 28th. This sudden move was caused by an alarm of a coming big German attack on the Loos salient. Nothing, however, happened and the Battalion remained at Allouagne quietly until the end of the month, though kept under orders of readiness to move at short notice.

During its year of active service the Battalion had gone through much hard work, had shared in hard fighting and had suffered heavy losses. It was, however, in high spirits and full of confidence, having been proved and found to be eager in the attack and staunch in holding its ground. It was now largely composed of old soldiers, and was considered equal to any strain.

A summary of the year's casualties gives perhaps the best idea of the stern initiation to war of a battalion which had had the good fortune to share in no reverse:—

|   |   |   |   |   |
|---|---|---|---|---|
| *Killed* | Officers | 7 | Other ranks | 118 |
| *Wounded* | ,, | 18 | ,, | 630 |
| *Missing* | ,, | — | ,, | 58 |
| Total | ,, | 25 | ,, | 806 |

The 7th Battn. East Surrey had, while at Allouagne, the good fortune to be given another complete month of training and preparation for the coming operations on the Somme. During the first week of June the 37th Brigade was in "Army Reserve," in readiness to move at short notice, and on June 8th it was transferred to "Corps Reserve" and still held ready. On the 13th the Battalion was inspected by Brigadier-General Cator, who expressed himself as delighted by its appearance and smartness, which he said went beyond what he thought possible. On June 16th the Battalion entrained at Lillers at one o'clock, and reached Amiens about 9.30 p.m. An hour later it marched off through Amiens to Flesselles, distant about twelve miles, getting in about 4 a.m. On the 19th and 20th the Battalion practised the attack on taped trenches, but this did not prove a satisfactory method. On the 21st the assault was practised. On the 22nd the Brigade carried out the attack, and on the 23rd the Division carried it out in the presence of General Sir Henry Rawlinson, Commanding the Fourth Army, and Lieut.-General Pulteney, Commanding III Corps.

June 24th was devoted to refitting and a rigid reduction of kit to the prescribed weight to be carried by Battalion transport. It was now known that the intended day of attack was June 29th, and on the 25th the preparatory bombardment of the German position opened. On the 27th the Battalion moved to St. Gratien and went into billets. The weather now became very wet, and the attack was postponed until July 1st, but the bombardment continued. On June 30th the Battalion marched to Bresle (four miles south-west of Albert), arriving there at about 3 a.m. on July 1st. There had been no casualties during the month of June, but 2 officers and 52 men had been admitted to hospital, leaving the Battalion on June 30th with a strength of 47 officers and 999 other ranks.

## CHAPTER XIII

SEPTEMBER, 1915, TO JUNE, 1916: THE 8TH BATTALION PASSES FIVE MONTHS IN THE FRONT LINE NEAR ALBERT; MOVES TO VAUX ON THE RIVER SOMME; AFTER A MONTH'S REST NEAR AMIENS, RETURNS TO THE FRONT LINE NEAR CARNOY, AND PREPARES FOR THE BATTLES OF THE SOMME, 1916.

THE close of September, 1915, saw the 8th Battn. East Surrey still in the trenches east of Albert. These trenches the Battalion held, alternately with the 7th Battn. "Queen's," until February, 1916. At first the reliefs between the two battalions took place every ten days, but as the winter advanced and weather conditions became more trying the periods of duty in the trenches were reduced to seven or eight days.

In the early days of October the Battalion while in the trenches suffered occasionally from a considerable variety of artillery fire to which no adequate reply could be made by the British guns owing to shortage of ammunition. After its relief on the 7th October the Battalion was inspected at Ville-sur-Ancre, where it spent its periods of "rest" in billets, by Sir C. Monro, Commander of the Third Army. At this parade General Monro presented to Lieut. C. Thorne and Pte. G. E. Hine the decorations awarded to them for gallant conduct on the 27th September, as already recorded.

October 17th found the Battalion again in the trenches, and early in the morning of the 20th October the Germans exploded a mine which cut off in a sap a party who were then gassed. Company Sergt.-Major A. Sterry, Sergt. A. Ashton and Ptes. C. Moore and W. P. Thurlow went under machine-gun fire to the mouth of the sap, unblocked the entrance and crawled in several times, rescuing Lieut. Eaton, R.E., and pulling out the entombed men until they themselves were overcome by the gas. They were all awarded subsequently the Distinguished Conduct Medal for their gallant conduct on this occasion. On the 21st October, Lieut. Soames was wounded in the head by a fragment of a trench-mortar bomb. The casualties during October were 5 other ranks killed and 1 officer and 6 other ranks wounded.

During November the Battalion was twice in the trenches, but no incident of special importance occurred, and there were only twelve casualties, including three men killed, during the month. Lieut.-Colonel Powell, D.S.O., left the Battalion on leave on the 17th November, and Major Irwin assumed temporary command.

The tour of trench duty which ended on the 18th December was marked by much activity in patrolling. Patrols were led with great enterprise by officers and N.C.O.'s, and did good service in examining various craters held by the Germans, locating their listening posts, testing their defences and exploring ground likely to be used in the event of an attack. On one occasion Sergt. H. G.

Ruffles, who was with a patrol commanded by 2nd Lieut. Jacobs, found his way to the German parapet, where he fired point-blank at the sentries. While making his way back Sergt. Ruffles was hit by a bullet which shattered his thigh. Notwithstanding this wound he crawled into cover, whence he was brought in by 2nd Lieut. Jacobs, who had twice searched the ground for him. For continuous gallantry on patrol duty Sergt. Ruffles received the Military Medal.

The 23rd December was observed as Christmas Day at Ville-sur-Ancre, as the Battalion was to return to the trenches on the 24th. The afternoon was a holiday, and after a good Christmas dinner 500 men were taken in motor lorries to the Divisional Cinematograph at Méricourt.

The first two days in the trenches were very quiet, but on the 26th our heavy artillery bombarded the south-west defences of Fricourt, apparently with good results. On December 29th the Tambour-du-Clos was heavily bombarded by the Germans for five hours in the afternoon. This was a very exposed work, the only thoroughly bad part of the sector, and was held by A Company, commanded by Captain T. A. Flatau. A similar bombardment took place on the 30th, the Germans being anxious to prevent our troops occupying the craters formed by mines exploded by us in front of the Tambour. The craters were, however, entrenched and held.

The Battalion was in its "rest" billets during the first week of January, 1916, practising various forms of attack, including a cutting-out expedition in the dark. On the 7th January the Battalion returned to the trenches, and on the night of the 8th five parties, totalling twenty-six men, started under Lieut. Frere to make their way across the craters to the German lines. A covering party under Lieut. Wingrave remained at the craters, and three men under 2nd Lieut. Pegg crossed the craters at a second point and bombed the German trenches before them.

Lieut. Frere's party was, however, held up by wire and were observed. Two men were wounded, but were brought in.

On the night of the 13th Captain Place took a patrol forward and, all being quiet, decided on examining the German trench. He crossed two German wire entanglements and went down five steps into the trench. Here the patrol was presently detected and fired on, one man being mortally wounded. On January 15th 1 man was killed and 2 wounded through the premature burst of the faulty cartridge of a rifle grenade. Later in the morning the Battalion was relieved and marched to its billets at Ville-sur-Ancre, where it remained until the morning of the 23rd January, on which date it returned to the trenches. Here it remained employed until the end of the month, with little incident to record. The casualties during December were 2 other ranks killed and 9 wounded.

After a week's rest in Ville-sur-Ancre, the Battalion returned to the trenches on the 8th February. No event of interest occurred till February 11th, on which day a number of patrols went out, both in the early morning and at night. In one of the latter Pte. Collis was shot through both legs by machine-gun fire when about 350 yards from our trench. He was dragged about 100 yards by Lce.-Cpl. W. Young, who had sent Pte. C. Castle, the other man of the patrol, back for help. Pte. Castle returned with 2nd Lieut. Hetherington, and Pte. Collis was then carried in under heavy fire. Lce.-Cpl. Young was subsequently awarded the Distinguished Conduct Medal, and Pte. Castle the Military Medal.

On February 12th, Lieut.-Colonel Powell assumed temporary command of the Brigade, and Captain and Adjutant O. C. Clare took command of the Battalion in addition to his own duties. The Battalion remained in the trenches, without further incident, until February 16th, when it proceeded to billets at Buire (4¼ miles south-west of Albert). The relief was carried out during very heavy rainstorms. February 17th was spent in bathing, and in cleaning and drying clothing and equipment. Major Irwin returned from leave and assumed command of the Battalion, being himself relieved in the command on the following day by Major Clifton. On February 23rd, Lieut.-Colonel Powell rejoined for duty. It had been ordered that the Battalion should return to the trenches on the 29th February, but no move took place.

On the 1st March the Battalion left Buire at 9.30 a.m. and marched past the Brigadier just outside the village. The midday halt was just outside Pont-Noyelle, and here the Battalion was inspected by Major-General Maxse. The Battalion then marched on to St. Gratien, where it billeted for the night. On March 2nd the Battalion marched to Allonville and went into billets. On March 5th A and B Companies marched to Flixecourt to join the 4th Army School; and on March 8th C and D Companies were ordered to Buire for roadmaking and defence work in the 7th Divisional area. The headquarters of the Battalion remained at Allonville. On the 16th March the Battalion concentrated at Corbie and on the following day marched to Etinehem Camp (two miles south-west of Bray), whence on the 19th it relieved the 18th Battn. Manchester Regt. in the trenches in Sub-sector Y.1, east of Vaux, on the River Somme.

On March 19th the enemy shelled Knowles Point at irregular intervals throughout the twenty-four hours, and on the morning of the 20th the shelling increased somewhat in violence. At 2.30 p.m. Knowles Wood was subjected to an intense bombardment lasting about a quarter of an hour; after this the hostile artillery fire lifted and formed a barrage to reinforcements. During the night a message was received at Battalion Headquarters that the Germans were attacking Knowles Point and Duck's Post, and Captain Paull was sent forward with two sections to reinforce Duck's Post. A platoon was ordered to hold the redoubt at the bridge-head, and a platoon at Vaux Wood was ordered to be in readiness to reinforce. The remainder of the Battalion in Vaux Wood and village stood to arms. The German attack was made by about 140 men, their object being to blow up the bridges of Vaux causeway. The East Surrey post held their ground successfully, and just before dawn on March 21st, Captain Pearce organized a counter-attack which cleared Knowles Wood, taking one unwounded prisoner and finding two dead Germans. The casualties of the Battalion in this affair were 1 man killed and 11 wounded, all belonging to C Company. For conspicuous gallantry in this action the Military Cross was conferred on 2nd Lieut. A. E. A. Jacobs; Distinguished Conduct Medals on Sergts. C. Beamish and J. Howard; and the Military Medal on Pte. J. Kenyon.

On March 22nd the enemy's artillery showed considerable activity, and two men were slightly wounded. On the 23rd one or more German guns were brought into Fries and shelling was renewed, Vaux village and Battalion Headquarters being the favoured target. A battalion orderly was killed on the road just outside Headquarters, which were in consequence moved early on March 25th into battle dugouts. During the remainder of the month no special incident occurred, but great vigilance was maintained by means of patrols.

During April, 1916, patrols, usually with an officer, went out every night except when the moonlight was too bright. On April 16th one of these patrols visited a German night post in order to verify a report by another battalion that it was still unoccupied by day. This proved to be incorrect, and as the patrol retired machine-gun fire opened on them and the French guide, Scholari, was killed. His body could not be removed, but Cpl. Ankertell and a lance-corporal of the 7th Battn. Royal West Kent Regt. dragged it under cover and removed all papers. The loss of Scholari, " a most excellent and brave soldier," was much felt by the Battalion. " He was a great favourite with our men, always being with them on any expedition that might be carried out, and he resented any patrol being sent out which did not include him " (Battalion Diary). Lieut.-Colonel Powell recommended that some English military honour should be conferred on him and given to his relatives.

On the 21st April, Major-General Maxse visited the Battalion's lines and expressed himself as well pleased with the work that had been done on the defences of Vaux village. On the 28th April, Vaux village and Vaux Wood were heavily shelled in the afternoon, C.S.M. Lane being killed and one man wounded. C.S.M. Lane was a great loss to the Battalion and to his company. He was a very good warrant officer and most popular.

For various acts of gallantry, mostly on patrol during the period of trench duty, the following N.C.O.'s and men, in addition to those already mentioned, received the Military Medal: Lce.-Sergt. C. Gathercole; Cpls. C. Anketell and W. A. Bone; Lce.-Cpls. L. Grossmith and E. Royal; Ptes. J. Collins, D. Mayes, F. Carter and C. A. Pearson.

As the 18th Division was now being withdrawn from the front line for six weeks' rest about Amiens, the 8th Battn. East Surrey was relieved on the 1st May by the 17th Battn. Manchester Regt. and marched to Etinehem Camp for the night. On May 2nd the Battalion marched to billets at Lahoussoye. On May 3rd a move was made to St. Sauveur, five miles north-west of Amiens, and on the following day the Battalion marched about three miles into billets at Picquigny. Here the Battalion remained for three weeks, the time being employed in a comprehensive and progressive course of training. On the 25th May the Battalion practised the attack in the morning and subsequently marched to Fourdrinoy, arriving about 5 p.m. On the 28th, Brigade Sports took place on ground midway between Picquigny and Fourdrinoy, the Battalion's representatives being very successful. At the end of the sports the prizes were presented by Major-General Maxse, the Brigadiers and some French Generals. The remainder of the month was devoted to practising various methods of attacking from trenches, in preparation for the coming British offensive now known as the Battles of the Somme, 1916.

The early days of June, 1916, were also devoted to active preparation for the coming attack on the German lines, and on June 3rd the Battalion was inspected at work by Generals Sir Douglas Haig, Sir Henry Rawlinson, commanding the Fourth Army, and Major-General Maxse and was afterwards reviewed. On the 6th June the Brigade practised the coming attack on trenches laid out to represent the German trenches about Montauban. The morning attack was carried out in a heavy rainstorm, and the attack was better performed in fine weather in the afternoon. In the Birthday Honours Lieut.-Colonel H. G. Powell, D.S.O., was appointed a Brevet Major in the Reserve of Officers.

As the 18th Division was now returning to the front line the Battalion entrained at Picquigny on the 9th June at 1.30 p.m. and arrived at Méricourt two hours later. Waiting until dark, the Battalion marched to Bray and billeted there for the night. On the 10th June the Battalion relieved the 10th Battn. Essex Regt. in Sub-sector A.1 near Carnoy, opposite the German trenches in front of Montauban, the relief being carried out without casualties. On the following day the enemy shelled the support trenches, a large dugout being blown in on the right, when 3 men were killed and 5 wounded. June 12th was quiet in the morning, but shelling took place in the afternoon. No material damage was done to the trenches and they were quickly repaired. On the 13th the morning was again quiet, but at night an intense bombardment of the front line started, which lasted about an hour. This fire was answered by our artillery, and unfortunately some of the British gun fire went short and caused a number of the casualties in the battalion. The killed and mortally wounded included 2nd Lieuts. W. A. Santler, G. Clarke and 9 men. There were also 42 other ranks wounded.

All ranks behaved with the utmost steadiness during the bombardment; A, B and C Companies in the firing-line lined the parapet and kept up a steady rifle and Lewis-gun fire on the German trench opposite. The evacuation of the wounded was helped by the 7th Battn. "Queen's," on the left, who had no casualties and placed their stretcher-bearers and dressing station at the disposal of the Battalion. The casualties above detailed were almost equally divided between the flank companies A and C, which were holding salients.

On the 15th June the Battalion was relieved in the trenches by the 7th Battn. Royal West Kent Regt., and from that date until the 19th dug three assembly trenches on the whole Brigade frontage. Each trench, that is, was about 800 yards long. The Battalion in the same period improved Coke Avenue and Merchiston Avenue. These were the two main communication trenches, and were about 700 yards and 400 yards long respectively. This was no light task, but was very quickly and efficiently carried out. On the 20th June the Battalion went into billets at Bray, leaving D Company and two platoons of A Company at Carnoy for fatigue duty. (See General Map of the Somme Battlefields facing page 198.)

On the 23rd June the Battalion relieved the 7th Battn. "The Buffs" in the trenches; A, B and C Companies taking over the trenches and D Company in reserve, being posted in Rail Avenue. Rail Avenue was a trench running east from Carnoy along the south side of the Carnoy–Trones Wood tramway. About 100 small shelters, roofed with semicircular sheets of corrugated iron and each capable of holding six men, had been dug in on the north side of the trench. This type of shelter was called a Lobin hut, after its inventor, Colonel Joly-de-Lotbinière, C.R.E., 18th Division. These huts were easily and quickly made, were comfortable and dry, and were of great value for housing troops required near the front line for digging parties.

On the 24th June the British artillery commenced the bombardment of the German positions, which continued daily until the infantry assault on the 1st July opened the Somme battle. At first the bombardment was chiefly confined to wire-cutting by field guns and mortars. The field guns were greatly assisted in their task of cutting the German wire by the 2-in. mortars, firing a 50-lb. bomb fitted with the new Newton fuse, which detonated as the bomb touched the ground and before it had time to sink below the surface. As a result none of the bomb was wasted in forming a crater, but burst laterally in all directions. The 2-in. mortars fitted with this fuse were extraordinarily effective, the wire not only being blown away, but the broken ends wrapped round the posts by the force of the explosion. Thanks to these mortars and to the R.F.A., the Battalion met with no wire at all during the assault.

It may be noted here that a large number of cylinders containing asphyxiating gas had been installed in the fire-trench in both the east and west salients, i.e. in the trenches held by C and A Companies. The intention was to release this gas as soon as possible, and every day orders were received that it would be released at such and such a time. As it turned out, the gas expert in the front line had constantly to report to Corps Headquarters that the wind was unfavourable, and the hour of release was postponed four or five hours, when the same thing occurred. To understand the effect of these orders and counter-orders on the troops in the front line it must be understood that, half an hour before the scheduled hours of release, the sandbags which had been built in on top of the cylinders to protect them had all to be removed, and all troops in the front line had to be withdrawn to a trench in the rear of it. Presently would come round the order postponing the hour of release, which meant that the men must at once be moved up again into the front line, and the sandbags all built up over the cylinders. This occurred twice and sometimes three times in the twenty-four hours for five consecutive days and nights, with the natural result that the men got very little sleep. Added to that were the facts that every man knew that the immediate result of releasing the gas would be to bring a heavy enemy barrage on to our trenches, and that gas cylinders are unpleasant things to have in one's trench at any time, being liable to be burst open by the enemy's shells or bombs. The tension caused by these circumstances and by the lack of sleep brought a heavy strain on a battalion ordered to hold the trenches for five days and to assault on the sixth. Unless all the conditions of the bombardment are thoroughly understood it is impossible to realize the endurance and courage of the men who carried out the assault of 1st July. Fortunately, owing to the postponement of the assault, they did in the end get two nights' rest before it took place.

On the 25th June the bombardment continued. On this day our "heavies" began shooting. It was observed and reported that the amount of heavy ammunition being used on the German positions opposite Sub-sector A.1 was very much less than that opposite the sector on our right, from which a brigade of the 30th Division was to assault. A fortnight later, when the Battalion occupied the German first- and second-line trenches immediately on the right of Sub-sector A.1, it was noticed that they had been most successfully pounded by our "heavies," whereas the German trenches opposite Sub-sector A.1 were very little damaged. This probably accounts for the fact that the 18th Division lost heavily during the assault, while the 30th Division suffered few casualties and met with a weak resistance. During the morning smoke bombs were lighted on the front-line parapet along the whole Corps front. It was a novel sight to see this vast volume of thick white smoke sweeping across to the German trenches. The enemy opened a brisk but harmless rifle and machine-gun fire. During the afternoon Lieut.-General W. N. Congreve, Commanding XIII Corps, went round the Battalion's lines.

On the 26th June the bombardment continued. The Battalion suffered heavy casualties on this day and on the two preceding days, both from our own and enemy fire. C Company in the east salient suffered most, partly owing to the fact that the 2-in. trench mortars were firing from positions close behind the company's fire-trench, and these the enemy searched for with 5.9-in. shells, which ultimately knocked out all but one of them, but not until they had completed their work of cutting the enemy wire. C Company was relieved during the afternoon by two platoons of D Company and were brought back to the support trench and Rail Avenue, but even there they suffered five casualties. During the night the headquarters of A Company, the left company, were most persistently shelled by one of our "heavies." This was reported several times, but it was found impossible to identify the offending battery until the following night, when the nuisance was stopped.

On the 27th June the bombardment continued. A platoon of D Company, under 2nd Lieut. E. C. Hetherington, attempted to raid Breslau Point at 10 p.m. They were spotted as soon as they left our trenches, but, in spite of heavy rifle and machine-gun fire, 2nd Lieut. Hetherington entered the enemy trench with twelve men, but found it filled with barbed wire. As he could not move in the trench, and could therefore do no good, he very wisely ordered his men to retire and got his platoon back to our lines with a loss of 1 man killed and 1 wounded. The latter was brought back with the party. It was only by extreme good fortune that this raid, which was planned and ordered by higher authority, escaped disaster. It was still quite light at 10 p.m., and the party was fired at before the greater part of it had even had time to climb out of our trench—a bad beginning, as the essence of successful raiding is surprise. In addition, the usual short hurricane bombardment prior to the raid had been cancelled, the result being that the enemy riflemen and machine gunners were at liberty to shoot at our men during both their advance and retirement without being interfered with by artillery fire. 2nd Lieut. Hetherington behaved with great courage and coolness, and was very fortunate in only losing one man.

During the morning of the 28th June, Lieut.-Colonel H. G. Powell handed over temporary command of the Battalion to Major A. P. B. Irwin and proceeded to Corps Headquarters, where he had been ordered to report himself as reserve Brigadier. Later in the day Major-General F. I. Maxse visited Battalion Headquarters and informed the Battalion that the assault had been postponed for two days. The Battalion was relieved that afternoon by the 7th Battn. " Queen's " and went back to dugouts in Billon Valley. During the last five days the enemy artillery had been extraordinarily quiet, the shelling being almost entirely confined to the east salient; but while this relief was in progress Coke Avenue and Battalion Headquarters were shelled for a short time with 4.2-in. shells. One N.C.O. was killed and two men were wounded during the relief.

While the Battalion had been in the trenches it had been called upon to furnish large carrying parties for the formation of dumps in the east and west salients. The dumps in the east salient were for the use of the Battalion, and contained iron rations, ammunition, bombs, rockets, flares, R.E. material, etc. The weather during this tour of duty had been fine on the whole, but on the night of the 28th/29th June it rained heavily, making the newly dug assembly trenches very wet. At this period the congestion of traffic on the Bray-Fronfay Farm–Carnoy road became worse and worse. It was the only good road, and it was no uncommon thing for a battalion's transport to have to wait three hours to get their place in the queue, and to take a further three hours to cover the three miles to Carnoy.

The 29th June was spent by the Battalion in Billon Valley. This day of rest and relief from strain was of the greatest value. What with the din of our own and the enemy's guns, the gas cylinders, the " P " bombs, attempted raids and incessant telephone messages, neither officers nor men had had any rest and very little sleep, and were badly in need of both. The day was hot and sunny, and the men lay about on the grass and slept most of the time. On the 30th June the Battalion moved off by companies during the afternoon to take up its battle positions in Sub-sector A.1. The day was warm and sunny, and there were no casualties. During the night B and C Companies removed all the wire in front of our trenches and ammunition, bombs, sandbags, flares, tools, etc., were issued.

## CHAPTER XIV

SEPTEMBER, 1915, TO JUNE, 1916: THE 9TH BATTALION ARRIVES IN FRANCE. IN THE BATTLE OF LOOS SUFFERS HEAVILY IN ACTION SOUTH-EAST OF HULLUCH. EIGHT AND A HALF MONTHS IN FLANDERS, IN THE TRENCHES NEAR ST. ELOI, NEAR HOOGE AND NEAR WULVERGHEM.

HAVING disembarked at Boulogne on the 1st September, 1915, the 9th Battn. East Surrey Regt. marched to its billeting area about Humbert, a village eighteen miles north-east of Montreuil-sur-Mer. Here it remained about a fortnight, spending the time in training, while parties of officers and N.C.O.'s were sent up to the front-line trenches to obtain an understanding of existing war conditions.

On the 20th September the 24th Division received orders to march that evening towards the front, but the move was postponed for some hours, and at 7 a.m. on the 21st the Battalion, with a strength of 30 officers and 901 other ranks, marched off from Humbert. The senior company commander, Major R. V. Bretell (an officer who had recently retired from the 1st Battalion after several years' service), left the 9th Battalion this day on promotion to the command of the 9th Battn. Suffolk Regt., which belonged to the 71st Brigade of the 24th Division. After moving off from Humbert the Battalion joined the remainder of the 72nd Brigade and made a march of about fifteen miles to Dennebroeucq. The weather was very hot and the road dusty, but billets were reached soon after midnight. There was a great shortage of water, particularly for animals. On the evening of September 22nd the march was resumed to Isbergues, about eighteen miles. The weather was equally hot, and, owing to the road being crowded, marching was slow, and consequently fatiguing. Isbergues was reached at about 2 a.m. on the 23rd, but the billets being very scattered, the companies took some time to settle down. In order to collect the Battalion it moved out later in the day, in heavy rain, a distance of about four miles to Berguette. Here it rested till the evening of September 24th, and at 6 p.m. had its last solid meal for over sixty hours. At 7 p.m. the 72nd Brigade marched for Béthune, distant about nineteen miles, and, arriving at about two the following morning, halted in the Rue de Beuvry. Arrangements had been made for breakfasts at about half-past four o'clock, but through an unfortunate order of a Staff Officer the transport was sent astray, and no food arrived.

A few words must first be said to explain the sudden move of the 24th Division to Béthune. The Battle of Loos, in which the 24th Division was about to play its part, was a remarkable episode from several points of view. For one thing, Field-Marshal Sir John French handled in it a much larger body of troops than any British General had previously commanded, either in peace or war; and, secondly, the battle, originally intended to be one of a number of subsidiary

## THE 9TH BATTALION IN THE BATTLE OF LOOS

attacks launched in the northern portion of the line of battle in order to aid the great French attack in Champagne, met with unexpected success, and even seemed likely for a time to result in a decisive victory.

The French southern attack, aimed at the very strong German positions on the heights east of Rheims, was opened on September 25th by the Fourth French Army. Simultaneously a northern attack was made by the Tenth French Army against the Vimy ridge, between Arras and Lens; while yet farther north the I and IV Corps of Sir Douglas Haig's First Army made the main British attack against Hulluch and Loos. Subsidiary British attacks were also made eastward from Ypres and about Neuve Chapelle.

Sir John French had in reserve, with other troops, the newly formed XI Corps, consisting of the Guards, 21st and 24th Divisions; and the attack of the 25th September having met with unexpected success, and the German General Staff being evidently in confusion, Sir John French placed the XI Corps at General Haig's disposal so that the success might be exploited to the utmost. The three divisions composing the Corps had been marched into the area of operations, but on the 25th September the Guards Division was somewhat farther away than the two New Army Divisions, and the latter were consequently first brought into action. On the 25th September the Battle of Loos had commenced at dawn, and the 24th Division being ordered to move up to the scene of action, the 9th Battn. East Surrey turned out of its billets in Béthune at 7 a.m. and was held in readiness to march at a moment's notice. After a long and wearisome halt in the street, the 72nd Brigade marched off at 11.15 a.m., via Beuvry, Sailly-Labourse and Annequin, to the Courant de Bully, a marshy rivulet just west of Vermelles. Arriving at this point at 3 p.m., the Brigade halted in the rain till about 4.30 p.m., when it moved on to Vermelles. Yet another advance brought the Brigade at 5.50 p.m. to the road junction 400 yards south of Le Rutoire Farm. From this point the Brigade advanced by compass-bearing, moving very slowly in consequence of the very heavy nature of the ground. At 6.50 p.m. the Brigade deployed into "artillery formation," and the slow advance continued under a scattered but regular shell fire from about Hulluch. The casualties were quite light. The 9th Battn. East Surrey was ordered to keep touch with the 8th Battn. Royal West Kent Regt. on its left and with a battalion of the 21st Division on its right. These orders were carried out, though with difficulty, and the Battalion kept its regular formation in spite of the difficulties of the advance. At 11.5 p.m. the left of the Brigade reached its point of direction, Lone Tree, and a few minutes later the West Kent and East Surrey crossed the German first-line system of trenches captured in the morning by the 7th Division (see sketch-map on page 167).

About this time the advanced scouts of the Royal West Kent Regt. reported that Hulluch was entirely in German hands, and Brigadier-General Mitford consequently ordered the Brigade to halt. The 9th Battn. East Surrey, in endeavouring to keep touch with the 21st Division, had spread out too far to its right, and was now ordered to close on its left and to dig itself in in two lines facing east and about half a mile south-west of the outskirts of Hulluch (FF in the sketch). The casualties in the Battalion so far were limited to 2nd Lieut. I. M. Johnson and two men wounded.

About midnight the rain ceased and the Battalion continued entrenching till near dawn, when a short retirement to the captured German second-line trench system was ordered. The Brigade remained halted in these trenches under a certain amount of shell fire which did no serious damage, until at 10 a.m. on September 26th the Brigadier received orders for an attack which was to commence an hour later.

Briefly, the orders received were as follows:—

1st Division to attack Hulluch.

72nd Brigade (with two battalions of the 71st Brigade and a Pioneer Battalion) to advance in a south-easterly direction past the southern outskirts of Hulluch and capture about 800 yards of German third-line trenches, which ran south from Puits No. 13 *bis*.

21st Division to prolong the attack of the 72nd Brigade to the right.

Brigadier-General Mitford disposed the force under his command as follows:—

*First Line.* 8th Battn. Royal West Kent Regt. on left; 9th Battn. East Surrey on right, and to maintain touch with the 21st Division.

*Second Line.* 8th Battn. "Queen's" on left; 8th Battn. "The Buffs" on right.

*Third Line.* 11th Battn. Essex on left; 9th Battn. Suffolk on right.

*Reserve.* 12th Battn. Sherwood Foresters.

Precisely at 11 a.m. all units of the 72nd Brigade jumped out of their trenches and advanced to the attack. The second line followed the first with from 400 to 500 yards' interval. The 9th Battn. East Surrey was on a two-company front, C and D Companies in first line, supported by A and B Companies. The distance from the German trenches was about 1700 yards. When the advance began there was no intensity of fire, but as soon as the Hulluch–Lens road had been crossed the artillery, rifle and machine-gun fire increased in volume, particularly from houses on the southern outskirts of Hulluch and from a trench lying close on the left of the advance and parallel to it. The line of advance was thus completely flanked at close range, and losses were unavoidably very heavy. Some snipers in the trees along the Hulluch–Lens road also caused many casualties in the Brigade, particularly among officers.

As the advance pressed steadily on, the 9th Battn. East Surrey, endeavouring to keep touch with the 21st Division as ordered, inclined somewhat to its right, leaving a gap between it and the 8th Royal West Kent Regt. This gap was at once filled by the 8th Battn. "The Buffs." At the same time the left of the West Kent suffered so heavily from the flanking rifle and machine-gun fire that the 8th Battn. "Queen's" pushed up to reinforce them, suffering the same fate. Brigadier-General Mitford then ordered the 11th Battn. Essex Regt. up to deal with the infantry and machine guns on the left, and this battalion did excellent service in the performance of the duty allotted to it.

## SOUTH OF HULLUCH

Shortly before noon the whole Brigade, in spite of heavy losses, reached the wire in front of the German third line, which proved to be a formidable obstacle. Though only made on the previous night, it was excellently constructed and from 15 to 25 yards deep. It was, moreover, quite undamaged by our artillery. Attempt after attempt was made to break through, but without success: a few strands of wire were cut here and there, but no practicable gaps could be made. While these attempts were in progress the Germans used bombs freely, and but little answer could be made, as at this time the British troops had but few bombs,

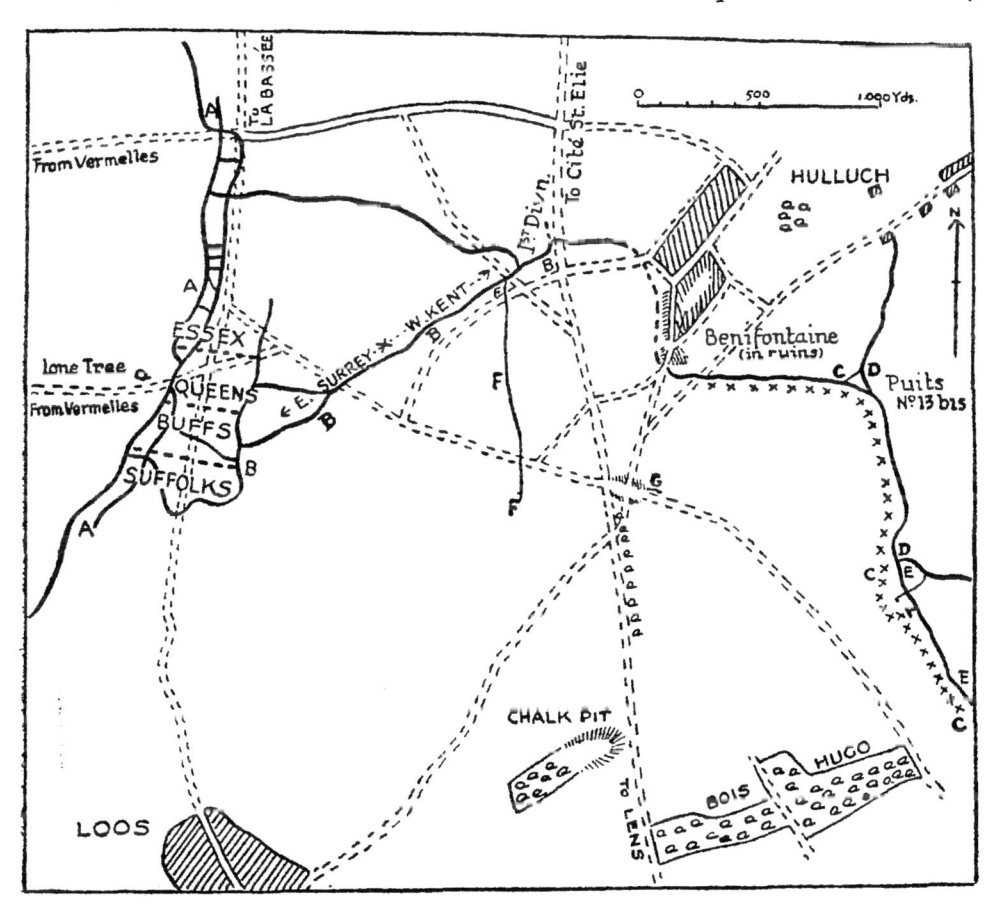

THE 9TH BATTALION IN THE ATTACK BY THE 72ND BRIGADE NEAR HULLUCH, 26TH SEPTEMBER, 1915.

A A = German first-line trench-system (captured during morning of 25th Sept., 1915).
B B = German second-line trench-system (from which the 72nd Brigade advanced to the attack at 11 a.m. 26th Sept.)
C C = German third-line trench-system.
D D = The objective of the 72nd Brigade.
E E = ,, ,, ,, ,, 21st Division.

x x x = Uncut German wire.
F F = Approximate line reached by 72nd Brigade at 1 a.m. 26th Sept.
- - - - = Approximate position of Battalions just before the advance to the attack.
G = Unfinished German trench manned by units of 72nd Brigade to cover the withdrawal.

and those of poor quality. After persisting for a long time in this hopeless attempt, which was now totally unsupported, as the divisions on either flank had not succeeded in reaching their objectives, the Brigade slowly fell back to the trenches from which it had advanced, where units at once set to work reorganising and preparing to meet counter-attacks.

The losses of the 72nd Brigade at Hulluch were very heavy, those of the 9th Battn. East Surrey amounting to 16 officers and 438 other ranks.

*The officers killed or mortally wounded* were: Major H. V. Welch (died of wounds 14th October, 1915, whilst a prisoner of war); Captains H. A. B. Dealtry, A. A. Collinson and C. E. Barnett; Lieuts. R. W. Elverson and A. C. P. Campbell; 2nd Lieuts. E. R. H. Bate, K. D. Murray and N. V. Coutts.

*Wounded:* Captains W. B. Birt (died 18th April, 1916, while a prisoner of war); B. A. Fenwick (prisoner of war) and D. P. O'Connor; Lieuts. J. H. S. Richards and S. W. Wills; 2nd Lieuts. D. G. O. MacLaren and E. M. Johnson.

It was the fortune of the Battalion to begin its war experience in an unsuccessful operation, in which its losses were very heavy. When all the circumstances in which it entered the Battle of Loos are considered—the long and trying march to the scene of action, the want of food and water and the unpromising nature of the attack, obvious to the youngest soldier—the staunchness of all ranks in the advance during the attack, and the steadiness of the Battalion in the final retirement, will be seen to deserve high credit. It is interesting to record that German officers who conversed with some of the wounded East Surrey officers who became prisoners spoke with the warmest admiration of the gallant advance of the Battalion.

Early in the morning of the 27th September (about 4 a.m.) the Battalion was relieved by a battalion of Guards and, with the rest of the Brigade, marched to bivouacs west of Vermelles. During the morning Brigadier-General Mitford visited the Battalion and expressed his satisfaction at the way in which the attack had been carried out. At 6 p.m. the 72nd Brigade marched to a new bivouac near Noeux-les-Mines, where it passed the night.

The Battalion rested all day on September 28th and entrained at 10.15 p.m. for Berguette, going into billets in that village and at Isbergues. The 29th and 30th September were occupied in refitting. 2nd Lieut. J. L. Vaughan (4th Battalion) arrived on the 29th and was appointed acting Adjutant, vice Captain O'Connor, wounded; and a draft of 30 men joined on the 30th.

The Battalion entrained on October 2nd for Godewaersvelde, marching thence to billets at Houtkerque. On the 3rd October a draft of 200 N.C.O.'s and men arrived from the 10th (Reserve) Battalion, and on the 7th another draft of 230 men joined from the 10th Battalion, making good the Loos casualties. The Battalion marched this day to Reninghelst, where Battalion training was taken in hand, combined with special instruction of machine gunners, bombers and signallers. On October 15th, Lieut.-Colonel F. L. Sanders handed over command of the Battalion to Captain C. T. Williams, and the Battalion marched from Reninghelst to Ouderdom Camp, south-west of Ypres. On the following day a draft of 50 men from the 10th Battalion joined. As will be seen from the succeeding pages, the Battalion, after its first experience of warfare in the Loos battle, had now before it eight and a half months of trench duty on the Flanders front, broken only by quieter periods in reserve or in rest behind the line.

On the 19th October, 1915, the Battalion undertook its first tour of regular duty in the trenches. Leaving its camp near Ouderdom at 3 p.m., the Battalion marched via Dickebusch and Kruisstraathoek to take over trenches U.24, U.25 and U.26, lying between the Bluff on the Ypres–Comines canal and St. Eloi. Two companies went into the firing line, a third company was in immediate support behind trench U.25, while the fourth company, together with Battalion Headquarters, was posted in the Spoil Bank dugouts.

The sector taken over was considered a quiet one, but it had serious disadvantages: the ground was very low-lying and badly drained, the trenches had been badly constructed, were not rivetted and were, moreover, overlooked by the German trenches, which were on higher ground. Battalion Headquarters and the reserve dugouts were very unhealthy, owing to the frequent mists which rose from the canal, and they were infested by innumerable rats, which popped in and out of the canal. During the relief Lieut. H. T. Barnett, the Battalion Lewis-gun officer, was killed and two men wounded.

On the above date Lieut.-Colonel H. V. de la Fontaine, who had been serving on the Staff as A.Q.M.G., I Corps, joined the Battalion and took over the command from Captain Williams. Lieut.-Colonel de la Fontaine had passed all his service in the Regiment and had done excellent work as a company commander and with the mounted infantry in the South African War, having been wounded and mentioned in despatches.

The tour of six days' duty in the trenches was chiefly employed in repairing the front-line and communication trenches, which were damaged by the considerable amount of rain which fell during that period. The enemy was fairly quiet, being content to snipe at night and to shell the communication trench from time to time. The casualties of the Battalion, in addition to those mentioned above, were 1 killed and 6 wounded.

On 25th October the Battalion, on being relieved, marched to Reninghelst, where it was accommodated in tents. This march of about fifteen miles in marching order was found very trying by a great number of the men, who had previously had little practice in wearing the equipment. The camp at Reninghelst was one of the worst in the district. It was pitched in a low-lying field, which recent rain had turned into a quagmire. Fortunately the parade ground was somewhat drier than the camp, and it was possible to give the men a certain amount of instruction. Owing to its very heavy losses at Loos, particularly in officers and N.C.O.'s, the Battalion was practically a new one, and all ranks were in great need of drill and training. Officers had been collected from various sources, and large drafts had been received from the 10th and 11th Battalions, so that neither officers, N.C.O.'s nor men knew one another or had been accustomed to working together. While numerically up to establishment, the Battalion was still without an Adjutant, a Quartermaster and an Orderly Room staff, and very few trained specialists remained.

However, through the energies of 2nd Lieut. Vaughan, who had taken over the duties of acting Adjutant, of the acting Quartermaster, of 2nd Lieuts. Hubbard and Rivers, who were appointed machine-gun officer and bombing officer respectively, things soon began to mend. Application was made to the Officer Commanding the 1st Battalion for a drill instructor, and he very kindly lent the services of Sergt. Hemmings for a month. This capable N.C.O. rendered invaluable service in instructing the newly promoted N.C.O.'s of the Battalion.

On the 27th October His Majesty the King came to Reninghelst to inspect the troops there. The Battalion was represented at the inspection by 2nd Lieut. F. G. Brown, 1 company sergeant-major, 2 corporals and 170 privates, who had all been present at the Battle of Loos. Later in the day, while inspecting another division, His Majesty unfortunately met with a serious accident.

The Battalion relieved the 8th Battn. "Queen's" in the same "U" trenches on the 30th October, and remained there for six days. Incessant rain again played havoc with the trenches. The main communication trench was partially destroyed, so that engineers' material and rations could only be brought up at night. The dugouts of the company in support collapsed entirely, so that the company had to be withdrawn to Spoil Bank, and the front-line parapet fell in in many places. Fortunately, the German trenches were in an equally bad condition, and the enemy were too busy repairing their own parapets to take much notice of our men when they exposed themselves to view. The drainage of the trenches was one of the chief difficulties. The ground in rear of the British trenches was so level that it was extremely difficult to find an outlet for the water which accumulated in them; and the problem was complicated by the fact that they received all the water pumped out of the German trenches.

It was only by working day and night that our men were able to prevent the whole of the front line from collapsing. They were so exhausted by their efforts that on the 4th November, when relieved by the 8th Battn. "Queen's," they had great difficulty in carrying out the long march to their camp at Reninghelst. Incessant rain had made the camp here, if anything, worse than before. Men now almost sank up to their knees in mud. However, a few huts built by prisoners in the Brigade, and a farm turned into a recreation room, made conditions somewhat more tolerable.

Symptoms of frostbite having made themselves felt, great care was taken to have all the men's feet well rubbed with anti-frostbite grease. This was the more necessary as the issue of gum boots in the trenches was still restricted to 200 per battalion.

On the 6th November news was received of the death of 2nd Lieut. Britts and Lce.-Sergt. Childs, as the result of an accident at the Army Grenade School at Terdeghem.

On the 9th November the Battalion again relieved the 8th Battn. "Queen's" in the "U" trenches, but on this occasion took over trenches U.27 and U.28 and handed over U.24 to another battalion. Three companies were now in the front line, the left of which rested on the Ypres–Comines canal, with the famous

Bluff immediately on the far side of it. Battalion Headquarters and the fourth company moved to the " Canal Bank " dugouts.

The following day, as Lieut.-Colonel de la Fontaine, Captain Williams and 2nd Lieut. Vaughan were passing a working party employed on the communication trench, the enemy suddenly opened fire on the working party with light field guns. Several men were killed, and Captain Williams was wounded. Beyond occasionally shelling the main communication trench and the reserve dugouts, the enemy was fairly quiet. The trenches were still much waterlogged, and all ranks had hard work in keeping them in order. The carriage of rations and of R.E. material from the Battalion dump at Château Langhof to the trenches entailed heavy labour. The rations and stores had to be carried along the muddiest of tracks for about a mile to Battalion Headquarters, thence for another mile at least through more mud to the front line. During the six days' tour in the trenches the casualties were two wounded, in addition to Captain Williams.

On the 14th November, when relieved by the 8th Battn. " Queen's," three companies of the Battalion moved into billets at Dickebusch, and the fourth company (A) occupied the dugouts at Spoil Bank, so as to be handy for furnishing working parties. On the following day the whole Battalion returned to the camp at Reninghelst, A Company not arriving till midnight, having been delayed by a heavy shelling of Château Langhof.

On the 19th November the Battalion was preparing to return to the trenches when the move was cancelled, as the 24th Division was ordered to proceed to rest billets on relief by another division. Never was news more welcome. The previous month had not been a pleasant one. The camp at Reninghelst, with its bare tents and inches of mud, was devoid of every comfort. The long, wearisome marches by night to and from the trenches through Dickebusch and Kruisstraathoek over *pavé* roads, or more often, owing to the enormous vehicular traffic, through the mud on either side of the road, were most exhausting. Finally, the trenches themselves, what with constant rain, the absence of dugouts and the need of continual repair, occasioned the greatest amount of discomfort.

When the 72nd Brigade had been relieved by the 9th Brigade in accordance with the above-mentioned orders, the Battalion, forming part of a composite brigade (two battalions of the 72nd and two of the 73rd Infantry Brigades), marched at 4 p.m. on the 20th November to Eecke, a distance of about ten miles. At Eecke, where the Battalion remained two days, the men were very comfortably billeted in large barns with plenty of straw. On the 22nd the march was continued over the steep hill at Cassel to Arneke, thence next day to Serques, and on the 25th Tournehem, the final destination, about ten miles north of St Omer, was reached.

Tournehem was fortunately an ideal resting-place for a weary and worn battalion. The headquarters settled themselves in a comfortable house belonging to an interned German; company officers found suitable accommodation for messes; while the N.C.O.'s and men were billeted in empty houses or barns in the village itself.

On the 25th November, Captain G. W. Thompson (4th Battalion) joined the Battalion and, being the senior captain present, took over the duties of Second-in-Command. The next day General Sir Herbert Plumer, commanding the Second Army, visited Tournehem to see if the Battalion was comfortably settled down. On the 29th the Brigadier (General Mitford) held a conference of Commanding Officers to arrange details of training and exercise during the month's rest. Immediate steps were taken for the construction of a rifle range, of a bombing pit and of an obstacle course. A suitable place was selected for a recreation room, a piano was hired and arrangements were made for the bathing of men in the local brewery.

Several officers joined the Battalion about this time from the Army Cadet School and the 10th Battalion. On 11th December, General Sir Herbert Plumer inspected the 72nd Infantry Brigade in column of route, and was pleased with the marching of the Battalion.

The training of all ranks was actively carried out, and included steady drill, route marches, physical training, bayonet exercises and musketry, as well as the instruction of specialists in signalling, Lewis-gun practice, bombing, sniping, scouting and sanitary duties. Inter-company football matches, cross-country runs, boxing and shooting competitions relieved the monotony of the training. An inter-battalion cross-country run limited to battalions of the 72nd Brigade was won by the Battalion.

On 22nd December the C.O., the Lewis-gun officer and one officer per company went by bus to visit the trenches in front of Pilkem, which were to be taken over by the Battalion. This party was heavily shelled whilst walking round the trenches, and 2nd Lieut. Hubbard (Lewis-gun officer) was sent to hospital suffering from severe concussion. The party arrived back at Tournehem on the 24th December.

On Christmas Day, which was observed as a holiday, special arrangements were made to have the men's dinners served in the various *estaminets* of the village. The menu included chicken, plum pudding and fruit, beer and mineral waters, and the arrangements made were much appreciated. On 28th December, Major-General J. E. Capper, commanding 24th Division, inspected the 72nd Infantry Brigade near Tournehem. On the 3rd January the C.O. and one officer per company proceeded to Ypres to visit trenches at Hooge, which were to be taken over by the Battalion, instead of those near Pilkem, as the 24th Division was returning to the line and the 72nd Brigade was taking over the Hooge–Sanctuary Wood sector.

At midnight on 5th/6th January the Battalion marched out of Tournehem to Audruick Station, there to entrain at 7 a.m. next morning for Poperinghe. It was with natural regret that all ranks left Tournehem. The five weeks' rest there had been as thoroughly enjoyed as they were needed; the inhabitants had been very friendly and had done their utmost to make officers and men comfortable. Letters were received from the Mayor and the parish priest expressing regret at the departure of the Battalion and testifying to the good behaviour of the men.

# IN THE TRENCHES NEAR HOOGE

After detraining at Poperinghe the Battalion marched to a camp about four miles south-east of that place, and on the evening of the 7th January relieved the 9th Battn. Northumberland Fusiliers in trenches C.4, C.5, C.6, C.7, the famous Hooge trenches in the Ypres salient.

The distribution of the Battalion was as follows: Two companies in the fire-trenches; one in dugouts and at the Culvert as immediate support; while the fourth company, together with Battalion Headquarters, was in the Half-way House dugouts, about one mile in rear of the firing-line.

Trenches C.6 and C.7 were found in a very bad state; they were full of water, and the parapet was very low. The ground on either side of the trench was so sodden that no sooner was the water pumped out of the trenches than it ran in again. Fortunately, every man was now provided with a pair of gum boots.

Just as the leading company was leaving the Menin road to go into the trenches an enemy trench mortar suddenly opened fire on it and killed the three leading N.C.O.'s and men, and also wounded another. Of the village of Hooge nothing was left except the cellars of one house, which were used as an aid post and afterwards also as Company Headquarters. A mass of bricks and iron girders represented the stables of the former Château of Hooge. These stables were immediately in front of Trench C.4, and on the far side of them were the German lines. At this particular point our lines and those of the Germans were only about twenty yards apart. Rations and R.E. materials were taken by the regimental transport as far as "Hell Fire Corner," a point on the Menin road where the railway crosses it; from there they were carried by hand to the trenches, a distance of about 2000 yards. The task of these carrying parties was by no means a pleasant one, as the Menin road by night was much exposed to rifle and machine-gun fire, especially in the vicinity of the Culvert.

The Battalion was six days in the trenches before being relieved, which was an exceptionally long time for that sector of the line. During that time the casualties were 6 men killed and Lieut. W. F. Bennett and 4 men wounded.

On 13th January, when relieved by the 1st Battn. North Staffordshire Regt., A, B and D Companies moved into the dugouts behind Zillebeke, and C Company into those at Belgian Château; and on 15th January, when the 73rd Brigade relieved the 72nd in the sector, all four companies marched to Camp "A," about two miles south-east of Poperinghe. This was an excellent camp, with good accommodation in huts for both officers and men. It was well drained, there were good facilities for washing and the divisional baths at Poperinghe were within reach. There was also an excellent parade ground.

On the 16th, Captain D. P. O'Connor, who had been wounded in the Battle of Loos and was subsequently awarded the Military Cross for his services in that action, rejoined the Battalion for duty.

On the 23rd January the 72nd Brigade relieved the 17th Brigade in the Railway Wood sector, and on the 26th the Battalion took over a new line of trenches which were immediately in prolongation to the north of the trenches at Hooge. These trenches, which were to the east of "Y" Wood, were numbered

H.13, H.14, H.15, H.16, H.17 and H.19. Trenches H.13, H.14 and H.15 were in a deplorable state, and could only be held by posts at wide intervals from one another. Here again two companies were in the firing line, one company in support, partly in dugouts and partly in the Menin road cellars; whilst the fourth company, in reserve, was posted in the cellars of a large school. Battalion Headquarters were also in the cellars of a house just south of the Menin road.

On the first night in the trenches 2nd Lieut. R. H. Marchant, with Sergt. Masters and one private, were out patrolling, when the two first were fired upon and wounded. 2nd Lieut. Marchant, who was only slightly wounded, refused to leave Sergt. Masters and sent the private back to our lines for assistance. The private unfortunately lost his way and only returned at daybreak. On the following night a search was made, but no sign could be seen of either 2nd Lieut. Marchant or Sergt. Masters. It was afterwards ascertained that Sergt. Masters had been taken prisoner and 2nd Lieut. Marchant killed—a sad sequel to his generous action. On 27th January another officer, 2nd Lieut. F. S. Handford, whilst out patrolling was also killed by the enemy's machine-gun fire. Lieut. J. L. Vaughan at once went out with a N.C.O., at great personal risk, to bring in 2nd Lieut. Handford's body, but was unable to find it in the dark. For this gallant action, and for good reconnaissance at other times in the Hooge sector, Lieut. Vaughan was awarded the Military Cross in June, 1916.

In this sector the enemy's snipers and machine gunners were particularly active, and the enemy's guns were continually shelling the front line, "Y" Wood and the support trench. On the 29th January a gunner laying telephone wires on the Menin road was badly wounded. 2nd Lieut. Youngman and Pte. Wright, a stretcher-bearer, in spite of very heavy shelling at this time, immediately went to his assistance and succeeded in bringing him in, thus saving his life.

On the 29th January three naval petty officers were attached to the Battalion for twenty-four hours, to gain some experience of trench life. Both going and returning from the trenches they were heavily shelled, and they had some narrow escapes in the trenches themselves. They were very much impressed with the behaviour of our men in the trenches, and declared that they had seen enough of trench life in twenty-four hours to last them a lifetime.

The casualties during the six days in the trenches amounted to 2 officers and 3 other ranks killed, 4 other ranks wounded, in addition to Sergt. Masters wounded and taken prisoner. The Battalion was relieved on the 30th January and returned to Camp "A." Among the officers who joined the Battalion during January was 2nd Lieut. C. A. Clark, who took over the duties of Adjutant from Lieut. Vaughan. 2nd Lieut. Clark had enlisted in 1896, served with the 2nd Battalion in South Africa and afterwards with the 1st Battalion at home, until he was promoted regimental sergeant-major in April, 1914, and posted to the 4th Battalion. He had received his commission in January, 1916.

On the 3rd February the Battalion returned once more to the trenches at Hooge. These were now in a worse state even than before. A bombardment on the 29th January had destroyed Trenches C.5, C.6 and C.7, and also the support Trench C.6.S. The front line, C.5, C.6 and C.7, was now held by a chain of sentry posts standing in crater holes full of water. Trench C.4 was in a slightly better condition, as was Trench C.3, which had been taken over from the Battalion on the right.

The support company was now placed partly in the Culvert and partly in a new trench, R.S.4. The partial destruction of the main communication trenches rendered it impossible to proceed from Headquarters to the front-line trenches by day. The Menin road had also become so unsafe for vehicles at night, owing to more frequent shelling, that the Battalion transport had now to come from Ypres along the Zillebeke road to Half-way House, whence the rations were carried, mostly across country, to the front-line trenches.

On the 6th February a good many shells fell near the Hooge crater, and the total casualties for the four days were nine wounded. On the night of the 6th the Battalion was relieved from the trenches and moved into Camp " B," near Poperinghe, the 72nd Brigade being relieved in the line by the 73rd.

On the 16th February, when the 72nd Brigade again relieved the 17th Brigade in the Hooge–Sanctuary Wood sector, the Battalion was in Brigade support and sent A, B and C Companies to the Zillebeke dugouts and D Company to Belgian Château. These dugouts were shelled on the 19th with " tear " shells, one of which struck the 72nd Brigade headquarters.

Next day the Battalion relieved the 1st Battn. North Staffordshire Regt. once more in the Hooge trenches. Beyond shelling C.3 and C.4 on 23rd February the enemy were fairly peaceful, and the Battalion returned to Zillebeke on the 24th without having suffered any casualties; but on the 25th the enemy suddenly opened artillery fire on a working party furnished by C Company near Gordon House, killing 2 men and wounding 10. The Battalion returned to the Hooge trenches on February 27th. The enemy had started constructing a new work behind the stable, the object of which was unknown; and during the night he bombed the East Surrey trenches at that point. The East Surrey men retaliated vigorously and damaged the new work considerably, timber and sandbags being scattered about.

On the 1st March the British artillery carried out a heavy bombardment, lasting about three-quarters of an hour, of the enemy's front line opposite Trenches C.4, C.5 and C.6, and repeated the performance at 4.15 a.m. on 2nd March. Later in the day the enemy retaliated on our front-line and support trenches. C Company, then under the command of 2nd Lieut. T. H. Yalden, was severely tried, but behaved extremely well. The parapets breached by trench mortars or shells were immediately repaired; posts destroyed were promptly re-established. Company Headquarters in the Hooge cellars all but collapsed under the stream of shells which fell on it, and its entrance was blocked up. Had these cellars been destroyed, the loss would have been considerably greater, as, in addition to the Company Headquarters and signallers, all the wounded had been brought in there for shelter and treatment. C Company in this bombardment had 7 killed, 10 wounded and many others severely shaken by being buried under fallen parapets, etc. For good work performed on this occasion 2nd Lieut. G. S. Tetley was awarded the Military Cross, and Ptes. F. Jewson and F. O'Connell the Distinguished Conduct Medal. D Company, under Lieut. White, holding C.6, C.7, the Culvert and R.S.3, had also a most trying time, about 1000 shells falling in the vicinity of the Culvert; but the damage to personnel was slight. The difficulty of maintaining communication with the front line was very great. The telephonic cable, buried five feet underground, was cut three times, and each time repaired by our signallers, who, under Cpl. Ericson, did excellent work that day.

On March 3rd the Battalion moved into the dug-outs at Zillebeke and Belgian Château, and on the following day to Camp "B." While in camp working parties were furnished almost daily for the front line, and also for building a reserve line along the canal bank near Ypres Station. At this time a train used to take these working parties by night as far as the Asylum, just west of Ypres, and bring them back again in the early morning. The casualties to these working parties were 1 man killed and 4 men wounded. On the 16th March the Battalion returned to the Zillebeke and Belgian Château dugouts, where on the 19thMarch it was relieved by the 4th Canadian Mounted Rifles. The Battalion then returned to Camp "B," and on the 21st March the 24th Division left the vicinity of Ypres and were billeted in farm-houses between Bailleul and the Mont des Cats, having handed over the Hooge sector to the Canadians.

The two and a half months spent in the neighbourhood of Hooge had been fairly trying, but far preferable to the time spent in the trenches near St. Eloi. The most unpleasant feature had again been the weather. In trenches perpetually full of water, which occasionally turned into ice, the greatest care was necessary to prevent the men's feet from becoming frostbitten. But the camps in rear were much more comfortable than that at Reninghelst. The Battalion, moreover, was fairly fortunate in not suffering greater casualties than it did.

The country round the Mont des Cats was very hilly and picturesque, and in complete contrast to the low-lying plains of Flanders. After a rest of five days in these pleasant surroundings the Battalion, on the 25th March, proceeded via St. Jans-Cappel and Dranoutre to relieve a battalion of the 1st Canadian Infantry Brigade as Brigade Reserve in its billets at Tea Farm (A Company and Headquarters), Aircraft Farm (B and C Companies) and Kandahar Farm (D Company), and next day took over from the 3rd Battn. Canadians the trenches astride of the Wulverghem–Wytschaete road, about one mile north-east of the former village. The front-line trenches were numbered D.2, D.4, D.5 and D.6, and a trench named E.1 connected D.6 with the Bull Ring on the left, which was held by a brigade of another division.

Three companies held the front line, whilst the fourth company was accommodated in dugouts near "R.E." Farm on the Wulverghem–Wytschaete road. The front-line trenches here, which had been occupied by the 2nd Battn. East Surrey in the summer of 1915, were the best that the 9th Battalion had taken over as yet. They were in good condition, with the exception of D.5, which had fallen in, owing to the rain. Another advantage of this portion of the line was that rations and engineer material could be taken in the regimental transport right up to "R.E." Farm, where the reserve company was billeted. The

Canadians, who had been holding this sector of the line for six months, had had a very quiet time of it and had suffered practically no casualties. The absence of shell holes in rear of the trenches was very noticeable, and nearly all the farms in the vicinity of the trenches had been left standing, and were used as billets for the troops in reserve.

There were two reasons to account for this: the desire of our military authorities to economize ammunition in this particular sector and the presence opposite the Canadians of Saxon troops, who were only too anxious to live and let live. With the arrival of the 24th Division an immediate change came over this peaceful scene. A Prussian division had just relieved the Saxons, and our artillery had now a plentiful supply of ammunition, which they used on every possible opportunity. In a very short time all the farms within view or easy range of the enemy's artillery were shattered or burnt. In the new trenches companies in the front line soon discovered that the enemy's chief form of aggression took the shape of rifle grenades and small aerial torpedoes (turnip bombs) sent over at intervals throughout the day.

Our companies at once set to work to establish rifle-grenade stands. Two 3.7-in. mortars were brought up to the trenches, and before long it became the rule to send over three missiles for every one fired by the enemy. The enemy's artillery also directed its fire at times on our supporting lines, but chiefly in retaliation to our own artillery fire. By night the enemy's snipers and machine guns were extremely active. Following the example of the Canadians, the Battalion sent out patrols all night in front of our own wires. These not only patrolled the front, but acted as listening posts. The Battalion snipers and bombers were chiefly employed on this duty. On 29th March, 2nd Lieut. R. H. Schooling, who had only joined the Battalion the previous day, was killed whilst assisting in strengthening a weak portion of the parapet in D.4. Other casualties during the six days' tour in the trenches were 4 men killed and 10 wounded.

On the 2nd April the Battalion was relieved by the 1st Battn. North Staffordshire Regt. and moved into Divisional Reserve at Dranoutre. Dranoutre as a billet was much liked by the men; the village itself has a good many shops and *estaminets*, and in addition there was a canteen and a Y.M.C.A. tent. The one drawback whilst in Divisional Reserve was the daily furnishing of working parties in the front line. On 3rd April, while burying an armoured cable near Tea Farm, a N.C.O. and three men were wounded.

On the 8th April the Battalion relieved the 1st Battn. North Staffordshire Regt. in the same trenches as before. Exchanges of rifle grenades and light trench-mortar bombs continued daily, and there was a certain amount of shelling on both sides. The Battalion snipers were very busy destroying the enemy's periscopes, of which there were a large number, and in shooting with armour-piercing bullets at his loopholed plates. Several German working parties were dispersed by our machine guns at night. The casualties during the week spent in the trenches were 1 man killed and 12 wounded.

On the 15th April the Battalion moved back into Brigade Reserve, with two companies and headquarters at Kandahar Farm, and two companies at Aircraft

Farm. Large working parties had to be found daily, and three men were wounded. On the 20th April the Battalion went back to the trenches north-east of Wulverghem. The enemy's trench mortars were now more active than ever. On the 22nd, for the first time, the enemy opened fire with a large "minenwerfer." The thirty rounds which came over fortunately fell just in rear of D.4 and D.3, making enormous craters, but otherwise doing no damage.

On the 24th, at 4.30 p.m., the enemy suddenly opened fire on D.5 and D.6 trenches with every rifle grenade, light trench mortar and aerial torpedo that he possessed. A regular hail of these missiles came over for half an hour. At the same time a few rounds of "minenwerfer" fell behind D.4, and the Wulverghem–Wytschaete road was shelled. A heavy retaliation on our side was decided on for the 26th, and at 3.50 p.m. on that date every available gun in the Division, together with the heavy artillery of the Corps, was turned on to the German trenches for twenty minutes. At the same time all our Stokes guns, 3.7-in. mortars and rifle grenades fired their hardest. The enemy were evidently much scared. Throughout the whole night they kept throwing bombs in front of their trenches, clearly expecting an attack.

On 25th April the dugouts at "R.E." Farm were heavily shelled with 4.2-in. and 5.9-in. howitzers, and had to be evacuated. Battalion Headquarters at Cooker Farm also came in for the enemy's attention. As communication by telephone between "R.E." Farm and Battalion Headquarters was no longer possible, signalling communication was established, during which Pte. R. J. Gibbs was severely wounded. For the courage and initiative he displayed on this occasion Pte. Gibbs subsequently received the Military Medal.

The casualties in the Battalion from 20th to 26th April were: 2nd Lieut. W. S. Howell killed and fourteen other ranks wounded. 2nd Lieut. Howell, the Battalion grenade officer, was killed by the blow-back of one of our heavy howitzer shells whilst observing the effect of our bombardment on the 26th April. He was a great loss to the Battalion. On the evening of the 29th April, shortly before the Battalion was relieved by the 1st Battn. North Stafford Regt., two Poles deserted from the enemy's lines and gave themselves up to the company holding the Bull Ring. They stated that the Germans opposite the D trenches, which the Battalion was holding, had intended the previous night, under cover of gas, to raid these trenches. The attack had not taken place, as there was not sufficient wind to release the gas.

As on the 29th the wind, though east, was very slight, there appeared to be little prospect of the enemy carrying out his threat on that night. However, the 1st Battn. North Stafford Regt., on arrival, were warned to be on the alert. The Battalion then moved back into Divisional Reserve at Dranoutre.

At 1 a.m. on the 30th April the promised gas attack took place, and Trench D.4 was raided. The 9th Battn. East Surrey had fifty N.C.O.'s and men under 2nd Lieut. Youngman working at "R.E." Farm, and they rendered material assistance in ejecting the raiding party. For his services 2nd Lieut. Youngman was awarded the Military Cross. The casualties in his working party were 1 man killed and 1 officer (2nd Lieut. W. S. Spurling) and 3 other ranks wounded.

As the North Staffordshires had suffered considerable casualties, the Battalion relieved them in the trenches on the night of the 2nd May. During the six days' tour of duty which followed the enemy's trench mortars and "minenwerfers" were very quiet, but their artillery shelled at intervals both front and support lines.

On the 6th May, between 2 p.m. and 5.30 p.m., the enemy heavily shelled Cooker Farm (Battalion Headquarters), Elbow Farm (regimental aid post) and Battle Axe Farm, about 150 yards north of Cooker Farm. Battle Axe Farm was set on fire, and the regimental aid post was partially destroyed. The casualties for the period 2nd to 8th May included the following: 1 man killed and 5 other ranks wounded. On the 8th May the Battalion went into Brigade Reserve at Aircraft Farm. From the 14th to 19th May the Battalion was once more in the trenches. A certain number of shells came over each day, and some trench mortars at midnight on the 18th.

On the 19th May Battalion Headquarters were shelled once more, the sentry in front of the Commanding Officer's dugout being killed. At the same time Elbow Farm was destroyed, and a new regimental aid post had to be constructed near "R.E." Farm. The casualties from the 9th to the 19th May were 4 men killed and 2nd Lieut. G. S. Tetley and 4 men wounded. The Battalion was in Divisional Reserve at Dranoutre from the 20th to 24th May, during which time as many men as possible were training in the Lewis gun, in grenade throwing, constructing wire entanglements, etc. The remainder of the men furnished the nightly working parties, which were never less than 220 strong. From the 24th to 30th May the Battalion was again in the trenches. The usual amount of shelling took place, and on 30th May the enemy fired a large number of rifle grenades, aerial torpedoes, trench mortars and "minenwerfer" shells all along our line. It was now becoming increasingly difficult for either side to put up a periscope. The German sniper had always been a good shot, and our snipers were improving rapidly with practice. At night, too, our Lewis gunners made it impossible for the enemy to work outside their parapet. The casualties during the six days in the trenches were 2 men killed and 5 wounded.

From the 30th May to the 5th June the Battalion was in Brigade Reserve about Aircraft Farm, during which time three men were wounded. From the 5th to the 13th June the Battalion once more held the Wulverghem trenches. The enemy's artillery, trench mortars and "minenwerfer" were particularly active on the 11th and 13th June. A "minenwerfer" crater on the Wytschaete road near the "Barrier" measured 12 feet in diameter and was 7 feet deep. An easterly wind caused anticipations of another gas attack, and everybody was fully on the alert. The casualties during the tour of trench duty were: 2nd Lieuts. E. L. Amies and F. G. Ball and eleven other ranks wounded.

The Battalion, relieved by the 1st Battn. North Stafford Regt., moved into Divisional Reserve at Dranoutre on 13th June. On the 17th the enemy again released gas from the trenches facing the North Staffordshires, but this time did not attempt a raid on the trenches. The Battalion had 250 men, under Lieut. Vaughan and 2nd Lieut. H. S. C. Jamieson, working in the front line at the time.

The party adjusted their gas helmets with such promptitude that only one man out of the 250 suffered from the effect of the gas. 2nd Lieut. Jamieson, accompanied by Sergt. Malins, whilst endeavouring to carry out his instructions to report himself to the nearest company commander in the event of a gas attack, was severely wounded, and Sergt. Malins was also wounded. The working party rendered great assistance in helping to remove the numerous casualties, both from gas and shell fire, and had five men wounded by shell fire, one of whom, " Cpl. Batchelor, though severely wounded, continued to issue instructions to the men under his command. He deserved the Military Medal, which unfortunately could not be awarded him " (Battalion Diary). The Battalion relieved the North Stafford Regt. in the trenches on the following night, the 18th June, and remained there until the 29th of the month.

Preparations were now being made to retaliate on the enemy by using gas and raiding his trenches. Boxes to contain cylinders were dug in under the firing steps of each bay in the front line and covered over with sandbags. The gas cylinders themselves were not to be placed in the boxes until the date for the raid had been decided on. The 8th Battn. " Queen's " were detailed to carry out the raid from trenches immediately on the right of those held by the 9th Battn. East Surrey.

From June 19th to 23rd there was considerable shelling of the area in rear of the front line, 1 man being killed and 6 wounded. A sniper at Spanbroekmolen was extremely active, and many officers and men had narrow escapes from his bullets. Spanbroekmolen was a prominent salient above the Bull Ring. It overlooked the whole of the country between Cooker Farm and " R.E." Farm, and the greatest precaution had to be taken by everyone proceeding to the front line or returning to Headquarters, in order not to be hit by the very vigilant German who had taken up an unassailable position with a commanding view. On the 23rd June, 1916, a shell destroyed the dugout at " R.E." Farm occupied by Regtl. Sergt.-Major W. Ladd and killed him, to the great regret of the whole Battalion. Sergt.-Major Ladd had always carried out his duties most efficiently and conscientiously. He was an old and experienced soldier, having served throughout the South African War with the 2nd Battalion. Sergt.-Major Ladd was succeeded as regimental sergeant-major by C.S.M. Lindsey.

At about 8.15 p.m. the enemy commenced an intense bombardment of the whole of the British front line with 5·9's, 4·2's, " whizbangs," every sort of trench mortars and numerous " minenwerfers." This bombardment lasted until 9.20 p.m., when it lifted on to the support line, and at 10 p.m. died down, with the exception of the " minenwerfer," which kept firing intermittently throughout the night. The parapets of D.5 and D.6 were solidly built, and the men crouching behind them escaped without many casualties, but those holding the salient D.4 had a terrible time. On this salient the majority of the enemy's " minenwerfers " were directed, and the parapet, though very high and thick, was levelled to the ground in several places. All the men holding the front face of the salient were either killed, wounded or buried. Lieut. J. M. Youngman (Battalion grenade officer), realizing the gravity of the situation, immediately rushed to the exposed spot with some of the Battalion grenadiers and attempted to rescue the men buried in one of the craters formed by a " minenwerfer " shell. Finding that he was exposed to the enemy's fire, Lieut. Youngman then commenced to rebuild the parapet, and was killed by a rifle bullet whilst doing so. Meanwhile 2nd Lieut. F. R. Ingrams, who was in charge of the salient, set to work with great energy to post fresh sentries and to rebuild the trench, which had lost all shape. He was subsequently awarded the Military Cross for his gallantry on this occasion.

When the enemy's fire lifted from the front line on to the support trenches an attack was expected and all were ready to meet it. But to the disappointment of all ranks no attack took place. About seven Germans advanced a few yards in front of their parapet towards the salient, but were driven back by a Lewis gun. Whether the enemy had intended attacking after their bombardment will never be known. The Battalion casualties on this occasion were Lieut. Youngman and 2 men killed, and 31 other ranks wounded.

In view of the projected raids to be carried out by the Canadians, 8th Battn. " The Buffs " and 8th Battn. " Queen's," our artillery were very active each day cutting wire. This led to constant retaliation on the part of the enemy, who evidently feared an attack. On the 27th June, in addition to shelling the front-line and support trenches, the enemy sent over about forty rounds of " minenwerfer," which practically destroyed " Stretcher Lane," a communication trench which ran along the upper portion of the Wytschaete road. " Minenwerfers " at the rate of one every three minutes also fell day and night on Deadman's Farm, which was about fifty yards in rear of the left of the line held by the Battalion. The casualties between the 24th and 28th June were eleven wounded. On the nights of the 25th and 27th June the gas cylinders were brought up by wagon to " R.E." Farm and carried from there to the bays, into which they were to be inserted, and it was decided to release this gas on the night of the 28th if the wind was favourable.

On the night of the 27th June a patrol under Sergt. W. G. T. Summers succeeded in getting right up to the enemy's parapet, and, looking over it, saw a German in the trench. This German caught sight of Sergt. Summers and shouted out, " Wer da ? " whereupon the sergeant shot him with his revolver and returned into our lines in safety. For this and other good work performed Sergt. Summers was awarded the Distinguished Conduct Medal.

During the afternoon of the 28th there was considerable shelling of our lines. The wind was watched with much anxiety, as it was very variable. However, towards the evening it blew with greater regularity from the right quarter, and it was decided to release the gas and carry out the raid that night.

At 11.31 p.m. the artillery bombardment began, from Peckham down to the Douve. At the same time gas was discharged, and smoke opposite the trenches to be raided. At 11.50 p.m. the three raiding parties advanced, that of the " Queen's " on the German trenches just south of the Wulverghem-Wytschaete road, that of the Canadians on Ontario Farm and that of the

"Buffs" on Anton Farm. All met with some measure of success, the "Queen's" bringing back six wounded prisoners.

At 12.15 a.m. on the 29th gas was discharged all along the front held by the Battalion. The white cloud moved fairly swiftly over the enemy's lines and, it is hoped, did much damage. The enemy put up red and green lights in large numbers and shelled our trenches, causing the following casualties: 1 man killed and 2nd Lieut. N. B. Morphy and 15 other ranks wounded.

On the night of the 29th June the discharge of gas by the Brigade on the right of the 72nd induced the enemy once more to bombard the trenches just at the time when the relief of the Battalion by the North Stafford Regt. was in progress. The relief, in consequence, which was not completed till 5 a.m. next morning, was effected under great difficulties, and both battalions suffered considerably. The casualties of the Battalion were 2nd Lieut. J. L. P. Denny and 21 other ranks wounded.

When relieved, the Battalion moved into Brigade Reserve at Aircraft Farm, where they were shelled for about an hour on the 30th June, and were consequently moved into the neighbouring trenches. Later in the day the 24th Division was relieved by the 20th Division and marched to Locre, about two miles north of Dranoutre. Thus its three months' sojourn in the Wulverghem sector came to an end.

Although the casualties suffered by the Battalion during this period amounted to nearly 200 killed and wounded, it was considered that this sector compared in many ways very favourably with the St. Eloi and Hooge sectors. The trenches were well constructed and well drained. The Battalion transport, under Lieut. Whiteman, though it had many narrow escapes, always succeeded in taking the rations as far as the reserve company at "R.E." Farm. The village of Dranoutre, as a billet for the Battalion when in Divisional Reserve, was much liked. On the other hand, the perpetual shelling and bombardments on the part of the enemy, their employment of "minenwerfers," of aerial torpedoes, of every kind of trench mortar and of gas, rendered the casualties of the Division and of the Battalion particularly heavy. Another great disadvantage of the sector was that so many working parties had to be furnished that there was little rest and hardly any opportunity for training newly arrived officers, N.C.O.'s and men.

In addition to those already mentioned, the following received Military Medals for good work performed on various occasions at this period: Sergts. E. Ericson, Oakey, H. Lee; Cpls. W. H. Batchelor, F. Halliday, C. W. Skinner; Lce.-Cpls. H. Hastings, A. Lee, W. Kerslake; Ptes. H. E. Braint, E. S. Matthews.

## CHAPTER XV

MAY AND JUNE, 1916: THE 12TH BATTALION ARRIVES IN FRANCE AND TAKES ITS FIRST TOUR OF TRENCH DUTY NEAR PLOEGSTEERT WOOD.

THE 12th Battn. East Surrey Regt. left Aldershot early on the 1st May, 1916, the strength of all ranks being 1018. It arrived at Havre without incident at 1 a.m. on May 2nd, and proceeded to No. 5 Rest Camp. Entraining at 3.30 a.m. on May 3rd, the Battalion reached Godewaersvelde, near Bailleul, after a train journey of twenty-four hours, and marched to billets at Outtersteene. Here it remained till May 9th, when it marched to billets immediately west of Steenwerck, whence parties of fifty officers and men proceeded for periods of forty-eight hours for instruction in trench duty in Ploegsteert Wood. General training continued at Steenwerck, the work including musketry and route marching, in addition to various courses for officers, N.C.O.'s and specialists.

On May 28th, this preliminary training being complete, the Battalion marched to its billets in Brigade Reserve at Soyer Farm, and on the 29th moved out by companies to perform its first tour of duty in the trenches, relieving the 7th Battn. Seaforth Highlanders in the Convent position. Two companies were in the firing line, one in support and one in reserve, with Battalion Headquarters at Lawrence Farm. The Battalion remained in the trenches from May 30th until the 4th June, sustaining one casualty from shell fire on the 31st May.

On the 4th June the Battalion was relieved by the 10th Battn. "Queen's" and went into reserve at Soyer Farm, where it remained till June 10th. The work here was principally fatigue duty in improving the trenches.

The Battalion spent the remainder of June either in the Convent trenches or in reserve at Soyer Farm, alternately with the 10th Battn. "Queen's," the reliefs taking place every seven days. A draft of 62 other ranks from the 3rd Battn. joined at Soyer Farm on the 20th June. While in the Convent trenches the Battalion heard the gas alarm for the first time at midnight, 16th/17th June, but sustained no casualty that night. On June 30th raiding parties were sent out by the 41st Division, that of the Battalion consisting of thirty-four N.C.O.'s and men, under Captain F. D. Jessop and Lieut. C. C. Fox. The men who formed the raiding party had before joining the Battalion belonged to a fraternity well known in Bermondsey as "The Black Hand Gang." Among them were some of the best fighting men in the Battalion. On this occasion they planted a board, with a black hand painted on it, in the German trench, to show where they entered. After performing their work effectively they returned, having sustained only four casualties. Captain Jessop was awarded the Military Cross for his conspicuous dash and gallantry and for his excellent leading, to which the light casualties of the raiding party were attributed by Lieut.-Colonel Lee. For gallant service in the raid, Sergt. J. Donnelly was awarded the Distinguished Conduct Medal, and the following received the Military Medal: Sergt. R. J. Calver and Ptes. W. C. Camp and H. V. Rice.

Major-General Lawford, commanding the 41st Division, expressed his entire satisfaction with the manner in which the raids of the 122nd Infantry Brigade were conducted, and in a special Brigade Order, Brigadier-General F. W. Towsey mentioned a soldier of the Battalion as follows :—

> "No. 12367 Private D. O'Sullivan, 12th East Surrey Regiment, was 46 years of age and two of his sons are fighting. He refused all jobs that would keep him out of the trenches and volunteered for the raid. While getting through the parapet he was wounded, but refused assistance, saying, 'Go on, lads, carry on without me.' When the party returned he was dying. Truly we mourn the loss of a gallant comrade."

The casualties of the Battalion during June were 18 other ranks killed and 3 officers and 38 other ranks wounded. The officers wounded were: Major L. Tenbosch, Lieut. E. C. Lambert, R.A.M.C. (mortally), and 2nd Lieut. J. F. Walton. Regtl. Sergt.-Major Nash was also wounded.

# SECTION III

JULY, 1916, TO MARCH, 1917

THE BATTLES OF THE SOMME, 1916, AND THE ADVANCE TO THE HINDENBURG LINE, 1917. OPERATIONS IN SALONIKA

## CHAPTER XVI

JULY, 1916, TO MARCH, 1917: THE 1st BATTALION IN THE BATTLES OF THE SOMME, 1916; AT LONGUEVAL IN THE BATTLE OF DELVILLE WOOD; IN THE BATTLE OF GUILLEMONT, IN AND NEAR LEUZE WOOD; IN THE BATTLE OF MORVAL; SIX MONTHS IN THE LINE IN THE LA BASSEÉ CANAL AREA.

DURING the afternoon of the 1st July news of the successful opening of the Battle of Albert, 1916, reached the 1st Battn. East Surrey at Wanquetin, near Arras. On the following day the 95th Brigade was ordered to move westward from Wanquetin, and the 1st Battn. East Surrey, marching at 5.30 p.m., arrived at Le Cauroy about midnight, settling quickly into billets and bivouacs. Headquarters of the 5th Division were also at Le Cauroy. For the next two days the Battalion was under orders to move at fifteen minutes' notice, so that little could be done, but on the 5th the notice was increased to three hours. Major Woulfe-Flanagan returned from leave and took over command of the Battalion, Captain Swanton being Second-in-Command.

On the 7th the Battalion returned to its former billets at Wanquetin, and on the following day marched to the training ground near Simencourt to practise the assault. For the next three days the Battalion furnished working parties of 500 men, who were employed in burying cables, and in the afternoon of the 13th it was conveyed in motor lorries to the little village of Oppy, consisting of six houses, which, however, provided cover for the whole Battalion.

Next day the Battalion marched to Longuevillette, near Doullens, where good billets were provided, the march being continued on the 15th in warm and cloudy weather to Hérissart, where were also Brigade Headquarters and the 1st Battn. D.C.L.I. Here Lieut. C. McH. Caffyn, who had performed most valuable work as sapper officer while with the Battalion, left it to join the Royal Flying Corps. On the 16th July the 1st Battn. East Surrey and the D.C.L.I. marched to Bresle, where the whole of the 95th Brigade was billeted; and on the 17th the Brigade marched through Albert south-eastwards to Bécordel-Becourt and bivouacked on the slopes of the hill just south of that village. The Battalion, which was now well in the battle area, was warned to be ready to go into action at two hours' notice after 4 a.m. on the 18th, and all officers were ordered to dress like the men and to carry rifles and bayonets. The arms were supplied by men of the transport; but the order to change into trousers and putties at such short notice caused some difficulty in the circumstances.

The situation at the time of the arrival of the 95th Brigade in the Somme area was as follows: The main attack by the Fourth Army on the 1st July, which opened the Battle of Albert, 1916, had extended from Maricourt round the German salient at Fricourt (two miles east of Albert) up to the River Ancre at

Pierre Divion. As the result of the ensuing fortnight's fighting the southern face of the German salient had been rolled back northwards to a depth of about two miles, and on the 13th July the Fourth Army held the line Boiselle–Mametz Wood—Trones Wood. The Battle of Bazentin Wood commenced on the 14th, and that day the Fourth Army overran the enemy's second system of defence and gained a footing on that part of the main ridge north of the Somme which overlooks the valley between Bazentin le Petit and Longuéval. Both of these villages were captured. On the 15th Delville Wood, just east of Longuéval, was also taken, and this action and the long struggle to hold it, which lasted till the 3rd September, are known as the Battle of Delville Wood.

To return to the story of the 1st Battn. East Surrey. On the 18th July the Commanding Officer, Adjutant, company commanders, machine-gun and medical officers went forward to reconnoitre. On reaching the front-line trenches in a copse close to the cemetery of Bazentin-le-Petit the party was held up for two hours by hostile shelling, and Captain Ponsford, the Medical Officer, was wounded in the wrist. On the 19th, the Commanding Officer, similarly accompanied, again went forward to reconnoitre trenches at Longuéval, but owing to the heavy fighting, incident on a strong German counter-attack in Delville Wood, the party was stopped in the valley north of Montauban, where later it was joined by the Battalion, whose previous movements had been as follows: At 12.45 it had moved under Major Swanton from its bivouac at Becordel to a field just east of Mametz. Here a halt of an hour was made, after which the Battalion proceeded to a valley near by, where it was ordered to make and improve cover for the night.

At 9 p.m., however, fresh orders were received to take over trenches in and west of Longuéval from the survivors of three battalions of the 27th Brigade. When this order had been carried out the 1st Battn. East Surrey was on the right of the 95th Brigade, with the D.C.L.I. next to it on the left. The Battalion was disposed as follows, with its right resting on the western side of the main square of the village: In the front line were B Company (Captain Streatfeild-James) on the right and C Company (2nd Lieut. Wright) on the left; D Company (Captain Gripper) was in support in the captured German support trench, and A Company (Captain King) was three-quarters of a mile back, in reserve in the valley between Longuéval and Montauban. During the relief Regtl. Sergt.-Major Murden, M.C., was wounded. At the commencement of the War Sergt.-Major Murden was company quartermaster-sergeant of B Company, and he had served since then with the 1st Battalion without a break. Loyalty to the Regiment and to his officers was the strongest characteristic of this good soldier.

The Battalion was not engaged on July 20th, but fighting took place on both flanks and its trenches were heavily shelled. Three officers were wounded, Lieut. Challacombe, 2nd Lieuts. Drake-Brockman and Parish, and the following six officers were sent back to the transport to be held in reserve in case of heavy casualties: Major Swanton; Lieuts. Druce and Fitz-Gerald; 2nd Lieuts. Stott, Pearce and Millar.

On the 21st July the Battalion was heavily shelled, particularly A Company, the casualties in the forenoon numbering 3 officers and 72 other ranks. This shelling was continued throughout the 22nd and developed great violence in the evening. At about 10 p.m. the enemy opened a fierce rifle and machine-gun fire on the trenches, at the same time sending up numerous red flares. Everything pointed to a coming attack, and the company commanders in the front line, in order to anticipate it, asked for artillery support. This was vigorously given, and no German assault was delivered.

The right of the Battalion, as already stated, rested on the western side of the main square of the village of Longuéval, but owing to the wholesale destruction that had been wrought by the artillery of both sides the former positions of houses and streets were indistinguishable from one another. From the right of the Battalion eastward the 18th Brigade had no regular line, but a series of posts at varying intervals, owing to the impossibility of digging in parts of the village. About midnight conditions became quieter. As on the 21st, A Company had again suffered heavily, as had also the Battalion cooks; one "cooker" was destroyed and another damaged. The total casualties on the 22nd were 2nd Lieut. O. W. Clark killed and 48 other ranks killed and wounded.

The Battalion had already received instructions as to the part it was to play in the renewed advance of the Fourth Army fixed for the 23rd July. These were to the effect that the 5th Division would co-operate with the 3rd Division and take by assault the portions of Longuéval and Delville Wood, which had been recaptured by the Germans on the 19th. The preliminary artillery bombardment was to lift at 3.40 a.m. on July 23rd, when the 9th Brigade of the 3rd Division would combine with the 95th Brigade in attacking certain strong points west and north-west of the village. The task allotted to the 1st Battn. East Surrey was to capture and hold two strong points known to contain machine guns.

The attacks on these two posts were led respectively by 2nd Lieuts. T. G. Stanyon and W. H. Matthews, and were conducted separately and in different circumstances. 2nd Lieut. Stanyon's attack was launched over ground swept by machine-gun fire, five minutes before the general assault, and met with misfortune from the outset. 2nd Lieut. Stanyon was mortally wounded as soon as the attack began; Sergt. J. W. Stacey, who afterwards received the Distinguished Conduct Medal, was wounded, and a large number of the men were shot down. It was clear that the post could not be carried by daylight.

2nd Lieut. Matthew's attack, on the other hand, was conducted as part of the general assault. It was carried out by a party of about forty, comprising Battalion snipers, bombers, R.E. sappers and a Lewis-gun team, supported by two platoons of D Company. The post, which was about 200 yards west of the northern end of Longuéval, was captured without the loss of a man; one machine gun was taken and five others put out of action, thirty to forty Germans were killed or captured wounded, and the post was successfully consolidated. 2nd Lieut. Matthews conducted the attack with great judgment and skill, and was awarded the Military Cross. Unfortunately, the troops on the right and left of the 1st Battn. East Surrey were compelled to fall back, and the post captured by 2nd Lieut. Matthews, being completely isolated, had to be evacuated.

The casualties of the Battalion on the 23rd were 2nd Lieut. T. G. Stanyon mortally wounded, Lieut. S. S. Horsley and 2nd Lieuts. H. Lonergan and E. F. Wentzel wounded, and 119 other ranks killed and wounded.

During the night of July 23rd/24th the Battalion was relieved by the 12th Battn. Gloucester Regt. and went into Brigade Reserve, occupying the old German trenches near Montauban and near Brigade Headquarters. These trenches were heavily shelled by the German artillery on the morning of the 24th and Captain W. V. T. Gripper (3rd Battn. attd.) was killed. He was very popular with all ranks and an excellent "emergency officer," thoroughly cool and clear-headed in action. His death was a great loss to the Battalion. All the officers held in reserve with the Battalion transport were brought up to replace casualties except Major Swanton, Lieut. Druce and 2nd Lieut. Pearce. On July 25th the Battalion, still in reserve, was again violently shelled, the casualties to noon being twenty-five other ranks. 2nd Lieut. Pearce was called up to the Battalion. The next day was fortunately somewhat quieter, and the men consequently got some much-needed rest. Casualties, however, continued to occur and at noon numbered thirteen.

On July 27th the Battalion received orders at midday to move an hour later, infantry fighting having been in progress since 7 a.m. At two o'clock the Battalion moved up to the old German trenches 1000 yards west of Longuéval, which were now occupied by the Devons and Cheshires. The enemy were shelling this line and the valley leading up to it from Montauban with heavies and shrapnel, and through this zone of fire the 1st Battn. East Surrey moved steadily to its new position. Three officers were wounded almost immediately: Lieuts. A. A. Wright, Hollingsworth and Stanbrook, all of C Company. Lieuts. Ovenden and H. C. Mason were also slightly wounded, but remained at duty. The losses in other ranks were estimated at from 40 to 60. Such were the casualties incurred in merely changing position behind the line under the enemy's terrific artillery fire.

Before daylight on the 28th the Battalion moved forward and occupied Longuéval and the north-west corner of Delville Wood, which had been recaptured on the previous day by the Norfolk and Bedford Regts. These Battalions had suffered so severely that it was necessary to relieve them without delay. The relief, which entailed passing through a heavily shelled area, seemed at the outset a desperate undertaking, but happily there was a lull in the barrage while the Battalion was passing through the main street of Longuéval. By 6 a.m. the relief was complete and the Battalion found itself on the immediate left of the 2nd Division, and supported by the D.C.L.I. Notwithstanding the good fortune which had attended the Battalion in its passage through Longuéval, the casualties during the relief were Lieut. W. H. Matthews and 2nd Lieut. Killick wounded and about seventy other ranks killed and wounded. Battalion Headquarters were near the main square of the village, which was a mere heap of smouldering ruins, streets being indistinguishable from houses. Dead and wounded British and Germans lay scattered amongst the ruins, and the storm of shells went on unceasingly. Delville Wood also was wrecked by shell fire and afforded but little cover from view.

## AN UNSUCCESSFUL ATTACK

July 29th was one of the most trying days experienced by the Battalion during the War, the enemy's shelling rendering communication from the rear almost impossible. To give an idea of the situation it may be mentioned that out of a water-carrying party of twenty-four of all ranks of the 14th Battn. Warwick Regt. one officer and six men only reached the 1st Battn. East Surrey, the remainder having been killed or wounded on the way. The water rendered available by such sacrifices was so tainted with petrol as to be barely drinkable, and increased rather than allayed thirst.

At 2 p.m. orders were received to attack two enemy posts north-west of Longueval, and an hour and a half later the attack was made by B, C and D Companies. It was known that the posts contained machine guns, and a preliminary bombardment was carried out with the intention of destroying them. This, however, was not accomplished, and when the assaulting troops left their trenches they encountered a hail of machine-gun bullets which cut down the leading waves before the attack was properly started. It was clear from the outset that the attack must fail, but the men would not admit defeat and pressed forward with increasing losses. 2nd Lieut. I. K. Millar led this advance with the greatest gallantry until he was killed and the attack came to a standstill. The survivors took shelter in shell holes, where they remained until darkness enabled them to return to their starting-point. The losses of the Battalion were very heavy. From noon on the 27th to noon on the 29th 12 officers and 308 other ranks were killed and wounded; and when the Battalion was relieved at Longueval at midnight on July 30th it had been reduced to a field strength of 9 officers (including the Commanding Officer and Adjutant) and 251 N.C.O.'s and men. Of the twelve officers mentioned above, the following were killed: 2nd Lieuts. N. M. Vernham, G. R. B. Mazengarb, I. K. Millar, L. F. Grigg and H. G. W. Clay. Captain T. S. King and Lieut. E. D. Fitz-Gerald were wounded.

On relief by the K.O.S.B., belonging to the 15th Brigade, at midnight on July 30th, the Battalion retired by platoons to the Pommiers Redoubt, south-west of Montauban. Here July 31st was passed in resting and cleaning up, a great relief to those who had come through the heavy strain of the uninterrupted shell fire during the past twelve days and nights.

In consequence of the decision to move the 5th Division to a rest area west of Amiens, the Battalion was relieved from the Pommiers Redoubt about 10.30 p.m. on August 1st and marched via Fricourt to Dernancourt, taking over a neighbouring camp at 4.30 in the morning of August 2nd. The company commanders were now Captain Streatfeild-James, Lieut. J. C. Druce, and 2nd Lieuts. H. G. P. Ovenden and L. L. Wight.

After a day of rest and bathing on the 3rd, the Battalion marched to Méricourt Station soon after noon on the 4th August, but, owing to disorganization of traffic, did not entrain till 1 a.m. on the 5th. It detrained at Airaines, twenty miles north-west of Amiens, and bivouacked some two miles west of that place at 5 a.m. A draft of 40 men joined, and 2nd Lieut. Ovenden left on transfer to the Royal Flying Corps, "a great loss to the Battalion," says the Diary. At 11 a.m. the Battalion marched from Airaines via Métigny and Croquoison to the rest area at Epaumesnil, where the billets were reasonably good, but there was a scarcity of water. On August 6th 18 men arrived, mostly recovered wounded. On the 8th a draft of 100 men of the 6th (Cyclist) Battn. Sussex Regt. joined after a very long march from Longpré. This was a severe strain in such hot weather, particularly as some of the men had had little or no training in marching or carrying a pack. On the 10th a draft of 35 men joined under 2nd Lieut. Whybrow, composed of 14 1st Battalion men who had been wounded and 21 men from the Service battalions of the Regiment.

On Friday, August 11th, a Memorial Service was held near the Officers' Mess in memory of the officers, N.C.O.'s and men who fell at Longueval and Delville Wood. On the 14th 3 more officers joined, and also 10 returned wounded men. The Battalion remained at Epaumesnil until the night of the 23rd August, reorganizing the companies after their heavy loss and preparing for further action.

The 5th Division was now under orders to return to the Somme front as part of the XIV Corps, and the 1st Battn. East Surrey accordingly marched late on the 23rd August for Longpré, arriving there early next morning. After a six hours' halt in the rain outside the station the Battalion entrained and arrived at Méricourt at noon. Marching thence via Dernancourt and Meaulte, Camp D.18, north of Buire, was reached at 2.30 p.m.

At seven in the morning of the 25th August orders were received to proceed to huts at "The Citadel" on the Fricourt–Bray road, and the Battalion arrived there early in the afternoon. On the following day a further move was made to Billon Farm, two miles south-west of Maricourt, and after a two hours' march in the morning the Battalion bivouacked in a field. There was no cover of any sort for the men, and only one or two dugouts for the officers. During the 28th, which was very wet, the whole Battalion was employed in digging an assembly trench behind the front line held by the Devon Regt. and D.C.L.I.; the Gloucesters were in support and the East Surrey in reserve. The next two days continued very wet, and on the night of the 30th August the 1st Battn. East Surrey was ordered to relieve the Devons in Lonely Trench, about 1000 yards south of Guillemont. The relief was carried out with great difficulty, several casualties being sustained, and was not completed until 2 a.m. on the 31st. Throughout the day the enemy's artillery was very active, and, owing to the recent rain, the trenches were in a bad state, causing several cases of trench-feet.

The Battle of Delville Wood was now nearing its end. In the last week of August the British line had been pushed forward to a certain extent north and east of the wood, but its possession was not secured so long as the Germans held the greater portion of Guillemont. It was, however, now evident that, to avoid heavy losses, a combined operation with the French Army on the British right was necessary to ensure the capture of that village. The first two days of September were therefore spent in preparation for the combined allied attack which at noon on the 3rd September opened the Battle of Guillemont.

On the 2nd September the 1st Battn. East Surrey received its orders for the task to be carried out on the following day by the 95th and 13th Brigades. In

# THE 1st BATTALION IN THE BATTLE OF GUILLEMONT

the 95th Brigade the 12th Battn. Gloucester Regt. and 1st Battn. D.C.L.I. were to form the assaulting line, with the 1st Battn. Devon Regt. and 1st Battn. East Surrey in support. The 13th Brigade was to advance at 9 a.m. against Wedge Wood and Falfemont Farm, which stands on the extremity of a prominent spur nearly a mile south-east of Guillemont and overlooks Wedge Wood and Angle Wood in the valley below. On the right of the 13th Brigade French troops were to attack simultaneously on the far side of the valley running up to Combles. The 95th Brigade, on the left of the 13th, was to attack the enemy's trenches between Guillemont and Wedge Wood at noon.

At nine o'clock on the night of the 2nd the two battalions which were to lead the 95th Brigade took up their assembly positions, and the Devons and East Surrey withdrew to the second-line trenches recently dug about half a mile west of Maltz Horn Farm. The East Surrey's orders were to move two companies up to the first-line trenches as soon as the D.C.L.I. advanced from them. The other two companies and two companies of the Devons were to form the Brigade Reserve.

At 9.30 a.m. on September 3rd, Battalion Headquarters moved forward to the road junction 300 yards north-west of Maltz Horn Farm. A furious bombardment opened at eleven o'clock, and at noon the attack commenced. A and C Companies moved forward to take over the original front-line trenches and support the D.C.L.I., and half an hour later B and D Companies filed past Battalion Headquarters. At 2 p.m. Headquarters moved forward to the position vacated by the D.C.L.I., where soon afterwards reports were received that the 95th Brigade had carried its first objective—the sunken road which runs south from Ginchy to Wedge Wood—without much difficulty or loss, but that the 13th Brigade had not succeeded in taking Wedge Wood or Falfemont Farm. During the night East Surrey Battalion Headquarters moved back to Lonely Trench.

The 1st Battn. East Surrey was now ordered to relieve the D.C.L.I. on the sunken road, and A and C Companies were, in fact, moved forward to that point by the Officer Commanding the D.C.L.I., under whose orders they had been placed. Owing, however, to the late arrival of guides for B and D Companies it was considered impracticable to send them forward also before the coming of daylight.

The morning of the 4th September was dull, and presently heavy rain came on. A and C Companies were now holding the trenches south-east of Guillemont dug on the preceding day by the D.C.L.I. These trenches were a few yards west of the above-mentioned sunken road. Headquarters and B and D Companies were still in Lonely Trench.

No sign of the enemy could be discerned by the leading East Surrey companies, nor were they troubled by hostile artillery fire, though the British guns were shelling the trenches and ground in their front. About 8 a.m. 2nd Lieut. E. R. H. Atkins with a small patrol examined the valley which lies between the sunken road and Leuze Wood and reported it clear of the enemy.

At 3 p.m., when the 15th Brigade, which had relieved the 13th, was ordered to renew the attempt to capture Wedge Wood and Falfemont Farm, A and C Companies of the East Surrey advanced and occupied without opposition the German trench running north-east up the valley from near Wedge Wood. At 7 p.m. the 1st Battn. Devon Regt. advanced from the sunken road to Leuze Wood and entrenched themselves a few yards within its southern edge. A and C Companies of the East Surrey followed and dug in in a position supporting the Devons, incurring as they did so some loss from artillery fire, which had now recommenced. Meanwhile the 15th Brigade had made considerable progress on the right of the 95th, though the capture of Falfemont Farm was not completed till the following day. The casualties during the 4th September included 2nd Lieut. L. C. Carey and Cpl. E. Dwyer, V.C., killed and 2nd Lieuts. E. R. H. Atkins and Carter wounded.

During the night of the 4th/5th September continual rain made rest impossible, though the enemy's shelling had nearly ceased. At 4 a.m. on the 5th orders arrived that the 1st Battn. East Surrey was to throw out patrols and form a chain of posts between the 95th Brigade and 15th Brigade on the right. The distance to be filled was found to be about 200 yards, and four posts, each of one N.C.O. and six men, were accordingly placed to fill the gap. At five in the afternoon the Devons made an advance in Leuze Wood, and A and C Companies East Surrey accordingly moved up to the trench inside the wood vacated by the Devon supports. At about 10 p.m. the Devons made a further advance in the wood and the two East Surrey companies were ordered to move up again to the trenches vacated by the Devons. Guides, however, were not provided and the night was very dark. The two company commanders, though personally reconnoitring, failed to find the position intended for them. They consequently remained in their trenches, which gave good cover and were well placed to support the front line.

Early in the morning of the 6th September the Battalion was relieved by the London Scottish. The companies were on the move at 5 a.m., and by ten o'clock all had arrived, tired and footsore, in Happy Valley. There were no tents, but the weather was fine and the men were able to get a partial wash. At about 7 p.m. the Battalion moved to its camp further north, where tents were available. The men were settled down by 9 p.m., and spent the whole of the following day resting and cleaning up. The 8th was also a day of rest, and about noon Major-General Stephens, commanding the 5th Division, addressed the 95th Brigade. After reading many congratulatory telegrams regarding the phenomenal successes of the Division, the General said that these were mainly due to the splendid vigour and determination shown by the 95th Brigade. He thanked all ranks most warmly for their individual efforts.

The decorations subsequently awarded to N.C.O.'s and men of the Battalion for conspicuous gallantry in the earlier battles of the Somme were as follows:—

*Distinguished Conduct Medal:* Cpl. E. Doel.

*Military Medal:* C.S.M. W. Hemmings; Sergts. G. Clapshaw, G. Fossey, G. W. Prosser and G. T. Wade; Cpls. H. Montgomery and W. A. Owers;

## 1st BATTN. TEMPORARILY ATTACHED TO THE 13TH BRIGADE

Lce.-Cpl. A. W. McGowan; Ptes. J. Brown, G. F. Brown, J. S. Golding, W. Smeeth and J. Solly.

On the 9th September, on which date Ginchy was captured by British troops, the 95th Brigade was ordered back to Morlancourt, south of Albert, less the Devons and East Surrey, who were now attached to the 13th Brigade, and moved into the Citadel Camp to await orders. On the morning of the 10th the 1st Battn. East Surrey again moved forward and reached its bivouac at Casement Trench at 11 a.m. Here grenades were issued, one to each man, and the reserve Lewis-gun ammunition was completed. Instructions as to the intended operations were given to the Commanding Officer at noon, and at 9 p.m. the Battalion, with guides provided by the 2nd Battn. London Regt., marched off for Wedge Wood. Headquarters and A and C Companies were posted in trenches just north-east of Angle Wood, and, as Wedge Wood was found to be full of troops, B and D Companies, which were to have been posted there, were settled in trenches half-way up the slope to Falfemont Farm, and about 150 yards north-east of those occupied by A and C. All were in position by 1 a.m.

September 11th was a comparatively quiet day, but in the afternoon a shell burst just outside Battalion Headquarters, killing one orderly and wounding Captain and Adjutant R. A. F. Montanaro, 2nd Lieut. H. W. Pearce (Lewis-gun officer) and Regtl. Sergt.-Major Hayes. Lieut. J. C. Druce took over the duties of Adjutant, and 2nd Lieut. Mason succeeded Lieut. Druce in the command of A Company.

The instructions as to the intended operations referred to above were cancelled very soon after they were issued, and on the 12th September the Devons and East Surrey were both warned that they might be called upon to relieve battalions in the first line during the night, though in the event only the Devons were required. Of the 1st Battn. East Surrey, D Company moved up to a trench in close support of the troops in Leuze Wood, and C Company moved up to the position vacated by D. The place of the Devons, on the right of the East Surrey, was taken by the 14th Battn. Royal Warwick Regt., commanded by Lieut.-Colonel L. Murray, a Captain in the Reserve of Officers of the East Surrey.

September 13th passed quietly for the 1st Battn. East Surrey; but the Devons in Leuze Wood suffered severely from shell fire. At night the two battalions were relieved and marched back to bivouac by companies. Next day the 1st Battn. East Surrey marched west across country to Ville-sur-Ancre and Treux, in which villages it found billets with some difficulty. It remained in these quiet quarters till September 18th, engaged in bathing and refitting, with a little steady drill. A draft of 95 men had joined on the 11th, bringing the strength of the Battalion slightly above 500, and on the 17th seven officers joined.

At 4.15 in the morning of the 18th September the Battalion marched from Treux and Ville-sur-Ancre for the Sandpits, south of Montauban, the rendezvous of the 95th Brigade. In the afternoon it moved on again to the Briqueterie, and in the evening again advanced as far as Brigade Headquarters, near Wedge Wood, where it was met by the Commanding Officer and company commanders, who had gone forward to reconnoitre. The latter then led their companies to the support trenches, which were taken over from the "Buffs" half an hour after midnight. The weather had been very wet and the roads were crowded and slippery, so this long day's work was very fatiguing to the men. The support trenches, which were half full of water, lay close to the Guillemont–Combles road, about a quarter of a mile west of Leuze Wood, and in them the Battalion remained till the night of the 22nd/23rd.

The intention had been that the 95th Brigade should attack Morval, which lay over a mile to the north-east on the 21st, and all arrangements were made accordingly; but, owing to the continued bad weather, the requisite supplies of gun ammunition could not be brought up in time and the attack was twice postponed. The treacherous weather conditions broke down a number of men, and on the 20th September the trench strength was only 450. Owing to the blocked state of the roads the cookers had been unable to get near the Battalion and, in consequence, no tea was available.

On the night of the 22nd September the 95th Brigade, less the 12th Battn. Gloucester Regt., was relieved for forty-eight hours' rest previous to the attack, which was now timed for the 25th. On relief, companies moved independently to Oxford Copse, near Maricourt, where there was cover for most of the Battalion. The two following days were fortunately fine, and the men rested; but the battalions of the 95th Brigade were all much weakened by heavy losses and the strain of prolonged fighting in bad weather. It was realized that the battalions were in no fit state of strength to carry out a desperate attack, and one battalion, which was more overworked than the remainder, was relieved and replaced by the 2nd Battn. K.O.S.B. The three other battalions were asked to do their best.

Operation orders were issued on the 24th and showed the task allotted to the three divisions of the XIV Corps, as part of the general attack to be launched by the Allies on the whole front from the Somme to Martinpuich, a village halfway between Albert and Bapaume. The 5th Division was temporarily attached to the XIV Corps, the XIII Corps having been for a time withdrawn from the line of battle. The 5th Division was ordered to capture Morval, and the Guards Division to capture Lesboeufs, half a mile further north, the 20th Division forming the Corps Reserve.

The distribution of the 5th Division placed the 95th and 15th Brigades in the first line, the former on the right; and the 95th Brigade operation order detailed the 1st Battn. East Surrey as right, and the 1st Battn. Devon Regt. as left, assaulting battalions, the 2nd Battn. K.O.S.B. being in support and the 12th Battn. Gloucester Regt. in reserve. The attack on Morval and Lesboeufs was to be made in conjunction with attacks by two French corps on Sailly-Saillisel on the right, and by the British Reserve Army on Gueudecourt on the left. The assaulting battalions of the 95th Brigade were ordered to advance each on a two-company front, and each company on a front of two platoons, which were to form the first wave. Three of the new heavily armoured cars known as "Tanks," which had made their first appearance in the Battle of Flers-Courcelette ten days previously, were placed at the disposal of the 5th Division.

## THE 1st BATTALION IN THE BATTLE OF MORVAL

The 1st Battn. East Surrey, with a strength of 19 officers and 437 other ranks, moved off at 5 p.m. on September 24th to the north-west corner of Faviere Wood, which lies a mile north-east of Maricourt. Here stores were drawn, including entrenching tools, bombs, sandbags and rockets. Thence it proceeded by Chimpanzee Valley to the south-east corner of Trones Wood, and through Guillemont to its assembly trenches. Here A and C Companies relieved the two right companies of the Royal West Kent Regt., while B and D Companies went forward to a newly dug assembly trench. During this relief the enemy, who was continually suspicious of attack, put down a heavy barrage which caused twenty-seven casualties in C Company. Soon afterwards Captain McLeod, the Brigade Major, visited Battalion Headquarters, gave out the last detail, the time of assault, 12.35 p.m., and synchronized watches. All arrangements for the assault were completed before dawn on the 25th, which removed any necessity for sending orderlies to the front companies, a service of considerable difficulty and danger, owing to their exposed position. During the morning of the 25th September the following message was received from Lieut.-General Lord Cavan, commanding the XIV Corps: "Special wishes of good luck to the 5th Division, who have already won highest honours on the Somme. Relief soon as possible faithfully promised."

At 12.35 p.m., under cover of a terrific bombardment, the whole line left their trenches and moved steadily forward across No Man's Land. The leading East Surrey companies at first sustained no serious loss, but so eagerly did the men press on that they outpaced the creeping barrage which protected them and thereby suffered some casualties. As they drew nearer to their objective, which lay midway between Bouleaux Wood and Morval, B Company suffered more severely by enfilade fire from the right and for a few seconds was checked. At that moment A and C Companies came up in support and the added impetus carried the assault up to the German trench line, which after a sharp bayonet fight was carried and passed.

The companies fought their way forward to the enemy's positions in rear, detaching a strong party to deal with the artillery dugouts, as the German occupants refused to come out until Mills grenades were thrown in amongst them. The work of clearing these dugouts was one of great difficulty and danger and entailed considerable losses, carried on as it was under heavy shell fire and continuous sniping at close range. 2nd Lieut. Smith, who was directing the clearing work, took prompt action against the snipers, who were soon completely disposed of. Eighty or more prisoners were taken at this point.

The action had been short but very severe. All the companies had suffered heavily, both in the last few moments of the assault and after that from the fire of the snipers; 2nd Lieut. H. A. Holgate had been killed and three out of the four company commanders had been seriously wounded. Captains R. Streatfeild-James, D.S.O., and G. D. Robinson, both most gallant and valuable soldiers, unfortunately died of their wounds—a heavy loss to the Battalion. 2nd Lieut. Wight, commanding D Company, another first-rate officer, was also severely wounded.

At 1.35 p.m. the Devons took the second objective nearer Morval, and the East Surrey, meeting with no resistance, worked up the trench on their left and got into touch with them; while on the right the London Scottish had established themselves on the railway embankment north of Bouleaux Wood. Fighting was now over as far as the Battalion was concerned, but it was subjected to a certain amount of shelling until the 2nd Battn. K.O.S.B. advanced through Morval to the third objective, the south-east edge of the village. 2nd Lieut. H. C. Mason was now the senior officer with the four companies, and the only officers remaining with him were 2nd Lieuts. S. A. Smith, C. S. Oswin and W. C. Roser. He was also well supported by Company Sergt.-Major J. V. Woolgar and Sergt. Silver. Every effort was now made to get the wounded away, and the prisoners were mostly found willing to carry the stretchers back to the advanced dressing-station, which was close to Battalion Headquarters. The work of removal, however, took a long time and was not completed till dusk. During the evening the following message from Lieut.-General Lord Cavan was received and circulated by the 5th Division: " Hearty thanks and sincere congratulations to you. A very fine achievement splendidly executed." The honours subsequently awarded for this fine action included the following:—

*D.S.O.*: Captain R. Streatfeild-James.
*M.C.*: Captain H. C. Mason (4th Battn. attd.) 2nd Lieut. L. L. Wight and Company Sergt.-Major J. V. Woolgar.
*Bar to D.C.M.*: Cpl. E. Doel.
*Military Medal*: Sergt. A. Silver; Cpl. J. Lane; Lce.-Cpls. J. Tracey and P. J. Ovenden.

September 26th proved to be on the whole a quiet day. The Battalion remained in its trenches and spent the day in improving them and in burying the dead. At night the 20th Division came up and relieved the 5th, the 1st Battn. East Surrey being relieved by the 6th Battn. Oxford and Bucks L.I. As Battalion Headquarters were going down they were caught by shrapnel, Regtl. Sergt.-Major Walker and two orderlies being wounded.

On relief, the companies marched back independently to Oxford Copse, mustering 7 officers and 200 men. The casualties during the forty-eight hours' fighting in the Battle of Morval were estimated at 12 officers and 191 other ranks, or nearly 50 per cent of all ranks; while the total war wastage, including sick, suffered by the 1st Battn. East Surrey in the battles of the Somme, 1916, is put at 40 officers and 1200 other ranks.

The following letter was received during the day from the G.O.C. 5th Division, Major-General Stephens: " The General Officer Commanding wishes to thank all ranks in the Division for their magnificent conduct yesterday. In spite of their heavy losses in previous actions and the hardships which they have endured during the recent bad weather they have shown that their spirit is as good as ever. No task is too hard for the 5th Division."

The Battalion rested at Oxford Copse until the evening of September 27th, when it marched to the Citadel once more. The weather was fine in the morn-

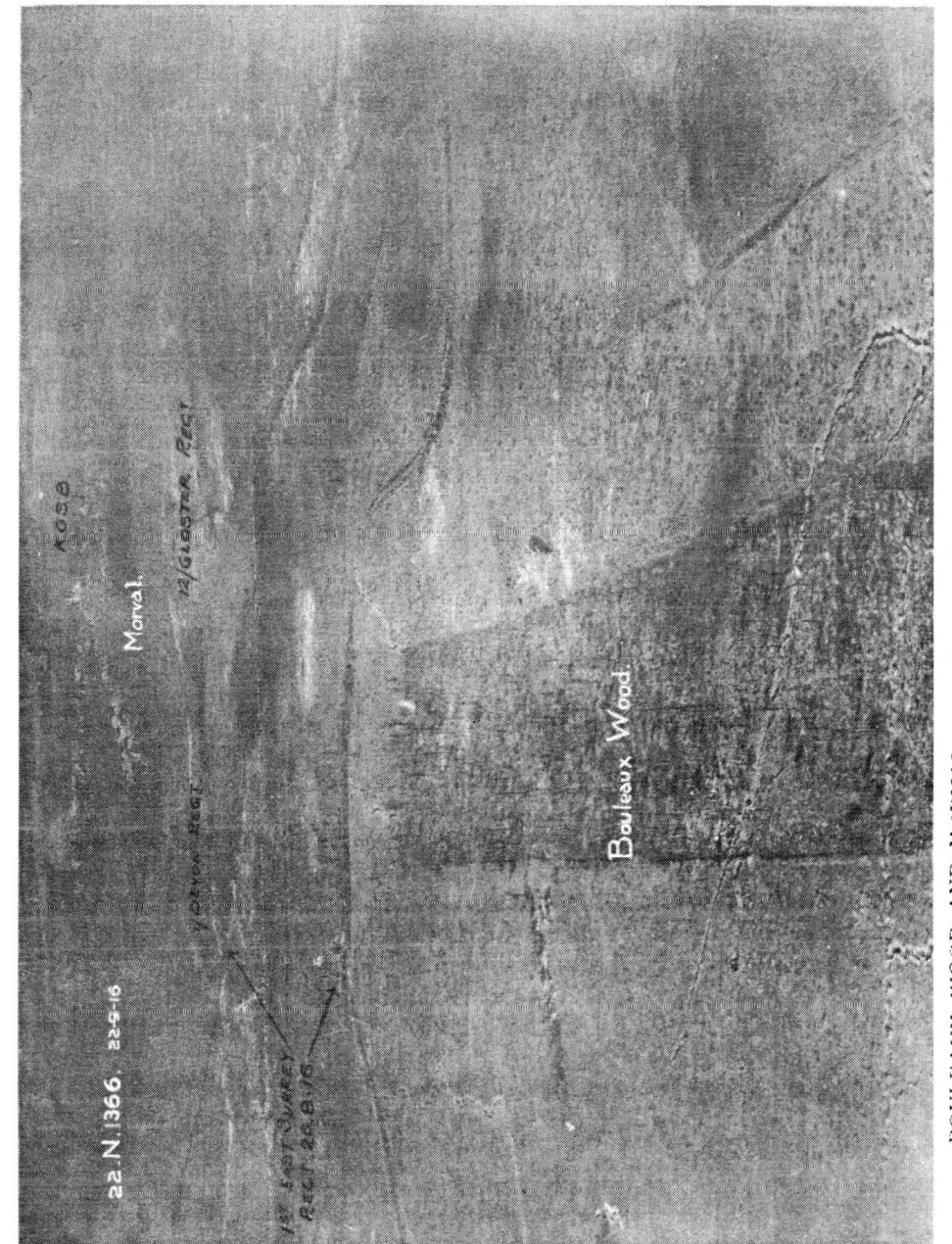

BOULEAUX WOOD AND MORVAL. FROM A PHOTOGRAPH TAKEN FROM THE AIR

## THE 5TH DIVISION TRANSFERRED TO LA BASSEE CANAL

ing, and a heavy thunderstorm in the afternoon happily did not break until the men were all under cover. In the early afternoon of the 29th the 1st Battn. East Surrey left the Citadel and, marching to Happy Valley station, entrained there. The train got under weigh at four o'clock and, after a tedious journey, arrived at Longpré an hour after midnight. Thence the Battalion marched to Liercourt, near Amiens, where it settled down in comfortable billets.

During the 30th September the following congratulatory letter from General Sir Henry Rawlinson, Commanding the Fourth Army, was circulated: "The conspicuous part that has been taken by the 5th Division in the Battle of the Somme reflects the highest credit on the Division as a whole, and I desire to express to every officer, N.C.O. and man my congratulations and warmest thanks. The heavy fighting in Delville Wood, the attack and capture of the Falfemont Farm line and Leuze Wood, and finally the storming of Morval are feats of arms seldom equalled in the annals of the British Army."

It should be explained that the series of operations referred to in the above letter as "The Battle of the Somme" is now officially designated "The Battles of the Somme, 1916." This designation includes a series of twelve battles, beginning with that of Albert, 1916, and ending on the 18th November with the conclusion of the Battle of the Ancre, 1916.

After its withdrawal to the Amiens area at the end of September, the 5th Division was not called upon to return to the Somme front, but was transferred to the La Bassée canal area for a spell of trench duty. The 1st Battn. East Surrey arrived accordingly in Béthune on the 2nd October, and spent the next few days reorganizing after its heavy losses.

On the 5th October the 5th Division took over the Givenchy-Cuinchy sector astride of the La Bassée canal, and the 1st Battn. East Surrey marched along the canal bank to Gorre, where the officers were billeted in the village and the men in the château buildings. Battalion Headquarters and the mess were in the château itself, and the transport in the grounds.

For a few days the Battalion occupied posts north of the La Bassée canal, but on the 10th October it left Gorre and took over the Cuinchy right sub-sector, known as "The Brickstacks," which lay south of the canal and had a frontage of 1000 yards. Owing to the weakness of the companies orders were received that all the transport except twenty men should be ready to reinforce the front line at half an hour's notice. The trenches were in a very damaged condition from trench-mortar fire, which was reported to be extremely violent at times; but casualties proved to be light, two men only being wounded during the tour, which ended on the 14th.

The 1st Battn. East Surrey then moved back into support in the village of Cuinchy on relief by the 1st Battn. Devon Regt. For the next six weeks—that is, till the 26th November—the 1st Battn. East Surrey and the Devons held the Cuinchy right sub-sector alternately, relieving each other every four days. The periods intervening between the tours of trench duty were passed either in support at Cuinchy in the "village line," or in Brigade Reserve at Le Quesnoy, three miles further back.

On the 20th October, when the East Surrey were in the trenches, the 18-pounders of the 5th Divisional Artillery fired forty rounds and unfortunately killed two men of B Company, though all proper precautions had been taken and registration had just been completed. On the 22nd, Lieut.-Colonel Woulfe-Flanagan went to England on leave, Captain H. A. Colt, 12th Battn. Gloucester Regt., taking over temporary command of the Battalion. On the 27th the 1st Battn. East Surrey, being then in the trenches, came in for a heavy bombardment with "minenwerfer" of all calibres and rifle grenades. Captain O. G. Norman and 2nd Lieut. Hill were wounded, the former very slightly; 2 men were killed and 2 wounded. At 3 a.m. on the 28th the enemy renewed his bombardment, using some very heavy mortars. The trenches were much damaged and two more men were wounded. Our artillery did not reply, but at 11 a.m. opened a very heavy retaliatory fire from a large number of guns and howitzers which had been collected for the purpose. The result was satisfactory. Enterprising patrol work was carried out on the 29th, in the early morning under 2nd Lieut. Waldron, and at night under Lieut. J. L. Lasenby. The latter was highly successful and inflicted several casualties on the Germans. Lieut. Lasenby and 2 men were slightly wounded, and 1 man was wounded and missing.

During its first tour of trench duty in November the Battalion had one man wounded by trench-mortar fire on the 3rd; and on the 5th a heavy "minenwerfer" opened fire in the evening, and by ill luck one shell destroyed a Lewis gun and killed or wounded the whole team. Lieut.-Colonel Woulfe-Flanagan returned from leave and resumed command, Captain Colt returning to his own regiment. A draft of 106 men joined at Le Quesnoy on the 9th, and a second draft of 80 on the following day. During the next tour in the trenches there was very little activity; in fact, the enemy showed a desire to be friendly, shouting several times over their parapet, "We are not Prussians," and similar ingratiating remarks. On the 20th, Lieut.-Colonel F. N. Butler, 5th Battn. Bedford Regt., joined the Battalion and assumed the duties of Senior Major.

2nd Lieut. L. O. Atkins was wounded on November 21st while wiring. On the 22nd a patrol of thirty N.C.O.'s and men, under 2nd Lieut. G. Gunning, attempted a raid against the Embankment Redoubt, with the intention of taking prisoners. The patrol remained out for a considerable time, but found the enemy very alert and met with no success. On the 23rd, Captains E. Crocker and O. G. Norman, who had been lent to the Battalion by the 13th Battn. East Surrey, returned to their unit, the 1st Battalion complement of captains being complete.

On November 26th the 5th Division took over the sector north of the Givenchy sector, and the Battalion moved in consequence to billets at Le Touret, where it remained until the 5th December in reserve to the 15th Brigade.

On the 3rd December, Lieut.-Colonel Woulfe-Flanagan went to England on one month's leave, the command devolving on Lieut.-Colonel Butler.

Early on December 5th the Battalion relieved the 1st Battn. Cheshire Regt. in the Ferme du Bois right sub-sector, just south of Richebourg l'Avoué, where the trenches resembled those occupied in the summer of 1915 near Verbranden-

Molen. The ground being damp and low lying, trenches had to be shallow, with breastworks and parados built up with sandbags and wooden frames. The front line was very thinly held and consisted of ten strong points, each garrisoned by twenty to thirty men with one Lewis gun. The support line, about 300 yards in rear, consisted of a nearly continuous fire trench. The sub-sector frontage was nearly 2000 yards. On December 7th, Captain E. G. Sulivan (4th Battalion), 2nd Lieut. Watts and 56 men joined the Battalion, and on the 9th the Battalion was relieved by the Devons and went back into Brigade Reserve at Senechal Farm and King's Road.

On December 13th the Battalion relieved the Devons in the Ferme du Bois sub-sector, and on the 17th went back into Brigade Reserve at Senechal Farm and King's Road as before. The tour of trench duty had been uneventful. Lieut.-Colonel F. N. Butler handed over command of the Battalion to Major Colt, of the Gloucester Regt., and left to take over command of the 1st Battn. Bedford Regt. On the 20th a draft of 139 " untrained " men arrived: this was a new and temporary arrangement. On December 21st the Battalion was relieved by a battalion of the 111th Infantry Brigade and marched to Béthune, where it was billeted with other troops in the Ecole des Jeunes Filles. The 95th Brigade was now in Divisional Reserve, the 13th and 15th Brigades holding the Givenchy and Cuinchy sectors. As Christmas approached, signs were not wanting that the enemy intended to attempt to fraternize, as he had done at the same season in 1914, and steps were taken to prevent anything of the sort happening. Christmas Day was observed by the Battalion as a holiday.

On the 29th December the 95th Brigade relieved the 13th in the Givenchy sector, north of the canal, and the 1st Battn. East Surrey took over the right sub-sector trenches. On the 30th, Captain G. A. E. Panter joined from the Third Army School and took over duty as Senior Major. The last day of the year was a quiet one in the trenches, but at midnight our artillery fired several salvoes as a New Year's greeting.

The Battalion was relieved on January 2nd by the Devons and moved back into support in the village line from Windy Corner to Festubert, one company being detailed as reinforcing company, and a second taking over the keeps and posts at Festubert. On the 3rd, Lieut.-Colonel Woulfe-Flanagan, who had been awarded the D.S.O. in the New Year's *Gazette*, returned from leave and resumed command of the Battalion. On the 4th, Major Minogue arrived from England and took over the duties of Senior Major. On January 6th the Battalion relieved the Devons in the Givenchy right sub-sector and remained in the trenches without incident until the 10th, when it went into Brigade Reserve at Gorre. Four days later the 95th Brigade went into Divisional Reserve at Beuvry, a mile and a half south-east of Béthune, and the 1st Battn. East Surrey carried out hard training in very cold weather until January 22nd, when it relieved the 1st Battn. Bedford Regt. in the Cuinchy left sub-sector south of the canal. The weather at the time was extremely cold and the trenches very wet. For the next eight weeks the 1st Battn. East Surrey and the Devons continued to hold this sub-sector, relieving each other in the trenches every four days and spending the intervening periods either in support in the village line or in reserve in Le Quesnoy. On the 24th 2 men were killed and 2 slightly wounded by a shell. On the 27th, 2nd Lieut. E. Hollingsworth rejoined. He had been wounded at Longueval, and was the first officer wounded on the Somme to return to duty.

Early in the morning of the 8th February, when the 1st Battn. East Surrey was in the trenches, a German raid was made on its left flank and on the battalion on its left. No losses were incurred by the East Surrey, but the Germans were stated by a prisoner to have had twenty casualties. The weather remained very cold until the 10th, on which day two companies of the Royal West Kent, the battalion on the left, made a very successful raid on the German trenches, inflicting many casualties and doing much damage. During the East Surrey's next tour of trench duty two mines were blown, after due preparation and warning, by the 254th Tunnelling Company at midnight on the 16th, in front of part of the line held by the Battalion. The left crater was to be held by a party of twenty-five men under 2nd Lieut. Crouch, and two working parties were ordered to dig a communicating and a connecting trench; owing, however, to the frozen state of the ground the task of digging the trench took longer than was expected, and 2nd Lieut. Crouch and his party in the crater were isolated throughout the 17th, but the Germans were inactive. On the 24th information was received that very large numbers of French and Russian prisoners of war were being made to work under the fire of the British artillery, and sentries were warned that some of these unfortunate men might try to escape into our lines.

At the beginning of March the Cuinchy sector was renamed Canal sector, the trenches held alternately by the Devons and East Surrey thus becoming the Left Canal sub-sector. On the 14th March, when the 1st Battn. East Surrey was in these trenches, the enemy's artillery became exceptionally active after a long period of comparative quiet, and the Battalion lost 3 men killed and 5 wounded during the morning. Next day it was relieved by the Devons for the last time in this portion of the line and went into support in the village line. On March 17th the 95th Brigade was relieved by the 198th Brigade and went into billets at Béthune and Essars, the 1st Battn. East Surrey being quartered in the Montmorency Barracks, which it had occupied in October, 1916, on its arrival in this district from the Somme area.

The 5th Division was now being withdrawn from the line in order to form the reserve of the Canadian Corps. Accordingly, on the 18th March the 1st Battn. East Surrey marched with the remainder of the 95th Brigade to Raimbert, eight miles west of Béthune, where a training programme up to April 6th was issued, of which the first day's work was carried out on the 20th March. The most important item in the course was instruction in the new normal formation for the attack, recently adopted from the French Army.

## CHAPTER XVII

JULY, 1916, TO MARCH, 1917: THE 2ND BATTALION WITH THE BRITISH SALONIKA ARMY ON THE STRUMA VALLEY FRONT, BETWEEN LAKE BUTKOVO AND LAKE TAHINOS.

THE epidemic of fever which had declared itself in the Battalion at Kurfali, on the Struma front, at the end of June, 1916, rapidly assumed alarming proportions. Work continued as usual on the 1st July, but on the 2nd and following days all ranks were detained in bivouac in an attempt to localize and check the disease. On the 4th 9 officers and 42 men were admitted to hospital, 2 officers and 94 men on the 5th, on which day a shade temperature of 112° is recorded in the War Diary. On the 6th and 7th another officer and 88 men went to hospital, and one man died. Several medical officers visited the Battalion's bivouac and pronounced its sanitary arrangements perfect. The epidemic was attributed to the tour of duty at Lozista. On July 8th the Battalion marched westwards across the Krusha Balkan to Hamzali, *en route* to Paprat. The march over steep hills and rough roads was executed with great difficulty, the transport being disorganized through sickness; 47 men were admitted to hospital.

The Battalion continued its march at 5 a.m. on the 9th, and reached Paprat at 8.20 a.m. One officer and 34 men were admitted to hospital this day; and on the 10th, when the Battalion was "at rest," 1 officer and 64 men were admitted. Two men died this day. On July 11th, 22 men were admitted to hospital, bringing total sick to date to 18 officers and 454 other ranks. The strength of the Battalion fit for duty was 12 officers and 278 other ranks. Every possible sanitary precaution had been taken, and it was now hoped that the turning-point had been reached; but for the time being the Battalion was rendered unserviceable, a condition shared by many other units of the Army. Happily the number of deaths did not exceed fourteen between the 7th and 27th July.

The Battalion remained at Paprat from the 9th July to the end of the month, and its history was necessarily uneventful. The first person to return to duty from hospital was Lieut. Voisin on the 15th, and 6 other officers and 38 men rejoined during the remainder of the month.

On July 17th, Lieut.-Colonel Gilbert-Cooper assumed command of the 85th Brigade during the absence on leave of Brigadier-General Carter. Major E. H. Nicholson, 3rd Battn. Royal Fusiliers, was temporarily appointed to command the Battalion, no East Surrey officer of sufficient seniority being available. On July 26th a change in the weather was noted, the nights becoming cold, and on the 31st the Diary records "weather distinctly better." No admissions to hospital are recorded on the last three days of the month, and on the 31st the Battalion resumed partial duty.

The Battalion remained in reserve at Paprat throughout August, and from the 1st to the 19th there was little to record. Twenty-seven men rejoined from hospital, and 2nd Lieuts. Clarke, Mears, Kitson, Cass and Card joined the Battalion from Egypt. The Battalion was employed in roadmaking, musketry and bombing practice. Cholera inoculation was effected on the 11th and 18th, and Salonika town was placed out of bounds.

On the 17th August the Bulgar troops, who had moved south as far as Demirhissar at the end of May, continued their advance into Greek Macedonia. Consequently, on the 20th sudden orders were received for the outpost-line now held by the other units of the 85th Brigade to be reinforced. This outpost-line ran along the narrow ridges and spurs of the Krusha Balkan. The surface was rock and all paths had to be made. The Battalion could only muster ninety rifles for duty, but took over from "The Buffs" three posts in the outpost-line northeast of Paprat, Battalion Headquarters remaining at Paprat. On the 21st and 22nd all hands worked at clearing the foreground; wiring was commenced, and stone sangars were constructed.

On the 23rd our guns shelled the villages occupied by the enemy, all of which were on the far side of the Struma. On the 25th the Battalion took over two more posts from "The Buffs." The five East Surrey posts were weakly held, but the arrival of a draft of 120 men was daily expected. The draft did, in fact, arrive on the 30th, but was only 100 strong; and on the 31st another post was taken over from "The Buffs."

The weather in the early part of September was stormy, thunder and heavy rain frequently occurring. Work continued assiduously, the sector of the outpost-line held by the Battalion being much strengthened, and Battalion Headquarters were moved forward from Paprat. A draft of 50 men arrived on the 5th, and on the 15th 8 officers and 89 other ranks rejoined from hospital. Further reinforcements, amounting to 2 officers and 100 other ranks, some from England and others rejoining from hospital, were received by the 20th, so that on the 21st the Battalion was able to take over charge of an extended line, its right resting on the left of "The Buffs" as hitherto, with its left reaching to, but not including, Rock Kopje (Hill 1004). The weather had by now considerably improved, and there were very few admissions to hospital during the month.

On the 24th September the outpost-line had been sufficiently strengthened for the construction of dugouts to be undertaken, and by the 28th cover for "practically all ranks" had been made—very quick work. There was a certain amount of artillery fire on our part during the month, but the Bulgars made no attempt to cross the Struma, which has a swift current, is full of sandbanks and not navigable. The plain of the Struma is fertile, with many villages. The principal crop is maize.

On the 1st October "The Buffs" were withdrawn from the outpost-line into Divisional Reserve, and their front was taken over by the 2nd Battn. East Surrey, in addition to the ground already held. This gave the Battalion a front of over five miles, extending from Demirhamlar on the right, round the head of the valley, to the foot of Rock Kopje (Hill 1004) on the left. Heavy rain fell at night, and most of the dugouts and bivouacs were flooded. On the 2nd, telephone communications through the Battalion line were completed and all supply arrangements were made. This was a heavy but successful day's work for all concerned. In different points of the Battalion line detachments of Royal Artillery, anti-aircraft gunners and Royal Engineers were posted, all of whom had to be supplied. From the position now held an excellent view of most of the Struma front was obtainable, and the artillery action could all be observed. Firing this day and on the 3rd October was very heavy, as another brigade further to the right was making an attack, which proved successful, on Yenikoi, a village on the left bank of the Struma River, about five miles from Lake Tahinos. On the 4th and 5th October much movement was observed among the enemy's troops and transport, and on the 6th cavalry patrols reported that the enemy was falling back, doubtless to get out of range of our guns, which had caused him considerable casualties. On the 7th October a draft of 141 men joined the Battalion, 81 of whom had served previously with it; 20 more men joined on the 8th from England. On the 8th the Royal Engineers with the Battalion were constructing rafts, aided by our men.

On the 9th the enemy was reported to have taken up the line Papalova–Homondos, and 2nd Lieut. Dell, with a patrol, crossed the river to ascertain if the enemy was holding Bursuk, which lay north-west of Papalova and opposite the outpost-line occupied by the East Surrey. 2nd Lieut. Dell located an enemy post in the wood south-west of Bursuk, and a stronger patrol sent out on the night of the 10th located another in the same locality.

On the 12th, 2nd Lieut. Dell was sent forward with a third patrol with orders to capture a sentry post near Bursuk, but found the post vacated. On October 14th 4 officers and 60 men passed the night at Big Tree Well, on the bank of the Struma, and crossed the river in four parties by raft and boat early on the morning of the 15th, with orders to advance on Bursuk and see if it were still held. The left party was fired on, showing that the village was held, and the Brigade Commander ordered the detachment to recross the river, which was effected under cover of the fire of a mountain battery. From the 18th to 21st inclusive wet weather prevailed.

On the 22nd October, A and B Companies, under Major Nicholson, proceeded a few miles south to the Gumus Dere district to form part of a reserve to the 83rd Brigade. Headquarters and C and D Companies proceeded to the village of Gurlimeli, just north of Demirhamlar, and remained there until the evening of the 23rd, when under cover of darkness they moved to a bivouac near Big Tree Well.

On the 25th it was decided that a camp should be formed, at the place where the Battalion was bivouacked, for Brigade Headquarters and certain Royal Artillery and Royal Engineers units; so from the 25th to 27th much work was done. On the nights of the 27th and 29th patrols under 2nd Lieut. Dell again visited Bursuk, and on the latter occasion were fired at from the village, and while returning to the river bank were followed up by hostile fire.

On the 30th and 31st operations were carried out by the 83rd and 84th

Brigades, in which the village of Barakli-Dzuma and Dolop Wood, three miles east of Bursuk, were captured. A and B Companies, under Major Nicholson, were employed as carrying parties during the operations. After the capture of Barakli-Dzuma a new defensive line was constructed on the left bank of the River Struma from Alipsa, a village near the junction of the Butkovo River with the Struma, through Haznatar, Barakli-Dzuma, Elisan and Yenikoi to Yenimah on Lake Tahinos.

On the 1st November a draft of 1 officer and 43 men joined, all from hospital in Egypt. The Battalion—still less A and B Companies—was warned that it would shortly go into the trenches at Haznatar, and on the 2nd the Commanding Officer, Adjutant, company commanders and signalling officer crossed the Struma and inspected the line held by the 1st Battn. Welsh Regt.

The relief was carried out on the night of the 3rd November. The line taken over was more than 3000 yards in length, and the left flank was much exposed. Up to the 8th November work on the trenches was carried out by day and drew a good deal of artillery fire; but subsequently all wiring was done by night. Three Bulgar deserters came into the Battalion's lines on the 12th November, and eight more on the 13th. That night a patrol of 1 officer and 15 men, covered by a party of 1 officer and 20 men with a Lewis gun, raided a Bulgar trench. The trench was found unoccupied, but the patrol came under heavy fire from another trench, somewhat in rear, which was strongly held. No casualties were sustained. On the 14th the Battalion extended its front to the left, so as to include the village of Alipsa on the bank of the Struma. From it three fords required guarding.

The 15th and 16th were very wet days. On the 17th, C and D Companies were relieved in their positions by A and B Companies, and went in Brigade Reserve at Ormanli. During the next three days the defences were being converted from trenches to breastworks, in consequence of heavy rains having set in. On the 20th November official news was received of the capture on the 18th of Monastir, in the south-west of Serbia, by the French and Serbian troops who were operating on the left of the Allied Salonika front. Leave to the United Kingdom was at once opened, and the 2nd Battn. East Surrey sent home eight N.C.O.'s and men, most of whom had never left the Battalion since it went on active service. For the next week the Diary records nothing of interest. Work went on daily on the defences, and frequent patrols were sent out to watch the enemy. On the 28th one of these patrols came under heavy fire and lost one man mortally wounded, who died on his way down to the field ambulance. The 19th and 30th were uneventful.

The Battalion retained its position about Haznatar throughout the month, and events were few. On the 4th December a patrol of 1 officer and 8 men, supported as before by a stronger party with a Lewis gun, left the lines at 4 p.m., with orders to locate an enemy machine gun. The patrol carried out its task, but had five men wounded, one severely. On the 6th another East Surrey patrol shot two Bulgar soldiers down from their observation post. On the 7th December the Diary notes that the roads by which supplies had to be brought up were becoming in a very bad state from the wet weather, in consequence of which the Battalion had no reserve rations in its possession.

On December 8th, Lieut.-Colonel Gilbert-Cooper received orders to proceed to England, and accordingly handed over command of the Battalion to Major E. H. Nicholson. On December 9th an East Surrey patrol again shot two Bulgar observers who were posted in a tree. The weather now improved for a time, and on the 12th gum boots were issued to the Battalion. Other precautions were taken to protect sentries and men on listening posts from frostbite and trench-feet. At this period small parties of the enemy deserted and came into our lines almost every day.

On December 16th patrol operations took place in which "The Buffs" and Middlesex also participated. It was found that the enemy had vacated his forward trenches, but "The Buffs" took "Ferdie" trench, killed 38 Bulgars and captured 6 prisoners. East Surrey casualties were two men wounded. On the 17th work was stopped, Sunday being now treated as a holiday; but the companies changed round at night. On the 22nd Lieut. and Quartermaster Percy proceeded to England on a well-earned leave of absence. Sunday the 24th was again a holiday, as was Christmas Day. Some additions were made to the rations at dinner; but very few of the Christmas purchases could be got up to the Battalion in consequence of transport difficulties. There was much activity on the part of hostile aircraft during the latter part of December, but no casualties were caused to the Battalion. The month and year closed without any further event.

The New Year opened with a bitterly cold day. The Battalion was still holding the Haznatar sector of the line and continued to dig communication trenches and improve the breastworks. The enemy's artillery was fairly active throughout the month. The Battalion had patrols out every night reconnoitring the enemy's advanced posts. On January 8th three other ranks were wounded while on patrol. In the early hours of the 13th the Struma overflowed its banks as a result of the downpour which had prevailed during the four days previous. The garrison at Alipsa had to be withdrawn at 4 a.m., the water between Alipsa and Haznatar being in places four feet deep. Haznatar was also flooded, and the Battalion was withdrawn to Ormanli, leaving fifty men to hold Haznatar Churchyard. On the 16th, the water having subsided, the Battalion reoccupied the Haznatar sector. Intense cold with snow followed the heavy rains. On the 26th a patrol of ten men, commanded by 2nd Lieut. B. F. Clarke, failed to return. It was ascertained later that 2nd Lieut. Clarke and one man had been killed and the remainder taken prisoners.

During the evening of the 26th the Battalion commenced to exchange sectors with the 3rd Battn. Middlesex Regt., who held the town of Barakli-Dzuma, and the relief was completed on the 28th. Leave parties, though small in numbers, were now going fairly regularly. The allotment for the Battalion was generally eight other ranks.

The heavy rains during the latter days of January had left the trenches in a very bad state, most of them being filled with water. However, an extensive system of draining was commenced at the beginning of February, with results which very soon justified the extra labour: more dugouts were constructed, and the general trench line was materially strengthened. On the 10th February the enemy's artillery obtained a direct hit on a bay where a sentry group, furnished by the Battalion, was posted. Two men were killed and three wounded. The ground was now drying up well and the weather greatly improved. Deserters were coming in fairly frequently from the enemy's lines, but their information could not be relied on.

During February malaria had broken out again: 223 cases in the Battalion came under medical treatment, and out of this number there were 64 admissions to hospital.

The epidemic continued during March, but anti-malarial precautionary measures were again undertaken on a large scale, with the result that in a few weeks the number of mosquitoes had been greatly reduced. On March 17th, when B, C and D Companies were holding the line, A Company being in reserve in Ormanli, the enemy started at 1.30 p.m. a systematic shelling of the entire British line from Stavros to Lake Doiran, and the town of Barakli-Dzuma came in for its full share. The bombardment was intense and lasted till 5 p.m. The front-line trenches held by the Battalion escaped most of the shelling, the enemy's plan apparently being to direct his fire on the supports, communication trenches and the town itself. At 2.30 p.m. the enemy demonstrated, but was soon scattered by rifle and Lewis-gun fire. There was a lull about 5 p.m., but at 6 p.m. the enemy opened fire again, and for half an hour the bombardment was intense, and then ceased. The casualties in the Battalion were 7 other ranks killed and 6 wounded. It was learnt afterwards that the enemy's activity on this day was in honour of King Ferdinand of Bulgaria, who had come to pay a visit to his troops on the Struma front.

Work was continued on the trench line, which was now becoming very strong, and communication trenches were dug under the houses, through the houses and under walls, which minimized observation from aeroplanes and afforded excellent cover.

# CHAPTER XVIII

JULY, 1916, TO MARCH, 1917: THE 7TH BATTALION IN THE BATTLES OF THE SOMME, 1916; AT OVILLERS IN THE BATTLE OF ALBERT, 1916, AND IN THE BATTLE OF POZIERES RIDGE; SIX WEEKS IN THE LINE SOUTH OF ARRAS; AT GUEUDECOURT IN THE BATTLE OF THE TRANSLOY RIDGES; FIVE MONTHS IN THE LINE ABOUT ARRAS.

AS already recorded in Chapter XII, the 7th Battn. East Surrey arrived at Bresle, near Albert, on the last day of June, 1916, and after a short rest in that village moved on to Millencourt, where it arrived on the 1st July. It was on that date that the Battles of the Somme, 1916, undertaken at the outset to relieve the German pressure on Verdun, commenced with the operations now known as the Battle of Albert, 1916.

The Battle of Albert began at 7.30 a.m., when the main attack by the Fourth Army was launched on a front extending from Maricourt, near the River Somme, round the German salient at Fricourt, two miles east of Albert, to St. Pierre Divion on the River Ancre, five miles north of Albert. By 5 p.m. the general results of this great attack were known to the Battalion. Briefly stated, the British right and centre had carried the German positions in front of them, but on the left, north of Albert, the strongly fortified villages of La Boisselle, Ovillers and Thiepval had resisted for the time being the attack of the III Corps. As a result of the day's fighting the British Commander-in-Chief decided to form a new army under Lieut.-General Sir Hubert Gough, consisting of the two left or northern corps, to operate on the front from La Boisselle near Albert northwards, in order that Sir Henry Rawlinson might push home the attack on the right and centre with the remainder of the Fourth Army. When, therefore, the 12th Division completed at 3.30 a.m. on the 2nd July the relief of the 8th Division, which had suffered heavy losses, it came under Sir Hubert Gough's orders.

On this occasion the 7th Battn. East Surrey was in Brigade Reserve, and at 2.30 p.m. it was ordered to move back to the railway cutting behind Crucifix Corner (see map opposite page 210), as the British artillery was about to open a fresh bombardment of Ovillers and La Boisselle, and it was desired to thin our line in order to lessen casualties. At 5 p.m. orders were issued that the 12th Division would attack Ovillers if an assault by the 19th Division on La Boisselle proved successful, and accordingly the Battalion moved up to its former trenches at 9 p.m., arriving there at 11 p.m.

The attack on Ovillers was launched at 3.15 a.m. on July 3rd, and the 6th Battn. "Queen's" and 6th Battn. Royal West Kent Regt., who formed the first line, both met with some success at first, but were bombed back and terribly cut up by enfilade machine-gun fire from both flanks. The 6th Battn. "The Buffs," who advanced in support, also suffered heavily, and the 7th Battn. East Surrey was not sent forward. The casualties in the 37th Brigade amounted to about 40 officers and 1050 other ranks, the 7th Battn. East Surrey naturally coming off comparatively lightly with 3 officers wounded (Captain J. L. Findlay and 2nd Lieuts. C. A. Wilson and I. T. Golds) and 50 other ranks killed or wounded.

By 1 p.m. all idea of continuing the attack on Ovillers by the 12th Division had been abandoned, and the 37th Brigade was ordered to hold its ground as a defensive flank. Its losses, however, had not been wasted, for the 19th Division had been helped in its operations against La Boisselle, which by the evening was completely captured. At 3 p.m. the 7th Battn. East Surrey took over the Brigade front, with the 6th Battn. "The Buffs" in support. The 6th Battn. "Queen's" were in reserve, and the 6th Battn. Royal West Kent Regt. (the heaviest sufferers) were at Albert in second reserve. The Battalion held this front line from the 3rd to the 6th July, and had a very heavy task. Not only was the front an extended one, but the trenches had been much knocked about and were full of dead and wounded. However, the men worked splendidly, and when the Battalion was relieved in the afternoon of the 6th the trenches were clear of dead, and the men had carried in from the front about 250 wounded, many of them in daylight. The trenches throughout this heavy work were above the boots in water and mud. On relief, the Battalion went back to the intermediate line just north of Albert.

During the five days in action the Battalion had had 10 other ranks killed, 3 officers and 80 other ranks wounded. The men came out very tired, and were thankful for a night's rest, the first for a week. They were also permitted to rest and attend to their feet on the morning of July 7th. This was much needed after working four days and nights in water.

The rest was fortunate, for at 6.30 p.m. on 7th July orders were received that the Battalion was lent to the 36th Infantry Brigade as a reinforcement to assist in consolidating the positions that had been captured in the outer defences of Ovillers. Sending his Adjutant, Captain Nicolls, on ahead to the headquarters of the 36th Brigade, Lieut.-Colonel Baldwin at 7.45 p.m. received orders to move quickly up to Ovillers Post, and on the way to draw two bags of bombs per man from the stores at Crucifix Corner. On arriving at the stores it was found that no bags were available, but by 11 p.m. the Battalion, about 350 strong, had reached Ovillers Post, every man carrying two *boxes* of bombs (weight 48 lbs.). Here Brigadier-General Boyd Moss, commanding 36th Brigade, explained to Lieut.-Colonel Baldwin the position of the trenches that he was required to consolidate, and also indicated a point, marked " X " in the sketch, supposed to be strongly held by the enemy, which was to be captured at all costs, as on its occupation depended to a great extent the advance of another division on the right up the Mash Valley.

The task of the 7th Battn. East Surrey was a difficult one, as the night was dark and trenches and ditches had to be crossed, but by 2.30 a.m. on July 8th the Battalion was close behind the Essex Regt., which was just entering the German trenches south-west of Ovillers, and by 3 p.m. the point " X " was

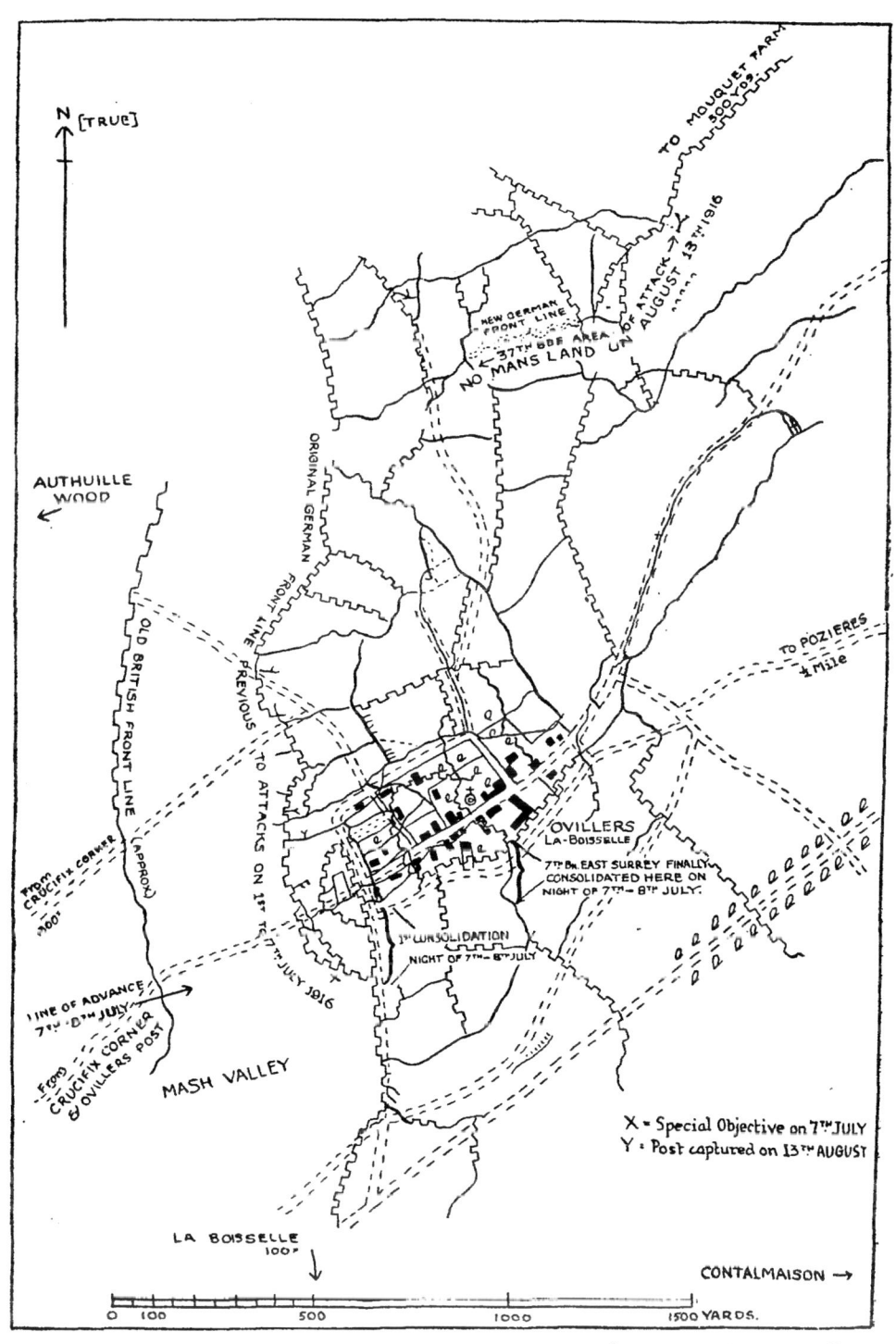

THE 7TH BATTALION IN THE BATTLES OF ALBERT, 1916, AND POZIERES RIDGE.

occupied without opposition. Further advance was prevented by our own artillery barrage, and at 6.15 a.m. Lieut.-Colonel Baldwin sent off a pigeon carrying a report as to his position to the 36th Brigade and also notifying that the barrage was holding up his advance. At 9 a.m. the barrage lifted, and the Battalion then pushed on along the southern outskirts of Ovillers, consolidating each trench in succession as it was won. By 12.45 p.m. the Battalion, in conjunction with the Essex Regt. on the left and South Lancashire Regt. on the right, had made considerable progress, which was eventually stopped by machine-gun fire from the eastern end of the village. At 4 p.m., Lieut.-Colonel Baldwin, who was in command of the three battalions, decided to consolidate. The left flank of his battalion was much exposed and the battalion on his right could go no further; moreover, he had been told to expect no reinforcements, and the men were absolutely exhausted owing to the heavy load of bombs that they had been carrying and the heavy mud through which they had been moving all day. What they had accomplished constituted indeed a fine feat of endurance. In this advance 2nd Lieut. G. A. Bentham was wounded. Three months later this officer was attached to the Royal Flying Corps, and on the 3rd November, 1916, was reported missing and is believed to have been killed in action.

At about 5 a.m. on July 9th the Battalion, having been relieved by the 15th Battn. H.L.I., moved out of Ovillers. Lieut.-Colonel Baldwin had the satisfaction of handing over more than 8000 bombs to the H.L.I. and, in addition, four boxes of Véry lights and telephone lines to Brigade Headquarters and the neighbouring battalion. Brigadier-General Boyd Moss afterwards warmly thanked Lieut.-Colonel Baldwin and his battalion for their invaluable services.

The Battalion arrived in Albert at 8.35 a.m., but were ordered to march at 9.30 to billets at Warloy, about eight miles west of Albert, as the 12th Division, having suffered over 5000 casualties, was to be kept out of the line until the arrival of reinforcements. Having rested at Warloy on July 11th, the 37th Brigade marched on the 12th to Vauchelles-les-Authie, about nine miles to the north, the Battalion being quartered there in huts with the 6th Battn. Royal West Kent Regt. On the 13th Major-General Scott, commanding 12th Division, inspected the two battalions and told them of the great satisfaction of himself and of the higher command with the work of the Division. To the 7th Battn. East Surrey he said that the Battalion had done splendidly throughout. On July 14th the Battalion found 6 officers and 324 men as its share of 1000 men which the 37th Brigade was ordered to furnish as a working party to the 29th Division. The next three days were uneventful so far as the 7th Battn. East Surrey was concerned, but during this period the Battle of Bazentin Ridge was fought, and on the 17th July British troops captured Ovillers.

On the 18th an unfortunate bombing accident cost the lives of Lieut. V. P. Knapp, the Battalion bombing officer, and of one man. Lieut. Knapp was a valuable and promising officer who had shown marked gallantry in action. Sergt. F. G. Evans, who had been awarded the D.C.M. and Croix-de-Guerre for his services on the 13th October, 1915, was wounded in this accident.

On the 21st July the 12th Division relieved the 4th Division in the line opposite Beaumont Hamel, some six miles north of Albert. The 37th Brigade being in reserve, the 7th Battn. East Surrey was quartered in huts five miles back at Bertrancourt, not far from Vauchelles. Its stay at Bertrancourt was a short one, as after three uneventful days the 12th Division was relieved from the line and the Battalion returned to its former billets in Vauchelles. Meanwhile, on the 23rd July, the Fourth Army and Sir Hubert Gough's Army had again attacked, and Pozières, a mile north-east of Ovillers, was captured on the 25th. Consequently, when the 12th Division again moved up to the line on that date it took over a position north of Ovillers, facing northwards towards Thiepval. The 37th Brigade, being still in reserve, remained on the west bank of the River Ancre, the 7th Battn. East Surrey and the 6th Battn. Royal West Kent Regt. being quartered in huts in Martinsart Wood.

The 7th Battn. East Surrey remained here until July 30th, as reserve battalion to the Brigade, when the latter moved up to the line, and found working parties of 200 men daily to assist in the work of consolidation and the construction of strong points near Ovillers. On the night of the 29th, C Company sustained thirty-two casualties through an 8-in. shell landing in the Brigade advanced store containing bombs, S.A.A., Véry lights and rockets. Several men were badly burnt by the Véry lights and rockets, but only a few bombs exploded. 2nd Lieut. J. A. B. Paul, who was in charge of the working party, showed great coolness in extricating his men from their dangerous position, and for this and other gallant acts was subsequently awarded the Military Cross. On the 31st July the Battalion relieved the 6th Battn. Royal West Kent Regt. in the left sub-sector, about half a mile north of Ovillers.

The casualties during July were 37 other ranks killed and 35 wounded, in addition to the 5 officer casualties already mentioned.

The 1st of August was a quiet day in the trenches, but at about midnight a patrol came in contact with the enemy and was bombed. 2nd Lieut. A. J. Martin was mortally wounded, but was brought in. The enemy then advanced down an old communication trench and bombed an East Surrey post with "egg" bombs, keeping out of range of the Mills bomb. After about five minutes' lively work the enemy was driven off. During the 2nd August the bombing post was advanced to within fifteen yards of the German barricade, and on the 3rd another bombing post was similarly advanced, in order to gain higher ground.

This night a successful attack was carried out by the 6th Battn. "The Buffs" on the right, and by the 36th Brigade beyond it. A Company was detailed as support to "The Buffs," but was not required till about 1 a.m. on August 4th, when it went forward under Captain Hubbard. The company returned at about 7.30 a.m., having done its work. Its casualties were 1 killed and 2 wounded. An ammunition-carrying party of D Company, under 2nd Lieut. D. H. Evans, was also employed and had two men wounded. In the afternoon the Battalion was relieved by the 6th Battn. "Queen's" and moved back into Brigade Support at Ovillers Post. The relief was carried out under a heavy shell fire, and five men were wounded.

On the 5th, B Company, under Captain Garnett, went forward as reserve to the 6th Battn. "Queen's," and returned on the 7th after a rather severe time. They had had 2 men killed and 6 wounded, and in addition 11 men had been buried in a wrecked dugout and were only rescued after two hours' hard work. In the afternoon of August 7th, A Company (Captain Hubbard) and C Company (Captain Cook) went up to Ovillers as "Brigade Tactical Reserve." On the 10th August the Battalion relieved the 6th Battn. "The Buffs" in the left sub-sector of the front line without casualty. A patrol under 2nd Lieut. K. Anns brought in very useful information as to the German dispositions which was required in view of a coming attack in which the Battalion was to participate.

This attack (see map opposite page 210) was made at 10.30 p.m. on the 12th August on a wide front extending from a point on the road 500 yards east of Moquet Farm to the German salient north of Ovillers. The 12th Division attacked in the centre, with the Australians on the right and the 49th Division on the left. In the 12th Division the 35th Brigade was on the right and the 37th Brigade on the left, and in the latter Brigade the 6th Battn. Royal West Kent Regt. attacked on the left and the 7th Battn. East Surrey on its right in a north-westerly direction about half a mile north of Ovillers. After three minutes' intense bombardment (i.e. at 10.33) B and D Companies (Captain Garnett and 2nd Lieut. D. H. Evans) went forward as the first line and, working up close to the barrage, moved up to assault. They, and particularly B Company, were, however, met by heavy machine-gun fire and also by a barrage of bombs all along the German trenches, which were very strongly held.

C Company (Captain Cook) was promptly brought up in support and with parties of B Company made two more attempts to carry the position, but failed to get through the bomb barrage. Captain Hubbard then brought up A, the reserve company, and Captain Cook, having reorganized the survivors of the three assaults (about 120 men), attempted to envelop the enemy's bombers. This attempt, however, failed. D Company, supported by two platoons of C, also attacked gallantly on the right and lost heavily. The assault failed, except for the occupation of a post at "Y" on the right flank of the Battalion, largely owing to the unexpected strength of the enemy. The German trenches were crowded with men, many of whom were wearing greatcoats and packs, and it seemed that a relief was in progress; also the enemy's artillery fire was exceptionally heavy.

During this action Pte. J. Casey, who has already been mentioned in connection with "The Buffs" attack on the Chord in the Hohenzollern Redoubt on the 7th March, 1916, again got separated from the 7th Battn. East Surrey and found himself with the 4th Australian Division. He and an Australian corporal attacked about thirty Germans, of whom they killed several and brought in twelve as prisoners. This gallant soldier was killed near Cambrai, when holding the rank of corporal, on the 20th November, 1917.

The losses of the Battalion in this unfortunate affair were severe. 2nd Lieuts. D. H. Evans, H. W. Striegler and C. Gennings were killed; Captains B. G. F. Garnett and R. B. Marshall, Lieut. H. R. Gaydon, and 2nd Lieuts. J. G. Wright and H. S. Pretious were wounded. 2nd Lieut. J. A. Ross was taken prisoner.

Ten other ranks were reported killed, 60 missing and 90 wounded. The casualties therefore numbered 9 officers out of 16, and 160 other ranks out of 360 who were actually in the attack.

As the 12th Division was now being withdrawn from this part of the line, the 7th Battn. East Surrey was relieved during the afternoon of the 13th August and marched to Albert, whence motor-buses conveyed it six miles north-west to Forceville. All the men were very tired after a trying tour of duty, and, as the Diary states, " everyone was soon asleep." Next day the Battalion started to march northwards, halting that night at Arqueves and the next night at Bus-les-Artois. The Battalion was played through Louvencourt by the band of the 4th Battn. Grenadier Guards. On August 16th the Battalion marched to Halloy, where it was comfortably accommodated in huts, and on the 17th the march was continued to Grand-Rullecourt, a fairly large village twelve miles west of Arras.

As the 12th Division was now to be employed for six weeks in holding the line near Arras, for that period it took no active part in the Battles of the Somme, 1916, and the list below gives the names of the officers and other ranks of the 7th Battn. East Surrey who were awarded decorations for conspicuous services in the earlier of those battles:—

*Distinguished Service Order:* Lieut.-Colonel R. H. Baldwin.
*Military Cross:* Lieut. J. A. B. Paul and 2nd Lieut. K. Anns. (2nd Lieut. Anns very gallantly volunteered to remain in the trenches, when the Battalion was relieved on the 13th August, in order to endeavour to bring in some of the wounded.)
*Distinguished Conduct Medal and 4th Class Russian Cross of St. George:* Pte. J. Casey.
*Bar to Military Medal:* Pte. A. E. Turner.
*Military Medal:* Sergts. W. F. Bird, H. Cator and J. R. E. Wilson; Cpls. A. E. Game and R. W. Park; Lce.-Cpls. A. W. Bennett, W. Bird, R. F. Chaney, F. Edwards, S. Fletcher, W. Gutheridge and F. Horswell; Ptes. A. Blundell, W. Eastman, C. Frowley, T. Findley, J. Hoare, A. Hobden and C. H. Wells.

After two quiet days in good billets at Rullecourt the 37th Brigade moved eastwards to Monchiet on August 20th, and next day relieved the 34th Brigade in the trenches east of Wailly and just south of Arras, the Battalion being posted at Rivière in Brigade Reserve. The billets were very good and the sector seemed remarkably quiet, a feature in the village being the Brigade tea-garden!

The Battalion relieved the 6th Battn. Royal West Kent Regt. in the front line on the 24th August, and remained so posted until the end of the month. Great quiet prevailed, there being one casualty only, and, although the trenches were in a good state, much work was done in order to get them ready for expected bad weather. Rain, in fact, set in on the 30th August.

The casualties during August had amounted to 4 officers and 67 other ranks killed and 5 officers and 135 other ranks wounded.

The Battalion remained in the trenches without any special incident and in very wet weather until the 6th September, during the early morning of which day it was relieved by the 6th Battn. "Queen's," and went back into reserve at Rivière. On the 10th the Battalion commenced another tour of duty in the centre sector, which was extremely quiet, one man only being wounded on the 21st September. On the 22nd the Battalion was relieved and moved back into reserve at Rivière, where a draft of 199 men joined from the base, bringing up the trench strength to nearly 600. Distinguished Conduct Medals were earned, while the Battalion was at Rivière, by Ptes. E. G. Champion and E. Reynolds for gallant conduct when putting up wire.

On the 27th September the 12th Division was relieved in the line by the 14th Division, and the Battalion, marching to Beaumetz, arrived there in the evening and went into billets. It was conveyed in motor-buses on the 28th to Lucheux, and thence on the following day to a camp two miles south-west of Albert.

Early in the morning of October 1st the Battalion moved by motor-bus from its camp to Montauban, on its way to join the Fourth Army and to take part in the Battle of the Transloy Ridges, the tenth of the Battles of the Somme, 1916. At Montauban guides were ready, who conducted the companies to dug-outs in Longuéval Valley. In the evening the Battalion moved up via Delville Wood to Gueudecourt, three miles south of Bapaume. Combles, Gueudecourt and Thiepval had all been captured on the 26th and 27th September, so that Gueudecourt now lay in the north-eastern salient of the British front line.

Thanks to a lull in the hostile artillery fire, which was intense, the Battalion was lucky in reaching its position at the cost of only four casualties, Lieut. R. A. C. Cholmeley and three men being wounded. The enemy's fire continued to be extremely heavy during October 2nd, but most of it happily went over the front-line trench which was on the north-eastern outskirts of the village and was very narrow and deep. Early in the morning 2nd Lieut. J. F. Hollingsworth (Royal Sussex Regt. attd.) was buried by a shell and also sustained very severe injuries in the head, of which he subsequently died. Throughout October 3rd the bombardment continued, with growing intensity. The Battalion was relieved by the 6th Battn. "Queen's" immediately after dusk, and during the night moved back into support in Gird Trench and Bull Road Trench (see map opposite). Both had been much knocked about, but some old German dugouts gave sufficient cover. During its short tour in the front line the Battalion had sustained between 50 and 60 casualties, all from shell fire. Shortly after midnight on October 5th the Battalion was relieved in support by the 6th Battn. Royal West Kent Regt. and moved back to the rest bivouacs near Longuéval, arriving there very tired at 9.30 a.m. on the 6th.

On the following day the Fourth Army was to attack along the whole front from Les Boeufs to Le Sars, in support of the operations of the French troops on its right. In the evening of the 6th, therefore, the Battalion, which was to act as Brigade Reserve, moved up to Switch Trench, south of Flers, vacated by the 6th Battn. "The Buffs," who had gone up to join the 6th Battn. Royal West Kent Regt. in the front line north of Gueudecourt. The night was quiet, and

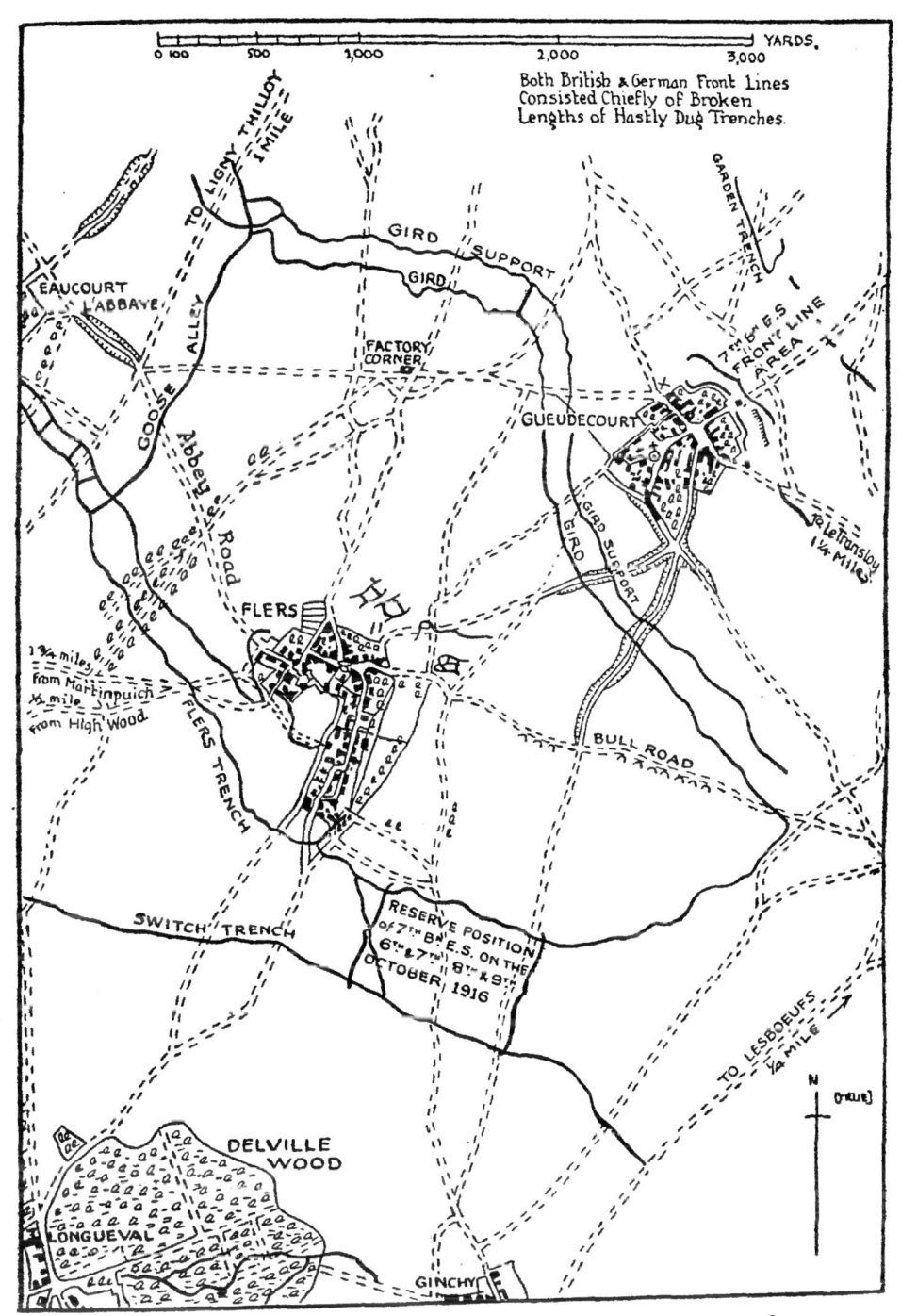

THE 12TH BATTALION IN THE BATTLE OF FLERS-COURCELETTE, SEPTEMBER, 1916, AND THE 7TH AND 12TH BATTALIONS IN THE BATTLE OF THE TRANSLOY RIDGES, OCTOBER, 1916.

during the morning of the 7th the British bombardment steadily increased in intensity until the attack was launched about 2 p.m. "The Buffs" got into Garden Trench and the troops on their right also gained some ground, but the Royal West Kent Regt. and the 36th Brigade on its left were held up by heavy machine-gun fire. During the evening the Battalion sent up several parties to carry wounded, both "The Buffs" and West Kent Regt. having suffered heavily.

The 8th October was a quiet day, carrying parties being again supplied for the wounded. In the evening of the 9th the Battalion relieved the 6th Battn. "Queen's" in the front line. The relief was successfully carried through, but shortly afterwards 2nd Lieut. J. A. B. Paul, M.C., was killed by a shell. He was an absolutely fearless officer and a great loss to the Battalion.

As the 12th Division was now being withdrawn from the line, the 7th Battn. East Surrey was relieved by the Newfoundland Regt. on the 10th October, and was fortunate enough to have no casualties in going out. The Battalion moved back to Longuéval Valley, where it remained until the 19th October, carrying on routine duties, and was frequently held in immediate readiness for action if required. The attacks north of Gueudecourt were renewed on the 12th and 18th, on both occasions with partial success, but the Battalion was not called upon.

On October 18th a draft of 50 men joined the Battalion, and at 2 p.m. on the 19th the Battalion moved off south-west across country to Fricourt, the roads being in so bad a state that it was almost impossible to march on them. From Fricourt the march was continued to Ribémont, which was reached at 9.30 p.m., after a trying march. Only four men fell out, which was creditable. In the afternoon of the 21st October the Battalion was conveyed by motor-bus via Amiens and Doullens to Wanquetin, and went into billets. On the 23rd, Major Nicolls arrived at Wanquetin with the Brigade transport, and a draft of 90 men joining on the same day brought the Battalion up to a fair strength again. On the 24th the Battalion marched to Monchiet, and on the following day went into reserve at Rivière, the Brigade having taken over "F" sector at Wailly, south of Arras. On October 26th the Battalion moved back a mile to Beaumetz-lez-Loges in Divisional Reserve.

The Battalion remained at Beaumetz-lez-Loges, undergoing various kinds of instruction, but without special incident, until the 31st October, on which day it relieved the 6th Battn. Royal West Kent Regt. in the left sub-sector of the Wailly trenches, which were greatly in want of repair. The casualties during October were 1 officer and 16 other ranks killed, and 2 officers and 32 other ranks wounded.

The Battalion occupied these trenches, alternately with the 6th Battn. Royal West Kent Regt., for about six weeks, the intervals between the tours of trench duty being passed either in Brigade Reserve at Rivière or in Divisional Reserve at Beaumetz-lez-Loges. Each tour of trench duty lasted six days. During the first tour in the early days of November the weather was very bad, and incessant rain greatly hindered the work of repairing the trenches. The casualties during this tour in the trenches were 1 killed and 3 wounded, all by shell fire.

On November 14th, when the Battalion was again in the Wailly trenches,

## THE 12TH DIVN. RESTING ABOUT GRAND RULLECOURT

the wind being favourable, gas was released against the German front line, which at one point was only 35 yards distant. No serious retaliation was made until the morning of the 16th, when all the Battalion's trenches were heavily bombarded. The damage done, which was considerable, was made good during the night.

During the trench tour at the end of November the Battalion was subjected to heavy bombing by trench mortars. The trenches were much knocked about and 2nd Lieut. D. G. Deslandes was killed. The 28th was a quieter day as far as the enemy was concerned, but his trenches were heavily shelled by our field guns and howitzers. The casualties during the month were 1 officer and 7 other ranks killed and 4 other ranks wounded.

The Battalion was at Rivière during the first five days of December, and on the 6th commenced another tour in the same trenches. Major Nicolls returned from leave on December 8th and took over command of the Battalion from Lieut.-Colonel Baldwin, who went to England on a month's leave. On the 9th the Diary records that, considering the time of year, the trenches were in splendid condition. On December 12th the Battalion was relieved in the Wailly trenches by the Royal West Kent Regt. and moved back to billets at Beaumetz-lez-Loges. This tour of duty had been fortunate, as there were only six other ranks wounded, although C Company's trenches had twice been violently battered by trench-mortar fire. On December 13th the Divisional Gas Officer inspected the box-respirators and highly approved of their condition.

The 12th Division was now being withdrawn from the line to rest, and on the 15th December the Battalion was relieved by a battalion of the King's Royal Rifles and marched after dinner to Grand Rullecourt, arriving there about 4.30 p.m.

The next two days were devoted to cleaning up clothing and equipment and a general smartening-up. The days following were fully employed in training, and while at Grand Rullecourt the Battalion was again brought up to establishment by the arrival of three drafts, 106 other ranks joining on the 22nd, 80 on the 24th and 90 on the 26th. The two former drafts were of particularly good quality and consisted mainly of men with about two years' service. Christmas Day was celebrated in great style; each company fitted up a barn very comfortably as a dining-room and excellent meals were provided. After church in the morning the officers played the sergeants at football, winning by 2 goals to 1. Instruction and drill parades filled up the remainder of the month.

On the 30th December, Major-General A. B. Scott presented medal ribbons to a number of N.C.O.'s and men of the Battalion. The names and decorations of these men have already been recorded in this chapter or appear in the subjoined list of awards for gallantry while on patrol or other duties during the period August to October, 1916:—

*Bar to Military Medal:* Pte. F. C. Fox.

*Military Medal:* Sergts. A. F. Comber and F. Fifield; Cpls. W. A. Leeds, W. Lobar and L. Townsend; Lce.-Cpl. A. E. Goddard; Ptes. V. Chard, W. R. Combes, W. J. Pratt, H. Tilling and E. Walton; also the Battalion interpreter, M. Jules Dubec.

In the New Year's *Gazette*, Lieut.-Colonel R. H. Baldwin was appointed Knight of the Order of St. Maurice and St. Lazarus (Italian), and Major E. H. J. Nicolls, Captain G. T. Wilkes and 2nd Lieut. C. W. Beadle were awarded the Military Cross; while Lieut.-Colonel Baldwin, Major Nicolls, Captain Wilkes, Captain and Quartermaster G. Rowe, Captain R. B. Marshall and Lieut. J. S. Hewat were mentioned in despatches.

The Battalion remained at Grand Rullecourt until January 13th, during which period little worthy of note happened. Lieut.-Colonel Baldwin returned from a month's leave in England on the 10th January and resumed command of the Battalion. On the 12th the Commanding Officer, Adjutant, company and platoon commanders went by motor-bus to Arras to visit the trenches about to be taken over by the Battalion, and on the 13th the Battalion "embussed" (to use its own word) in the evening, but, owing to the leading driver losing his way, did not reach Arras till 3 a.m. on the 14th.

The 12th Division was now returning to the line after its month of rest, and during the morning of January 14th the Battalion took over the left subsector trenches at Blangy, just east of Arras. It continued to occupy the same trenches alternately with the 6th Battn. Royal West Kent Regt. until the 6th February. The reliefs took place every four days, and when out of the trenches the Battalion was either in Divisional Reserve in Arras or in Brigade Reserve in the eastern outskirts of Arras. The tours of duty in the trenches were comparatively uneventful, though the enemy's trench-mortar activity was constant and always punished by artillery retaliation. The casualties during the month were 5 other ranks killed and Lieut. J. R. Bridgewater and 1 man wounded.

The Battalion was in the Blangy trenches until the early morning of February 3rd, when it was relieved and returned to Arras. The tour of duty had not been eventful. After four days in Divisional Reserve, finding the usual ammunition fatigue and digging parties, the Battalion moved on the night of February 6th to Agnez-lez-Duisans, settling down in huts shortly after midnight in bitter cold. On February 7th and 8th the whole Battalion was employed in levelling a track for a new railway, and in the afternoon of the latter day made a ten-mile march to Manin, eleven miles west of Arras. The weather was very cold, and the men marched well.

As the Division was again out of the line for a month's rest and training, the 7th Battn. East Surrey passed the remainder of the month at Manin, carrying out a full programme of trench-making and progressive instruction. Working parties of from 400 to 600 men constructed trenches near the neighbouring village of Ambrines which were an exact copy of a section of the British line with the German section facing it. This was, of course, in anticipation of the coming offensive, and on these trenches careful instruction in the attack was carried out. When not so engaged the companies practised physical training, bayonet fighting, drill and musketry. On the two last days of the month a Brigade assault on the Ambrines trenches was carried out.

The casualties during the month had been 2nd Lieut. C. S. Chettoe and three men killed. About the middle of the month Pte. F. C. Fox was awarded the Médaille Militaire. He had been brought to notice for his conspicuous services on several occasions and had already received the Military Medal and Bar. He was selected for the French decoration as being one of the most gallant soldiers in the Division.

Brigade attacks at Ambrines were repeated on March 1st and 2nd. On the latter date all the officers were withdrawn from the companies, and the attack was carried out by the N.C.O.'s. On the 4th the Battalion marched eastward to Montenescourt. The billets allotted were bad, but the worst were changed on March 5th, on which day Lieut.-Colonel Baldwin went to the officers' rest station at Habarcq, suffering from bronchitis, Major Nicolls taking over command. Montenescourt was, the Diary states, the muddiest village in France, and snow fell on the 7th and 8th March, but training continued as usual. Lieut.-Colonel Baldwin returned from hospital and resumed command on the 12th. On March 14th the Battalion did a heavy day's work, marching about twenty miles and carrying out a practice attack, both in pouring rain.

On the 15th, as the 12th Division was moving back into the line, the Battalion marched for Arras at 5 p.m. and relieved the 6th Battn. "Queen's" in the trenches near Arras. Working parties were provided on March 16th and 17th, and on the latter day the Battalion sustained 24 casualties: 20 of these were caused by one shell, which fell into a platoon, killing 6 and wounding 14. 2nd Lieut. W. S. Johnson, among others, was mortally wounded, dying later of his wounds at Habarcq. All available men were employed daily on working parties, and on March 19th the Battalion Diary records that everyone was greatly excited by reports of the German retreat to the Hindenburg Line. The Battalion remained at Arras until the evening of that day, having had every man out on working parties in the morning and afternoon. It was relieved by a battalion of the 36th Brigade, which had come up from the training area. During the night the Battalion marched about fifteen miles, arriving at Manin at 9 a.m. on the 22nd March.

On the 23rd and 24th March the Battalion practised the assault, on the 25th it marched in the evening to Agnez and on the 26th to Arras, taking over billets in the Museum. Here the Battalion finished the month, finding daily all available men for tunnelling and working parties. Arras was constantly shelled at this time, and from the 27th to 31st March the Battalion had 8 men wounded, in addition to 2nd Lieut. S. Parker, who was killed by a shell in his billet. The casualties during the month were 2 officers and 6 men killed and 3 other ranks wounded.

# CHAPTER XIX

JULY, 1916, TO MARCH, 1917 : THE 8TH BATTALION IN THE BATTLES OF THE SOMME, 1916 ; IN THE BATTLE OF ALBERT, 1916, AT MONTAUBAN ; IN THE BATTLE OF THIEPVAL RIDGE AT THE SCHWABEN REDOUBT ; IN THE BATTLE OF THE ANCRE, 1916, CAPTURES DESIRE TRENCH ; IN THE WINTER OPERATIONS ON THE ANCRE, IN ACTION NEAR MIRAUMONT ; TRANSFERRED TO THE HAZEBROUCK AREA.

THE conclusion of Chapter XIII left the 8th Battn. East Surrey in the trenches near Carnoy, with all preparations completed for the commencement of the operations now known as the Battles of the Somme, 1916. These operations, which were undertaken primarily to relieve the German pressure on Verdun, were initiated by the main attack by the Fourth Army on a front which extended from Maricourt (about seven miles east-southeast of Albert and three miles north of the Somme) to St. Pierre Divion on the River Ancre, some five miles north of Albert. This attack opened the Battle of Albert, 1916. The enemy's lines, which formed the objective of the Fourth Army, ran along the high, undulating ground situated between the two above-named rivers. From the southern crest of this high ground long spurs and deep valleys run southwards to the Somme, and it was in this locality that the 8th Battn. East Surrey was to take part in the Battle of Albert, 1916.

During the night of the 30th June, 1916, the enemy had kept up a desultory shelling of the trenches held by the Battalion, killing 3 men and wounding 10. This shelling was chiefly directed on the line held by C Company, who had held the right half of the trenches during the first five days of the preliminary bombardment and had proved themselves to be consistently steady, in spite of heavy losses during that period. This was largely due to the courage and energy of Captain C. S. Pearce, who commanded the company, and invariably displayed the greatest cheerfulness and contempt for danger. The night of the 30th was fine, but the previous three days had been very wet and there were several inches of water in the trenches. This, coupled with the shelling, prevented the men from getting much rest or sleep, but in no way damped their cheerfulness.

At 4.30 a.m. on July 1st breakfasts were brought up by carrying parties of the 7th Battn. Royal West Kent Regt., who were in Brigade Reserve. Rum was issued, and the men had on them their bread and also a quarter of a pound of biscuits and some chocolate, which had been provided regimentally. By 5.30 a.m. all companies had reported that they were in their correct battle positions, and that all extra ammunition, grenades, rations, water, etc., had been issued. The morning was very misty, it being impossible to see more than a few yards; but this mist lifted about 6.30 a.m., and for the rest of the day the weather was perfect, with a clear blue sky and a hot sun. At 6.30 the enemy opened a barrage on our trenches which was maintained for several hours, and appeared to indicate that the date and time of our assault was known to them. This barrage caused several casualties and a considerable amount of damage to our trenches, particularly those held by B Company (Captain W. P. Nevill), the left assaulting company, whose trench was completely flattened out in three or four places.

The first objective of the Battalion was the Breslau Trench (see General Map of the Somme Battlefields), and its final objective was 300 yards of the road from the west end of Montauban, running along the ridge towards Mametz. The plan of attack was as follows: The leading companies were C Company on the right and B Company on the left. They held a frontage of 300 yards, and occupied respectively the salient abutting on the railway and the re-entrant to the point of junction with the 7th Battn. "Queen's." Of each of these two companies, two platoons were in position in the front-line trench (1st Assembly Trench), to form the first and second waves, the men of the two platoons of each company being placed alternately, so that when the first platoon of each company got out to form the first wave the second platoons were in position to follow them as second wave. The third and fourth platoons of C and B companies were in the 2nd Assembly Trench. The third platoon in each company advanced in line, covering the company frontage, as a support to the platoons in front, and formed the third wave. The fourth platoons advanced in line of sections in file and were in company reserve. The distance between waves was laid down as 50 yards, but actually the companies suffered such heavy casualties in No Man's Land that the officers quite rightly hurried their men on, in order to reach the comparative shelter of the enemy trenches as quickly as possible. D Company (Captain C. L. S. Bowen) was in support to C and B Companies, and advanced from the 3rd Assembly Trench in line of sections in file covering the Battalion frontage. A Company (Captain T. A. Flatau) in Battalion Reserve advanced from the 4th Assembly Trench in line of platoons in file. In consequence of the very heavy enfilade rifle and machine-gun fire, this company was extended when half-way across No Man's Land.

C Company had suffered so heavily during the week prior to the attack that two of its platoons were reduced to ten or twelve N.C.O.'s and men apiece. Captain C. S. Pearce was therefore ordered to combine these two platoons to form one wave, and his company was reinforced by 2nd Lieut. H. W. Pegg's platoon of D Company. The "operation orders" for the attack were admirably clear and complete. One paragraph may be quoted: "All ranks are reminded that it is absolutely forbidden to use the word 'Retire' for any purpose. It can only originate from the enemy."

B Company, which was holding the re-entrant, had to cross about 400 yards of No Man's Land, whereas C Company had but 120 yards. With the idea of helping to keep up his men's spirits during this trying initial advance, Captain Nevill had provided each platoon of B Company with a football, which was to be kicked across No Man's Land, subject to the proviso that proper formation and distance was not to be lost thereby.

At 7.27 a.m. Captain Nevill climbed out of the trench, kicked off one of the footballs and started to advance, closely followed by his two leading platoons.

They were met by very heavy machine-gun fire from the craters on their left, but made steady progress. The British barrage was very hot on the enemy's front line opposite the Battalion, and was intensified by Stokes mortars which were executing rapid fire, with the result that Breslau Trench disappeared in a cloud of dust and smoke.

As B Company came abreast of C Company's trench the leading platoons of the latter company moved out and prolonged B's line, and the advance was continued in spite of heavy losses. Captain W. P. Nevill (East Yorkshire Regt. attd.) and Captain R. E. Soames were killed just outside the German wire, in which two of B Company's footballs were picked up next day. Captain C. S. Pearce, Lieut. G. H. S. Musgrove, and 2nd Lieuts. T. E. Evans and T. P. Kelly were killed in No Man's Land; while Captain T. A. Flatau was killed on the parapet of Breslau Trench. 2nd Lieut. H. W. Pegg was mortally wounded, and 2nd Lieuts. G. G. Morse and E. C. Hetherington were wounded. Amongst the other ranks the casualties were so heavy that not more than 250 men reached Breslau Trench unwounded.

It ought to be noted here that two "Russian saps" had been exploded at 7.28 a.m. opposite the salient. These had been prepared by making horizontal borings, at a depth of from 6 to 8 feet, from beneath the British front-line parapet to within about 40 feet of the German trenches. This was no easy work, as the drill was of very small diameter and was apt to be deflected by any unusually hard substance. These borings had been filled with high explosive, and the result after explosion was that two ready-made communication trenches were formed, which were immediately improved and consolidated by parties of the 8th Battn. Royal Sussex Pioneers.

The very heavy casualties sustained while crossing No Man's Land had the inevitable result that the troops in their further advance, instead of going forward steadily by waves at stated intervals, as had been practised, were split up into a series of small parties who bombed or bayoneted their way forward with the greatest gallantry, but with no order or cohesion.

At 8.10 a.m., 8.25 a.m. and 8.40 a.m., Captain Clare, returning from the front trench, reported heavy rifle and machine-gun fire from the craters and the high ground behind them. The Battalion bombing section under Sergt. Wileman, and a section of Stokes mortars under 2nd Lieut. P. G. Heath, were sent forward soon after 8 a.m. to assist in the bombing attacks.

At about 8.40 a.m. a message was sent to the Officer Commanding the 7th Battn. "The Buffs," asking him to reinforce the Battalion with one company, which request was promptly complied with. At 9 a.m., 2nd Lieut. M. A. Stimson, who had been wounded in the arm, reported at Battalion Headquarters. He stated that parties of the enemy were on the railway line, and were bombing along Valley Trench and Valley Support on the Battalion's right flank. A message was therefore sent to the 7th Battn. "The Buffs," asking them to send reinforcements up the valley to Train Alley, and the reply was received at 9.20 a.m. that one platoon, which was all that could be spared, had been sent forward.

At 9.21 a.m., Pte. Bilson, a Battalion runner, brought back a report that some of the East Surrey men were in the Pommiers Line (i.e. the German 4th line), and at the same time 2nd Lieut. Griffin, R.F.A., reported by telephone that the East Surreys were in Train Alley, a portion of the Pommiers Line. 2nd Lieut. Wightman also reported that the Brigade on the right was making good progress. At 9.45 a.m. Major Irwin went forward to get a closer view of the situation and, if possible, to reorganize the attack and carry it forward. On his way he met Captain E. C. Gimson, R.A.M.C., the Battalion Medical Officer, who had been in the front-line trench since the commencement of the attack dressing the wounded. Captain Gimson displayed the greatest courage and devotion to duty throughout the action, and undoubtedly saved many lives. He was recommended for the Victoria Cross by the Divisional Commander, but was awarded the Distinguished Service Order.

On reaching the German trenches, Major Irwin made his way forward up Back Lane, meeting no one until he came to the junction of Back Lane and Back Trench, in the German 3rd line, where he met two small parties, one of three men under 2nd Lieut. C. W. Janion, and one of ten men under Sergt. Griffin, of A Company. 2nd Lieut. Janion was the only unwounded officer of C Company, and had displayed great courage and determination in bombing his way forward, although his company had been reduced to about twenty N.C.O.'s and men.

Major Irwin instructed 2nd Lieut. Janion to construct a bomb-stop a little way in advance of the point where they had met. He then started to collect a mixed party of about seventy East Surreys and "Buffs," sending them forward to the Pommiers Line (4th line) as he came across them, and telling them to reverse the parapet there. This work of collecting small parties and reorganizing in the Pommiers Line took a long time to carry out, and it was not until 11.45 a.m. that Major Irwin considered that a further advance was possible. He then sent the party forward in two waves, putting Sergt. Willis, of A Company, in command of the first wave; and, having seen them well started, he went back to the telephone to report the situation to the Brigade. A forward telephone station had meanwhile been established at the junction of Middle Alley and Back Trench, and here Major Irwin met Captain Clare and the headquarter details.

From this point a clear view could be obtained of the long slope up to the Montauban Ridge, and it could be seen that the party led by Sergt. Willis had reached the junction of Breslau Alley and Mill Trench and had lined the parapet of Breslau Alley south of that point. The Brigade on the right had already reached Montauban, having met with very little resistance, and Major Irwin therefore sent Captain Clare and Lieut. Thorley forward to lead Sergt. Willis's party on to the Montauban Ridge. He also sent orders to Captain Bowen, whose company (D) was still engaged in a brisk bombing fight on the left flank, to disengage and take his company forward.

At 12.22 p.m. the advance party, led by Captain Clare, reached their objective on the Montauban Ridge and dug in along the road from the two westernmost houses of Montauban to the Windmill. The 7th Battn. "Queen's" on the left were still engaged in the Pommiers Line, so that the left flank of the

Battalion was quite in the air. Sergt. Willis was therefore sent with a small party to form a defensive flank and to hold the Windmill, where he took 1 officer and 2 men prisoners. At 12.35 p.m. the situation was reported to Brigade Headquarters, and shortly afterwards Captain Bowen, with D Company, arrived on the Montauban Ridge. A German machine gun, which had been found by Pte. Osborn, of the Battalion runners, was brought into action with good effect.

Soon after 1 p.m. a few of the "Queen's," under Captain Heaton, came up; but it was not until about 4 p.m. that the left flank of the Battalion became secure. A reorganization was then possible, and A and D Companies, with a combined strength of 2 officers and about 130 rank and file, took over the whole Battalion line, while B and C Companies were withdrawn to Mine Alley. These two companies had borne the brunt of the preliminary bombardment and of the attack, and were reduced to one officer and about twenty other ranks apiece. The place to which they were withdrawn seemed to be the safest available spot; but at about 5 p.m. the enemy commenced to shell it most accurately with 5.9's, causing about a dozen casualties, two sergeants being killed and several men wounded. The two companies were therefore moved a little higher up Mine Alley, where the shelling was less effective.

At 9 p.m. Major Irwin was called to a conference with the Brigadier at the junction of the Pommiers Line and Mine Alley, and returned with the news that the Battalion would be relieved at daylight by the 7th Battn. Royal West Kent Regt. The shelling was not very heavy, but continued steadily all night, and about midnight 2nd Lieut. A. B. Derrick received a severe shell wound.

At dawn on the 2nd July the Battalion was relieved and, after a somewhat hazardous journey down Mine Alley, reached the comparative security of the Pommiers Line, where they received their rations and slept all the morning.

The casualties included 7 officers and 140 other ranks killed, 7 officers (1 mortally) and 272 other ranks wounded, and 20 missing. The two wounded officers not already mentioned were Lieut. J. R. Ackerley and 2nd Lieut. C. W. Alcock. The conduct of all ranks of the Battalion was most creditable. While all the brave dead were much to be lamented by the Battalion, special mention must be made of the loss sustained by the deaths of Captains Pearce, Nevill and Flatau.

The dogged determination with which the task allotted to the 8th Battn. East Surrey in the assault on Montauban Ridge was carried out, regardless of loss and in the face of most formidable difficulties, deserved and obtained the highest praise, and was soon afterwards practically recognized by the award of the honours specified in the subjoined list:—

*Distinguished Service Order:* Major A. P. B. Irwin and Captain C. Janion.
*Military Cross:* Captain O. C. Clare and Company Sergt.-Major C. Hanks.
*Distinguished Conduct Medal:* Sergt. J. Lancaster and Lce.-Sergt. G. Brown.
*Bar to Military Medal:* Sergt. J. Kenyon.
*Military Medal:* Sergt. H. Griffen; Lce.-Cpls. A. Rowe and A. Williams; Ptes. C. Alexander, S. Catton, M. Dumpleton, H. Smith and A. E. Watts.

## THE 55TH BRIGADE ORDERED TO CAPTURE TRONES WOOD

After dinner on the 2nd July the Battalion marched to huts in Carnoy Valley, where it rested for the remainder of the day. Volunteers from each company went up to the battlefield and brought in the seven dead officers, who were buried in Carnoy Valley on July 3rd. All the Battalion wished to be present, but this was thought inadvisable as the valley was shelled from time to time. In the afternoon Major-General Maxse visited Battalion Headquarters. He expressed the greatest pride and admiration for the work done by the Battalion on the 1st July, and said that on that day the Battalion had made for itself an immortal name.

On July 4th the Battalion went in the morning to Bray, to bathe in the River Somme. A letter was received by the C.O. from Lieut.-Colonel Blois, R.F.A., commanding Right Group R.F.A., 18th Division, from which the following passage is taken: "It is indeed gratifying to be told that every help was given by the artillery to the magnificent infantry we were privileged to support that day. The attack by the 8th Battn. East Surrey was the admiration of the whole Group, especially, if I may be allowed to say so, the advance on the Mill led by yourself in person. I need hardly say how much we all deplore the loss of so many very gallant officers and men that you have unavoidably sustained in carrying out such an attack to a completely successful issue against such a determined enemy."

On July 6th the Battalion marched to Grovetown Camp, near Bray, headed by the pipers of the 10th Battn. Argyll and Sutherland Highlanders, who played the "Lass o' Gowrie," the ancient quick-step of the 2nd Battn. East Surrey since 1758. On the 8th a further move was made to a prettily situated but dirty camp at Bois Celestins, overlooking the valley of the Somme. Here the Battalion remained until the 11th July, when it moved up to the support trenches in Z.1 sub-sector at Maricourt. Three N.C.O.'s who had been sent forward to act as guides to the trenches were wounded. On the night of the 12th the Battalion moved to the old German front line (Silesia Trench and Silesia Support) in relief of a battalion of the 89th Brigade. The relief was completed without loss by 9.45 p.m., and the night was quiet.

On the 8th of July British troops had succeeded in gaining a footing in Trones Wood, which lay a mile to the east of Montauban, and about midday on the 13th the 55th Brigade received orders to attempt to complete the capture of the wood by midnight, 13th/14th July. If this attempt were successful, a straight "jumping-off line" would be obtained for the 3rd and 9th Divisions, who were to assault the Longuéval, Bazentin-le-Grand, Bazentin-le-Petit Line at 3 a.m. on the 14th July.

The orders for the attack of the 55th Brigade on the enemy's positions in Trones Wood were as follows: The 7th Battn. Royal West Kent Regt. and the 7th Battn. "Queen's" were to attack simultaneously; the former in a northerly direction from the south edge of the wood, the "Queen's" to attack the west edge of the wood from Longuéval Alley. The 7th Battn. "The Buffs" was to form the Brigade support with the exception of one company, which was to be in close support of the 7th Royal West Kent Regt. The 8th Battn. East Surrey (which formed the Brigade Reserve) was much split up, being disposed as follows: D Company (Captain Bowen) at the Briqueterie, for carrying R.E. material to the north-east corner of Bernafay Wood and for consolidating the north edge of Bernafay Wood. A Company (Captain Rhodes) in the Sunken Road running south-east from the Briqueterie, with orders to hold it at all costs in the event of a successful enemy counter-attack. B Company (Captain Thorne), two platoons in Bernafay Trench and two platoons in Dublin Trench. C Company (Captain Paull), two platoons to report at the Hairpin Corner for carrying forward R.E. material. One platoon to report at Brigade Headquarters at Cambridge Copse for carrying forward bombs. One platoon to be in reserve in Dublin Redoubt. Battalion Headquarters to be at the point where Silesia Support crosses the eastern Maricourt–Briqueterie road. All units of the Battalion were ordered to move to their new positions between 5 and 5.30 p.m. The assault to take place at 7 p.m. The evening of July 13th was a quiet one and the moves were carried out quickly and smoothly, the Battalion sustaining no casualties.

The assault on the German positions in Trones Wood resulted in very heavy fighting, as they were powerfully defended, and the attackers were subjected to the heaviest bombardment experienced so far in the War. The three companies of the 8th Battn. East Surrey chiefly employed (A, B and D) were all handled boldly and skilfully by their captains and did valuable service. They were, however, altogether detached from their own Battalion and worked mainly under the orders of the Officer Commanding 7th Battn. Royal West Kent Regt., and on some occasions under those of the Officer Commanding " The Buffs." All were exposed to an extremely heavy shell fire, and it was chiefly owing to the fact that their successive movements were made principally through trenches that their casualties were comparatively light, amounting only to 2nd Lieut. J. Wightman and 23 other ranks wounded.

Early in the morning of July 14th, on which date the Battle of Bazentin Ridge opened, the 54th Brigade relieved the 55th in Trones Wood. The latter Brigade was withdrawn from the line, and the East Surrey companies were ordered to move independently to Méricourt (five miles south-west of Albert), where the whole Battalion assembled by midday. In the afternoon the Battalion marched by companies to Grovetown Camp, finding on arrival there a draft of 408 N.C.O.'s and men, who were immediately allotted to companies. The work of reorganization was busily carried out on July 15th, which was also utilized for bathing and the issue of clothing and necessaries. A further draft of 93 other ranks arrived in the afternoon, which fortunately included some old N.C.O.'s and men of the Battalion. The Battalion remained at Grovetown Camp, while the rest of the 18th Division was being withdrawn from the line, busily engaged in training, until July 21st, and during that brief period made astonishing progress under Lieut.-Colonel Irwin, who had been promoted to that temporary rank in recognition of his distinguished conduct at Montauban. Captain and Adjutant O. C. Clare had also been promoted to the rank of Major.

The Battalion left Méricourt Station by train at 1.30 p.m. on July 21st, arriving at Longpré two hours later. At 9 p.m. it set out for Doudelainville, arriving there about 3.30 a.m. on the 22nd. At 4 a.m. on the morning of the 23rd the Battalion marched to Pont Rémy, where it entrained and reached St. Omer at 3.30 in the afternoon after a quick journey via Étaples, Boulogne and Calais. From St. Omer the Battalion marched south-east to Arques and thence to Wardrecques, where it went into billets.

The Battalion remained at Wardrecques from July 24th to 28th, marching on the latter date, in very sultry weather, to Hondeghem, near Hazebrouck. The march was long and trying, and many men fell out; as was the case on the 29th in another long march to Flêtre, where a Sunday rest on the 30th was welcome. On the 31st progressive company training began with special attention to instruction in bomb-throwing for the benefit of the 500 newly arrived men.

The Battalion continued its training at Flêtre on the 1st and 2nd August, and on the 3rd marched via Steenwerck to Erquinghem, two miles south-west of Armentières. The march was long and the weather sultry, but the men marched well, owing to recent training and the help of the drums and silver bugles, which had just been presented to the Battalion by certain members of the Stock Exchange who were friends of Captain Clare. On the evening of August 4th the Battalion found itself once more in the trenches, relieving the 1/3rd New Zealand R.B. The exceptionally clean state of the trenches was specially noted by all ranks and recorded in the Battalion Diary.

The enemy artillery was found to be very active and the trenches were constantly shelled, one man being killed on 5th, and 2nd Lieuts. J. S. Bottrill and C. E. Carrall being wounded. About midnight on the 7th the enemy opened an intense bombardment on the trenches (or rather, breastworks) held by the Battalion, and B Company suffered heavily, having 2nd Lieut. A. E. A. Jacobs, M.C., and 15 men killed, 39 men wounded and 2 men missing. About 200 yards of the fire trench were obliterated, as were the heads of the communication trenches leading into it. The enemy then raided the trench, but left it almost immediately. The two missing men were signallers, who were seized and dragged away. The company commanders had the situation well in hand and took immediate steps to hold the shattered portion of the line. The 8th and 9th August were quiet days, and in the latter evening the Battalion was relieved by the 7th Battn. "The Buffs." One man was killed during the relief. At 3 a.m. on the 10th August the Battalion was assembled in billets in the La Rolanderie area, where it rested for the day. The Battalion remained at La Rolanderie until August 12th, when Headquarters moved to Erquinghem, where they remained till the 15th, on which day the Battalion went into camp for special training at the Bois des Vaches. After four days' progressive training in wood-fighting, the Battalion moved back on the 19th August into billets in the La Rolanderie area.

On the 21st August the 18th Division commenced its return to the Somme theatre of operations, and the Battalion, while awaiting its turn to entrain, moved into billets at Erquinghem, and on the 22nd into billets at Estaires for three days' final training. On the 25th August the Battalion marched in the early morning to Merville Station, where it entrained at 5.30 a.m., arriving at Brias three hours later. Thence it marched to Magnicourt-en-Comté, about twelve miles north-west of Arras, where training was resumed in accordance with a Brigade programme.

The Battalion remained at Magnicourt until September 9th, on which date it marched in a highly efficient state to Houvin-Houvigneul, some ten miles in a south-westerly direction. On the 10th the march was continued to Lucheux, and on the 11th to Puchevillers, about eleven miles north-west of Albert. Here information was received that Sergt. John Kenyon had been awarded a bar to his Military Medal for gallant conduct at Montauban on July 1st. The Battalion remained at Puchevillers, completing its training, until the 23rd September, by which date, in the opinion of a very competent critic, it had reached an even higher state of efficiency than it was in at the opening of the Battles of the Somme, 1916. In view of its heavy casualties at Montauban, and particularly remembering its losses in officers on that occasion, this result speaks highly for the Commanding Officer's powers of instruction and discipline.

On the 23rd September the Battalion was conveyed in motor lorries to Aveluy, a mile north of Albert, being the first battalion of the 18th Division to arrive in the new area. During the absence of the 18th Division the operations on the Somme had entered on their third phase, at the commencement of which the successes of the Fourth Army south of Bapaume had brought the British advance to a stage at which the capture of the Thiepval Ridge became advisable. In the resulting operations the 18th Division was now to take its part.

During the nights of the 23rd to 25th September the 8th Battn. East Surrey was employed in digging assembly trenches preparatory to the attack on Thiepval. Its casualties during this period were 1 man killed and 5 wounded. Soon after noon on September 26th Thiepval was attacked and captured by the 53rd and 54th Brigades, the 55th being held in reserve. A further advance against the Schwaben Redoubt made by the two first-named brigades was, however, unsuccessful, which was not surprising, considering the strength of the position and the heavy casualties sustained in the capture of Thiepval.

The Schwaben Redoubt (see Map opposite) stood on the western extremity of the Thiepval Ridge and overlooked Thiepval to the south and the valley of the Ancre to the west and north. Its possession was of vital importance. In shape it was a rough oblong, about 500 yards from east to west, and 300 yards from north to south. The south face of the Redoubt was about 700 yards north of Thiepval.

On the 27th September the Battalion, which was then lying in bivouac at " South Bluff," had 1 man killed and 9 wounded by shell fire. On September 28th the 53rd Brigade, reinforced by the 7th Battn. " Queen's " from the 55th Brigade, again attacked the Redoubt at 1 p.m. The assault was led by the 7th Battn. " Queen's," who captured and were able to maintain their footing in the south face. Casualties were heavy, and the remaining faces of the Redoubt were not taken. That evening the 8th Battn. East Surrey was ordered to relieve the " Queen's " on the following night. It was decided at a conference, at which

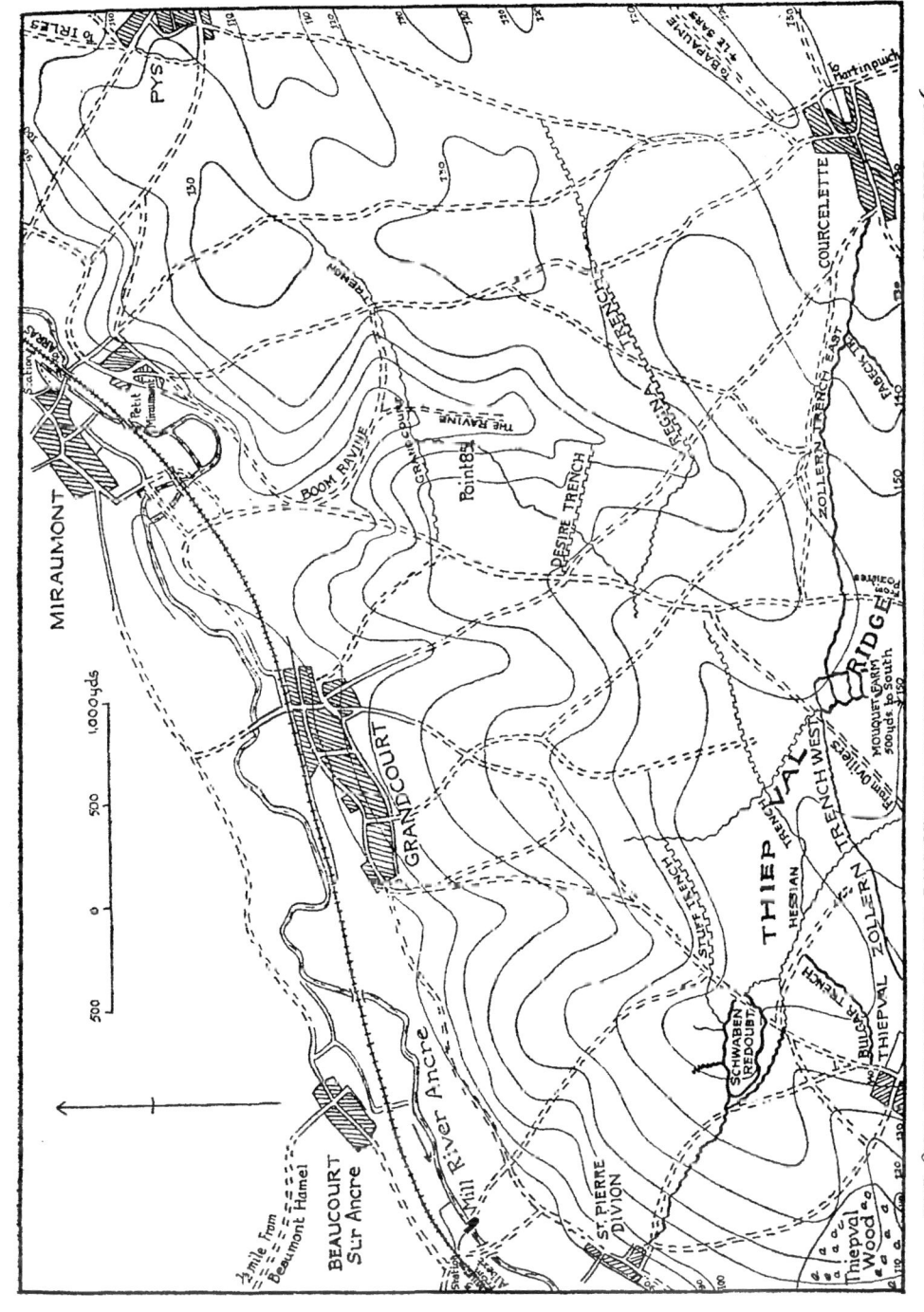

THE 8TH BATTALION IN THE BATTLES OF THIEPVAL RIDGE AND THE ANCRE, SEPTEMBER–NOVEMBER, 1916.

Major-General Maxse (Commanding the 18th Division) and Brigadier-General Sir T. Jackson (Commanding the 55th Brigade) were present, that the 8th Battn. East Surrey should advance from the south face of the Redoubt against the north face at 4 p.m. on the 30th September, and should also furnish a bombing party to deal with the east face. The west face was to be attacked simultaneously by two platoons of the 7th Battn. Royal West Kent Regt. It appears from these orders that the east and west faces were assumed to be weakly held, which proved not to be the case.

Pursuant to the above decision, C and D Companies of the 8th Battn. East Surrey were detailed as right and left assaulting companies respectively. B Company, detailed as support, was short of half its strength, two platoons being employed on a divisional working party; it was promised that these platoons should be sent to the Battalion in time for the assault, but very unfortunately this was not done. A Company was to be posted in reserve at Thiepval.

The south face of the Redoubt was occupied by D Company by midnight of the 29th/30th September; but it was decided that C Company should pass the night in Bulgar Trench, in which the two platoons of B Company were also posted. At six o'clock in the morning of the 30th September the enemy put down a barrage to the south of the Schwaben Redoubt to stop reinforcements coming up, and launched a strong bombing attack on the left of D Company. The East Surrey men here were attacked from two directions and were outranged through the use by the Germans of the small egg-bomb. Captain Wightman, commanding D Company, however, organized a counter-attack which he himself led, and, "being a powerful man and throwing Mills bombs like cricket-balls," he got the better of the enemy. In this attack he was well supported by flanking parties in the open under 2nd Lieuts. Milner and Barford. The supply of bombs having been exhausted, Captain Wightman ordered bayonets to be fixed for a charge, when the enemy broke and the trench was regained. At this moment a misleading message (not sent by the Battalion) had caused our heavy guns to open fire on the south face, and from this fire Captain Wightman's company unfortunately suffered heavily. Lieut.-Colonel Irwin, who had gone forward to visit the companies, had ordered the two platoons of B Company, under Captain C. Thorne, to reinforce the right of D Company; but as the situation was well in hand when they arrived, B Company was ordered to withdraw to a trench in rear and to garrison the south face of the Redoubt as soon as it was vacated by the assaulting companies. During this operation Captain Thorne was unfortunately killed by a shot through the head. His death, which was a heavy loss to the Battalion, occurred exactly a year after he earned the Military Cross by carrying in the dead body of his brother. Both were most gallant officers.

D Company, having been reduced by the fire of the enemy and by that of the British heavy guns to a strength of seventy-five men, A Company (Captain Rhodes) took its place as left assaulting company, D going into reserve in Thiepval. A Company, it should be mentioned, had been on fatigue through the night and early morning, and only ceased work just before it was ordered forward for the attack. Two platoons of the 7th Battn. "The Buffs" were lent to the Battalion to assist in the attack on the west face of the Redoubt; but this face proved to be very strong, and messages asking for artillery action against its garrison failed to get through. Throughout the day the German artillery shelled the positions held by the Battalion, with such effect that two platoons of C Company had, before the assault, been reduced to 10 and 17 men respectively.

On the 30th September, at 4 p.m., the time fixed for the attack, the barrage started, and the assaulting companies, sadly reduced in strength, advanced in two waves at about 50 yards interval. On the right, C Company advanced on either side of the eastern face and immediately came under a heavy enfilade fire from it. A small party, under Lce.-Cpl. Theedom, detailed to bomb up this trench, was stopped at once by rifle fire at point-blank range and fell back to renew their attempt over the open from a flank. Meanwhile, Sergt. Palmer, who had seen what was happening, took with him Lce.-Cpl. Smith, who had a Lewis gun, and, making a dash for the eastern face, they entered it at a bomb-stop. Looking over it, they saw the German infantry thickly lining the parapet, and brought the Lewis gun into play with great effect. Thirty Germans were at once killed and the rest driven into dugouts. Lce.-Cpl. Theedom, with his party, then joined Sergt. Palmer, and they pushed slowly along the eastern face; while the remainder of C Company swung to the right and successfully assaulted it, taking 2 officers and 70 men prisoners and occupying the whole face. "In this assault the Battalion suffered another great loss in the death of Captain B. D. Paull (R. Irish Rifles attd.), who was in command of C Company. He had been promoted to the rank of Captain at the age of nineteen, and, besides being a most capable officer, was held in great affection by everyone in the Battalion. Another gallant young officer of this company, 2nd Lieut. M. A. Stimson, was also killed, and the remaining officers were wounded" (Battalion Diary).

Meanwhile on the left, the first wave of A Company had come under heavy enfilade fire from the west face on which its left flank rested. The two officers with it, 2nd Lieuts. S. G. Barder and A. A. Bartrum, were killed, and the few unwounded men lay in shell holes until after dark, when they got back to our lines. The second wave kept more to the right, to fill the gap caused by the movement of C Company to the right in assaulting the east face. They were assisted by a Lewis gun in the south face that Captain R. H. Rhodes had detailed, under C.S.M. Hopkins, to keep the west face under fire. The Lewis gunners were hit, but C.S.M. Hopkins kept the gun going, and it made the enemy fire somewhat erratic. Captain Rhodes was wounded on the way over, leaving 2nd Lieut. Maund the only officer, who got into the middle of the north face with a small party of men and worked along to the right, finding a few of the enemy for whom they accounted, and getting touch with C Company at the north-east corner of the Redoubt.

A few men of A Company were seen to enter the German trench further to the left, and later those who were unwounded also worked along to the right to get touch, some of the wounded getting back to our lines over the top. Further on the left, the two platoons of the 7th Battn. "The Buffs" had made a gallant effort to reach the west face; but this position, untouched by our barrage and strongly held by the enemy, was too much for them. Besides a heavy fire from the front, they were enfiladed, and taken almost in rear, by the enemy in trenches west of Schwaben Redoubt that were not affected by our barrage. Though supported by two platoons of the 7th Battn. West Kent Regt., none of the "Buffs" were able to reach the west face, and of their two platoons all but five men were killed or wounded. Whilst the assault was in progress the Germans tried again to bomb down the south face from the west, and, if they had been successful, would have cut off the assaulting companies. C.S.M. Hopkins, with some men of a bomb-carrying party of D Company, however, constructed a bomb-stop and kept the enemy off until the arrival of the two platoons of B Company.

The enemy put down a heavy barrage on the rear face of the Redoubt, the communications to it, and on Battalion Headquarters in Thiepval, which lasted for about two hours. It was then reported that B Company, in the south face of the Redoubt, had only twenty-five men left, and as there was great risk of this being an insufficient force to deal with further enemy attacks from the west face, Captain Wightman was sent up with what was left of D Company to reinforce B Company and take over the defence of the south face of the Redoubt. Lieut. Tillard was also sent up to take command of A and C Companies, with whom there was now only one subaltern officer. There were three communication trenches leading from the north-east corner of the Redoubt, and to block and defend these, to do the same with about 150 yards of the north face and to garrison the east face, took all the men at Lieut. Tillard's disposal. The enemy had not then returned to the north face, out of which A Company had cleared them, but at this time it was only possible to occupy about a quarter of it in sufficient strength to ward off counter-attacks.

At about 9.30 p.m. the Officer Commanding the 7th Battn. "The Buffs" arrived at Battalion Headquarters with three companies less two platoons at his disposal. It was a very dark night, and the ground was one mass of shell holes that made the trenches barely distinguishable even by day. Under these conditions the Officer Commanding "The Buffs" decided against any attempt to make any further ground that night, so that the 8th Battn. East Surrey was not relieved until the dawn of the following day. The Battalion had succeeded in taking its objectives, the north and east faces of the Redoubt, and if the two platoons of B Company had been returned to them in time, might have been able to hold all the ground they had gained. As it was, they handed over to the relieving troops the whole of the east face, and of the north face about 150 yards which the enemy had not reoccupied.

In view of its heavy losses, and the gravity of the task with which it was entrusted, it will be realized that the Battalion owed its success, partial though it was, to the individual fighting quality of its officers and men. The casualties at the Schwaben Redoubt were very heavy, amounting to nearly 70 per cent of the numbers actually engaged. Five officers and 43 other ranks were killed, 4 officers and 234 other ranks were wounded, and 34 other ranks were reported missing, of whom most were killed. The wounded officers not already mentioned by name were 2nd Lieuts. O. F. Madox-Hueffer, B. M. Stanton and S. H. Mallet. Lieut.-Colonel Irwin specially brought to notice the services of the officers killed and of Captain J. Wightman, Lieut. P. A. Tillard and Lieut. Corman, 7th Battn. "The Buffs," the last named "for his gallant attempt to carry out the attack on the left."

The honours subsequently awarded for the fighting in the Schwaben Redoubt were as follows:—

*Military Cross:* Captain J. Wightman; 2nd Lieuts. W. M. Barfoot, R. A. Maund and P. G. Heath.

*Distinguished Conduct Medal:* Sergt. C. Palmer; Pte. J. H. Houghton (attd. 55th T.M.B.).

*Bar to Military Medal:* Sergt. H. Griffen.

*Military Medal:* Sergts. H. Gould and R. Hopkins; Cpls. P. Simon and A. Wood; Lce.-Cpls. W. James, F. Simcoe and E. R. Theedom; Ptes. J. J. E. Bagg, J. T. Barthropp, F. W. Bartlett, W. Byrne, V. Cobbold, C. Finnis, N. Norris and J. Smith.

On being relieved at the Schwaben Redoubt early on the 1st October the Battalion took over dugouts at Wood Post, but later in the day moved to safer ground in Blighty Valley, where it remained until noon on October 5th, finding working and fatigue parties daily. On the 5th the Battalion marched to Bouzincourt, where it halted for dinners, marching thence to Acheux, where it entrained, arriving at Candas, about twenty miles west of Albert, at midnight. Here the Battalion remained, going through a steady course of instruction and reconstruction, until the 15th October, when it made a short march to Gezaincourt. On the 16th it marched to billets at Rubempré, and on the 17th to Albert, where it bivouacked outside the town, no billets being available. This was unfortunate, as heavy rain came on, and on the night of the 18th the shelters occupied by the men were flooded out. On the evening of the following day billets in the town were allotted to the Battalion, and in them it remained until the 25th.

The long-drawn-out Battle of the Ancre Heights had commenced on the 1st October, and on the 21st, British troops captured "Stuff Trench" and "Regina Trench," extending from the Schwaben Redoubt to the Courcelette-Pys road, which was about two miles to the east of the Redoubt. Into this area the 8th Battn. East Surrey moved via Pozières on the 26th October and occupied "Fabeck" and "High" trenches between Mouquet Farm and Courcelette. Owing to the possibility of a German counter-attack, A Company was ordered forward to Zollern Trench and attached to the 7th Battn. Royal West Kent Regt.

The front-line tour of duty of the 8th Battn. East Surrey on this occasion was uneventful and short, as the Battalion was relieved during the morning of the 29th October, and by 3 p.m. was settled in billets at Albert. On the 30th clothing was issued to the companies, and woollen gloves, mittens and other winter comforts received from the Regimental Depot were distributed. On the last day of the month the Battalion marched to Warloy, eight miles west of Albert, arriving there about noon and resting for the remainder of the day.

The Battalion remained at Warloy, carrying out company training, until the 4th November. During the afternoon of this day it moved into billets in Albert, company training continuing until the 8th, when the Battalion relieved the 7th Battn. "The Buffs" in the trenches north of Mouquet Farm. It was relieved on the night of November 10th and returned to Albert after another uneventful tour of duty.

About this time the long-continued spell of bad weather ceased and preparations were made for a further advance up the left bank of the River Ancre. This advance developed into the Battle of the Ancre, 1916, which was the last of the Battles of the Somme, 1916. On the 13th November the 8th Battn. East Surrey moved forward to the Fabeck Trench. An attack planned for the 15th, in which the Battalion had its duties assigned, did not take place till the 18th, preparatory to which the Battalion was posted as follows: *Regina Trench*, two platoons of B Company and two platoons of D Company; *2nd Assembly Trench*, remainder of these companies; *Hessian Trench*, A Company; *Fabeck Trench*, C Company; *Zollern Trench*, Battalion Headquarters.

The battalion on the right was the 38th Canadians, and on the left the 75th Battn. Royal West Kent Regt. The objective was Desire Trench, which lay 400 yards north of Regina Trench and about a mile south-east of Grandcourt. The assault was timed for 6.10 a.m. on the 18th November, and an hour previously the leading wave had advanced 150 yards, and the second wave 50 yards from Regina Trench. At 6.10 the barrage moved forward and the attacking waves closely followed it. As was usual all over this area between the Ancre and the Somme, a fog hung over the ground, making it very difficult to keep touch and direction, nevertheless this was achieved. At 6.40 the trench was captured, and ten minutes later the leading waves were consolidating 150 yards beyond it. A written report was at once sent back by Captain Place, describing the position held by B and D Companies, and stating that he was in touch with the Canadians and West Kent. As all the officers of B Company except one were casualties, Captain Place took command of both assaulting companies, until 2nd Lieut. B. C. Carrall was sent forward to take command of B Company.

At about 8 a.m. on the 19th November sniping became violent in front, and Lieut.-Colonel Irwin went forward to examine the situation and inspect the work of consolidation. Having done this, he was about to return, soon after 9 a.m. to his headquarters when he was wounded in the leg by a sniper's bullet. The command of the Battalion then devolved on Captain J. Wightman.

Eighty prisoners were captured by the Battalion during the assault and subsequently during the morning, and by noon the two front companies had dug an excellent trench 5½ feet deep and constructed a well-wired strong point in a ravine close to their trench. At night A Company was sent forward from Hessian Trench to relieve as many men as possible of the two front companies, the men relieved being kept as an immediate local reserve. The enemy's artillery was inactive, and ration parties, except for the intense darkness, found little difficulty in getting up.

During the 20th November hostile sniping continued to be heavy in the morning, but was reduced by intermittent shelling in the afternoon. The night also was fairly quiet, and the men of the Battalion, though naturally much fatigued, were very cheerful. The 21st was a very misty day, and at 6.30 p.m. the relief of the Battalion by the 2/5th Battn. Gloucester Regt. began. The relief was completed by 11.40 p.m., and the Battalion had reached the huts at Ovillers by 4 a.m. on the 22nd.

The casualties at the capture of Desire Trench were as follows:—

*Killed:* Captain P. A. Tillard (Shropshire Yeomanry, attd.); 2nd Lieuts. J. B. Stacey and A. M. Wilson and 21 other ranks.

*Wounded:* Lieut.-Colonel A. P. B. Irwin; 2nd Lieut. Milner and 96 other ranks.

The following honours were awarded subsequently for gallant conduct at the capture of Desire Trench:—

*Military Cross:* Captain C. G. M. Place; 2nd Lieuts. J. F. MacMillan, G. Milner (4th Battn. attd.) and F. J. Gaywood (attd. 55th Trench Mortar Battery).

*Distinguished Conduct Medal:* Company Sergt.-Major G. Theedom; Lce.-Cpls. F. Cammell and W. James.

*Bar to Military Medal:* Pte. J. J. E. Bagg.

*Military Medal:* Sergt. W. Carter; Cpl. A. Kernott; Lce.-Cpls. H. Hilder, G. Simmons, R. C. Springett and A. Walker; Ptes. E. Dewell and E. Poulton.

During the morning of the 22nd clean clothing was served out, and in the afternoon the Battalion was conveyed in motor lorries to Contay, marching on the 23rd November to its old billets at Candas. After a hard tour of three months in the line the 18th Division was now being withdrawn for a rest, so on the 25th the Battalion marched in heavy rain to Beaumetz and thence via Noyelles-en-Chaussée to Canchy, near Abbeville, where it arrived on the 27th and spent the rest of the month and the first fortnight of December in company training.

On the 10th December a draft of 111 men joined the Battalion, chiefly composed of men from the 2/5th Battn. East Surrey Regt. On the 14th the Battalion moved to Neuf Moulin, where billets were found to be widely scattered. Christmas Day and Boxing Day were kept as holidays, and on December 29th the Battalion moved into the Le Titre area, billeting at Forest L'Abbaye, and here it remained without incident until the 11th January, 1917, on which date the 18th Division commenced to return to the Thiepval Ridge, and the 8th Battn. East Surrey marched from Forest L'Abbaye to Henchy, arriving there at 5 p.m.

The honours *Gazette* of the 1st January, 1917, notified the award of the Distinguished Conduct Medal to Sergts. N. J. Cossey and G. Jones for good service in the field during 1916. On the 12th the Battalion marched to Huezecourt and remained there in billets until the 14th, when it marched to Terramesnil, halting there on the following day. On the 16th January the Battalion marched to Varennes, seven miles north-west of Albert, where it was accommodated in huts; but on the following day B and C Companies moved into huts at Donnet's Post and Tramway Huts, where they were at the disposal of the IV Corps Tramways for work on the communications, principally in the vicinity of Thiepval. The remainder of the Battalion carried out various forms of instruction at Varennes until January 24th, on which day Battalion Headquarters, with A and D Companies, proceeded also to Donnet's Post.

During the rest of January and the first ten days of February the whole Battalion was employed in tramway and light railway construction in the Thiepval area and the Ancre Valley line. On February 9th, Lieut.-Colonel Irwin returned from sick leave, having recovered from his wound. In consequence, Captain (acting Lieut.-Colonel) Wightman relinquished the command and took over the duties of Second-in-Command, with the acting rank of Major. Captain C. J. Lonergan at the same time relinquished the acting rank of Major.

On the evening of February 11th the Battalion once again reoccupied its old position in Fabeck Trench, a mile east of Thiepval. The operations on the Ancre had been in progress since the 11th of January, and the British had already gained ground on both banks of that river to the north of Thiepval. On February the 14th three platoons of the 8th Battn. East Surrey were detailed to attack a German post known as Point 85, which was situated on the western slope of " The Ravine " Valley, 600 yards north of Desire Trench and a mile south of Miraumont. The attacking force, three platoons commanded by 2nd Lieuts. Ackerley, Doble and Cranham, were in position at 5.20 a.m., and the attack started, following a barrage, at 5.45. 2nd Lieut. Cranham's platoon, acting as a flank guard, reached its objective, but the other two platoons came under heavy fire and had both their commanders wounded. After holding on for a time in shell holes in the open, the platoons fell back to their starting-point.

At about 5.30 a.m. a renewed attack on Point 85 by the same company was organized under Captain C. J. Lonergan, a platoon of C Company, under 2nd Lieut. D. W. N. Taylor, being sent forward, supported by a platoon of B Company, under 2nd Lieut. H. S. Single. Captain Lonergan, soon seeing a prospect of success, promptly ordered the supporting platoon to advance also. Point 85 was captured at once, and four dugouts in the Point were bombed and the occupants killed, five German prisoners were also taken and the captured post was consolidated during the night. The Battalion was relieved from the trenches during the night of February 15th, and had returned without casualties to the Wellington Huts by midnight. The casualties in the attack on Point 85 were: 2nd Lieuts. P. R. Ackerley, A. A. Doble and A. E. Bell wounded; 6 privates killed and 18 wounded; 8 men, in addition, were wounded during this tour of trench duty, making 35 casualties in all.

On February 16th the Battalion moved to Warwick Huts, as reserve to the 54th Brigade, and on the 18th moved into the Grandcourt Trench in Boom

Ravine about 500 yards north of Point 85. The weather being misty, it was ordered that the relief should be carried out by daylight. While passing up "The Ravine" Valley, 2nd Lieut. H. J. Newland was killed and six men were wounded. Intermittent shelling occurred during this tour of duty, and on the 19th February 3 men were killed and 2nd Lieut. H. S. Single and 10 men wounded. The Battalion was relieved by the 7th Battn. Royal West Kent Regt. on the afternoon of February 20th and returned to Warwick Huts.

In the early morning of February 23rd the Battalion moved up to trenches in and near the Zollern Redoubt in support of the 7th Battn. "Queen's," who were holding the left half of the Brigade sector. On the following day it was ascertained by patrols that the German positions before Miraumont had been evacuated, and on the morning of the 25th the 7th Battn. "The Buffs" advanced on a front of about 1500 yards, and by the evening held a line extending from Miraumont passenger station to a point about 500 yards north-east of Pys. The 8th Battn. East Surrey was then warned that on the following morning it would advance in support of the 7th Battn. "Queen's," who were to relieve the "Buffs." This was duly carried out on the 26th February, and in the evening of the 27th the Battalion in turn relieved the "Queen's" in the front line.

Early on the morning of the 28th February a patrol of six men, under 2nd Lieut. T. J. Astington, was sent out northward. No news was heard of this patrol for a considerable time, when it was ascertained that 2nd Lieut. Astington had been killed. During the day a platoon under 2nd Lieut. Hall, while holding Miraumont goods station, was reinforced by a second platoon under 2nd Lieut. Smith, both being placed in charge of Lieut. W. M. Barfoot. At midnight this detachment successfully attacked and captured a German trench about 200 yards long, with a loss of one man killed. In this attack Cpl. T. W. Williams, with a party of bombers, drove back the enemy and made a "stop" at which he held them off while the captured trench was being consolidated. For this good service he received the Distinguished Conduct Medal. A very heavy fire from the German artillery followed this attack, the Battalion losing 1 man killed and 2 wounded. For rescuing two wounded men under heavy machine-gun fire on this day, Cpl. E. W. Cordell and Pte. D. W. Martin were awarded the Military Medal.

An attack to extend the ground captured on February 28th was planned for March 1st, and was eventually executed in the early morning of March 2nd. Two platoons of D Company, under 2nd Lieut. Williams and Sergt. Fidgett, were detailed for the attack, under the orders of Captain Place. It had not been practicable for Captain Place or either of his platoon commanders to reconnoitre the ground by daylight; the trench to be attacked was a small one, and difficult to identify. The attack was made over broken ground at 2.30 a.m.; it was therefore not surprising that it failed. Sergt. Fidgett's platoon lost its way in the dark, and 2nd Lieut. Williams' platoon sustained fifteen casualties.

The Battalion was relieved in the evening by the 7th Battn. "Queen's" and withdrew to the Zollern Redoubt and Trench and Mouquet Farm, and in the afternoon of March 3rd moved to Warwick Huts. Here it remained until the 12th March, employed in working parties under the Royal Engineers and in various forms of training. On the 11th March, Major Wightman and a private were wounded by the premature burst of a defective bomb. In the evening of March 12th the Battalion moved to Thiepval Wood, where it found pleasant quarters in dugouts and bell tents.

The German retreat to the Hindenburg Line had commenced on the 14th March, but the 18th Division was not called upon to take part in the pursuit, as it was about to be transferred to the Hazebrouck area. The 8th Battn. East Surrey marched on the 18th February to new quarters at Hessian Camp, where duties under the Royal Engineers, road-making, etc., continued until the 21st, when the Battalion marched to Contay. On the 22nd it marched to Bertangles, and on the 23rd to Ailly-sur-Somme, where it halted on the 24th. On March 25th the Battalion marched to Saleux Station, and entraining there at 3 p.m., arrived at Steenbecque, near Hazebrouck, at 8.30 p.m. on the 26th. Detraining at Steenbecque, it marched to billets at Wittes, where it arrived at midnight. Here the remainder of the month was spent in various forms of training.

## CHAPTER XX

JULY, 1916, TO MARCH, 1917: THE 9TH BATTALION IN THE BATTLES OF THE SOMME, 1916; ITS ATTACK ON A STRONG POINT NEAR GUILLEMONT, AND ITS HEAVY LOSSES IN THE BATTLE OF DELVILLE WOOD; IN THE TRENCHES ON THE VIMY RIDGE AND NEAR HULLUCH AND LIEVIN.

AS already recorded, the 9th Battn. East Surrey moved at the end of June, 1916, to Locre, in the Bailleul area, after completing a lengthy tour of trench duty in the Wulverghem sector. From Locre about 500 men were employed daily on burying cable. This work continued until the 8th July, when the Battalion marched through Neuve Eglise and with two companies took over Winter Trench and Trenches 134 and 135, opposite the Petite Douve Farm, which is about half a mile south of Messines. Battalion Headquarters were at Red Lodge, and the two remaining companies were in a farm and huts near Red Lodge. On the 12th July the Battalion's front was extended northwards, and Trenches 136, 137 and 138 were taken over by one of the companies from Red Lodge. Battalion Headquarters and the remaining company were moved from Red Lodge to " Stinking Farm."

This sector was relatively a very quiet one. The German trenches lay at some distance from the British line, the nearest point being the Petite Douve Farm, which was 200 yards from Trench 134. The enemy's action lay chiefly in the use of rifle grenades, small aerial torpedoes and the smaller type of " minenwerfer " known as " oil drums," and also in shelling support and communication trenches in rear of the front line. The casualties of the Battalion during the ten days in these trenches were: 2nd Lieut. L. G. Hadenham and 1 man killed and 2 men wounded. 2nd Lieut. Hadenham was killed at night by a stray bullet. He was the Battalion Sniping Officer, and had also had great experience in scouting. He was a very valuable officer, and his loss at this time was irreparable. On the 18th July the Battalion returned to Red Lodge, and on the following day proceeded by motor-bus to the billets they had occupied once before between Bailleul and the Mont des Cats.

It was now rumoured that the 24th Division was about to be sent down to the Somme, and, in fact, after four days' rest, the Division commenced entraining at Bailleul Station. The Battalion, leaving Bailleul at 2.30 p.m., arrived at Longneau, three miles south of Amiens, about ten o'clock at night. There they were informed that they were to be billeted in the village of Saisseval, fifteen miles from the station. The Battalion marched all night, and arrived at Saisseval at 6 a.m. next morning. After a day's rest all four companies set to work to practise the attack and bayonet fighting. All ranks were making rapid progress in these practices, when the order was received that the Division was to proceed to Morlancourt, four miles south of Albert, on 31st July. At 2 p.m. on that day the Battalion marched from Saisseval to Ailly Station to entrain there for Méri-

## 242  THE 24TH DIVISION ARRIVES IN THE SOMME AREA

court. The train, however, which was timed to start from Ailly at 5 p.m. that day, did not arrive till 5 a.m. next morning, so meanwhile all ranks settled down to sleep as best they could on the railway platform. On arrival at Mericourt Station, at 9 a.m. 1st August, tea was provided for the men, after which the Battalion marched to Morlancourt. On reaching that village, it found that the Brigade was moving that day to the Sandpits, about two and a half miles south of Albert. After a rest of about five hours, the Battalion left Morlancourt at 7.30 p.m. and reached the Sandpits at 10 p.m., where the officers were accommodated in tents and the N.C.O.'s and men went into bivouac.

On the 3rd August, Major-General J. E. Capper, Commanding 24th Division, addressed the Battalion. Training was continued, and a visit paid to the vicinity of Fricourt, in order that officers, N.C.O.'s and men might inspect the captured German trenches and dugouts. On the 7th August orders were received that the 24th Division was to relieve the 2nd Division in the front line facing Guillemont. These orders were cancelled during the afternoon. The next day it was announced that the 24th Division was to relieve the 65th Division in a sector of the line opposite Guillemont and in front of Trones Wood, which lies about half a mile south of Delville Wood (*vide* General Map of the Somme Battlefields). In accordance with the latter order the Battalion left the Sandpits at 4.30 p.m. on the 10th August and relieved the 1/5th Battn. North Lancashire Regt. in the reserve trenches at Talus Boisé, one mile north of Maricourt.

At this point it may be well to give a brief outline of the progress of the Battles of the Somme, 1916, up to the time of the arrival of the 24th Division. Previous to the commencement of the Battle of Albert on the 1st July, 1916, the British front line had run roughly southwards from opposite Thiepval to Fricourt, which lies two and a half miles east of Albert. At Fricourt the British line turned due east for nearly five miles to a point just north of Maricourt, whence it bent southwards again to join up with the French front line in the Somme Valley. There existed, therefore, a German salient at Fricourt, and a British salient about Maricourt. The opening attack on the 1st July was made by the Fourth Army from the River Ancre near Thiepval round the Fricourt salient to Maricourt. The subsequent British operations from the 2nd to the 17th July, now known officially as the Battle of Albert (1st to 13th July) and the Battle of Bazentin Ridge (14th to 17th July), took the form of attacks north and slightly east from the Fricourt-Maricourt line, which resulted in an advance of over two miles and the establishment of the new British front on the line Ovillers-Bazentin le Petit-Delville Wood. At the end, therefore, of this, the first phase of the Somme Battle, there was a pronounced German salient about Thiepval and a British salient at Delville Wood. The enemy's hold on the main plateau between the Somme and the Ancre, at the western extremity of which stood the Thiepval salient, was thus threatened, and during the remainder of July and August he fought obstinately to maintain his position, with the result that the British could make no advance on the eastern face of the Delville Wood salient, though the northern face of the salient was meanwhile pushed forward to the line Pozières-High Wood.

## THE 9TH BATTN. IN THE BATTLE OF DELVILLE WOOD 243

On 11th August a good many of the officers and N.C.O.'s visited the trenches near Guillemont to be taken over by the Battalion. Whilst walking round the trenches, Captain D. P. O'Connor was wounded. A working party of 400 men was furnished that night for work in the front-line trenches. On 12th August, 400 men were employed in digging an advanced trench (Lamb Trench in map opposite page 244) parallel to the existing "New" trench, which ran north and south, passing east of "Arrow Head" Copse. Just as this party reached the trenches the enemy opened a bombardment, and the work could not be commenced until 2 a.m. on the 13th August. The digging took place under very difficult conditions, as the enemy were sniping the whole time. The Battalion's casualties were 2 men killed and 2nd Lieut. J. H. Royal and 12 men wounded.

Late on the 13th August, A and B Companies and Battalion Headquarters relieved the 8th Battn. "Queen's" in the front-line trenches near Arrow Head Copse; while C and D Companies, under Captain Vaughan, remained behind to practise an attack which was to be made in a few days' time on a strong point held by the enemy opposite Arrow Head Copse, in conjunction with an attack on Guillemont by the 3rd Division and other attacks by the French further south. On the 14th and 15th August, A and B Companies in the trenches carried out an immense amount of work, in spite of frequent shelling on the part of the enemy. The casualties in these two companies were seven wounded.

On the 16th August the intended attack took place. The general plan of the attack was as follows: The 3rd Division, on the east side of the sunken road, was to attack the trench marked BEF; while C and D Companies of the Battalion were to attack the strong point at C and seize the quadrilateral A, B, C, D. Trench ABE was known to be a very deep trench, which had been but little damaged by artillery fire, and the sunken road, together with the strong point at C, had resisted several previous attempts at assault. In the sunken road there were known to be many dugouts, whilst the strong point at C, built of concrete and iron rails, had not been damaged by artillery fire. Lieut.-Colonel de la Fontaine, recognizing the strength of the position to be attacked, requested that the strong point should first be shelled and destroyed by 9.2-ins. It was shelled by a 6-in. gun on the 14th and again on the 16th, but without much effect.

The artillery barrage also presented considerable difficulty, as the front to be attacked was L-shaped at CAE. It was feared that if a barrage were applied to the sunken road from C to A, the shells might hit some of the 3rd Division when attacking the line BE from the south. It was therefore decided to have an oblique barrage on the line AD, which should creep forward towards the line AE during the advance. This barrage was not a success, since not only did it fail to prevent the enemy from firing, but it generally interfered with the British advance.

The attack of C and D Companies was to be made in three waves, each with an approximate strength of 80 men. The first and second waves formed up in Lamb Trench. The third wave was in New Trench. There were also 15 men at the Barrier, under 2nd Lieut. Lawrence, who were to advance towards the strong point, keeping touch with the 3rd Division. C and D Companies, numbering 9 officers and 240 N.C.O.'s and men, came up to the trenches on the morning of the 16th August and, after their dinners, took up their assigned positions. Captain Vaughan took up his station at point Y, and a telephone was laid thence to Battalion Headquarters in Scottish Lane. At 5.10 p.m. our artillery commenced a heavy bombardment of the enemy's position, which continued for half an hour. Unfortunately, several of our 18-pounders fired short and caused some casualties in the attacking party in Lamb Trench.

At 5.40 p.m. our artillery barrage commenced, and units of the 3rd Division, who had about 200 yards further to advance than C and D Companies, left their trenches. Their advance, however, was soon stopped; mown down by machine-gun fire, they were forced to retire to their lines, and it devolved on the two East Surrey companies to carry out unaided the assault on the strong point. At 5.42 p.m. the three waves left their trenches and advanced in perfect lines towards their objective, but the barrage of the British artillery, for the reasons given above, was defective. Not only was it difficult to detect, but it did not even prevent the enemy from firing over their parapet.

The East Surrey companies had barely left their trenches before they came under a withering rifle fire from the front, and machine-gun fire from both flanks, and as they approached the sunken road they were met with a tremendous volley of bombs. 2nd Lieuts. H. L. Matheson and F. P. O'Brien, Sergt. Garrish and one or two others succeeded in getting into the enemy's trench, and were no doubt killed at once. Almost all the remainder were killed or wounded in the advance, the few who escaped being some men of the third wave, whom Captain Hilton, seeing that the first two waves had been destroyed, ordered to retire into Lamb Trench.

Soon after, a party of about thirty Germans with fixed bayonets came out of the sunken road near the strong point, probably with a view of counter-attacking; but one of our Lewis guns at the barrier was immediately turned on to them and, accounting for a large number, forced the remainder to retire under cover.

Out of the 9 officers who took part in the attack on the strong point, 6 were killed or died of wounds and 1 was wounded; and out of about 240 N.C.O.'s and men, 31 were killed, 116 were wounded and 29 were missing. In addition, 2 officers (2nd Lieuts. Ball and Spurling) were killed who did not take part in the attack. The officers killed on the 16th August, 1916, were: Captain J. L. Vaughan, M.C.; Lieut. W. C. Metcalfe; 2nd Lieuts. J. R. M. Lawrence, H. L. Matheson, F. P. O'Brien, C. L. Cuthbert, F. G. Ball and H. S. Spurling. 2nd Lieut. J. L. P. Denny was wounded. Captain C. Hilton and 2nd Lieuts. J. A. Picton and Schofield were the only officers who came unwounded out of this action.

The loss of so many valuable officers, N.C.O.'s and men was a great blow to the Battalion. Captain Vaughan was a first-class officer. Lieut. Metcalfe was an excellent instructor in the Lewis gun. 2nd Lieut. Spurling had trained the Battalion bombers with great care; and 2nd Lieut. Matheson had shown marked

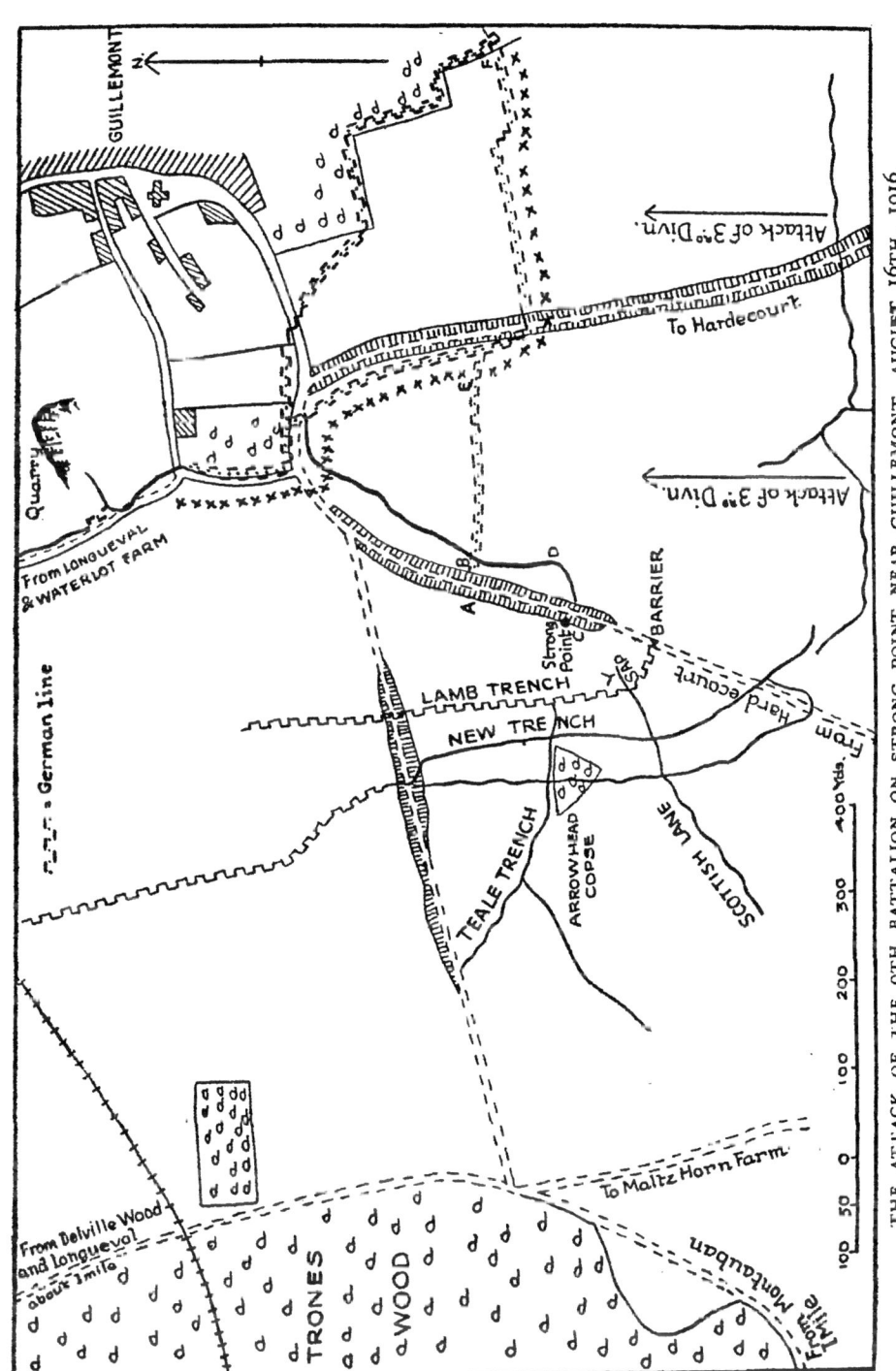

THE ATTACK OF THE 9TH BATTALION ON STRONG POINT NEAR GUILLEMONT, AUGUST 16TH, 1916.

skill in training the Battalion scouts and snipers. 2nd Lieuts. Lawrence and O'Brien were also exceptionally good officers.

During the night the wounded who had dropped into shell holes crawled in, and patrols were sent out to search the ground for any men unable to get back unaided. In the end all the wounded were carried back to the Battalion Aid Post.

During the early hours of the 17th August the Battalion was relieved by the 8th Battn. "Queen's," when A and B Companies moved back to Montauban, and the remnants of C and D Companies and Battalion Headquarters to the Talus Boisé. Here Major-General Capper, the Divisional Commander, inspected the survivors of C and D Companies and made them a very sympathetic speech.

On the 18th August the Battalion was ordered up to the Briqueterie, near Montauban, in support of the 73rd Infantry Brigade, who, together with the 17th Brigade, attacked and captured the western outskirts of Guillemont. On the 21st the Battalion, together with the 8th Battn. "Queen's," moved up into the new front line, the "Queen's" occupying the trench just west of the quarry in Guillemont, whilst the Battalion held the trenches in rear of the "Queen's." Violent shelling on the part of the enemy during the day led to the following casualties:—*Killed*: 2nd Lieut. C. C. Rivers and 3 men. *Wounded*: Captain C. Hilton, 2nd Lieuts. C. Lillywhite and A. A. Matthews and 8 men.

On the 22nd August the relief of the 24th Division commenced, and the same day the Battalion marched back to a camp called the Citadel, about one and a half miles south of Fricourt. Casualties: 1 killed and 5 wounded.

On the 25th August the Battalion marched to a place about one mile north-west of Dernancourt, where it bivouacked, exchanging ground with the 1st Battn. East Surrey Regt., who were proceeding to the Citadel. This was the first meeting between the two battalions.

The weather being very wet, the 72nd Brigade moved on the 25th August into billets at Ribémont, where the Battalion remained until the 30th August, when the 72nd Brigade relieved the 43rd Brigade in Delville Wood, the 9th Battn. East Surrey moving into the reserve trenches at Montauban.

On 31st August the enemy attacked and seized some trenches to the east, and also the north-west of Delville Wood. Several 12-in. shells fell on the ruins of Montauban, but without doing much damage. The total casualties for the month were:—*Killed or died of wounds*: 9 officers and 53 other ranks. *Wounded*: 6 officers and 175 other ranks. *Missing*: 29 other ranks. The fighting strength of the Battalion on the 31st August was thus reduced to about 325 of all ranks.

On the 1st September the Battalion relieved the 1st Battn. North Stafford Regt. in the front-line trenches along the eastern edge of Delville Wood. On the way up the companies had to pass through a very unpleasant barrage of gas and tear shells. During the relief a counter-attack just to the north by the 17th and 73rd Infantry Brigades caused the enemy to bombard Delville Wood, and the Battalion lost 2 men killed and 8 wounded.

The 2nd September was spent in deepening the trenches occupied by the Battalion. Ten Germans belonging to the 118th Infantry Regt. surrendered to

A Company. The Battalion Lewis gunners accounted for a good many of the enemy in Ale Alley, a trench which ran north-east from the easternmost point of Delville Wood. The casualties this day were:—*Killed:* 2nd Lieut. A. Urban and 4 other ranks. *Wounded:* Lieut. C. F. Pullen, 2nd Lieuts. S. K. Grant and J. D. Monro and 15 other ranks.

The 3rd September saw another general attack by the British, and in the Delville Wood area the 7th Division on the right of the 24th Division was ordered to attack the village of Ginchy, which lay half a mile south-east of the East Surrey trenches. The Battalion was ordered to assist by attacking Ale Alley from the north-west, and it was arranged that at the same time a bombing party from the Brigade on the right would attack that trench from the south. The Battalion was also ordered to seize Beer Trench, which ran south from Ale Alley at a distance of about 300 yards from Delville Wood. In Beer Trench the enemy at the moment had only one post. The attack on Ale Alley, which was to be launched at 12 noon, was to be supported by heavy artillery from the rear, by a Stokes' gun and a 2-in. trench mortar, firing smoke.

In accordance with the above instructions, Captain Ingrams and 2nd Lieut. Tetley, with about forty N.C.O.'s and men of A and B Companies, attacked Ale Alley from the north-west. The attack would undoubtedly have been successful had the Brigade on the right been able to combine. As it was, the attack just failed; but a large number of the enemy were killed, and a German officer who surrendered next day stated that he had only twenty men left. During this attack Captain Ingrams, M.C., was killed, and Lieut.-Colonel de la Fontaine very severely wounded. Meanwhile, Lieut. R. C. Gold and 2nd Lieut. Castle sent forward parties to seize and hold Beer Trench as ordered. A party of thirty Germans who approached one of these posts from the north-east was driven back by Sergt. Robertson with his Lewis gun, and suffered very heavily. As soon as the 7th Division commenced its attack on Ginchy the enemy opened a terrific bombardment on Delville Wood, and in consequence casualties in the Battalion were very severe. Major G. G. Ottley (Royal Fusiliers attd.), 2nd Lieut. E. A. Haines and 28 other ranks were killed; Lieut. R. C. Gold and W. F. Bennett and 90 other ranks were wounded and 25 other ranks missing. In addition, 3 officers and 40 men of the 8th Battn. "The Buffs," who had been sent up in support of the Battalion, were nearly all killed.

As a result of the casualties in the day's fighting the Battalion, now commanded by the Adjutant, Lieut. Clark, was reduced to a strength of 9 officers and 100 to 150 other ranks. Lieut.-Colonel Dugmore, commanding the 1st Battn. N. Stafford Regt., was therefore sent up after dark on the 3rd September with two of his companies and took over command of the section. The remnant of the 9th Battn. East Surrey, though very exhausted, remained in the section holding a portion of front line until the 5th September, when it was relieved by the 5th Battn. N. Lancashire Regt., as the 24th Division was being taken out of the line, and was moving back to a training area near Abbéville. During the 4th September, 2nd Lieuts. H. B. G. Castle, P. M. Yonge and A. A. Matthews had been wounded, the last named mortally, as he died of his wounds on the 12th.

On the morning of the 5th, Major-General Capper visited Battalion Headquarters. He expressed his gratitude for all that the officers and men of the Battalion had done, and said he fully realized what a trying time they had had. It was satisfactory also to hear from General Mitford, the Brigade Commander, that Lieut.-General Horne, the XV Corps Commander, had written to him to express his satisfaction at the way in which the 72nd Brigade had behaved at Delville Wood. On being relieved on the 5th September, the Battalion, under the command of Lieut. Clark, marched to Fricourt. The following company officers alone were left: 2nd Lieuts. G. S. Tetley, J. M. Royal (again slightly wounded on this date), S. W. Taylor, E. W. Davies and A. M. Douglas.

The casualties in the Battalion during the first five days of September had been:—

*Killed or died of wounds:* 4 officers and 42 other ranks.
*Wounded:* 10 officers and 112 other ranks.
*Missing:* 25 other ranks.

The following decorations were awarded to the Battalion for the fighting in the Somme Battle —

*Distinguished Service Order:* Lieut.-Colonel H. V. M. de la Fontaine.
*Military Cross:* Lieut. and Adjutant C. A. Clark; Lieut. R. C. Gold.
*Distinguished Conduct Medal:* Lce.-Cpl. G. Webb.
*Military Medal:* Company Sergt.-Major W. W. White; Sergt. D. O. L. Robertson; Lce.-Sergt. F. G. Dyke; Cpl. J. Daniels; Lce.-Cpls. C. W. Lambert, B. Allam and A. W. Andrews; Ptes. J. W. Bashford, H. Kimber, E. W. Wigg, J. Wright, C. W. Pocock and D. Husk.

From Fricourt, where Lieut.-Colonel H. S. Tew, East Surrey Regt., assumed command, the Battalion marched on the 6th September to Dernancourt, where it bivouacked. On the 7th it entrained at Edgehill near its bivouac, where it met the 12th Battn. East Surrey going up to take part in the Battle of Flers-Courcelette. On detraining at Longpré, near Amiens, the 9th Battn. East Surrey marched to billets at Francières, near Abbéville. When Lieut.-Colonel Tew took over the Battalion it had a strength of 10 officers and about 200 men; there were hardly any N.C.O.'s, and nearly all of them were quite inexperienced as instructors. Officers and drafts of men joined very rapidly, and before long the Battalion was raised to a strength of 40 officers and about 700 men. Lieut.-Colonel Tew, a most able infantry officer, was admirably assisted by Lieut. Clark, the Adjutant, also a first-rate instructor, and a strenuous course of detailed instruction was at once started. At first, Colonel Tew found it necessary to take the companies in turn, acting himself as instructor to each while the remaining officers watched the proceedings. Aided by the great keenness of the officers and the high order of intelligence of the men, progress was extremely rapid.

The Battalion remained in the Abbéville training area till September 19th, when it entrained for Valhuon, near St. Pol. The 24th Division was now about to take over a sector on the western slopes of the Vimy Ridge, with the 72nd Brigade in the Berthonval section, some five miles north of Arras. The Battalion accordingly marched on the 24th September from Valhuon to Bruay, where it was billeted, and on the 26th it moved on to Estrée-Cauchie (ten miles north-west of Arras), where it remained in Brigade Support for the rest of the month, employing its time in training from 7 a.m. till 4 p.m. daily.

The 1st of October was a Sunday, and on the 2nd the Battalion went into Divisional Reserve near Souchez, midway between Arras and Lens, two companies, under Captain St. John Spencer, being posted at Cabaret Rouge, while Battalion Headquarters and the other two companies were in the Maistre Line near Berthonval Wood. While so posted the Battalion daily found working parties of 400 men, which were employed on the front support line. On the 10th October the Battalion relieved the 8th Battn. "Queen's" in the front-line trenches, about one mile south-east of Souchez, on the Vimy Ridge. There was considerable artillery activity on nearly every day of the week spent by the Battalion in these trenches, the casualties being 6 other ranks killed and 10 wounded. On the 17th October, Lieut.-Colonel Tew, who was in temporary command of the 72nd Brigade whilst Brigadier-General Mitford was in command of the Division, was severely injured as the result of his horse falling with him. He was admitted to hospital, and Lieut.-Colonel T. H. Swanton, East Surrey Regt., assumed command. During the afternoon of the 18th October the Battalion was relieved by the 13th Battn. Middlesex Regt. and marched back to its former billets at Estrée-Cauchie, where it remained till the 25th. On the 24th October the 24th Division commenced to vacate the Vimy Ridge sector and to move to the Hulluch-Loos sector; and on the 25th October the 9th Battn. East Surrey relieved the 11th Battn. K.O.R. Lancaster Regt. in Brigade Support at Noeux-les-Mines in the new sector, remaining so posted until the last day of the month, when it relieved the 8th Battn. "Queen's" in the front line of the left sub-section of the Hulluch-Loos sector. Here three companies were in the front line, with the fourth in local reserve.

From the 31st October, 1916, to the 10th February, 1917, the Battalion occupied the same front-line trenches in the Hulluch sector alternately with the 8th Battn. "Queen's," the reliefs taking place every six days. During the six-day periods when the Battalion was out of the front-line trenches it was either in Brigade Support about a mile west of Hulluch, or in Brigade Reserve at Philosophe, near Vermelles. During the tours of trench duty the Battalion was frequently bombarded by hostile artillery and by aerial darts and "minenwerfer." Retaliation with rifle grenades and light trench mortars frequently earned for the Battalion some respite from these bombardments, but the casualties were frequent, viz.:—

During November, 1916. *Killed:* 7 other ranks. *Wounded:* 2nd Lieuts. H. C. Buchanan and M. S. Blower and 17 other ranks.

During December, 1916. *Killed:* 7 other ranks. *Wounded:* 12 other ranks.

During January, 1917. *Killed:* 2nd Lieut. N. C. Le Poer Trench and 15 other ranks. *Wounded:* 2nd Lieut. A. A. D. Toplis and 36 other ranks.

During the first eleven days of February, 1917. *Killed:* 1 man. *Wounded:* 13 other ranks.

## 250 A SUCCESSFUL RAID FROM THE HULLUCH TRENCHES

The Battalion was in Brigade Support on Christmas Day, which was treated as a holiday and made as enjoyable as circumstances would allow.

The month of January was one of arduous trench duty. During the tour which commenced on December 30th, New Year's Day was memorable on account of the activity of the enemy's artillery, which gave the companies no respite from dawn to dusk. On the 23rd January, when the Battalion was again in the Hulluch trenches, a party of the enemy attempted to capture No. 2 Crater Post. The garrison of the post was alert and held its fire, allowing the enemy to come close before it opened rapid fire. The Germans fled, leaving two of their number dead and two wounded.

At midday on the 25th January the Battalion carried out a very successful raid against the enemy. The strength employed was 3 officers and 50 other ranks 9th Battn. East Surrey, with 6 sappers of the 103rd Field Company, and the party was divided into six squads, each of 1 officer or N.C.O. and 8 privates. Commanded with great judgment and coolness by 2nd Lieut. E. W. Davies, and gallantly led by 2nd Lieuts. L. C. Thomas and W. H. Lindsay and Sergt. W. G. T. Summers, the whole raiding party carried out its task with the utmost confidence and skill. No Man's Land, 100 yards in width, was crossed with the loss of two men killed by machine-gun fire, and the enemy's trenches were explored and various dugouts bombed, in strict accordance with the prearranged plan. Heavy losses were inflicted on the enemy, over 20 men being killed or wounded in the trench and dugouts, and 3 prisoners being taken and brought in. Great gallantry and determination was shown by several members of the raiding party in bringing in the wounded and the bodies of two of the men killed. In this duty the following were conspicuous: 2nd Lieuts. E. W. Davies, W. H. Lindsay and M. S. Blower, Lieut. G. C. Hartley (R.A.M.C.), 2nd Lieut. Robens, R.E., Sapper Yirrel and Cpl. J. W. Perry. The enemy's casualties have been mentioned. Those of the raiding party were 3 killed and 4 wounded, only one of the latter being seriously wounded.

This gallant raid, the first conducted in broad daylight, met with much approval by the higher command. The Army Commander, First Army, in a minute dated 31st January, expressed " to all concerned his appreciation of this raid. The conception, careful preparation and soldier-like manner in which it was brought to a successful issue reflects credit on the 72nd Infantry Brigade and the 9th East Surrey Regiment."

Having completed its last tour of duty in the trenches of the Hulluch sector, and having been relieved by the 8th Battn. " Queen's," the Battalion moved back on the 10th February to Philosophe. On the 11th February the Battalion paraded at 11.45 and marched to Noeux-les-Mines, where it spent the night. On the 12th February the 24th Division came out of the line and began to move to a training area about Allouagne, five miles west of Béthune. Accordingly, on that date the 9th Battn. East Surrey continued its march at 9 a.m., moving in column of route for the first time for many a long day. The Battalion went via Marles-les-Mines and Lozinghem to Bas-Rieux and Cautrainne, north of Allouagne.

Here the companies were reorganized into two fighting, one reserve and one training platoons; and after two days' rest a thorough course of company training was begun on the 15th. On the 16th, 2nd Lieuts. L. C. Thomas and W. H. Lindsay and Lieut. G. C. Hartley, R.A.M.C., the Battalion Medical Officer, were awarded the Military Cross for their gallant services in the raid of the 25th January; while Sergt. W. G. T. Summers and Pte. C. A. Baker were granted shortly afterwards the Military Medal for their conduct on the same occasion.

The remainder of the month was spent in training at Bas-Rieux, much time being devoted to practice on the rifle range and to bombing instruction. On the 26th February, 2nd Lieut. S. K. Grant and two men were wounded in the bombing pit by the premature burst of a rifle grenade.

As the 24th Division was now about to take over the Calonne sector opposite Lens, the Battalion paraded at 9.15 a.m. on March 1st and marched east again to Fouquereuil, where it went into billets. On the following morning it marched at the same hour via Nocux-les-Mines to Bully-Grenay, where it arrived about 1 p.m. and rested till 5.30 p.m. It then proceeded to the right sub-section Calonne and relieved the 15th Canadian Highlanders in the trenches facing Liévin, the western suburb of Lens. Here it remained until the 8th March, when it was relieved by the 8th Battn. " Queen's," and went back to Divisional Reserve at Bully-Grenay, where Lieut.-Colonel de la Fontaine resumed command, having sufficiently recovered from his dangerous wound received on the Somme. Lieut.-Colonel Swanton, who had ably commanded the Battalion for five months, consequently reverted to Second-in-Command.

The Battalion remained at Bully-Grenay from March 8th to 14th, relieving the 8th Battn. " Queen's " in the right sub-section in the evening of the latter day. The 15th and 16th were days of considerable artillery activity on both sides, and on the 17th the Battalion snipers were very active, and at night the enemy showed great nervousness, apparently expecting a raid. On the 18th the enemy's artillery was very active, causing a number of casualties. The 19th and 20th were quieter days, and on the 20th the Battalion was relieved by the 8th Battn. " Queen's " and went into Brigade Support at Calonne, where it remained till the 25th, when it again relieved the " Queen's " in the right sub-section.

During the ensuing tour of duty there was much artillery activity. Artillery and aircraft activity continued throughout the month, increasing on the enemy's part on the 31st. The casualties for March were 5 other ranks killed and 20 wounded.

# CHAPTER XXI

JULY, 1916, TO MARCH, 1917: THE 12TH BATTALION IN THE LINE NEAR PLOEGSTEERT WOOD: IN THE BATTLES OF THE SOMME, 1916; THE CAPTURE OF FLERS; FIVE MONTHS IN THE LINE NEAR ST. ELOI.

AT 5 a.m. on July 1st the 12th Battn. East Surrey was relieved in the Convent trenches by the 10th Battn. "Queen's" and returned to Soyer Farm. The Battle of Albert, the first of the Battles of the Somme, 1916, commenced this day, and there was consequently a great increase of artillery and other activity all along the western front. At 10.30 p.m. on July 6th the Battalion moved into new billets about Grande Munque Farm, west of Ploegsteert Wood. On the 8th the Battalion went into the trenches, taking over a new line from the 11th Battn. Royal West Kent Regt. The line lay north of the wood and ran from a point 200 yards north of Anton's Farm to La Douve Brook.

There was now no special hostile activity, and the weather was very fine. On July 13th, Lieut.-Colonel H. H. Lee was wounded in the foot and removed to hospital at Bailleul and subsequently to England. Major H. J. Walmisley-Dresser, of the Royal Warwick Regt., was appointed to the command during Lieut.-Colonel Lee's absence and received the acting rank of Lieut.-Colonel. Artillery activity was considerable on both sides on the 14th and 15th. During the night of the 15th the Battalion was relieved by the 11th Battn. Royal West Kent Regt. and went back into billets at Grande Munque Farm, where Headquarters and two companies were accommodated, the remainder being placed in the wood in front of the farm. The Battalion remained in this position, finding working parties as usual, until the evening of July 27th, when it moved to Soyer Farm remaining there till the end of the month. The casualties during the month were 1 man killed and 2 officers (Lieut.-Colonel Lee and 2nd Lieut. B. F. Dodd) and 36 other ranks wounded.

The Battalion remained in billets on August 1st and 2nd, finding working parties as before, and early on the 3rd moved into the trenches, having the 123rd Infantry Brigade on its right and the 15th Battn. Hampshire Regt. on its left. The Battalion remained in the trenches until August 9th, the enemy being generally inactive. On relief by the 10th Battn. "Queen's," the Battalion returned to Soyer Farm. Here it remained, finding working parties as before, till August 15th, when the 41st Division was withdrawn to rest billets, prior to moving down to the Somme theatre of operations. On the 15th the Battalion moved to La Crèche, 16th to Meteren, 17th to Flêtre. Here it remained till August 22nd, engaged in hard training for the coming active work.

On August 23rd the Battalion entrained at Bailleul, with a strength of 40 officers and 934 other ranks. It arrived at Longpré, near Amiens, at 10 a.m. on

## THE 12TH BATTN. IN THE BATTLE OF FLERS-COURCELETTE

the 24th and marched to Mouflers, where it went through a further course of field training, practising the attack and consolidation, wood fighting, etc. This training continued vigorously to the end of the month. The casualties during the month were 1 man killed and 3 wounded.

The period of training approaching its close, the Battalion was inspected on September 2nd by Major-General Lawford, Commanding the 41st Division, who expressed himself well pleased with all he had seen. Major-General Lawford added an expression of his entire confidence that the 122nd Infantry Brigade when called on would do its duty. The Battalion remained in its billets at Mouflers until September 6th, when it proceeded with the remainder of the 122nd Brigade to Longpré railway station and entrained for Méricourt, which place was reached at 10 a.m. Here A Company (Captain Jessop) rejoined the Battalion from the Fourth Army School, where it had undergone a special course of instruction. After inspection by Lieut.-General Horne, the Battalion left its camp near Albert on September 11th, and marched to the vicinity of Fricourt, its field strength being 36 officers and 777 other ranks. Here it lay in readiness till 4.30 p.m. on September 14th, when it was ordered to take up its battle position near Longueval at the north-west corner of Delville Wood. The prescribed battle strength was 17 officers and 634 other ranks, the remainder of the Battalion being sent to the vicinity of Fricourt.

The 41st Division, together with the New Zealand and 14th (Light) Divisions, now formed the XV Corps, under Lieut.-General Horne, and was a part of the Fourth Army. This Army, in conjunction with the Reserve Army (General Sir Hubert Gough) and the Sixth French Army, had orders to capture the German defence system on and including the line Morval–Lesboeufs–Gueudecourt–High Wood. The resulting operations are known as the Battle of Flers-Courcelette, the seventh of the Battles of the Somme, 1916.

The 122nd Infantry Brigade, on the left of the 41st Division, was ordered to capture the village of Flers, which lies about one mile north of Delville Wood, and a double line of trenches beyond it, Flers being the third objective, and the trenches beyond, the fourth. The Brigade put the 15th Battn. Hampshire Regt. and 18th Battn. King's Royal Rifle Corps in front line, with the 11th Battn. Royal West Kent Regt. and the 12th Battn. East Surrey in second line. The Battalion's place was therefore on the left of the second line in its brigade, and it followed close on the 18th Battn. K.R.R.C.

Lieut.-Colonel Walmisley-Dresser's orders for the attack, which are perfectly clear, were that the Battalion was to advance in four waves on a four-company front, moving off in successive lines of half-platoons in file. Distances between waves were not to exceed 70 yards.

The Battalion reached its prescribed position at the north-west corner of Delville Wood (*vide* Map opposite page 216) at 2 a.m. on September 15th, when the half-platoons concealed themselves in shell holes, and during the night were intermittently under lachrymatory shell fire. At 6.15 a.m. the Brigade advanced, aided by a heavy artillery barrage and by "Tanks," which were now brought into action for the first time. The 18th Battn. K.R.R.C., after an advance of about 1000 yards, captured the advanced German trenches, where the 12th Battn. East Surrey joined them, after suffering heavy losses though in second line. When the K.R.R.C. resumed their advance over the 600 yards which separated them from the village, the East Surrey men went forward with them and were the first to enter Flers, which was being heavily shelled. Inside the village there was much confused fighting, a result of the heavy losses in officers and N.C.O.'s, but eventually small parties fought their way through and occupied a line of German trenches some 300 yards north of the village, where they held on. Sixteen out of the seventeen officers were killed or wounded, while the casualties among the N.C.O.'s and men were 286. Lieut.-Colonel Walmisley-Dresser was mortally wounded, dying on September 17th. Captains F. D. Jessop, M.C., J. L. Buckman, C. York-Davis; Lieuts. C. C. Fox and J. R. Chesters were killed; and of the remaining officers only 2nd Lieut. W. J. Palk was unwounded when at 7.30 p.m. the Battalion was ordered back to the reserve trenches, where it remained on September 16th and 17th. On the 16th, Major H. de C. Blakeney brought up a reinforcement of 6 officers and 60 men from Fricourt and took over command of the Battalion.

On September 18th the Battalion was relieved by a battalion of the Royal Lancaster Regt. and proceeded to a camp near Albert, where on the following day Major C. H. Kitchin, 15th Battn. Hampshire Regt., took over the command. The strength of the Battalion this day was 29 officers and 606 other ranks. The Battalion remained in the Albert camp till the end of the month, in wet and cold weather, reorganizing and preparing for further work.

The Battles of the Somme, 1916, were on so large a scale, and the number of officers and men who distinguished themselves so great, that rewards were given on a very meagre scale, particularly to regimental officers. To the 12th Battn. East Surrey the following awards were made for service at Flers:—

*Military Cross:* Lieut. H. S. Openshaw; 2nd Lieuts. J. F. Tamblyn, W. J. Palk and Company Sergt.-Major B. P. Horswell.

*Distinguished Conduct Medal:* Lce.-Cpl. W. Carter; Ptes. A. B. Giles and P. Huggett.

*Military Medal:* Sergt. C. Maguire; Lce.-Cpl. L. C. Southall; Ptes. F. A. Butler, W. Hammond, P. J. Budd, J. Newton, G. Jones and F. Cole.

Lieut. J. W. Staddon was also recommended for reward for conspicuous gallantry at Flers and in the trench beyond the village. Sergt. R. A. Langley was twice recommended for gallant conduct: (1) In the raid at Ploegsteert on June 30th, and (2) at Flers on September 16th, 1916. He was awarded the Military Medal in January, 1917. The casualties during September were:— *Killed or mortally wounded:* 6 officers and 112 other ranks. *Wounded:* 10 officers and 224 other ranks. The officers wounded were Captains R. A. McCulloch (Adjutant) and A. D. Crow; Lieut. J. W. Staddon; 2nd Lieuts. J. E. M. Crowther, F. Beard, S. Stimson, H. T. Pike, A. G. Howitt and W. M. Edwards and Lieut. G. W. Young (R.A.M.C.).

After two more days of reorganization and preparation, the Battalion (consisting of three companies and fifteen men only of the 4th Company) returned via Mametz Wood to the Flers area and received orders to relieve a New Zealand battalion in the portion of Gird Support Trench north of Factory Corner.

During the Battalion's stay near Albert, the Battle of Morval (25th to 28th September) had been fought and the village of Gueudecourt had been taken by British troops on the 26th September. On the 1st October the Battle of the Transloy Ridges commenced, and on the 3rd Eaucourt L'Abbaye was captured also. The 41st Division was now to attempt a fresh advance towards Ligny-Thilloy, and in this operation the 122nd Brigade was held in Divisional Reserve.

The guides who were to lead the 12th Battn. East Surrey to Gird Support Trench were met at Thistle Dump at 4.30 p.m. on the 3rd October. Unfortunately, the guides quitted the recognized route and led the Battalion across the open for some 600 yards south of Factory Corner. Very heavy shell fire was encountered, and the companies suffered unnecessary casualties. The relief also took a long time and was not completed till 10.45 p.m. There was continuous shelling of the whole front throughout the night, and this continued all day and night on the 4th October and rendered the provision of food and water very difficult. Happily, the fire slackened considerably between noon and 6 p.m. on the 5th, and carrying parties took full advantage of the opportunity, all necessary supplies being brought up to the front line.

The French were now attacking Sailly-Saillisel, three miles south-east of Gueudecourt, and, in order to support them, the Fourth Army was preparing to attack along the whole front from the Albert–Bapaume road to Lesboeufs. During the night of 5th/6th October the 12th Battn. East Surrey was withdrawn to Flers Trench, which was very heavily shelled by the enemy during the morning of the 7th. At 12.30 p.m. on that day the Battalion received orders to occupy Goose Alley at once, and to act as Brigade Support in the coming attack. Moving by way of Abbey road, the Battalion reached Goose Alley at 1.15 p.m. The attack opened at 1.45 p.m. on the 7th October, and soon afterwards Goose Alley was heavily shelled; but it was not until 2.10 p.m. that the Battalion was able to leave it and to occupy the newly dug trench from which the 18th Battn. King's Royal Rifles had advanced to the attack. At 4.30 p.m. the Battalion moved up to reinforce the 11th Battn. Royal West Kent Regt., who had succeeded in advancing about 100 yards. Difficulty being experienced in finding the way, patrols were sent forward by whom the Battalion was led by the sunken road east of Eaucourt l'Abbaye. A heavy hostile barrage was encountered, but the Battalion was fortunate enough to arrive at the front line without loss.

On reaching the 11th Battn. Royal West Kent Regt., the Battalion consolidated and held the ground gained. Throughout the night the enemy's machine guns and snipers were very active, and at dawn on October 8th all working parties, scouts and covering patrols were called in. The whole of this day was devoted to improving the trenches dug during the previous night, and, to prevent congestion, 20 per cent of the Battalion was withdrawn to the Gird Support Trench. The Battalion was to have been relieved at 8 p.m., but owing to an exceptionally heavy barrage, lasting $4\frac{1}{2}$ hours, the relief did not begin till

1 a.m. and was not completed till 3.30 a.m. on October 9th. The Battalion then moved back to Switch Trench, where reinforcements from Mametz Wood joined Headquarters in the evening. Conditions on the 10th were normal, and at 7.30 a.m. on October 11th the Battalion left Switch Trench for Mametz Wood.

The 41st Division, after its gallant services and heavy losses, was now to be withdrawn for a time from the battle front, and at 9.30 a.m. on October 11th the 12th Battn. East Surrey left by train for Dernancourt rest camp, but on arrival there was ordered to Ribémont. The strength on arrival here was 530 of all ranks; but on October 14th a draft of 259 men joined, followed by 191 of the Surrey Yeomanry on the 15th. On this day Lieut.-Colonel Lee rejoined from hospital, having recovered from his wound, and resumed the command. Lieut.-Colonel Kitchin was consequently struck off the strength and rejoined his own battalion. On the 17th the Battalion entrained at Ribémont and proceeded to Oisemont, where it arrived early on the 18th October and went into billets at Hoppy, six miles away. Lieut.-Colonel H. H. Lee took over command of the 122nd Brigade, and Major H. de C. Blakeney assumed that of the Battalion.

The Battalion left Hoppy on October 20th and marched to Pont Rémy Station, where it entrained for Goedewaersvelde. Here guides were met who led the way to billets at Eecke, which were reached early on the 21st. After two days' company training here the Battalion marched on the 24th to Goedewaersvelde, and on the 25th to the rest camp at Reninghelst; strength, 46 officers and 1014 other ranks. Training continued here till October 28th, and in the afternoon of the 29th the Battalion took over trenches in the St. Eloi sector from the 20th Battn. Durham L.I. Here the front line was held by two companies, the remainder being in reserve. The Diary mentions that the support line could not be held, "being under water for the most part." The enemy's attitude was quiet, and the month closed without incident. The casualties during October were —*Killed:* 2nd Lieut. P. J. Gibbons and 12 other ranks. *Wounded:* 2nd Lieut. A. V. Reiner and 51 other ranks.

On November 1st the enemy shelled the trenches, the Battalion having 1 man killed and 6 wounded. During the 3rd the relief by the 20th Battn. Durham L.I. took place and was completed by 4.15 p.m., the Battalion returning via Reninghelst to Ontario Camp. On the 8th, Lieut.-Colonel Lee rejoined and resumed command of the Battalion on the return of Brigadier-General Towsey from leave. On November 10th the Battalion, with a trench strength of 756, again relieved the 20th Battn. Durham L.I. in the St. Eloi sector. The enemy was generally quiet during the early part of the tour. During the night of November 11th/12th a patrol under Captain C. O. Slacke, consisting of 2nd Lieut. J. F. Walton, Sergt. T. G. Mackenzie and three privates, on approaching the enemy's wire came under heavy machine-gun fire. Both the officers were wounded and two of the men were killed. Sergt. Mackenzie, assisted by Lce.-Cpl. A. Kitchen and Pte. T. J. Young, who went out to aid him, attempted to bring in the wounded officers; but 2nd Lieut. Walton was again wounded, this time mortally, and Captain Slacke, it is supposed, fell into a large shell hole and was drowned. Sergt. Mackenzie, Lce.-Cpl. Kitchen and Pte. Young were subsequently awarded the Military Medal.

On relief by the 20th Battn. Durham L.I. on the 16th November the Battalion returned to Ontario Camp, where it remained in reserve till the 23rd. On the 20th, Lieut.-General Sir T. L. N. Morland, Commanding X Corps, presented the ribbon of the Military Medal to Sergt. G. W. Simpson, Lce.-Sergt. J. Dawe, Lce.-Cpls. E. Morris and R. Collins, Ptes. E. E. Williams and F. C. Coombes. These rewards were granted in recognition of exceptionally gallant and valuable services in action north-west of Flers on October 6th and 7th.

On November 23rd the Battalion relieved the 20th Battn. Durham L.I. in the Diependaal sub-sector between St. Eloi and Bois Confluent, where it remained until the afternoon of the 28th. The tour was quiet, and both reliefs were effected without casualties. The month closed without incident at Ontario Camp, the Battalion doing steady training. The casualties during November were: 1 officer and 7 other ranks killed, 13 wounded, and 1 officer and 4 men missing. The strength on November 30th was 38 officers and 997 other ranks.

Training continued on the 1st and 2nd December, and on the 3rd the Battalion again took over the Diependaal sub-sector from the 20th Battn. Durham L.I. and occupied it alternately with that battalion for the rest of the month, the reliefs taking place weekly and the periods between the tours of trench duty being passed at Ontario Camp in reserve. The Battalion was at Ontario Camp for Christmas, and returned to the trenches on the 29th December. The casualties during the month were: 4 other ranks killed, and 2nd Lieuts. J. W. Barrow and H. E. Winder and 23 other ranks wounded. The strength on December 30th was 35 officers and 1019 other ranks.

The Battalion was to pass nearly four months more in the then quiet St. Eloi region, and our narrative during that period must consequently be brief. The New Year found the Battalion in the St. Eloi trenches, which they occupied during January, as in the previous month, alternately with the 20th Battn. Durham L.I. On the 17th, Brigadier-General Towsey returned from leave and resumed command of the Brigade. Lieut.-Colonel Lee consequently reverted to the Battalion, but went on leave to England on the 18th. Fatigue duties at Ontario Camp now became heavier than ever, and on January 31st the Diary records that the whole Battalion less specialists were on fatigue, of course much to the detriment of training. The casualties during the month were: 2 men killed and 2nd Lieuts. J. W. Barrow, O. E. Woollard, J. H. H. Pritchard and 12 other ranks wounded. Of these, the two last-named officers and 3 men were injured in a bombing accident on the 18th.

On February 2nd, Lieut.-Colonel Lee returned from leave and assumed command of the 122nd Brigade, Brigadier-General Towsey being in temporary command of the Division. The same routine as regards trench duty near St. Eloi and training while in reserve at Ontario Camp continued throughout February. Lieut.-Colonel Lee resumed the command on the 8th, and on the 15th, Ontario Camp was inspected by Major-General Lawford, who was accompanied by Brigadier-General Towsey. On the 25th, Captain McCulloch, having recovered from his wounds, returned to duty and resumed the Adjutancy from Captain Reynard. On February 27th the Battalion returned to the trenches, where the month was ended. The casualties during the month were: 4 other ranks killed and 11 wounded. The strength at the end of February was 44 officers and 1097 other ranks.

March 1st was quiet, but on the 2nd, 2nd Lieut. A. T. Duncan was killed by a sniper and one private was killed by a shell. There was much counter-battery work during this trench tour, and two more casualties occurred on the 4th March. On the 5th the Battalion was relieved by the 20th Battn. Durham L.I. and returned to Ontario Camp, Reninghelst. Training was now being carried out with special reference to a proposed raid. The Battalion returned to the trenches on March 11th, and on the following day the wire in the enemy's front was fired on from 2 to 3.30 p.m. by trench mortars and 18-pounders. This was repeated on the 13th, with the result of a very heavy reply from the enemy. Major L. A. Hickson, Royal West Kent Regt., joined this day and took over duty as Second-in-Command.

At 10.30 p.m. on the 14th our guns opened an intense bombardment. The advance party with tapes, under 2nd Lieut. Puttock, went out, but were seen and fired on by the enemy, who was thoroughly alert and evidently expecting the raid. Eight more men were wounded, and eventually the raid was judged impossible and was abandoned. The damage to the trenches done by the German guns was quickly made good.

On March 17th the Battalion was relieved by the Durham L.I. and returned to Ontario Camp, for the usual six days' training, instruction and inspection. On the 23rd it again relieved the Durham L.I. in the trenches, coming in for a heavy bombardment on the 24th lasting 3½ hours. The front-line trench was considerably damaged and 2nd Lieut. Bennett was severely shaken, but returned to duty four days later.

On March 30th the Battalion was relieved in the trenches by the Durham L.I. and returned to Ontario Camp, where it was visited on the 31st by Lieut.-General Sir T. Morland, Commanding X Corps. Lieut.-Colonel Lee returned from leave this day and resumed the command. The casualties during the month were:—*Killed*: 1 officer and 4 other ranks. *Wounded*: 1 officer and 17 other ranks.

## CHAPTER XXII

JUNE, 1916, TO MARCH, 1917: THE 13TH BATTALION ARRIVES IN FRANCE; IN THE TRENCHES OPPOSITE LENS AND NORTH OF ALBERT; THE BATTALION MOVES TO THE SOMME VALLEY AND IS IN THE FRONT LINE NEAR BOUCHAVESNES WHEN THE GERMAN RETREAT TO THE HINDENBURG LINE COMMENCES.

THE 13th Battn. East Surrey landed at Havre early on June 4th, 1916, went into camp for the day and entrained early on June 5th for an unknown destination. This proved to be Lillers, where the Battalion detrained, moving into billets in the neighbouring villages of Fancquenhem and Lières, where the next ten days were passed in field training and route-marching. On June 16th the Division marched to Sailly-Labourse and Noyelles, whence the units were sent forward for instruction by the 15th Division, which was holding the Hulluch and Hohenzollern Redoubt sectors. The Battalion was attached to one of the brigades of this Division, one company being taken in hand by each battalion of the Brigade. After ten days' instruction the Battalion marched to Bruay, five miles south-west of Béthune. Here Lieut. F. S. Ainger took over the appointment of Adjutant, which he held until taken prisoner in April, 1918.

After a further fortnight's training at Bruay, viz. about the middle of July, 1916, the 40th Division relieved the 1st Division in the line near Lens, chiefly in the Loos section, remaining there for three months, after which it spent a further period of two months in the line near Albert and Hebuterne, and thus had not the opportunity of taking part in the Battles of the Somme, 1916. When the 40th Division took over the line near Lens, the 13th Battn. East Surrey was at first in Brigade Reserve at Calonne. Afterwards it went into the trenches in the Hulluch, Maroc and Calonne sectors alternately, the intervening periods in reserve being spent in billets in or near Bully Grenay. There were no special incidents during this period of trench warfare except for one raiding party, under 2nd Lieuts. L. I. Deacon and R. Thompson, which, in the Calonne sector, reached the enemy's lines and inflicted considerable damage, though it did not succeed in capturing a prisoner. While in the line near Lens the Battalion sustained about 100 casualties, including the following officers:—*Killed or died of wounds*: Captain L. R. Merryfield and Lieuts. E. B. Buckland and W. J. Chambers. *Wounded*: Captain M. J. Pemberton and 2nd Lieuts. G. K. Fielding and C. J. Noakes.

Towards the end of October the 40th Division was relieved in the line near Lens, and the 13th Battn. East Surrey was withdrawn in consequence to Averdoingt (near St. Pol), where it spent a short time at training.

On the 2nd November the Battalion marched south from Averdoingt to billets in and near Rebreuve, and on the 4th to Mézerolles, near Doullens. On

## 260  THE 40TH DIVISION ARRIVES IN THE SOMME VALLEY

November 5th the march was continued southward to Vacquerie, near Candas, where training went on until the 12th November. The 40th Division was now transferred to the XIII Corps and formed part of the Fifth Army. On the 12th the Battalion marched to billets at Doullens, and on the 14th to Souastre, the 120th Infantry Brigade being now posted as Brigade in Reserve to the 49th Division.

On November 15th the 120th Brigade commenced a short tour of duty in the front line, and the 13th Battn. East Surrey relieved the 4th Battn. K.O.Y.L.I. in the left sector Hebuterne, eight miles north of Albert, and became the left battalion of the Fifth Army in the line. The Battalion remained in the trenches for six days without special incident, casualties being light. On the 19th, Company Sergt.-Major R. T. Padget went forward under heavy fire to an advanced post and rescued a number of men who had been buried in shelters. On relief, on November 21st, the Battalion marched to camp at Couin, near Souastre, where the 120th Brigade rejoined the 40th Division. Three more marches to the westward followed, the Battalion moving on the 22nd to Amplier, on the 23rd to Bonneville and on the 24th to Bussus-Bussuel, near Abbéville, where it was billeted for the remainder of the month, carrying out a programme of work of its own. The casualties during the month were 3 other ranks killed and 9 wounded.

The Battalion continued training, without special incident, until the 14th December, when the 40th Division returned to the front line. Accordingly, the Battalion marched to Pont Rémy, and on the 15th entrained there for Dernancourt, near Albert. After detraining, the Battalion marched to huts in Camp 112, on the Bray–Mcaulte road.

On Sunday, December 20th, Brigadier-General the Hon. C. S. H. Drummond-Willoughby, Commanding the 120th Brigade, presented the ribbon of the Distinguished Conduct Medal to Company Sergt.-Major R. T. Padget for his gallant action on the 19th November. On the 26th the 120th Brigade relieved the 108th Brigade in the Bouchavesnes north sub-sector, just north of Peronne. The Battalion, with a strength of 20 officers and 600 other ranks, proceeded in motor lorries to Maurepas Halte, and marched thence to its post as Brigade Support, the remainder of the Battalion having joined the Brigade details in camp near Suzanne. While in support the Battalion occupied dugouts in a valley about a mile south-east of Maurepas. On the 30th December the Battalion, less one company, relieved the 14th Battn. H.L.I. in the left sub-sector, Bouchavesnes North, the remaining company being attached to the 14th Battn. A. and S. Highlanders and posted on the right of that battalion. This company was thus on the extreme right of the British Army.

On the last day of the year the 120th Brigade was relieved. Owing to mud and water the communication trenches were impassable, and the 13th Battn. East Surrey took seven hours to get down to Maurepas. Thence it was conveyed in lorries to Camp 21 on the Suzanne–Maricourt road. One man was wounded during the relief. The casualties during the month were 1 man killed and 1 wounded.

## THE NEW YEAR (1917) OPENS WITH SEVERE WEATHER

The weather conditions during the first three months of 1917 were exceptionally severe. The Battalion arrived at Maricourt during the early hours of New Year's Day, but the last company did not get in till 9 a.m. The next two days were spent in resting and cleaning off the mud of the trenches. On January 4th the 120th Brigade took over the Rancourt sector, north of Bouchavesnes, the Battalion taking over the left sub-sector. The front line consisted of a number of detached posts, held by Lewis guns and a few rifles. The relief had therefore to be carried out in the dark. The Battalion remained in the line until January 8th, when it was relieved and went into Brigade Reserve at Maurepas. One man was killed and one wounded during the tour of duty.

On January 12th the 120th Brigade returned to Maricourt, and on the 18th took over the Bouchavesnes North sector, the 13th Battn. East Surrey again taking charge of the left sub-sector. Two companies were in first line, one in support and one in reserve. The Battalion remained in the line until January 22nd, during which period there was considerable artillery activity on both sides. On relief, on January 22nd, the Battalion moved into Brigade Support, being accommodated in dugouts at Asquith Flats.

The supply of food, water, ammunition, etc., to the companies in the line in the Bouchavesnes area was a matter of great difficulty, as, owing to the mud, everything had to be carried on pack-mules. For this purpose the transport was brigaded, and a convoy of some eighty drivers with mules was sent up with supplies nightly from the 26th December to the 26 January, the journey lasting from twelve to fifteen hours owing to the mud, which in places was waist deep. On the 26th January the 120th Brigade was relieved by a brigade of the 8th Division, and the 13th Battn. East Surrey proceeded in lorries to a camp near Sailly-Laurette, where it was joined by the details from Suzanne. On the 27th it marched to billets at Corbie, near Amiens, where it remained in G.H.Q. Reserve for the rest of the month. During this period "Fighting Platoons" were organized and training was carried out. The casualties during the month were 3 other ranks killed and 8 wounded.

The story of the Battalion during February may be told quite briefly, as it was almost devoid of incident. During the first nine days the Battalion remained at Corbie, carrying out physical training, bayonet fighting, musketry instruction and trench work. On the 10th it marched to Camp No. 3, on the Meaulte-Bray road. On the following day it made a further march to the Bray-Toubière railhead, where it furnished working parties, Battalion Headquarters being located at Bray-sur-Somme. Here the Battalion continued to be employed till the 24th February, when it was relieved by the 19th Battn. Royal Welsh Fusiliers and proceeded to its old quarters in Camp 21 near Maricourt, where it continued its programme of training till the 6th March. The only casualties during February were 3 other ranks killed on 14th February.

From the 6th March, when the 120th Brigade returned to the line, until the 17th March, the 13th Battn. East Surrey, alternately with the 14th Battn. A. and S. Highlanders, held the front-line trenches just south of Bouchavesnes. Each tour of trench duty lasted three days, the intervening periods being passed either in support at Road Wood, a mile south-west of Bouchavesnes, or in Brigade Reserve at Howitzer Wood. About midnight of the 13th/14th, when the Battalion was in the trenches, its headquarters were shelled and Regtl. Sergt.-Major A. Seymour, who had been awarded the D.C.M. two months previously, was killed. The transport, which had just arrived with supplies, had a lucky escape, as the pack-mules were off-loaded under a heavy fire and led away to a safer spot without a single animal being touched.

The month of March, 1917, witnessed the result of the British operations on the Ancre during the winter of 1916/17, viz. the retreat of the enemy on the Arras–Soissons front to the Hindenburg Line, the new German line of defence which ran from near Arras in a general south-easterly direction to St. Quentin. It was, however, the fortune of the Battalion to be but little concerned in the operations of following up the Germans. On the 15th March, Brigade Orders were received giving instructions to be taken in the event of the enemy's withdrawal; but it was not until the 17th, when the A. and S. Highlanders had relieved the Battalion in the front line, that the expected retreat commenced. The A. and S. Highlanders pushed forward at once and established themselves in the enemy's third line of trenches. On the following day the 13th Battn. East Surrey also advanced and on the 19th occupied Allaines and established east of that village an outpost line, in touch with the A. and S. Highlanders on the left and the 20th Battn. Middlesex Regt. on the right. While following up the Battalion to Allaines the transport was among the first troops to pass through Peronne, which had been set on fire by the Germans before their retirement and was still burning.

The Battalion was relieved on the 20th March and moved back to Curlu, where the 40th Division was assembled by the 25th March and became Corps Reserve of the XV Corps. The casualties during March were 2 other ranks killed, 2nd Lieut. N. W. Hagger and 12 men wounded and 1 man missing.

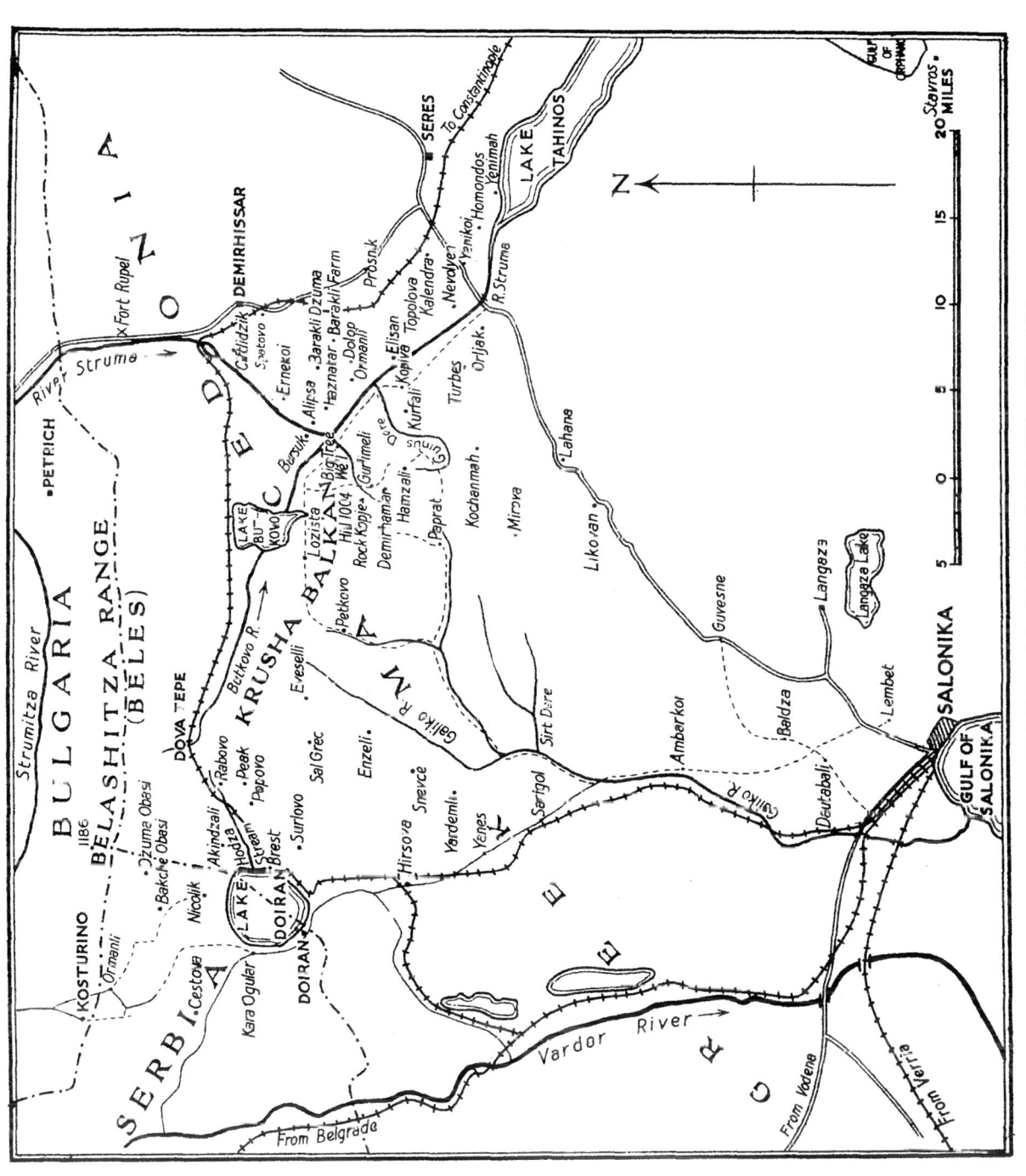

THE 2ND BATTALION ON THE SALONICA FRONT

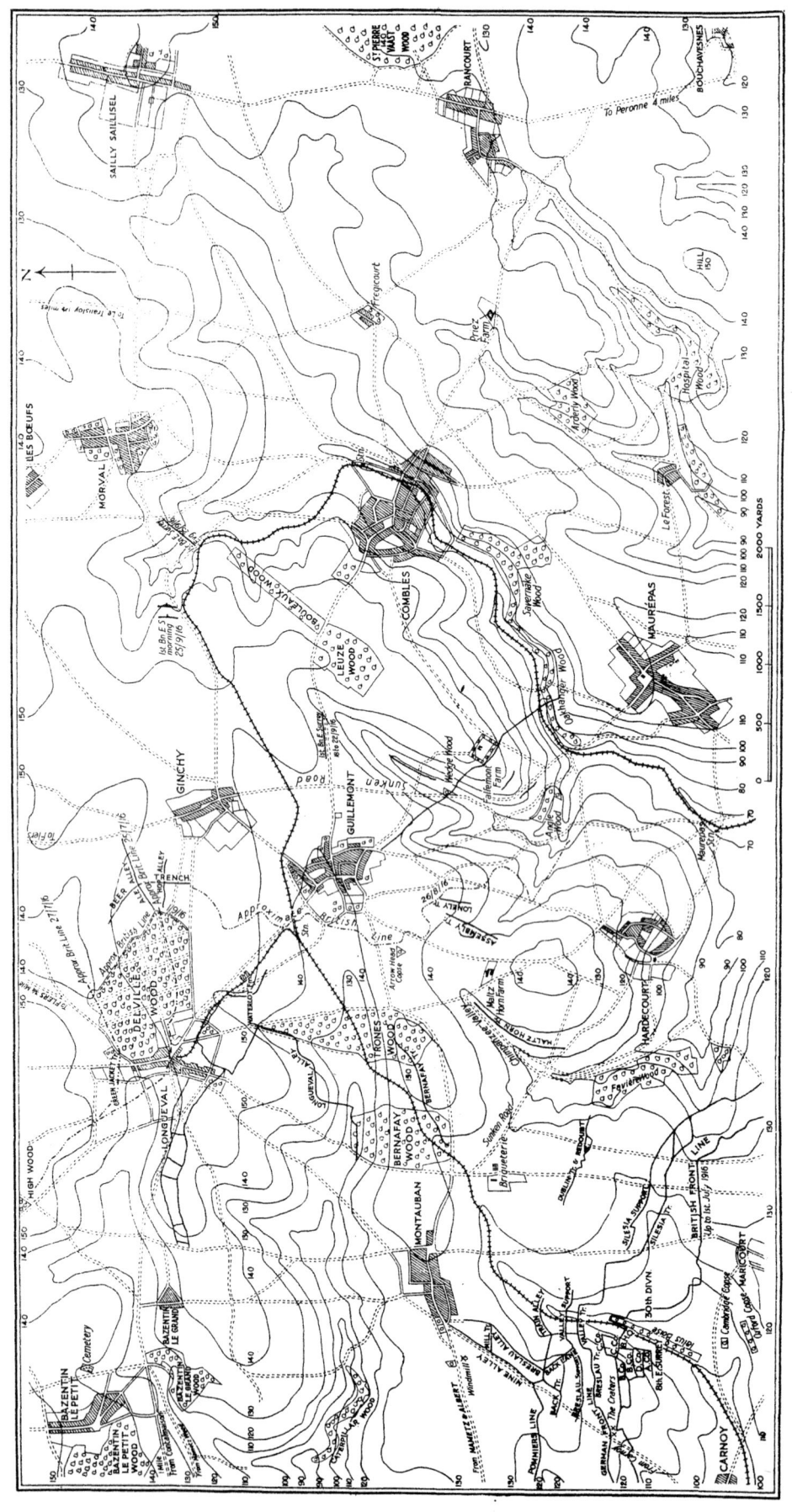

GENERAL MAP OF THE SOMME BATTLEFIELDS